1971

The
Continental
Short Story

An Existential Approach

The
Continental
Short Story

An Existential Approach

THEODORA L. WEST

WEST CHESTER STATE COLLEGE

Odyssey Press   •   New York

Library of Congress Catalog Card Number: 69–11184

A 0 9 8 7 6 5 4 3 2 1

ACKNOWLEDGMENTS

The author is grateful to the following writers, publishers, and literary agents for permission to use the materials listed below.

A. S. Barnes & Company, Inc.: "Ivan Fyodorovitch Shponka and His Aunt" by Nikolai Gogol from *Old Russian Stories,* selected by J. I. Rodale, 1960.

Barron's Educational Series, Inc.: "Juan Manso: A Dead Man's Tale" by Miguel De Unamuno, from *Classic Tales from Modern Spain,* translated by William E. Colford, Copyright © 1964 by Barron's Educational Series, Inc.

A. and C. Boni: "Every Inch a Man" and "The Marquis of Lumbría" from *Three Exemplary Novels,* translated by Angel Flores. Copyright 1930 by A. and C. Boni.

Valentino Bompiani & Co.: "The Fall" from *Bitter Honeymoon* by Alberto Moravia. Copyright © 1956 by Valentino Bompiani & Co. "Triple Looking Glass" from *The Fetish* by Alberto Moravia. English translation copyright © 1964 by Martin Secker & Warburg Ltd. From *L'Automa* copyright © 1963 by Casa Editrice Valentino Bompiani. "The Go-Between" from *Roman Tales* by Alberto Moravia. Copyright © 1956, 1957 by Valentino Bompiani.

Chatto & Windus Ltd.: "The Man in a Case" from *The Wife and Other Stories* by Anton Tchekov, translated by Constance Garnett. Permission granted by Chatto & Windus, Ltd., and Mr. David Garnett.

Farrar, Straus & Giroux, Inc.: "The Fall" from *Bitter Honeymoon* by Alberto Moravia, translator Bernard Wall, Farrar, Straus & Cudahy, 1956. "The Triple Looking Glass" from *The Fetish and Other Stories,* translator Angus Davidson, Farrar, Straus & Giroux, 1965. "The Go-Between" from *Roman Tales* by Alberto Moravia, translator Angus Davidson, Farrar, Straus and Cudahy, 1957. "The Old World Landowners" from *Mirgorod* by Nikolai

Gogol, translator David Magarshack. Copyright © 1962 by David Magarshack. Reprinted by permission of Farrar, Straus & Giroux, Inc. "A Fragment" and "A Visit to Friends" by Anton Chekov, reprinted with permission of Farrar, Straus & Giroux, Inc. from *Unknown Chekov*, translated and with an Introduction by Avrahm Yarmolinsky. Copyright © 1954 by Avrahm Yarmolinsky.

William Heinemann Ltd. Publishers: "An Honest Thief" by Fyodor Dostoevsky translated by Constance Garnett.

Alfred A. Knopf, Inc.: "The Dilletante," "The Wardrobe," and "A Gleam" from *Stories of Three Decades* by Thomas Mann and translated by H. T. Lowe-Porter. Copyright 1936 by Alfred A. Knopf, Inc. Reprinted by permission. "Theseus" from *Two Legends: Theseus and Oepidus* by Andre Gide and translated by John Russell. Copyright 1950 by Alfred A. Knopf, Inc. Reprinted by permission. "The Guest" from *Exile and the Kingdom* by Albert Camus. Justin O'Brien translator. © Copyright 1957, 1958 by Alfred A. Knopf, Inc. by permission of the publisher.

The Macmillan Company: "The Man in a Case" from *The Wife and Other Stories* by Anton Chekov, translated by Constance Garnett. Copyright 1918, The Macmillan Company, copyright renewed 1946 by Constance Garnett. Reprinted with permission of The Macmillan Company. "The Dream of a Ridiculous Man" and "The Peasant Marey" from *An Honest Thief and Other Stories* by Fyodor Dostoevsky, translated by Constance Garnett. First printed in Great Britain. Reprinted with permission of The Macmillan Company.

Martin Secker & Warburg Ltd. Publishers: Andre Gide's "Theseus" from *Oedipus and Theseus*. Permission granted by Martin Secker & Warburg Ltd. Alberto Moravia's "The Fall" from *Bitter Honeymoon*, "The Triple Looking Glass" from *The Fetish* and "The Go-Between" from *Roman Tales* Reprinted with permission from Martin Secker & Warburg Ltd.

New Directions Publishing Corporation: "The Room" from *Intimacy* by Jean-Paul Sartre, translated by Lloyd Alexander. Copyright 1948 by New Directions. Reprinted by permission of New Directions Publishing Corporation.

Random House, Inc.: "The Cloak" by Nikolai Gogol. Reprinted from *Great Russian Stories*, edited by Isai Kamen, by courtesy of Random House, Inc.

Schocken Books, Inc.: "The Judgement" and "An Old Manuscript" reprinted by permission of Schocken Books, Inc. from *The Penal Colony* by Franz Kafka. Copyright © 1948 by Schocken Books, Inc. "The Refusal" and "Give It Up!" reprinted by permission of Schocken Books, Inc. from *Description of a Struggle* by Franz Kafka. Copyright © 1958 by Schocken Books, Inc.

Charles Scribner's Sons: "A Joke" is reprinted with the permission of Charles Scribner's Sons from *Russian Silhouettes* by Anton Chekov. Translated by Marian Fell. Copyright 1915 by Charles Scribner's Sons; renewal copyright 1943 Olivia Fell Vans Agnew.

Simon & Schuster, Inc.: "Cinci," "The Soft Touch of Grass," "The Rose," and "Mortal Remains" by Gli Eredi di Luigi Pirandello from *Short Stories by Pirandello*, translated by Lily Duplaix. Copyright © 1959 by Gli Eredi di Luigi Pirandello. Reprinted by permission of Simon & Schuster, Inc.

To W. R. W.

CONTENTS

The
Continental
Short Story

An Existential Approach

THE SHORT STORY

An Aesthetic Approach

The Nature of Aesthetics

A serious study of the short story as an art form must begin with a basic understanding of aesthetics, and to paraphrase Emerson, aesthetics is its own excuse for being. Although it serves no practical purpose in perpetuating man's physical existence, aesthetics is a large part of man's experience, and man's universal sense of beauty cannot be denied. It does exist, and it exists in each man through a unique combination of emotions and intellect: John Donne's oxymoron the "thinking heart" figuratively expresses this dichotomy of the aesthetic experience. Man's contemplation of a work of art results in his aesthetic awareness—an awareness of the existence of beauty, for aesthetics is the exercise of the Mind and the Emotions in consideration of the Beautiful. Beauty, in turn, is an Ordering pleasurably perceived by the observer.

A reevaluation of the terms *beauty, ordering,* and *pleasure* must occur in order to include modern art forms which are frequently marked by bizarre, shocking, irrational, dissonant, or irregular and asymmetrical features. Beauty, for example, too frequently connotes "prettiness"; but, if beauty is in the eye of the beholder, such a limiting definition obviates individual taste. The term is amorphous: it is all things to all people, *provided* those people can delineate their concepts of beauty in terms of its ordering and the pleasure received from that ordering.

1

The ordering or arrangement or selection of a painting, play, or short story may appear beautiful to an observer because it presents a particular point of view or vision of life that is deeply meaningful to him. It touches an inner response in him. It pleases him. And the general term "to please" in art is analogous to the specific one "to entertain" in drama, where entertainment may consist of shocking and revolting self-torment or obscene accusation or even a good cry. Beauty is not always pretty, order is not always symmetrical and rational, and pleasure is not always fun.

The Role of Subjective Evaluation

Pleasure, which is always a part of the aesthetic experience, depends largely upon subjective experience, both emotional and intellectual. For example, it is a pleasurable experience to project one's feelings in contemplating a work of art, that is, a painting, a piece of music, a short story. But the emotional response should not be overemphasized to the detriment of the intellectual one. It would seem impossible to dissociate the intellectual from the emotional response. While a person reacts emotionally to a painting or a short story with pity or joy or anger, at the same time he is intellectually ordering his ideas, values, concepts, and judgments. The pleasure results from this simultaneous union of complex emotional and intellectual reactions in the observer.

The Need for Objective Criteria

In addition to bringing a subjective emotional and intellectual experience to a work of art, a person must also employ certain objective critical criteria in explicating a short story or analyzing a painting. In interpreting fiction, for example, a reader would analyze an author's level of diction, mode of character development, use of point of view, setting, tone, mood, and the like. Too frequently, however, when a student approaches a short story he either relies heavily on purely personal "opinion" and emotional response or else he accepts in toto a critic's explication.

Or he may wait for a teacher's analysis of it. For there can be only one interpretation, and that one, of course, must come from the all-knowing or know-it-all instructor. The student may find it difficult and confusing to admit to opposites existing simultaneously: how can there be a subjective, personal interpretation of a story and, at the same time, an objective set of tools for interpretation, or an established critic's opinion, or an apparently definitive textbook explication of the work?

Aesthetic appreciation of a work of art lies within the individual beholder and his capacity for subjective experience and objective evaluation. His rapport with and understanding of a work of art depend upon his state of physical well-being at the time, his mood, his values, his capacity for human experience in general. Aesthetic appreciation occurs upon a propitious union of beholder and work of art. But, lest this statement be misconstrued as advocating a kind of "noble savage" standard of evaluation, it must be made clear that untutored appreciation is not enough. Art is difficult. An artist may have worked painstakingly for many years to create one work—a short story, for example. This cannot be totally appreciated (as no work of art can ever be totally appreciated by an individual) in a kind of intuitional trance. Hence, a reader must employ objective standards simultaneously with subjective appreciation.

Once the student of the short story or any other art form becomes convinced that his own experience is valid background for interpreting the work, he frequently balks at accepting critical tools for analytical approach or the critical taste and judgments of authorities in the field who earnestly strive to arrive at standards of excellence. It is not enough to feel deeply about art. Nor is it sufficient to say, "I know what I like." A person must be humble, open, and receptive to a work of art. He must be able to provide proof of his opinion, proof based on objective analysis of the internal components of the work. His freeborn political rights do not extend to the right of an inadequately-arrived-at opinion. So his own subjective responses, both emotional and intellectual, must work with his objective standards of excellence in order to arrive at a just evaluation of a work of art.

The Nature of the Short Story

Is a short story a work of art? It does fulfill significant criteria. It has form or design which is of a permanent nature: a writer can leave behind a body of work consisting of short stories. Like any work of art, a short story calls for an enormous amount of technical skill. In respect to its aesthetic appeal, the short story is not primarily a tool of communication—rather, it is one of emotional-intellectual expression. As a tool of expression, the short story performs a main artistic function—it presents a particular vision of life, whether philosophical or psychological. It offers this vision for contemplation, for rumination, not necessarily as irrevocable truth. It presents itself for scrutiny to expand the reader's experience, whether he chooses to accept or reject the proffered vision.

Herein lies the beauty of the short story. Whether dealing with intrinsically beautiful subject matter or with the sordid and ugly of the world, the truly excellent short story selects and dramatizes the stuff of life into an ordered whole so that the resulting experience is so complete, so consistent within itself, that it appears a beautifully wrought whole. This is not to assume an art-for-art's-sake attitude, however, even though the aesthetic appeal of the short story as a work of art is of prime importance. In addition to the reader's appreciation of a short story as a work of artistic ordering, any moral, ethical, biographical, political, social, or religious comment of universal significance enrich the total experience for the reader.

Interrelationship of Form and Content

Once a reader becomes aware of the principles of aesthetics and recognizes the necessity for subjective experience and objective standards of judgment, he is prepared to approach the short story form in particular. What is a short story? A short story is a piece of short fiction that tells a story. The dramatic action of the story may be physical, psychological, or emotional. Because of its brevity, the short story is best approached through a discussion of the intimate relationship that exists between its form and content. The marriage of form and content is more critical in the short story than in any other type of literature because it combines the loose, narrative techniques of the novel with the condensed, metaphorical ones of the poem.

Revising the words or changing the punctuation in a tightly knit, well-constructed, and well-organized short story would alter, or perhaps even destroy, the aesthetic unity of it. The aesthetic unity or aesthetic experience of a particular short story is the result of a closely integrated form–content relationship. This relationship results in the artist's particular style, which is uniquely his, consistent and recognizable. STYLE is the union of FORM (design, point of view, tone, mood, and all other compositional or formal elements) and CONTENT (theme and plot or dramatic incident). While a short story may be dissected into its formal elements and its plot discussed, the resulting aesthetic experience arising from its union of form and content is nondiscursive. The whole is greater than the sum of its parts; that is, the aesthetic effect arising from this union somehow transcends the technical skill of the artist working through his own experience and creates a new vision of life. It would be impossible to separate what a great artist has to say from the way he says it. At what point can Franz Kafka's content be separated from his form in his dream-narratives?

If the coming-together of form and content, the nondiscursive, aesthetic experience of the short story, transcends its own informing artist, then the possibility of a reader's subjective interpretation becomes tenable. The reader's subjective reactions to the short story, combined with his objective set of critical tools, produce his own private interpretation of the work. The short story seems thus to have three distinct lives: its own, the artist's, and the reader's.

The Integrity of the Short Story

Each short story must be considered from these points of view: its own essential being, the artist's informing skill, and the reader's interpretation. A short story is complete in itself: its content perfectly expresses its form and its form adapts perfectly to its content, so it may be said to have an existence of its own. A reader should be able to work out a complete and satisfactory explication within the confines of the short story alone, an explication which may be a multilevel, allegorical one. Once the umbilical cord has been cut, the short story must be able to survive of itself. Any short story bound so closely to the life of its author or to its socio-political or religious background that it can not tolerate internal analysis, is stillborn. Of course, it is impossible to separate the life of a short story from its author's, but it is equally erroneous to assume that biographical study of an author will reveal a particular work. While the creative impulse moves through the artist as a man, the finished product, the short story itself, is a separate entity. This is not to suggest that a short story is greater than its creator, but rather that it is separate from him.

The Nature of the Writer

Paradoxically, one must look to the writer himself for proof that a short story has a separate being and integrity of its own. The proof lies in the nature of a writer. What is a writer? He is an artist, and as such is a superb technician. He is capable of mastering the craft of writing. But in addition to his technical skill, he possesses certain nondiscursive qualities: sensibility, imagination, and intuition. The artist must possess all three of these qualities because each of them interacts dependently upon the other in the conscious and unconscious faculties of the artist. His technical skill and these three nondiscursive abilities result in a work of art, the finished form of which frequently goes beyond the conscious endeavor of the man. If a short story is partially the result of unconscious experience and selection, then it may be said to have a certain being and integrity of its own.

The interrelationship of these three nondiscursive qualities grows out of their functions. The artist must first of all possess great SENSIBILITY, that is, a capacity for emotional experience and intellectual concepts. His mental and emotional acuteness make him more open, more aware, more appreciative, more conscious of the world around him than is the ordinary man. Through his

IMAGINATION the artist transcends the visual world, the "real" world, and sees shockingly new relationships. He "imagines" or envisions a world of his own making, a heightened reality. He is daring in his point of view and unbounded in his search for a new way to reveal truth that would otherwise go unnoticed.

But his imagination is dependent upon his sensibility. It can work only upon experience previously gathered through an alert sensibility. Indeed, it might even be regarded as an outgrowth of a refined sensibility, for it is his active imagination that translates the experience of the real world, the sensible world, into the aesthetic experience of the contrived world of the short story. For to be successful, the short story must be artistically contrived. Fiction is not a mirror of life; rather, it is a highly selective vision of life wrought with all the technical skill of the artist and adorned with all the formal compositional elements of creative writing.

Between the direct experience of the writer-artist and the finished product nurtured by the imagination there is a crucial step. INTUITION is the catalyst that actually transmutes raw experience into art. Intuition is an immediate apprehension of past experience and observation; it is an unconscious insight which allows the writer to select with great sureness the proper word, phrase, or symbol. It is the sense of rightness all great artists possess. Intuition is interdependent upon the other two faculties, however. The writer must be acutely sensible to the world of experience around him, he must have the imagination and the vision to reorder this "real" world, and he must have the intuitive gift of selection to realize in an art form his concept of the real world. One could have technical facility and any one or two of the nondiscursive faculties, but without all three of them working interdependently with the technical skill, he would not be an artist.

Through his sensibility, imagination, and intuition, then, a great deal of the unconscious experience of the artist finds its way into a work. The possibility of these unconscious, nondiscursive forces at work in creative writing raises some doubts about a writer's total intent and any precise "meaning" of a given short story. It is useless to debate the artist's intent, because such an approach mercilessly delimits the short story's total experience—conscious and unconscious, the writer's artistry, and the reader's interpretive freedom.

The Responsibility of the Reader

Without interpretive freedom, the reader may find a short story quite meaningless. But the reader has special responsibilities toward the short story as an art form. He must first of all be aware that he is engaging in aesthetic experience when he looks to the world of the short story for some comment on life. He must be open to this aesthetic experience emotionally and intellectually. He must be aware of the ingredients of the short story, the artist's own experience, his technical skill, and his sensibility, imagination, and intuition. He must be willing to explore the short story's form and content in order to determine their interrelationship and the degree to which each contributes to the total aesthetic unity of the story. But before the reader is fully equipped for such subtle investigation, he must possess a set of fine critical tools with which to explicate. These tools and their use to the writer as well as to the reader can be discussed more fully in the next section, which is on the mechanics of the short story.

THE SHORT STORY

A Mechanical Approach

Reading a short story is not easy. There are no short cuts to its interpretation. In order to penetrate a particular short story, five, ten, perhaps even twenty readings must be given it before the reader can "get inside" it. A reader's aesthetic enjoyment begins in these readings and continues to develop throughout repeated examination. In fact, it is not a final, comprehensive reading of a short story that one necessarily works toward: rather, it is the process of experiencing and explicating the story that provides the fullest pleasure.

The first several readings of a short story should be for general impressions, before beginning the process of analyzing or explicating. Some students (even graduate students) object to "tearing apart" a short story, a widely used synonym for explicating. What they really object to is learning to read. To read does not mean to summarize. To read means to analyze every word choice, every use of punctuation, every symbol, and to work and rework them in their total context.

While the ultimate hope is for a totally integrated explanation —possibly one of many—that would account for all loose ends, this total explanation can be arrived at only through detailed analysis of a particular theme, scene, symbol, allegory, or character development in a given short story. Analysis of the separate components of a short story appears to some students to be dis-

secting or "tearing apart," but such dissection is absolutely necessary for complete understanding and aesthetic appreciation. Those
who regard close analysis as an assault upon a short story miss
the exciting experience of exploring the individually meaningful
nuances of the highly complex vision of life presented in the
short story.

Style

Because of the powerfully condensed style of the short story, an
intimate relationship exists between a story's form and content.
A writer's style is the result of his merging what he has to say
(content) with the way he says it (form). Unfortunately, these
three terms are used interchangeably by some critics to the confusion of most readers. Form and content must be separated,
clarified, and recombined in order for a reader to understand how
the finished short story can be greater than its individual parts.
The intuitive choice of the artist of refined sensibility and imagination results in the successful union of form and content.
Various mechanical elements of form or formal elements will
provide the student with certain technical terms and analytical
skills with which to explicate the writer's total short story: point
of view, diction, methods of character development, mood, tone,
setting, symbol, poetic devices, sentence structure, and punctuation.

Point of View

While no absolute order in terms of importance can be given the
formal elements, the author's selection of point of view must be
considered first because it provides the most significant insight
into the total vision of life inherent in the work. The author's
role in selecting point of view seems highly ambiguous: if the
reader separates an author from his work, is it valid to discuss
"an author's point of view"? It is, providing the reader distinguishes between the author as a person and the author as an
informing artist. An author's very anonymity is of his own crea-

tion. Whatever particular point of view he chooses, the author should never be identified with the story. One should refer to the "narrator" of a short story rather than to its author, since the writer orders his particular vision of life through his impersonal manipulation of point of view. Point of view is always carefully contrived and consistent, calculated to reveal best the character, plot, and theme of the short story. While literally the term refers to the narrator's position in time and space, philosophically it is the key to the whole aesthetic experience.

Several points of view are involved in every short story: the author's (which probably could never be known), the narrator's, the characters', and the reader's. The author may remove himself from a story to varying degrees depending on the point of view he chooses to employ. Possibly the most remarkable control of point of view occurs in Jonathan Swift's *Gulliver's Travels*, where the unique figure of Gulliver the gullible proceeds from the rational, naive, and reserved figure of Part I to the irrational, uncontrolled misanthrope of Part IV, as the calculated control of Swift the informing artist goes unnoticed in the final outbursts of invective. Swift should never be confused or identified with Gulliver.

The point of view to be considered as a crucial mechanical device is the narrator's point of view, which may take one of several approaches or a combination of these. (1) "*I*" *as the main character* provides a consistent point of view, but it may be a heavily biased or warped one. "I" can never be totally relied upon to tell the truth about himself because he doesn't always know it; he may even be a child or a moronic person. "I" must be interpreted through the use of diction, mood, other characters' opinions and descriptions of him and his own actions. This point of view must be carefully scrutinized in relation to the overall philosophical experience of the story. The world of "I" must present a carefully selected and consistent vision of life, one possibly antithetical to the author's beliefs, but a proffered vision to be experienced by the reader. Consistency, the great advantage of this technique, is also its greatest hazard—the main character selects *only* the details he chooses to reveal to the reader. The reader must be on constant guard against this inherent bias; he must learn to look for the main character's concealed motives, self-delusions, unconscious reactions, or stunning epiphanies and relate them to the overall purpose of theme of the story.

Another possible point of view would be (2) "*I*" *as a minor character.* This "I" can witness, describe, or relate without assuming an active part in the story. Since the author is one step further removed from the action and theme of the story, it is especially important for the reader to recognize this kind of author–narrator separation. The remote point of view must somehow tie in with the theme of the short story itself. A detailed analysis of one example may demonstrate the complex and integrated machinations of point of view. Joseph Conrad's "Youth" is a superb example of such craftsmanship in which the theme of man in isolation, proving himself, is accented by a unique manipulation of point of view: "I," a minor character never named or visualized, is seated at a table with four other aging seafarers, among whom is one "Marlow." "I," the chief narrator, writing in the present, recounts a story told at a past reunion of five men: Marlow, taking over the narrative and speaking in the present tense while getting drunker throughout the story, relates a total action which took place twenty-two years prior to the evening's meeting.

The story presents this interesting complication of time and place: Conrad as controlling artist> "I" (in the present, writing of a past meeting of five men seated at a table)> Marlow (speaking in the present tense)> Marlow (getting drunk throughout the narration)> Marlow (speaking entirely of a past experience)> "I" (again seated at the table at the end of the narration by Marlow)> "I" (presumably back in the present, setting down on paper his tale within a tale). The careful framing and the complicated use of point of view separate the author from the work so totally that the tale is forced to stand alone; it is a complete and whole experience within itself. Close examination of all the other formal elements would enforce the verisimilitude and authenticity of the unique experience. The reader could never begin to comprehend the complexity and brilliance of the story without first exploring the contribution of its point of view toward theme and the overall aesthetic experience.

Several other points of view are technically possible: (3) *the omniscient narrator,* (4) *the narrator-observer,* and (5) *the third person impersonal.* The point is, however, that every short story offers a slight variation of approach and relates the use of point of view uniquely to the overall purpose and experience of the story. Mere definitions of terms are meaningless unless the techniques themselves are worked out in an individual short story in order to gain an insight into the total experience through an analysis of its point of view. By definition, the omniscient narrator knows all, sees all, thinks all. He can "get inside" all the characters. Functioning at its best, this type can provide direct insight into the motivation of characters; however, it also runs the risk of delimiting a reader's interpretation by telling him exactly what to think.

The narrator-observer circumvents this limitation: the reader sees the observer who in turn sees the action. The reader can judge more easily the bias of the narrator. The most unbiased, objective technique of them all is the third person impersonal point of view. The author forces the reader to deal directly with the story through the words and actions alone of the characters. This type of short story is usually marked by a great amount of dialogue. Ernest Hemingway and Shirley Jackson both employed the stark objectivity of this approach to enforce their general themes. Point of view is not idly conceived by the informing artist—it is the chief clue providing direct insight into the total purpose of the short story.

Point of view not only provides the key to the philosophical experience of a short story, but it also functions as a structural cohesive device. It has many uses, any number of which may occur simultaneously in a short story: point of view may remove an author *per se*, provide a consistent narrator and level of diction, encourage the reader to identify with the narrator, conceal or reveal particular bias, create a microcosm, "frame" a story in time and space, condense through careful selection of details, or unify through a consistent tone. All of these uses contribute to the vision of life contained within the short story.

Diction

While point of view is essential to "getting into" a short story, it is difficult to adjudge the relative importance of the remaining formal elements. Certainly the first line of every short story presents another major element of an author's style as he yokes together his form and content—his use of diction. The reader must answer the question: why did the author use this particular level of diction? It may be archaic, stilted, formal, common, abstract, regional, illiterate, colloquial, slangy. It may be used symbolically or metaphorically; it may sound cacophonous, alliterative, or onomatopoetic. The necessarily close relationship between an author's choice of diction and his choice of narrator and point of view is obvious. The choice of diction must be analyzed and classified by the reader and then interrelated with his accumulated perceptions of the story. An author's vocabulary may differ only slightly from the reader's; however, his selection and placement of words and his use of that vocabulary differ greatly.

Character

Character, mood, and tone grow out of selective word choice. Characters, whether "originals" or types, are either described by the artist or revealed dramatically from the inside out through their use of diction. Depending upon the story's total purpose, a character may appear realistically drawn or may function symbolically or abstractly. While the main character may actually appear in a minor role, he is generally the one who changes, the one who moves from unawareness to self-realization, from innocence to experience, from ignorance to enlightenment. The characters of a short story, all of them, are extremely significant since they represent the dramatic working out or enactment of the author's vision of life.

Mood and Tone

Mood is the atmosphere generated by the characters in their attitudes toward one another. It can be detected through their choice of words, their actions, their descriptions of each other. Mood frequently is antithetical to the tone or the attitude of the narrator toward theme and character. Tone is intimately related to point of view. An author's choice of a particular point of view reveals the narrator's tone or attitude toward life, an attitude that may be ironic, pessimistic, sarcastic, sentimental, or bitter. For example, the mood of drunken camaraderie around the table in "Youth" is quite different from the bitter, despairing attitude that emerges from Marlow's reminiscences and the narrator's final comment.

Setting

Because the author must work very fast in the short story form, his choice of one setting out of all possible settings to be imagined is pertinent to his overall theme and design. In some short stories, setting almost assumes the proportions of another character. It becomes a palpable entity which not only provides a convenient locale but becomes an objective correlative for the total experience of the story. The South, a jungle, the marketplace—as symbolic settings each must be analyzed in terms of its overall contribution to the rest of the story. Time—the century, the year, the day or the hour—is frequently closely related to setting and often plays a crucial role in connoting theme. A short story writer must make every formal element do double duty in enforcing, enriching, and dramatizing his particular vision of life.

Symbol

Not only do characters and setting frequently function as symbols, but any particular word can assume symbolic value. Recognizing and interpreting symbolism in literature is a habit of mind which the reader must cultivate. Literature is an art and art is difficult. Literature presents a heightened or condensed reality and symbolism is a useful tool for signaling short cuts, for sustaining multiple allegorical levels, for opening up new areas of richness and experience. A word becomes a symbol upon tacit agreement between artist and reader, and the artist always supplies adequate signs pointing toward possible symbolic interpretation. But the reader must learn to read these signs.

"It all seems perfectly clear when the symbolism is pointed out" is a complacent excuse. As soon as a reader develops a habit of mind which questions the choice of a particular setting, he is interpreting symbolism. There are several signposts pointing toward symbolism: ambiguity, repetition, and connotation. When the reader encounters a term which is being used ambiguously, he should automatically explore its symbolic potential. When a story or even a paragraph repeats a key word or numerous synonyms, a reader should be attuned to possible symbolic comment. And finally, there is a common body of words—such as *water, youth,* and *cross*—so steeped in connotation that they should engage the reader's speculation and expand his interpretation of the short story.

The symbolic level of any work of art exists outside, above, and beyond the concrete level of perception. Through ambiguity, repetition, connotation, implication, allusion, metaphor, or allegory, an author goes beyond his primary level of narration to imply abstract truths. The author's intuitive use of symbol may be the result of his unconscious selection. By alluding to outside ideas and experiences, symbols can economically suggest those ideas which are essentially inexpressible, nondiscursive. Only after a reader has developed this sophisticated level of perception can he fully appreciate the artistry of a great writer.

Poetic Devices, Sentence Structure, and Punctuation

Finally, in analyzing the formal elements of style, the reader must consider the writer's use of poetic devices, his sentence structures, and his use of punctuation. Sounds and rhythms resulting from alliteration, consonance, assonance, or onomatopoeia subtly enforce the total style and the total comment. Metaphorical language influences tone and mood, reveals character, or enforces theme. The presence or the absence of such devices is significant. Except in a translation, a reader should try to analyze a passage strictly for its structural mechanics. A great deal can be learned from the way an artist puts one word behind another, the parts of speech he prefers to emphasize, the sentence order, the extravagant or conservative use of punctuation. Sentence structures frequently reveal a certain order that reflects the artist's aesthetic vision. An examination of Hemingway's terse sentences or Henry James' more latinate structures can only enforce understanding of the authors' overall themes and visions of life.

Content

All these formal elements, each interacting with the others, constitute half of an author's style; the content, consisting of story, plot, and theme, provides the narrative element through which they all function. A story is merely the record of what happens; plot implies why it happens. Plot connotes character motivation, narrative complication, and causal action. A typical plot line develops in five steps; proportionate emphasis on each step varies in every short story. (1) the *introduction* generally quickly establishes point of view, time, setting, level of diction, tone, mood, characters, and sometimes even theme. (2) A *conflict* or entanglement is suggested or begun between two characters, two philosophies, or even two opposing forces within a single character. (3) The *climax* is the point at which one side yields inevitably to the other. (4) The *resolution* works out the result of the action, conflict, and climax, and the (5) *denouement* quickly ties off and concludes the main action.

Merely noting mechanical divisions of plot is useless unless the reader tries to relate the author's choice of one particular plot (chosen out of unlimited combinations of character and action) to his application of formal elements. By the time the reader has successfully merged form and content, he should have arrived at a satisfactory interpretation of theme, one which consistently accounts for all the questions raised in the short story and enforces all the other stylistic elements. He should also be aware that it is not the final interpretation that provides full satisfaction; rather, it is the process of explicating the artist's total vision that provides the fullest aesthetic pleasure. Theme, of course, also appears inextricably interwoven with plot. It is the point toward which all the explication is directed and seems worthy of separate and lengthy consideration as part of the fabric of a short story's content.

THE SHORT STORY

A Thematic Approach

> It would begin from some point, some little thing, at times unnoticed, and then by degrees there would rise up a complete picture, some vivid and complete impression.

This excerpt from Dostoevsky's "The Peasant Marey" describes the process of artistic creation: it begins in the particular and then spirals out to include the artist's total vision. This quote also suggests the thematic unity of the short stories to follow—an existential unity. The existential attitude begins in the assertion and affirmation of an individual's identity and then spirals out to encompass the total man in his concrete existence. The purpose of this thematic approach is to define the existential attitude and to make specific comment upon existential themes as they occur in the various stories of this collection.

Roots of Existentialism

While the roots of modern existentialism may extend far back in time, the existential attitude that marks the modern era could only flourish when the total historical period was ready for it. Soren Kierkegaard (1813–1855) was the first man to use the term "existence" in the modern sense of the word—as it has resolved itself into the basic existential tenet that man's existence precedes

19

his essence. This principle stresses the individual's awareness of freedom and his responsibility for making his own existence in the face of death. In order to trace the roots of this existential attitude, however, several questions must be posed with little hope for precise answers. When did modern man begin to question the eternal, immutable body of Platonic essences or ideas? When did man begin to question the Aristotelian theory of the supremacy of reason as the chief way of knowing? When did modern man begin to notice the unreasonable, the irrational, and the absurd around him?

Something is absurd when it appears to be unresolvable and unreasonable. But the modern world is not just now becoming absurd; rather, modern man is becoming more aware of certain irrational, inexplicable forces around him. Dante's carefully ordered world did not appear absurd because of the powerfully constraining order he imposed on his classical cosmos; but, modern man's cosmos, limitless and infinitely expanding, appears absurd because it seems to be without cause and without resolution. A brief examination of previous eras may illustrate the history of changing attitudes toward life that culminated in that of modern existentialism.

During the Middle Ages St. Thomas Aquinas (1225?–1274?) reconciled medieval faith with Aristotelian reason, and this happy marriage sustained itself into the Renaissance. In retrospect the Renaissance seems to have been the best of all possible worlds: the religious dedication of the Middle Ages combined with Renaissance Platonic Idealism. The revival of classical learning created a period of high aesthetic values, and the revival of classical order neatly contained the boundaries of the Renaissance universe. In the seventeenth century, however, science shattered existing boundaries and Protestantism fragmented the solidarity of the Church. As the Church splintered and science made great strides, man began to feel the tension created by this dichotomy. Milton's weighty justification of "the ways of God to men" already needed more than the anachronistic Ptolemaic universe to convince his readers of his great argument.

A temporary stabilizing return to order was effected in the eighteenth century through the exaltation of reason and belief in the great chain of being. Many eighteenth-century thinkers purported to know through rational perception that man existed in a neatly ordered position of superiority to the beasts and inferiority to the angels. There remained those skeptics of pure reason, however. In Part IV of *Gulliver's Travels* Jonathan Swift saw Gulliver ultimately alienated from those of his kind—nauseated— because of his stubborn attempt to adhere to the principle of pure reason.

The Romantics, revolted by the cold, dehumanizing effects of elevating reason as the primary if not the sole way of knowing, seem in retrospect to have made a frantic effort to revive the total human spirit. Wordsworth's " . . . we are laid asleep / In body, and become a living soul" reflects a total response to Nature. The Romantic thinkers emphasized the subjectivity of experience, elevated the power of the imagination, and eulogized the passionate feelings of the individual. The Romantic vision of infinite perfectibility was one of the total Man in Nature. But this same romantic spirit could not survive the overpowering thrust of science that leveled the entire nineteenth century in its inevitable drive toward a modern, mechanized society. The Dickens' urchin, linking the two centuries, is not a sentimental figure so much as he is an alienated, despairing one, standing alone, dehumanized by the impersonal forces of the twentieth-century machine.

The continental expansion of industrialization and mechanization clashed with the simultaneous shrinking of global boundaries and aggravated the growing tension of modern times. But as industrialization and scientific experimentation spread over Europe they carried with them new ideas, new attitudes, and new values. The long shift from the agrarian economy of the Middle Ages to the industrial economy of the twentieth century was being completed. The resultant mass secularization of society into everexpanding cities was effected throughout Europe and Russia. New social ideas, attitudes, and values found fertile ground in Russia where the will to revolution was ripening among the new intelligentsia as well as among the peasants. By mid-nineteenth century the demonic power of the Russian bear was being meaningfully translated into Russian literature. The modern existential themes of absurdity and irrationality were emerging in the works of the great Russian original, Nikolai Gogol. In his works we see the insignificant little clerk, lost in the vast city, crying out for his individual dignity. After Gogol, the vision of Russian writers dramatically and irrevocably altered.

Nikolai Gogol (1809–1852)

The bizarre world of Nikolai Gogol reveals a frightening and irrational vision of the universe. Ordinary values and incidents are distorted until trivia assumes importance and important actions become absurd. In "Shponka and His Aunt" a remote, unidentified, dotty narrator presents the first half of a story written down for him by one obscure Stepan about a nonentity, Ivan Fyodorovitch, called Shponka. Between absurd digressions on hallway tables, farmyards, turnips (absurd because they are seemingly pointless), the main theme of the story unfolds. A dream book which Shponka frequently consults (comforting because it always says the same thing) becomes the unifying symbol which ties together Shponka's existence. He looks to it, to the unreal, irrational, magical world, to give the "real" world meaning. Shponka, a misfit, alone, alienated in this "real" world ever since his childhood, recoils in nausea from the threat of marriage, of union with another person. In a dream which abruptly terminates the short story, Shponka has the terrifying vision of endless, anonymous wives being spun off a reel of coarse material. His fortune-teller–dream book had " . . . absolutely nothing in it that remotely resembled this incoherent dream." There can be no help and no answer to a vision of life at once irrational, horrifying, alien, meaningless.

"The Cloak," a chilling ghost story, presents the same anti-hero, this time called Akaki, an insignificant, grotesque little clerk, lost in the anonymous masses of bureaucratic St. Petersburg. His cry, "Why do you insult me?" hurled against his inimical world, becomes man's cry for identity and stability in a purposeless universe. The story is the paradox of Akaki, the nonhuman, in an inhuman world. While Gogol was dramatically working out the plight of the little man's struggle to assert his identity, the Danish philosopher Soren Kierkegaard (1813–1855) was passionately exalting the individual man in the face of a rapidly approaching mechanized, collectivist society. Kierkegaard believed that in an individual's struggle in mass society he confronts the possibility of nothingness, the annihilation of his own identity. The resulting tensions of fear, anxiety, and despair constitute the sickness unto death, and these threaten the spirit as collectivized society threatens the social body. Before this yawning gulf of death, man can only resort to living out fundamentally, elementally, his individual Christian existence.

While Gogol deals with the Kierkegaardian theme of annihilation, he does not effect Akaki's salvation through the application of Christian principles. The dehumanization and ultimate annihilation of Akaki is an inevitable process: Akaki worked as though alone; he never noticed the activity in the streets; he never tasted his food; he never felt the cold; he walked lightly on stones to save his shoe leather; he tried to be invisible at parties; he ceased feeling his body after his precious new cloak was stolen; he fell into a dream fit and breathed his last. It were " . . . as though he had never lived there." But surprisingly enough, it is at that point the story really begins, because Akaki, that most insignificant of humans, becomes more "real" after his metamorphosis from life to death to ghost than he had ever been as a man. In a short story filled with symbols of faceless, anonymous people, Akaki ultimately finds his salvation as a rumor, a ghost.

The absurdity of Gogol's little men who live out their lives of quiet desperation is dramatized again in his Ukranian tale of the old Russian landowner Afanasy and his simple wife Pulcheria. The empty, futile lives of the old couple, the senselessness of their living and dying, the decay and misuse of the fruits of the land, the indifference of the heir and trustees, the terrible waste of human and natural resources, the isolation and lack of communication among humans—all punctuate Gogol's existential theme of the futility of existence. When the gray cat (Death) came, they succumbed to it stoically.

Fyodor Dostoevsky   (1821–1881)

Like all the Russians to follow Gogol, Fyodor Dostoevsky was affected by the original genius of Gogol which taught him the value of the single detail, bequeathed him a new vision of life, and freed him to explore the agony of the soul in an existential universe. Dostoevsky's "The Peasant Marey" might almost be viewed as the objective correlative for his existential view of life, a view which did attempt to resolve themes of fear, anxiety, guilt, and despair in the context of Christian ethics. Marey, a man of simple faith and love, dramatizes the need to be strong, independent, responsible, hardworking, free in spirit. Marey dispensed his love and his strength in a strangely detached, impersonal, and impartial manner. He carried his burden of mortality in good faith and expected nothing in return. He was an isolated figure in the center of a field, working with his hands in nature, doing his job responsibly.

In a more complex story," An Honest Thief," the simpleminded vagrant Emelian repeats his agonized denials of the theft of a pair of trousers from the self-righteous Astaphy, who grandly absolves him of guilt. He says in effect to Emelian, "Even if you are guilty, I forgive you." This smug, sadistic, self-righteous pronouncement is humbly received by the ignorant but kindly Emelian, who rewards his tormentor by the greatest gift he can make him—his false confession of guilt. This is a great act of freedom in the face of an all-pervading, nameless, and unjustified guilt.

In his immense allegory of man which concretely sets forth Dostoevsky's Christian existentialism, the unnamed, absurd hero in "The Dream of a Ridiculous Man" proclaims his belief that to live is always better than to die. The narrator clearly favors the existential choice over the essential one. Life and happiness are more important than the ideas of life and happiness. Because of his unique position in time and history, Dostoevsky had the vision and the power to state man's religious place in the universe in modern, existential terms, making the shift from an essential to an existential vision of life. In this short story Dostoevsky substitutes individual responsibility for the destructive will to power. The will to power leads to despair, and man must triumph in living.

About this time in Germany Friedrich Nietzsche (1844–1900) was denying this possibility of man's triumphing in life, love, and happiness. He began by repudiating Kierkegaard's Christian ethic and Christian existentialism. He believed that modern man, in dynamically asserting his own existence over the possibility of eternal essences, had killed the Christian God. Nietzsche recognized in modern man only the dynamic will to power as his driving force; and the will to power is the will to control. This same will to power extended indefinitely breeds hopelessness and nihilism. So Nietzsche looked the other direction from Kierkegaard and Dostoevsky—to nothingness. Affirmatively speaking, however, Nietzsche did force nineteenth- and twentieth-century thinkers to examine their past values—moral, ethical and religious—under the naked light of nihilism.

In a remarkably prophetic vision of twentieth-century man, the narrator of "The Dream of a Ridiculous Man" anticipates the spread of Nietzschean nihilism:

> Regular wars sprang up over this idea [of a harmonious society]. All the combatants at the same time firmly believed that science, wisdom, and instinct of self-preservation would force men at last to unite into a harmonious and rational society . . . But the instinct of self-preservation grew rapidly weaker; there arose men, haughty and sensual . . . There arose religions with a cult of non-existence and self-destruction for the sake of everlasting peace of annihilation. At last these people grew weary of their meaningless toil, and signs of suffering came into their faces, and then they proclaimed that suffering was a beauty, for in suffering alone was there meaning.

But the narrator refutes this distorted and un-Christian concept of man. He offers instead a life of freedom, choice, responsibility, and happiness. He concludes his doctrine of love with:

> I know that people can be beautiful and happy without losing the power of living on earth. I will not and cannot believe that evil is the normal condition of mankind.

While accepting the Christian ethic, Dostoevsky emphasizes the existential credo that man must make his own existence and that he can easily effect a happy existence through responsible choice.

Anton Chekhov   (1860–1904)

The Chekhovian short story shifts to a cerebral, self-contained, carefully structured consideration of man's solitude in the immense natural universe. Nature frequently assumes the proportions of another character as the reader is made constantly aware of man in his physical setting: torrential rains, vast plains, icy slopes. In "A Joke" the narrator is left alone many years later after cruelly tormenting Nadia with successive frantic and terrifying sled rides down icy slopes during which he would whisper hauntingly "I love you, Nadia." Actually, he was incapable of touching, contacting, communicating with another human in that frigid setting, and the symbols of excessive cold and terror underscore that inability of man. A perilous ride into a terrifying abyss is a recurrent symbol in existential literature.

The extent to which man will go to insulate himself from his natural world and human contact is bizarrely illustrated in Chekhov's "The Man in a Case." Byelikov, an absurd-looking man subjected to countless insulting and humiliating experiences in life, is surrounded by numerous objects of encasement: coats, galoshes, umbrellas, watch cases, collars, dark glasses, earplugs, rolled-up windows, coverlets, dressing gowns, nightcaps, blinds, bolts, bed curtains, closed doors and, ultimately, his casket. He once was tempted to reject fear and death for life and Varinka, but contemplation of marriage and human contact had a " . . . depressing effect on him. He grew thinner and paler, and seemed to retreat further and further into his case." He chose death as his final release from a life which rigidly encased and contained him. Byelikov died of humiliation, and for those remaining, " . . . life went on as in the past, as gloomy, oppressive, and senseless . . . . "

Another story by Chekhov, "A Visit to Friends," also deals with the lonely figure of alienated man, unable to involve himself existentially in human affairs, repelled by human contact. In a story filled with images of sterility, loneliness, isolation, and boredom, Chekhov presents the anti-hero, Podgorin, as a symbol of the emancipated but sterile new Russia. He repudiates Sergei, the buffoonish Russia of the past, but anticipates nervously the collectivist Russia of the future. Ten minutes after returning from his visit to friends, he forgets them and retreats into his dead present, caught between the two worlds.

Miguel Unamuno   (1864-1936)

Miguel Unamuno was both philosopher and writer. As an existentialist philosopher, Unamuno found the short story form an excellent aesthetic vehicle in which to dramatize various facets of his existential credo. Each of the stories presented here illustrates the theme of "Juan Manso": "Man has to fight his way through life on earth!" In "The Marquis of Lumbría" the weak-fleshed Tristan does not have the courage to become one of Unamuno's "real men." Overwhelmed by the fanatic maternal instincts of his second wife, he is crushed by his own weakness and does not fulfill himself as a man. In the male–female struggle for power, he is emasculated by his own lust. Alejandro in "Every Inch a Man" is destroyed by his pride and, unlike Tristan, his inability to admit human passion. He justifies denying his wife an answer to her repeated question, "Do you love me," by reasoning that love must be lived between the two of them, not talked about. Love itself, not a romanticized idea of love, must be lived: There can be no compromise; and Alejandro's unyielding pride destroys both himself and his wife. But in the grimly humorous "Juan Manso: A Dead Man's Tale," Juan finds the answer—miraculously, he is given a second chance on this earth and he lives it as a real man. He learns that the meek shall not inherit the earth. Only the wise, the honest, the dedicated, and the committed man who dares to realize himself on this earth will extend his existential being beyond the grave and beyond "the lonely wastelands." Unamuno dramatizes the necessity for an affirmative and dynamic approach to life.

Luigi Pirandello   (1867-1936)

In a story typical of Luigi Pirandello's theme of passionate life struggling against the reality of death, "Cinci" grimly unfolds the roots of the modern *angst*. It is a cancer permeating even the young. Cinci, angry, cruel, anxious, unloved, and alone, ricochets back and forth between violence and boredom. When, "outraged and infuriated" by the dirt hurled at him, he kills the country boy, "Cinci foundered in a backwash of man's eternal solitude from which he wanted to flee." But there is nowhere to flee but to death. Cinci's isolation and rejection are complete. Death comes to the lizard, to the country boy, and to the old inmates of the nearby hospital alike under the "unheeding," unwitting, and cruel moon.

In "The Rose," a sensual fable of physical love, Pirandello brutally underscores the transitoriness of love. The men, the sensualists, symbolically violate the fragile beauty of Lucietta as death violates and terminates love. Pirandello's recurrent use of "eyes" painfully and terribly suggests man's tenuous porthole of life.

André Gide   (1869–1951)

In a kind of reverse anthropomorphism in "Theseus," André Gide elevates the human being. Man is his ultimate triumph: "Man has not yet said his last word." Man, in his human condition, can only struggle against his earthbound limitations by living the good life: religion and sex in just proportions. Myth suited Gide's purpose superbly, for through Greek mythology he was able to create a divinely sensual creature in Theseus. As a sincere man struggling to know himself, Theseus remains the antithesis of Oedipus, the self-deceiver. Theseus seeks disciplined life of action based on courage, love, wit, freedom, candor, humor, and perseverance. The crippling labyrinths of reason, law, and dogma can stultify human existential freedom. As Daedalus advises Theseus in an existential credo of physical immortality:

> Keep on the move. Regard indolence as treachery. Seek no rest until, with your destiny completed, it is time to die. It is only thus that, on the farther side of what seems to be death, you will live, forever re-created by the gratitude of mankind.

In proof of his acceptance of Daedalus' advice, Theseus gently and respectfully reproves Oedipus for his belief in a preordained sense of guilt; he feels that Oedipus yielded luxuriously to his sense of Sin:

I remain a child of this world, and I believe that man, be he what he may, and with whatever blemishes you judge him to be stained, is in duty bound to play out his hand to the end.

The existential thesis of self-realization and responsibility is thus fulfilled in "Theseus."

Thomas Mann   (1875–1955)

While one does not think of Thomas Mann as an existentialist, his novels, novellas, and short stories provide excellent insights into the history of twentieth-century values—moral, ethical, political, social. The enormous scope of this artist's works suggests his rather staggering ability to see life whole. Even his vision of life within a single short story is vast. His storytelling ability, detailed character development, psychology of the masses, and social comment sustained through simultaneous allegorical levels characterize his enormous, all-encompassing talent. Several of Mann's favorite themes are illustrated in the stories anthologized here. "A Gleam" portrays Baron Harry, one of the blessed of society: debonair, self-confident, duel-scarred, but vain, boorish and utterly dissolute. At all times is Mann concerned with man in society, man among other men, man responsible for decent behavior. Society frequently breeds a special brand of hero, however, which is distasteful to Mann—the "outwardly successful" Baron Harry.

"The Dillettante" psychologically traces the self-destructive power of artistic talent that dissipates itself in the faustian pursuit of total proficiency in all the arts. The artist is tempted to self-destruction because in the conflict of two worlds, the creative artist can be destroyed, diverted, or perverted through the humiliating mockery of the affluent and materialistic business world. The narrator of "The Dilettante" is held in ineffectual isolation by a society intolerant of his talents. The early parental disapproval of a strong, domineering, businessman father psychologically emasculates the more gentle, artistic spirit of the young boy. The repeated themes of disgust, suicide, ridicule, passing time, anxiety, boredom, fear, isolation, and absurdity are the thoroughly existential ones of the displaced twentieth-century man and artist.

The existential dream world of Mann's "The Wardrobe" begins with a familiar device, a train ride to nowhere. The station where Albrecht van der Qualen impulsively debarks bares no name. The gloomy, empty square of the town suggests the nightmare world of Franz Kafka. Herr van der Qualen's dream walk takes him over a bridge where the water is " . . . rolling slow and turbid below." People pass dreamlike, inexpressive. The time of day is nebulous, but then he has banished Time—he wears no watch. He knows he is going to die soon. He passes the closed shops and arrives at the edge of town, where an unreal but highly explicit sign hangs on a strange house: "In this house on the third floor there are rooms to let."

A repulsive old lady with "beautiful long white hands" beckons him to his strange room. From a very special wardrobe in his room there nightly emerges a breathtakingly exquisite creature, "quite nude." When van der Qualen attempts to escape time and death in his dream world of sensual experience, the mysterious lady proves elusive physically and entertains him only with tales of death and treachery. "The Wardrobe" explores the unconscious levels of man's existence in concrete terms: his fears, his desires, his loneliness. It is an eerie, brooding allegory of suspended time and imminent death.

Franz Kafka   (1883–1924)

The world of Franz Kafka is a world of protest in which man struggles in frustration against empty symbols of authority. "Give It Up!" typifies in title and theme Kafka's cry of despair. It is a shockingly bizarre vignette of modern man lost, modern man asking the way in time and space, modern man being scornfully derided by the sardonic laughter of authority, itself lost.

In "The Refusal," man appears far removed from the traditional "truths" he seeks. The narrator is abandoned in an ancient, isolated little town, quite remote from the "frontier." Even the vested "authorities" have forgotten whatever answers once held true. But paradoxically, the authority's refusal (his repudiation of the idea that there is a higher authority to answer man's grievances) comes as a relief in its consistency. There seems little consolation in the young peoples' questioning of the colonel's right to refuse to hear grievances—because, unfortunately, they are the least capable of comprehending the answers should they be forthcoming.

The sense of alienation from a rational image of the world permeates "An Old Manuscript." Ravaging, barbaric, obscene foreign soldiers terrorize a town because they are unknown, irrational forces that threaten annihilation. In a kind of nightmare, a cobbler stands by helplessly, alone, as these forces destroy his ordered world. The authoritarian figure, the king, is but vaguely and uncertainly seen: " . . . he was standing, or so at least it seemed to me, at one of the windows . . . . " This impotent figure may symbolize the father image, civil authority, or perhaps God. The great irony of this fable lies in the cobbler's final understatement: "This is a misunderstanding of some kind; and it will be the ruin of us." The jarring use of the word "ruin" underscores the absurd possibility that life may indeed be a very bad joke.

In "The Judgment" Kafka soars beyond the personal and autobiographical into artistic objectivity. The ultimate failure of the father (or God) symbol to give meaning to life symbolizes the social and spiritual isolation and despair of twentieth-century man. Kafka's "dream" world is the very real nonrational world lurking below man's level of consciousness. In this dream allegory Kafka brilliantly delineates the schizoid Georg Bendemann through his tormented guilt and self-inflicted punishment—death by water. Georg's struggle begins when his efforts to conform to society and its mores are pitted against his essential estrangement: his feelings of alienation, his guilt at not having loved his mother sufficiently, his fear of marriage, his resentment against his aging father.

In his dream world, it is Georg who dominates his father, who still looms a "giant" of a man. Georg's carefully undressing his father (unmanning him) reduces his father to the helpless babe he becomes as Georg carries his father to bed while he lies on Georg's "breast . . . playing with his watch chain." His repeatedly covering his father indicates his desire for his father's death. But even in the dream Georg's father sees through him and humiliates him. So, because of his own feelings of sexual inadequacy, his sublimated hatred of his parents, and his sense of isolation, Georg sentences himself to death by drowning. This thoroughly pessimistic existential work opens up speculations about the other Georg Bendemann, the one the reader never meets—Georg Bendemann awake, alive, and in the "real" world.

Jean-Paul Sartre   (1905-   )

In the existential philosophies of Martin Heidegger and Jean-Paul Sartre, a specifically atheistic dimension appears. Heidegger feels that an anxious fear of nothingness results from man's essential estrangement from his own being; therefore, man must be open to his own human existence. He must be open to his human condition and must assert his own destiny. Since truth does not lie in preconceived judgments of a thing, but rather in things in the world being allowed to reveal themselves, man must be open to experience—he must not accept the anxiety or nausea prompted by the finite termination of one's being: death. Sartre, however, accepts the palpable reality of nothingness and is nauseated by man's very existence in an inimical universe. Man's existence in this alien universe is absurd, that is, without justification or resolution. For Sartre, Milton's justification did not work. But if man is alone in the absurd consciousness of his atheistic situation, he is at least free—and freedom is a great responsibility for Sartre. The responsible man of good faith is needed to act within the finite framework of man's existential being. Both Sartre and Heidigger claim the primacy of the individual over the universal, the subjective over the objective, while recognizing at the same time the omnipresence of nothingness, fear, anxiety, despair, estrangement, absurdity—death.

In his short story "The Room," Sartre explores the sickness of the soul. His multileveled use of point of view explores the characters' consciousness of "reality." The graduated levels of spiritual decay terminate in the genuine madness of Pierre, Eve's husband. The room is their microcosm, their madhouse, where they patiently await death, alienated and withdrawn from a society which worships physical well-being while suffering spiritual malaise. In the story Eve's father, M. Darbedat, one of the unaware, thinks the problem of his son-in-law's madness simple: instead of giving him another fork, it would have been better to have reasoned quietly and made him understand that the first was like all the others. M. Darbedat does not comprehend the impossibility of reason in an irrational world—Pierre had escaped the terrible knowledge of life. When M. Darbedat confronts his daughter with "You don't want to admit he's sick," Sartre is dramatizing the general sickness of the world—its inability to recognize its own sickness.

Eve's repugnance at returning to "the room" symbolizes her burden of awareness; her retreat into the black-draped room is a descent into the underworld where the only meaningful act remaining is the murder of her husband. When meaningless existence becomes too intolerable, death and oblivion are salvation. Pierre's flying, buzzing statues are the furies, the harpies, the flies, the plague, the irrational madness called life. The statues are imitations of humans, themselves spectres and mockeries of the human condition. Eve's great gift and responsibility to her husband is to retreat with him into the union of oblivion.

Alberto Moravia   (1907-   )

The significance of Alberto Moravia as a writer in the existential tradition rests with his themes of alienation, sex, adolescence, and guilt. "The Fall" is a modern allegory of an adolescent's loss of innocence. The Garden of Eden is a tangled, rubbish-cluttered enclosure outside the villa where young Tancredi is staying for his health, a young victim of "obsessions," "fear," "remorse," "anguish," and "chronic apprehension." The snake is in attendance in the form of a cat, and Tancredi's willful and senseless blinding of it portends his sense of shame and verifies a haunting sense of guilt which he constantly feels brooding over him.

Tancredi's fantasies (both sacred and profane, aroused by the pictures of saints, Judith, and Danaë) transfer to the maid Veronica, and emerge in his dream world in explicit sexual symbols. Moravia presents the modern adolescent's sexual anxiety in an indifferent world (symbolized by his callous, card-playing mother) through a moral allegory of the loss of innocence. One is constantly reminded of the mythos of man's Fall and his subsequent eternal punishment in this world—guilt and shame. Moravia's extensive use of "fall" images and symbols emphasizes modern man's torment perpetuated by his sense of sin.

Albert Camus   (1913–1960)

Camus' existential view of life in "The Guest" is chilling, icy, contemptuous. It lacks the nausea of Sartre and the passionate guilt of Kafka. It is utterly bleak. In a totally subjective manner man can account only for his own existence. In this manner is man free—but, since he is without appeal, freedom *in vacuo* is absurd. It is absurd that the free man is aware of his own consciousness, responsibility, and freedom; therefore, paradoxically, the free man is like a prisoner: to live is an act of revolt on the individual's part—this is a free act. But he is bound to revolt, to live, since there is nothing beyond life; hence his freedom to revolt in full consciousness of his existential limitation is absurd. If man were a stone, he would have no consciousness to evoke. But instead, man is free and, consequently, absurd.

Camus' short story "The Guest" superbly illustrates his philosophy: Daru, the schoolteacher, presumably a rational man, is alone in a "remote schoolhouse" in a "cruel," snow-covered, mountainous region, a " . . . solitary expanse where nothing had any connection with man." As a free man, Daru is alienated from Nature by his own consciousness of his alienation. A bound Arab is delivered to him, to be turned over by Daru to authorities in the next town. "Daru felt a sudden wrath against the man, against all men with their . . . blood lust." Blood, lust, passion have no meaning among the snow, rocks, and wastelands of his world because they seem to have no purpose. "No one in this desert, neither he nor his guest, mattered." They were absurd figures. The guest in his "restless and rebellious" passion was perhaps more absurd than Daru. When the Arab unfortunately does not flee when given a chance to escape, Daru frees his prisoner only to see him dutifully trudging off alone to his fate in the town. The Arab's freedom was absurd because he could only choose death—sooner or later, but death ultimately. For Camus, death is the only reality.

The existential attitude revealed by these authors is varied and complex and one peculiar to the twentieth century, one that could not have existed at any other time in history. Science is expanding into ever-receding vistas of experimentation, vistas without end, extending *ad infinitum* into oblivion, nothingness. At a time when man is turning to the terrifying and tentative exploration of inner and outer space, the microcosm of the molecule reflects the macrocosm of the universe. But this infinitude is frightening to modern man because it is boundless and man is left essentially alone. A symbolic image of modern man might be a lonely individual chained in his seat in a darkened movie theatre, staring straight ahead at animated unreality, not touching, not contacting his fellow theatregoers, experiencing vicariously. It is an absurd picture. Modern man would seem to have come full circle from Plato's "allegory of the cave."

Selected Readings: Existentialism

Barrett, William. *Irrational Man: A Study in Existential Philosophy.* Garden City, N.Y.: Doubleday and Company, Inc., 1958.

————. *What Is Existentialism?* New York: Partisan Review, 1947.

Collins, James. *The Existentialists.* Chicago: Henry Regnery Company, 1952.

Friedman, Maurice (ed.). *The World of Existentialism.* New York: Random House, 1964.

Heinemann, Frederick H. *Existentialism and the Modern Predicament.* New York: Harper & Row, Publishers, 1953.

Kaufmann, Walter. *Existentialism from Dostoevsky to Sartre.* New York: Meridian Books, 1956.

Winn, Ralph B. *A Dictionary of Existentialism.* New York: Philosophical Library, 1960.

NIKOLAI GOGOL

(1809–1852)

Like Akaki Akakiyevich, Nikolai Gogol, born March 19, 1809, in a Ukranian township, wasted away and died. Spiritually, intellectually, artistically, Gogol had already died. Like a good true believer, Gogol's zealous attachment to a dying cause helped destroy him.

Gogol was, in the fullest sense, an "original." His works represent a shocking innovation in the continuity of Western literature. Works like "Ivan Fyodorovitch Shponka and His Aunt" (1832), "The Terrible Vengeance" (1832), "Diary of a Madman" (1835), and "The Nose" (1836) heralded not only a new literary style but a whole new attitude toward the world. Gogol was the first great modern writer. His influence extends through Dostoevsky and Chekhov to Kafka and all the modern spokesmen of the absurd.

Gogol's background as civil servant and teacher in St. Petersburg from 1828 to 1831 provided him with the raw material for his absurd, irrational world. He writes "My subject was always the same: my subject was life, and nothing more." By the time he was twenty-two he was already an accomplished and acclaimed writer. The next eleven years, culminating in the publication of *Dead Souls* in 1842, produced some of the world's most original literary works. But the last ten years of Gogol's life trace the gradual deterioration of a great and unique spirit.

Gogol's lifelong passion was Mother Russia; Gogol's great paradox was his advocacy of a return to traditional, conservative, patriarchal forms of government, religion, and society. He did not pause to realize that he no longer believed in them himself. While he advocated serfdom as part of the necessary "system," his works proclaim the principles of dignity and equality of man. Gogol is a perfect example of the ambivalence that frequently exists between an artist and his work: caught between his conflicting social-political beliefs and his aesthetic integrity, Gogol systematically starved himself to death. He died February 21, 1852.

Ivan Fyodorovitch Shponka
and His Aunt

There is a story about this story: we were told it by Stepan Ivan-ovitch Kurotchka, who came over from Gadyatch. You must know that my memory is incredibly poor: you may tell me a thing or not tell it, it is all the same. It is just pouring water into a sieve. Being aware of this failing, I purposely begged him to write the story down in an exercise-book. Well, God give him good health, he was always a kind man to me, he set to work and wrote it down. I put it in the little table; I expect you know it; it stands in the corner as you come in by the door . . . . But there, I forgot that you had never been in my house. My old woman, with whom I have lived thirty years, has never learnt to read—no use hiding one's shortcomings. Well, I noticed that she baked the pies on paper of some sort. She baked pies beautifully, dear readers; you will never taste better pies anywhere. I happened to look on the underside of a pie—what do I see? Written words! My heart seemed to tell me at once: I went to the table, only half the book was there! All the other pages she had carried off for the pies! What could I do? There is no fighting at our age! Last year I happened to be passing through Gadyatch. Before I reached the town I purposely tied a knot in my handkerchief that I might not forget to ask Stepan Ivanovitch about it. That was not all, I vowed to myself that as soon as ever I sneezed in the town I

Reprinted from *Old Russian Stories,* selected by J. I. Rodale. Published by A. S. Barnes, 1960.

would be sure to think of it. It was all no use. I drove through the town and sneezed and blew my nose too, but still I forgot it; and I only thought of it nearly five miles after I had passed through the town gate. There was no help for it, I had to print it without the end. However, if any one particularly wants to know what happened later on in the story, he need only go on purpose to Gadyatch and ask Stepan Ivanovitch. He will be glad to tell the story, I daresay, all over again from the beginning. He lives not far from the brick church. There is a little lane close by, and as soon as you turn into the lane it is the second or third gate. Or better still, when you see a big post with a quail on it in the yard and coming to meet you a stout peasant woman in a green petticoat (it may be as well to mention that he is a bachelor), that is his yard. Though indeed you may meet him in the market, where he is to be seen every morning before nine o'clock, choosing fish and vegetables for his table and talking to Father Antip or the Jewish contractor. You will know him at once, for there is no one else who has trousers of flowered linen and a yellow cotton coat. And another thing you may know him by—he always swings his arms as he walks. Denis Petrovitch, the assessor, now deceased, always used to say when he saw him in the distance, "Look, look, here comes our windmill!"

I

Ivan Fyodorovitch Shponka

It is four years since Ivan Fyodorovitch retired from the army and came to live on his farm Vytrebenki. When he was still Vanyusha, he was at the Gadyatch district school, and I must say he was a very well-behaved and industrious boy. Nikifor Timofyevitch Dyepritchastie, the teacher of Russian grammar, used to say that if all the boys had been as anxious to do their best as Shponka, he would not have brought into the class-room the maplewood ruler with which, as he owned himself, he was tired of hitting the lazy and mischievous boys' hands. His exercise-book was always neat, with a ruled margin, and not the tiniest blot anywhere. He always sat quietly with his arms folded and his eyes fixed on the teacher, and he never used to stick scraps of paper on the back of the boy sitting in front of him, never cut the bench and never played at shoving the other boys off the bench before the master came in. If any one wanted a penknife to mend his pen, he immediately applied to Ivan Fyodorovitch knowing that he always had a penknife, and Ivan Fyodorovitch, at that time simply Vanyusha, would take it out of a little leather case attached to a buttonhole of his grey coat, and would only request that the sharp edge should not be used for scraping the pen, pointing out that there was a blunt side for the purpose. Such good conduct soon attracted the attention of the Latin master, whose cough in the passage was enough to reduce the class to terror, even before his frieze coat and pockmarked countenance had appeared in the doorway. This terrible master, who always had two birches lying on his desk and half of whose pupils were always on their knees, made Ivan Fyodorovitch monitor, although there were many boys in the class of much greater ability. Here I cannot omit an incident which had an influence on the whole of his future life. One of the boys entrusted to his charge tried to induce his monitor to write *scit* on his report, though he had not learnt his lesson, by bringing into class a pancake soaked in butter and wrapped in paper. Though Ivan Fyodorovitch was usually conscientious, on this occasion he was hungry and could not resist the temptation: he took the pancake, held a book up before him and began eating it, and he was so absorbed in this occupation that he did not observe that a deathly silence had fallen upon the class-room. He only woke up with horror when a terrible hand protruding from a frieze overcoat seized him by the ear and dragged him into the middle of the room. "Hand over that pancake! Hand it over, I tell you, you rascal!" said the terrible master; he seized the buttery pancake in his fingers and flung it out of window, sternly forbidding the boys running about in the yard to pick it up. Then he proceeded on the spot to whack Ivan Fyodorovitch very painfully on the hands; and quite rightly—the hands were responsible for taking it and no other part of the body. Anyway, the timidity which had always been characteristic of him was more marked from that time forward. Possibly the same incident was the explanation of his feeling no desire to enter the civil service, having learnt by experience that one is not always successful in hiding one's misdeeds.

He was very nearly fifteen when he moved up into the second class, where instead of the four rules of arithmetic and the abridged catechism, he went on to the longer one, the book of the duties of man, and fractions. But seeing that the further you went into the forest the thicker the wood became, and receiving the news that his father had departed this life, he stayed only two years longer at school, and with his mother's consent went in the P——— infantry regiment.

The P——— infantry regiment was not at all of the class to which many infantry regiments belong, and, although it was for the most part stationed in country places, it was in no way inferior to many cavalry regiments. The majority of the officers drank neat spirit and were quite as good at dragging about Jews by their curls as any Hussars; some of them even danced the mazurka, and the colonel of the regiment never missed an opportunity of mentioning the fact when he was talking to any one in company. "Among my officers," he used to say, patting himself on the belly after every word, "a number dance the mazurka, quite a number of them, really a great number of them indeed." To show our readers the degree of culture of the P——— infantry regiment, we must add that two of the officers were passionately fond of the game of bank and used to gamble away their uniforms, caps, overcoats, swordknots and even their underclothes, which is more than you could find in every cavalry regiment.

Contact with such comrades did not, however, diminish Ivan Fyodorovitch's timidity; and as he did not drink neat spirit, preferring to it a wineglassful of ordinary vodka before dinner and supper, did not dance the mazurka or play bank, naturally he was bound to be always left alone. And so it came to pass that while the others were driving about with hired horses, visiting the less important landowners, he sitting at home spent his time in pursuits peculiar to a mild and gentle soul: he either polished his buttons, or read a dream-book or set mouse-traps in the corners of his room, or failing everything he would take off his uniform and lie on his bed.

On the other hand, no one in the regiment was more punctual in his duties than Ivan Fyodorovitch, and he drilled his platoon in such a way that the commander of the company always held him up as a model to the others. Consequently in a short time, eleven years after becoming an ensign, he was promoted to be a second lieutenant.

During that time he had received the news that his mother was dead, and his aunt, his mother's sister, whom he only knew from her bringing him in his childhood—and even sending him when he was at Gadyatch—dried pears and extremely nice honeycakes which she made herself (she was on bad terms with his mother and so Ivan Fyodorovitch had not seen her in later years), this aunt, in the goodness of her heart, undertook to look after his little estate and in due time informed him of the fact by letter.

Ivan Fyodorovitch, having the fullest confidence in his aunt's good sense, continued to perform his duties as before. Some men in his position would have grown conceited at such promotion, but pride was a feeling of which he knew nothing, and as lieutenant he was the same Ivan Fyodorovitch as he had been when an ensign. He spent another four years in the regiment after the event of so much consequence to him, and was about to leave the Mogilyev district for Great Russia with his regiment when he received a letter as follows:

"*My Dear Nephew, Ivan Fyodorovitch,*—I am sending you some linen: five pairs of thread socks and four shirts of fine linen; and what is more I want to talk to you of something serious; since you have already a rank of some importance, as I suppose you are aware, and have reached a time of life when it is fitting to take up the management of your land, there is no reason for you to remain longer in military service. I am getting old and can no longer see to everything on your farm; and in fact there is a great deal that I want to talk to you about in person.

"Come, Vanyusha! Looking forward to the real pleasure of seeing you, I remain your very affectionate Aunt,

"*Vassilissa Tsuptchevska.*

"P.S.—There is a wonderful turnip in our kitchen garden, more like a potato than a turnip."

A week after receiving this letter Ivan Fyodorovitch wrote an answer as follows:

"*Honored Madam, Auntie, Vassilissa Kashparovna,*—Thank you

very much for sending the linen. My socks especially are very old,
my orderly has darned them four times and that has made them
very tight. As to your views in regard to my service in the army,
I completely agree with you, and the day before yesterday I sent
in my papers. As soon as I get my discharge I will engage a chaise.
As to your commission in regard to the seed wheat and Siberian
corn I cannot carry it out; there is none in all the Mogilyev province. About here pigs are mostly fed on brewers' grains together
with a little beer when it has grown flat. With the greatest respect,
honored madam and auntie, I remain your nephew,

"Ivan Shponka."

At last Ivan Fyodorovitch received his discharge with the grade
of lieutenant, hired for forty roubles a Jew to drive from Mogilyev
to Gadyatch, and set off in the chaise just at the time when the
trees are clothed with young and still scanty leaves, the whole
earth is bright with fresh green, and there is the fragrance of spring
over all the fields.

II
The Journey

Nothing of great interest occurred on the journey. They were
travelling a little over a fortnight. Ivan Fyodorovitch might have
arrived a little sooner than that, but the devout Jew kept the
Sabbath on the Saturdays and, putting his horse-cloth over his
head, prayed the whole day. Ivan Fyodorovitch, however, as I
have had occasion to mention already, was a man who did not
give way to being bored. During these intervals he undid his trunk,
took out his underclothes, inspected them thoroughly to see
whether they were properly washed and folded; carefully removed
the fluff from his new uniform, which had been made without
epaulettes, and repacked it all in the best possible way. He was
not fond of reading in general; and if he did sometimes look into
a dream-book, it was because he liked to meet again what he had
already read several times. In the same way one who lives in the
town goes every day to the club, not for the sake of hearing anything new there, but in order to meet there friends with whom

it has been one's habit to chat at the club from time immemorial. In the same way a government clerk will read a directory of addresses with immense satisfaction several times a day with no ulterior object, he is simply entertained by the printed list of names. "Ah! Ivan Gavrilovitch So-and-so . . . " he murmurs mutely to himself. "And here again am I! h'm . . . !" and next time he reads it over again with exactly the same exclamations.

After a fortnight's journey Ivan Fyodorovitch reached a little village some eighty miles from Gadyatch. This was on Friday. The sun had long set when with the chaise and the Jew he reached an inn.

This inn differed in no respects from other little village inns. As a rule the traveller is zealously regaled in them with hay and oats, as though he were a post-horse. But should he want to lunch as decent people do lunch, he keeps his appetite intact for some future opportunity. Ivan Fyodorovitch, knowing all this, had provided himself beforehand with two bundles of breadrings and a sausage, and asking for a glass of vodka, of which there is never a shortage in any inn, he began his supper, sitting down on a bench before an oak table which was fixed immovably in the clay floor.

Meanwhile he heard the rattle of a chaise. The gates creaked but it was a long while before the chaise drove into the yard. A loud voice was engaged in scolding the old woman who kept the inn. "I will drive in," Ivan Fyodorovitch heard, "but if I am bitten by a single bug in your inn, I will beat you, on my soul I will, you old witch! and I will give you nothing for your hay!"

A minute later the door opened and there walked in—or rather squeezed himself in—a stout man in a green frock-coat. His head rested immovably on his short neck, which seemed even thicker, from a double chin. To judge from his appearance, he belonged to that class of men who do not trouble their heads about trifles and whose whole life has passed easily.

"I wish you good day, honored sir!" he pronounced on seeing Ivan Fyodorovitch.

Ivan Fyodorovitch bowed in silence.

"Allow me to ask, to whom have I the honor of speaking?" the stout newcomer continued.

At such an examination Ivan Fyodorovitch involuntarily got

up and stood at attention as he usually did when the colonel asked him a question. "Retired Lieutenant Ivan Fyodorovitch Shponka," he answered.

"And may I ask what place you are bound for?"

"My own farm Vytrebenki."

"Vytrebenki!" cried the stern examiner. "Allow me, honored sir, allow me!" he said, going towards him, and waving his arms as though some one were hindering him or as though he were making his way through a crowd, he folded Ivan Fyodorovitch in an embrace and kissed him first on the right cheek and then on the left and then on the right again. Ivan Fyodorovitch was much gratified by this kiss, for his lips were pressed against the stranger's fat cheeks as though against soft cushions.

"Allow me to make your acquaintance, my dear sir!" the fat man continued: "I am a landowner of the same district of Gadyatch and your neighbor; I live not more than four miles from your Vytrebenki in the village of Hortyshtche; and my name is Grigory Grigoryevitch Stortchenko. You really must, sir, you really must pay me a visit at Hortyshtche. I won't speak to you if you don't. I am in haste now on business . . . . Why, what's this?" he said in a mild voice to his postilion, a boy in a Cossack tunic with patched elbows and a bewildered expression, who came in and put bags and boxes on the table. "What's this, what's the meaning of it?" and by degrees Grigory Grigoryevitch's voice grew more and more threatening. "Did I tell you to put them here my good lad? Did I tell you to put them here, you rascal? Didn't I tell you to heat the chicken up first, you scoundrel? Be off!" he shouted, stamping. "Stay, you fright! Where's the basket with the bottles? Ivan Fyodorovitch!" he said, pouring out a glass of liqueur, "I beg you take some cordial!"

"Oh, really, I cannot . . . I have already had occasion . . . ." Ivan Fyodorovitch began hesitatingly.

"I won't hear a word, sir!" the gentleman raised his voice, "I won't hear a word! I won't budge till you drink it . . . ."

Ivan Fyodorovitch, seeing that it was impossible to refuse, not without gratification emptied the glass.

"This is a fowl, sir," said the fat Grigory Grigoryevitch, carving it in a wooden box. "I must tell you that my cook Yavdoha is fond of a drop at times and so she often dries up things. Hey, lad!" here

he turned to the boy in the Cossack tunic who was bringing in a
feather-bed and pillows, "make my bed on the floor in the middle
of the room! Mind you put plenty of hay under the pillow! And
pull a bit of hemp from the woman's distaff to stop up my ears
for the night! I must tell you, sir, that I have the habit of stopping
up my ears at night ever since the damnable occasion when a
cockroach crawled into my left ear in a Great Russian inn. The
confounded long-beards, as I found out afterwards, eat their soup
with beetles in it. Impossible to describe what happened to me;
there was such a tickling, such a tickling in my ear . . . . I was
downright crazy! I was cured by a simple old woman in our district, and by what do you suppose? Simply by whispering to it.
What do you think, my dear sir, about doctors? What I think is
that they simply hoax us and make fools of us: some old women
know a dozen times as much as all these doctors."

"Indeed, what you say is perfectly true, sir. There certainly
are cases . . . "Here Ivan Fyodorovitch paused as though he could
not find the right word. It may not be amiss to mention here that
he was at no time lavish of words. This may have been due to
timidity, or it may have been due to a desire to express himself
elegantly.

"Shake up the hay properly, shake it up properly!" said Grigory
Grigoryevitch to his servant. "The hay is so bad about here that
you may come upon a twig in it any minute. Allow me, sir, to wish
you a good night! We shall not see each other to-morrow. I am
setting off before dawn. Your Jew will keep the Sabbath because
tomorrow is Saturday, so it is no good for you to get up early.
Don't forget my invitation; I won't speak to you if you don't come
to see me at Hortyshtche."

At this point Grigory Grigoryevitch's servant pulled off his
coat and high boots and gave him his dressing-gown instead, and
Grigory Grigoryevitch stretched on his bed, and it looked as
though one huge feather-bed were lying on another.

"Hey, lad! where are you, rascal? Come here and arrange my
quilt. Hey, lad, prop up my head with hay! Have you watered the
horses yet? Some more hay! here, under this side! And do arrange
the quilt properly, you rascal! That's right, more! Ough . . . !"

Then Grigory Grigoryevitch heaved two sighs and filled the
whole room with a terrible whistling through his nose, snoring so

loudly at times that the old woman who was snoozing on the settle, suddenly waking up, looked about her in all directions, but, seeing nothing, subsided and went to sleep again.

When Ivan Fyodorovitch woke up next morning, the fat gentleman was no longer there. This was the only noteworthy incident that occurred on the journey. Two days later he drew near his little farm.

He felt his heart begin to throb when the windmill waving its sails peeped out and, as the Jew drove his nag up the hill, the row of willows came into sight below. The pond gleamed bright and shining through them and a breath of freshness rose from it. Here he used to bathe in old days; in that pond he used to wade with the peasant lads, up to his neck, after crayfish. The covered cart mounted the dam and Ivan Fyodorovitch saw the little old-fashioned house thatched with reeds, and the apple trees and cherry trees which he used to climb on the sly. He had no sooner driven into the yard than dogs of all kinds, brown, black, grey, spotted, ran up from every side. Some flew under the horse's hoofs, barking, others ran behind the cart, noticing that the axle was smeared with bacon fat; one, standing near the kitchen and keeping his paw on a bone, uttered a volley of shrill barks; and another gave tongue in the distance, running to and fro wagging his tail and seeming to say: "Look, good Christians! what a fine young fellow I am!" Boys in grubby shirts ran out to stare. A sow that was promenading in the yard with sixteen little pigs lifted her snout with an inquisitive air and grunted louder than usual. In the yard a number of hempen sheets were lying on the ground covered with wheat, millet, and barley drying in the sun. A good many different kinds of herbs, such as wild chicory and swine-herb, were drying on the roof.

Ivan Fyodorovitch was so occupied in scrutinizing all this that he was only roused when a spotted dog bit the Jew on the calf of his leg as he was getting down from the box. The servants who ran out, that is, the cook and another woman and two girls in woolen petticoats, after the first exclamations: "It's our young master!" informed him that his aunt was sowing sweet corn together with the girl Palashka and Omelko the coachman, who often performed the duties of a gardener and watchman also. But his aunt, who had seen the sack-covered cart in the distance, was already on the spot. And Ivan Fyodorovitch was astonished when she almost lifted him from the ground in her arms, hardly able to believe that this could be the aunt who had written to him of her old age and infirmities.

III
Auntie

Auntie Vassilissa Kashparovna was at this time about fifty. She had never been married, and commonly declared that she valued her maiden state above everything. Though, indeed, to the best of my memory, no one ever courted her. This was due to the fact that all men were sensible of a certain timidity in her presence, and never had the spirit to make her an offer. "A girl of great character, Vassilissa Kashparovna!" all the young men used to say, and they were quite right, too, for there was no one Vassilissa Kashparovna could not get the whip hand of. With her own manly hand, tugging every day at his topknot of curls, she could, unaided, turn the drunken miller, a worthless fellow, into a perfect treasure. She was of almost gigantic stature and her breadth and strength were fully in proportion. It seemed as though nature had made an unpardonable mistake in condemning her to wear a dark brown gown with little flounces on weekdays and a red cashmere shawl on Sunday and on her name-day, though a dragoon's moustaches and high topboots would have suited her better than anything. On the other hand, her pursuits completely corresponded with her appearance: she rowed the boat herself and was more skilful with the oars than any fisherman; shot game; stood over the mowers all the while they were at work; knew the exact number of the melons, of all kinds, in the kitchen garden; took a toll of five kopecks from every wagon that crossed her dam; climbed the trees and shook down the pears; beat lazy vassals with her terrible hand and with the same menacing hand bestowed a glass of vodka on the deserving. Almost at the same moment she was scolding, dyeing yarn, racing to the kitchen, brewing kvass, making jam with honey; she was busy all day long and everywhere in the nick of time. The result of all this was that Ivan Fyodorovitch's little property, which had consisted of eighteen souls at the last census, was flourishing in the fullest sense of the word. Moreover, she had a very warm affection for her nephew and carefully accumulated kopecks for him.

From the time of his arrival at his home Ivan Fyodorovitch's life was completely transformed and took an entirely different turn. It seemed as though nature had designed him expressly for looking after an estate of eighteen souls. Auntie herself observed that he would make an excellent farmer, though she did not yet permit him to meddle in every branch of the management. "He's but a young child yet," she used commonly to say, though Ivan Fyodorovitch was as a fact not far off forty. "How should he know it all!"

However, he was always in the fields with the reapers and mowers, and this was a source of unutterable pleasure to his gentle heart. The sweep of a dozen or more gleaming scythes in unison; the sound of the grass falling in even swathes; the carolling songs of the reapers at intervals, at one time joyous as the welcoming of a guest, at another mournful as parting; the calm pure evening—and what an evening! How free and fresh the air! How everything revived; the steppe flushed red then turned dark blue and gleamed with flowers; quails, bustards, gulls, grasshoppers, thousands of insects and all of them whistling, buzzing, churring, calling and suddenly blending into a harmonious chorus; nothing silent for an instant, while the sun sets and is hidden. Oh, how fresh and delightful it was! Here and there about the fields camp-fires are built and cauldrons set over them, and round the fires the mowers sit down; the steam from the dumplings floats upwards; the twilight turns greyer . . . . It is hard to say what passed in Ivan Fyodorovitch at such times. When he joined the mowers, he forgot to try their dumplings, though he liked them particularly, and stood motionless, watching a gull disappear in the sky or counting the sheaves of corn dotted over the field.

In a short time Ivan Fyodorovitch was spoken of as a great farmer. Auntie was never tired of rejoicing over her nephew and never lost an opportunity of boasting of him. One day—it was just after the end of the harvest, that is at the end of July—Vassilissa Kashparovna took Ivan Fyodorovitch by the arm with a mysterious air, and said she wanted now to speak to him of a matter which had long been on her mind.

"You are aware, dear Ivan Fyodorovitch," she began, "that there are eighteen souls on your farm, though, indeed, that is by the census register, and in reality they may reckon up to more, they may be twenty-four. But that is not the point. You know the copse that lies behind our vegetable ground, and no doubt you know the broad meadow behind it; there are very nearly sixty acres in it; and the grass is so good that it is worth a hundred roubles every year, especially if, as they say, a cavalry regiment is to be stationed at Gadyatch."

"To be sure, Auntie, I know: the grass is very good."

"You needn't tell me the grass is very good, I know it; but do you know that all that land is by rights yours? Why do you look so surprised? Listen, Ivan Fyodorovitch! You remember Stepan Kuzmitch? What am I saying: 'you remember'! You were so little that you could not even pronounce his name. Yes, indeed! How could you remember! When I came on the very eve of St. Philip's Fast and took you in my arms, you almost ruined my dress; luckily I was just in time to hand you to your nurse, Matryona; you were such a horrid little thing then . . . ! But that is not the point. All the land beyond our farm, and the village of Hortyshtche itself belonged to Stepan Kuzmitch. I must tell you that before you were in this world he used to visit your mamma—though, indeed, only when your father was not at home. Not that I say it in blame of her—God rest her soul!—though your poor mother was always unfair to me! But that is not the point. Be that as it may, Stepan Kuzmitch made a deed of gift to you of that same estate of which I have been speaking. But your poor mamma, between ourselves, was a very strange character. The devil himself (God forgive me for the nasty word!) would have been puzzled to understand her. What she did with that deed of gift—God only knows. It's my opinion that it is in the hands of that old bachelor, Grigory Grigoryevitch Stortchenko. That pot-bellied rascal has got hold of the whole estate. I'd bet anything you like that he has hidden that deed."

"Allow me to ask, Auntie: isn't he the Stortchenko whose acquaintance I made at the inn?" Hereupon Ivan Fyodorovitch described his meeting with Stortchenko.

"Who knows," said his aunt after a moment's thought, "perhaps he is not a rascal. It's true that it's only six months since he came to live among us; there's no finding out what a man is in that time. The old lady, his mother, is a very sensible woman, so I hear, and they say she is a great hand at salting cucumbers; her own serf-girls can make capital rugs. But as you say he gave you such a friendly welcome, go and see him, perhaps the old sinner will listen to his conscience and will give up what is not his. If you like you can go in the chaise, only those confounded brats have pulled out all the nails at the back; you must tell the coachman, Omelko, to nail the leather on better everywhere."

"What for, Auntie? I will take the trap that you sometimes go out shooting in."

With that the conversation ended.

IV
The Dinner

It was about dinner-time when Ivan Fyodorovitch drove into the hamlet of Hortyshtche and he felt a little timid as he approached the manor-house. It was a long house, not thatched with reeds like the houses of many of the neighboring landowners, but with a wooden roof. Two barns in the yard also had wooden roofs: the gate was of oak. Ivan Fyodorovitch felt like a dandy who, on arriving at a ball, sees every one more smartly dressed than himself. He stopped his trap by the barn as a sign of respect and went on foot towards the front door.

"Ah, Ivan Fyodorovitch!" cried the fat man Grigory Grigoryevitch, who was crossing the yard in his coat but without cravat, waistcoat and braces. But apparently this attire weighed oppressively on his bulky person, for the perspiration was streaming down him.

"Why, you said you would come as soon as you had seen your aunt, and all this time you have not been here?" After these words Ivan Fyodorovitch's lips found themselves again in contact with the same cushions.

"Chiefly being busy looking after the land . . . . I have come just for a minute to see you on business . . . . "

"For a minute? Well, that won't do. Hey, lad!" shouted the fat gentleman, and the same boy in the Cossack tunic ran out of the kitchen. "Tell Kassyan to shut the gate tight, do you hear! make it fast! And take this gentleman's horse out of the shafts this minute. Please come indoors; it is so hot out here that my shirt's soaked."

On going indoors Ivan Fyodorovitch made up his mind to lose no time and in spite of his shyness to act with decision.

"My aunt had the honor ... she told me that a deed of gift of the late Stepan Kuzmitch ... "

It is difficult to describe the unpleasant grimace made by the broad countenance of Grigory Grigoryevitch at these words.

"Oh dear, I hear nothing!" he responded. "I must tell you that a cockroach got into my left ear (those bearded Russians breed cockroaches in all their huts); no pen can describe what agony it was, it kept tickling and tickling. An old woman cured me by the simplest means .... "

"I meant to say ... " Ivan Fyodorovitch ventured to interrupt, seeing that Grigory Grigoryevitch was intentionally changing the subject; "that in the late Stepan Kuzmitch's will mention is made, so to speak, of a deed of gift .... According to it I ought ... "

"I know; so your aunt has told you that story already. It's a lie, upon my soul it is! My uncle made no deed of gift. Though, indeed, some such deed is referred to in the will. But where is it? No one has produced it. I tell you this because I sincerely wish you well. Upon my soul it is a lie!"

Ivan Fyodorovitch said nothing, reflecting that possibly his aunt really might be mistaken.

"Ah, here comes mother with my sisters!" said Grigory Grigoryevitch, "so dinner is ready. Let us go!"

Thereupon he drew Ivan Fyodorovitch by the hand into a room in which vodka and savories were standing on the table.

At the same time a short little old lady, a regular coffee-pot in a cap, with two young ladies, one fair and one dark, came in. Ivan Fyodorovitch, like a well-bred gentleman, went up to kiss the old lady's hand and then to kiss the hands of the two young ladies.

"This is our neighbor, Ivan Fyodorovitch Shponka, mother," said Grigory Grigoryevitch.

The old lady looked intently at Ivan Fyodorovitch, or perhaps it only seemed that she looked intently at him. She was good-natured simplicity itself, though; she looked as though she would like to ask Ivan Fyodorovitch: "How many cucumbers have you salted for the winter?"

"Have you had some vodka?" the old lady asked.

"You can't have had your sleep out, mother," said Grigory Grigoryevitch. "Who asks a visitor whether he has had anything. You offer it to him, that's all: whether we have had any or not, that is our business. Ivan Fyodorovitch! the centaury-flavored vodka or the Trofimov brand? Which do you prefer? And you, Ivan Ivanovitch, why are you standing there?" Grigory Grigorye-vitch brought out, turning round, and Ivan Fyodorovitch saw the gentleman so addressed approaching the vodka, in a frock-coat with long skirts and an immense stand-up collar, which covered the whole back of his head, so that his head sat in it, as though it were a chaise.

Ivan Ivanovitch went up to the vodka and rubbed his hands, carefully examined the wineglass, filled it, held it up to the light, and poured all the vodka at once into his mouth. He did not, however, swallow it at once, but rinsed his mouth thoroughly with it first before finally swallowing it, and then after eating some bread and salted mushrooms, he turned to Ivan Fyodorovitch.

"Is it not Ivan Fyodorovitch, Mr. Shponka, I have the honor of addressing?"

"Yes, certainly," answered Ivan Fyodorovitch.

"You have changed a great deal, sir, since I saw you last. Why!" he continued, "I remember you that high!" As he spoke he held his hand a yard from the floor. "Your poor father, God grant him the kingdom of Heaven, was a rare man. He used to have melons such as you never see anywhere now. Here, for instance," he went on, drawing him aside, "they'll set melons before you on the table—such melons! You won't care to look at them! Would you believe it, sir, he used to have water-melons," he pronounced with a mysterious air, flinging out his arms as if he were about to embrace a stout tree trunk, "upon my soul as big as this!"

"Come to dinner!" said Grigory Grigoryevitch, taking Ivan Fyodorovitch by the arm.

Grigory Grigoryevitch sat down in his usual place at the end of the table, draped with an enormous tablenapkin which made him resemble the Greek heroes depicted by barbers on their signs. Ivan Fyodorovitch, blushing, sat down in the place assigned to him, facing the two young ladies; and Ivan Ivanovitch did not let slip the chance of sitting down beside him, inwardly rejoicing that he had some one to whom he could impart his various items of information.

"You shouldn't take the bishop's nose, Ivan Fyodorovitch! It's a turkey!" said the old lady, addressing Ivan Fyodorovitch, to whom the rustic waiter in a grey swallow-tail patched with black was offering a dish. "Take the back!"

"Mother! no one asked you to interfere!" commented Grigory Grigoryevitch. "You may be sure our visitor knows what to take himself! Ivan Fyodorovitch! take a wing, the other one there with the gizzard! But why have you taken so little? Take a leg! Why do you stand gaping with the dish? Ask him! Go down on your knees, rascal! Say, at once, 'Ivan Fyodorovitch, take a leg!' "

"Ivan Fyodorovitch, take a leg!" the waiter with the dish bawled, kneeling down.

"H'm! do you call this a turkey?" Ivan Ivanovitch muttered in a low voice, turning to his neighbor with an air of disdain. "Is that what a turkey ought to look like? If you could see my turkeys! I assure you there is more fat on one of them than on a dozen of these. Would you believe me, sir, they are really a repulsive sight when they walk about my yard, they are so fat . . . !"

"Ivan Ivanovitch, you are telling lies!" said Grigory Grigoryevitch, overhearing these remarks.

"I tell you," Ivan Ivanovitch went on talking to his neighbor, affecting not to hear what Grigory Grigoryevitch had said, "last year when I sent them to Gadyatch, they offered me fifty kopecks apiece for them, and I wouldn't take even that."

"Ivan Ivanovitch! I tell you, you are lying!" observed Grigory Grigoryevitch, dwelling on each syllable for greater distinctness and speaking more loudly than before.

But Ivan Ivanovitch behaved as though the words could not possibly refer to him; he went on as before, but in a much lower voice: "Yes, sir, I would not take it. There is not a gentleman in Gadyatch . . . "

"Ivan Ivanovitch! you are a fool, and that's the truth," Grigory Grigoryevitch said in a loud voice. "Ivan Fyodorovitch knows all about it better than you do, and doesn't believe you."

At this Ivan Ivanovitch was really offended: he said no more, but fell to putting away the turkey, even though it was not so fat as those that were a repulsive sight.

The clatter of knives, spoons and plates took the place of conversation for a time, but loudest of all was the sound made by Grigory Grigoryevitch, smacking his lips over the marrow out of the mutton bones.

"Have you," inquired Ivan Ivanovitch after an interval of silence, poking his head out of the chaise, "read the 'Travels of Korobeynikov in the Holy Land'? It's a real delight to heart and soul! Such books aren't published nowadays. I very much regret that I did not notice in what year it was written."

Ivan Fyodorovitch, hearing mention of a book, applied himself diligently to taking sauce.

"It is truly marvellous, sir, when you think that a humble artisan visited all those places: over two thousand miles, sir! over two thousand miles! Truly, it was by divine grace that it was vouchsafed him to reach Palestine and Jerusalem."

"So you say," said Ivan Fyodorovitch, who had heard a great deal about Jerusalem from his orderly, "that he visited Jerusalem."

"What are you saying, Ivan Fyodorovitch?" Grigory Grigoryevitch inquired from the end of the table.

"I had occasion to observe what distant lands there are in the world!" said Ivan Fyodorovitch, genuinely gratified that he had succeeded in uttering so long and difficult a sentence.

"Don't you believe him, Ivan Fyodorovitch!" said Grigory Grigoryevitch, who had not quite caught what he said, "he always tells fibs!"

Meanwhile dinner was over. Grigory Grigoryevitch went to his own room, as his habit was, for a little nap; and the visitors followed their aged hostess and the young ladies into the drawing-room, where the same table on which they had left vodka when they went out to dinner was now as though by some magical transformation covered with little saucers of jam of various sorts and dishes of cherries and different kinds of melons.

The absence of Grigory Grigoryevitch was perceptible in everything: the old lady became more disposed to talk and, of her own accord, without being asked, revealed several secrets in regard to the making of apple cheese, and the drying of pears. Even the young ladies began talking; though the fair one, who looked some six years younger than her sister and who was apparently about five-and-twenty, was rather silent.

But Ivan Ivanovitch was more talkative and livelier than any one. Feeling secure that no one would snub or contradict him, he talked of cucumbers and of planting potatoes and of how much more sensible people were in old days—no comparison with what people are now!—and of how as time goes on everything improves and the most intricate inventions are discovered. He was, indeed, one of those persons who take great pleasure in relieving their souls by conversation and will talk of anything that possibly can be talked about. If the conversation touched upon grave and solemn subjects, Ivan Ivanovitch sighed after each word and nodded his head slightly: if the subject were of a more homely character, he would pop his head out of his chaise and make faces from which one could almost, it seemed, read how to make pear kvass, how large were the melons of which he was speaking and how fat were the geese that were running about in his yard.

At last, with great difficulty and not before evening, Ivan Fyodorovitch succeeded in taking his leave, and although he was usually ready to give way and they almost kept him for the night by force, he persisted in his intention of going—and went.

V

Auntie's New Plans

"Well, did you get the deed of gift out of the old reprobate?" Such was the question with which Ivan Fyodorovitch was greeted by his aunt, who has been expecting him for some hours in the porch and had at last been unable to resist going out to the gate.

"No, Auntie," said Ivan Fyodorovitch, getting out of the trap: "Grigory Grigoryevitch has no deed of gift!"

"And you believed him? He was lying, the confounded fellow! Some day I shall come across him and I will give him a drubbing with my own hands. Oh, I'd get rid of some of his fat for him! Though perhaps we ought first to consult our court assessor and see if we couldn't get the law of him . . . . But that's not the point now. Well, was the dinner good?"

"Very . . . yes, excellent, Auntie!"

"Well, what did you have? Tell me. The old lady, I know, is a great hand at looking after the cooking."

"Curd fritters with sour cream, Auntie: a stew of stuffed pigeons . . . "

"And a turkey with pickled plums?" asked his aunt, for she was herself very skilful in the preparation of that dish.

"Yes, there was a turkey, too . . . ! Very handsome young ladies Grigory Grigoryevitch's sisters, especially the fair one!"

"Ah!" said Auntie, and she looked intently at Ivan Fyodorovitch, who dropped his eyes, blushing. A new idea flashed into her mind. "Come, tell me," she said eagerly and with curiosity, "what are her eyebrows like?" It may not be amiss to observe that Auntie considered fine eyebrows as the most important item in a woman's looks.

"Her eyebrows, Auntie, are exactly like what you described yours as being when you were young. And there are little freckles all over her face."

"Ah," commented his aunt, well pleased with Ivan Fyodorovitch's observation, though he had had no idea of paying her a compliment. "What sort of dress was she wearing? Though, indeed, it's hard to get good material nowadays, such as I have here, for instance, in this gown. But that's not the point. Well, did you talk to her about anything?"

"Talk . . . how do you mean, Auntie? Perhaps you are imagining . . . "

"Well, what of it, there would be nothing strange in that? Such is God's will! It may have been ordained at your birth that you should make a match of it."

"I don't know how you can say such a thing, Auntie. That shows that you don't know me at all . . . . "

"Well, well, now he is offended," said his aunt. "He's still only a child!" she thought to herself: "he knows nothing! We must bring them together—let them get to know each other!"

Hereupon Auntie went to have a look at the kitchen and left Ivan Fyodorovitch alone. But from that time forward she thought of nothing but seeing her nephew married as soon as possible and fondling his little ones. Her brain was absorbed in making preparations for the wedding, and it was noticeable that she bustled about more busily than ever, though the work was the worse rather than the better for it. Often when she was making the pies, a job which she never left to the cook, she would forget everything, and imagining that a tiny great-nephew was standing by her asking for some pie, would absently hold out her hands with the nicest bit for him, and the yard-dog taking advantage of this would snatch the dainty morsel and by its loud munching rouse her from her reverie, for which it was always beaten with the oven fork. She even abandoned her favorite pursuits and did not go out shooting, especially after she shot a crow by mistake for a partridge, a thing which had never happened to her before.

At last, four days later, every one saw the chaise brought out of the carriage house into the yard. The coachman Omelko (he was also the gardener and the watchman) had been hammering from early morning, nailing on the leather and continually chasing away the dogs who licked the wheels. I think it my duty to inform my readers that this was the very chaise in which Adam used to drive; and therefore, if any one gives out that some other chaise was Adam's, it is an absolute lie, and his chaise is certainly not the genuine article. It is impossible to say how it survived the Deluge. It must be supposed that there was a special coach-house for it in Noah's Ark. I am very sorry that I cannot give a living picture of it for my readers. It is enough to say that Vassilissa Kashparovna was very well satisfied with its structure and always expressed regret that the old style of carriages had gone out of fashion. The chaise had been constructed a little on one side, so that the right half stood much higher than the left, and this pleased her particularly, because, as she said, a stout person could sit on one side and a tall person on the other. Inside the chaise, however, there was room for five small persons or three such as Auntie herself.

About midday Omelko, having finished with the chaise, brought out of the stable three horses which were a little younger than the chaise, and began harnessing them with cord to the magnificent equipage. Ivan Fyodorovitch and his aunt, one on the left side and the other on the right, stepped in and the chaise drove off. The peasants they met on the road seeing this sumptuous turn-out (Vassilissa Kashparovna rarely drove out in it) stopped respectfully, taking off their caps and bowing low.

Two hours later the chaise stopped at the front door—I think

I need not say—of Stortchenko's house. Grigory Grigoryevitch was not at home. His old mother and the two young ladies came into the dining-room to receive the guests. Auntie walked in with a majestic step, with a great air stopped short with one foot in front, and said in a loud voice:

"I am delighted, dear madam, to have the honor to offer you my respects in person; and at the same time to thank you for your hospitality to my nephew, who has been warm in his praises of it. Your buckwheat is very good, madam—I saw it as we drove into the village. May I ask how many sheaves you get to the acre?"

After that followed kisses all round. As soon as they were seated in the drawing-room, the old lady began:

"About the buckwheat I cannot tell you: that's Grigory Grigoryevitch's department: it's long since I have had anything to do with the farming; indeed, I am not equal to it, I am old now! In old days I remember the buckwheat stood up to my waist; now goodness knows what it is like, though they do say everything is better now." At that point the old lady heaved a sigh, and some observers would have heard in that sigh the sigh of a past age, of the eighteenth century.

"I have heard, madam, that your own maids can make excellent carpets," said Vassilissa Kashparovna, and with that touched on the old lady's most sensitive chord: at those words she seemed to brighten up, and she talked readily of the way to dye the yarn and prepare the thread.

From carpets the conversation passed easily to the salting of cucumbers and drying of pears. In short, before the end of an hour the two ladies were talking together as though they had been friends all their lives. Vassilissa Kashparovna had already said a great deal to her in such a low voice that Ivan Fyodorovitch could not hear what she was saying.

"Yes, would not you like to have a look at them?" said the old lady, getting up.

The young ladies and Vassilissa Kashparovna also got up and all moved towards the maids' room. Auntie made a sign, however, to Ivan Fyodorovitch to remain and said something in an undertone to the old lady.

"Mashenka," said the latter, addressing the fair-haired young lady, "stay with our visitor and talk with him, that he may not be dull!"

The fair-haired young lady remained and sat down on the sofa. Ivan Fyodorovitch sat on his chair as though on thorns, blushed and cast down his eyes; but the young lady appeared not to notice this and sat unconcernedly on the sofa, carefully scrutinizing the windows and the walls, or watching the cat timorously running round under the chairs.

Ivan Fyodorovitch grew a little bolder and would have begun a conversation; but it seemed as though he had lost all his words on the way. Not a single idea came into his mind.

The silence lasted for nearly a quarter of an hour. The young lady went on sitting as before.

At last Ivan Fyodorovitch plucked up his courage. "There are a great many flies in summer, madam!" he brought out in a half-trembling voice.

"A very great many!" answered the young lady. "My brother has made a flapper out of an old slipper of mamma's on purpose to kill them, but there are lots of them still."

Here the conversation dropped again, and Ivan Fyodorovitch was utterly unable to find anything to say.

At last the old lady together with his aunt and the dark-haired young lady came back again. After a little more conversation, Vassilissa Kashparovna took leave of the old lady and her daughters in spite of their entreaties that they would stay the night. The three ladies came out on the steps to see their visitors off, and continued for some time nodding to the aunt and nephew, as they looked out of the chaise.

"Well, Ivan Fyodorovitch, what did you talk about when you were alone with the young lady?" Auntie asked him on the way home.

"A very discreet and well-behaved young lady, Marya Grigoryevna!" said Ivan Fyodorovitch.

"Listen, Ivan Fyodorovitch, I want to talk seriously to you. Here you are thirty-eight, thank God; you have obtained a good rank in the service—it's time to think about children! You must have a wife . . . ."

"What, Auntie!" cried Ivan Fyodorovitch panic-stricken, "a

wife! No, Auntie, for goodness' sake ... You make me quite ashamed .... I've never had a wife .... I shouldn't know what to do with her!"

"You'll find out, Ivan Fyodorovitch, you'll find out," said his aunt, smiling, and she thought to herself: "what next, he is a perfect baby, he knows nothing!" "Yes, Ivan Fyodorovitch!" she went on aloud, "we could not find a better wife for you than Marya Grigoryevna. Besides, you are very much attracted by her. I have had a good talk with the old lady about it: she'll be delighted to see you her son-in-law. It's true that we don't know what that reprobate Grigoryevitch will say to it; but we won't consider him, and if he takes it into his head not to give her a dowry, we'll have the law of him .... "

At that moment the chaise drove into the yard and the ancient nags grew more lively, feeling that their stable was not far off.

"Mind, Omelko! Let the horses have a good rest first, and don't take them down to drink the minute they are unharnessed; they are overheated."

"Well, Ivan Fyodorovitch," his aunt went on as she got out of the chaise, "I advise you to think it over well. I must run to the kitchen: I forgot to tell Soloha what to get for supper, and I expect the wretched girl won't have thought of it herself."

But Ivan Fyodorovitch stood as though thunderstruck. It was true that Marya Grigoryevna was a very nice-looking young lady; but to get married ... ! It seemed to him so strange, so peculiar, he couldn't think of it without horror. Living with a wife ... ! Unthinkable! He would not be alone in his own room, but they would always have to be two together ... ! Perspiration came out on his face as he sank more deeply into meditation.

He went to bed earlier than usual but in spite of all his efforts he could not go to sleep. But at last sleep, that universal comforter, came to him; but such sleep! He had never had such incoherent dreams. First, he dreamed that everything was whirling with a noise around him, and he was running and running, as fast as his legs could carry him .... Now he was at his last gasp .... All at once some one caught him by the ear. "Aie! who is it?" "It is I, your wife!" a voice resounded loudly in his ear—and he woke up. Then he imagined that he was married, that everything in their little house was so peculiar, so strange: a double-bed stood in his room instead of a single one; his wife was sitting on a chair. He felt queer: he did not know how to approach her, what to say to her, and then he noticed that she had the face of a goose. He happened to turn aside and saw another wife, also with the face of a goose. Turning in another direction, he saw yet a third wife; and behind him was still another. Then he was seized by panic: he dashed away into the garden: but there it was hot, he took off his hat, and—saw a wife sitting in his hat. Drops of sweat came out on his face. He put his hand in his pocket for his handkerchief and in his pocket too there was a wife; he took some cotton-wool out of his ear—and there too sat a wife.... Then he suddenly began hopping on one leg, and Auntie, looking at him, said with a dignified air: "Yes, you must hop on one leg now, for you are a married man." He went towards her, but his aunt was no longer an aunt but a belfry, and he felt that some one was dragging him by a rope on the belfry. "Who is it pulling me?" Ivan Fyodorovitch asked plaintively. "It is I, your wife. I am pulling you because you are a bell." "No, I am not a bell, I am Ivan Fyodorovitch," he cried. "Yes, you are a bell," said the colonel of the P—— infantry regiment, who happened to be passing. Then he suddenly dreamed that his wife was not a human being at all but a sort of woolen material; that he went into a shop in Mogilyev. "What sort of stuff would you like?" asked the shopkeeper. "You had better take a wife, that is the most fashionable material! It wears well! Every one is having coats made of it now." The shopkeeper measured and cut off his wife. Ivan Fyodorovitch put her under his arm and went off to a Jewish tailor. "No," said the Jew, "that is poor material! No one has coats made of that now...."

Ivan Fyodorovitch woke up in terror, not knowing where he was; he was dripping with cold perspiration.

As soon as he got up in the morning, he went at once to his fortune-teller's book, at the end of which a virtuous bookseller had in the goodness of his heart and disinterestedness inserted an abridged dream-book. But there was absolutely nothing in it that remotely resembled this incoherent dream.

Meanwhile a quite new design, of which you shall hear more in the following chapter, was being matured in Auntie's brain.

The Cloak

In the department of ——, but it is better not to mention the department. The touchiest things in the world are departments, regiments, courts of justice, in a word, all branches of public service. Each individual nowadays thinks all society insulted in his person. Quite recently, a complaint was received from a district chief of police in which he plainly demonstrated that all the imperial institutions were going to the dogs, and that the Tzar's sacred name was being taken in vain; and in proof he appended to the complaint a romance, in which the district chief of police is made to appear about once in every ten pages, and sometimes in a downright drunken condition. Therefore, in order to avoid all unpleasantness, it will be better to designate the department in question, as a certain department.

So, in a certain department there was a certain official—not a very notable one, it must be allowed—short of stature, somewhat pock-marked, red-haired, and mole-eyed, with a bald forehead, wrinkled cheeks, and a complexion of the kind known as sanguine. The St. Petersburg climate was responsible for this. As for his official rank—with us Russians the rank comes first—he was what is called a perpetual titular councillor, over which, as is well known, some writers make merry and crack their jokes, obeying the praiseworthy custom of attacking those who cannot bite back.

His family name was Bashmachkin. This name is evidently derived from bashmak (shoe); but, when, at what time, and in

Reprinted from *Great Russian Short Stories*, edited by Isai Kames, by courtesy of Random House, Inc.

what manner, is not known. His father and grandfather, and all the Bashmachkins, always wore boots, which were resoled two or three times a year. His name was Akaki Akakiyevich. It may strike the reader as rather singular and far-fetched; but he may rest assured that it was by no means far-fetched, and that the circumstances were such that it would have been impossible to give him any other.

This was how it came about.

Akaki Akakiyevich was born, if my memory fails me not, in the evening on the 23rd of March. His mother, the wife of a Government official, and a very fine woman, made all due arrangements for having the child baptized. She was lying on the bed opposite the door; on her right stood the godfather, Ivan Ivanovich Yeroshkin, a most estimable man, who served as the head clerk of the senate; and the godmother, Arina Semyonovna Byelobrushkova, the wife of an officer of the quarter, and a woman of rare virtues. They offered the mother her choice of three names, Mokiya, Sossiya, or that the child should be called after the martyr Khozdazat. "No," said the good woman, "all those names are poor." In order to please her, they opened the calendar at another place; three more names appeared, Trifily, Dula, and Varakhasi. "This is awful," said the old woman. "What names! I truly never heard the like. I might have put up with Varadat or Varukh, but not Trifily and Varakhasi!" They turned to another page and found Pavsikakhi and Vakhtisi. "Now I see," said the old woman, "that it is plainly fate. And since such is the case, it will be better to name him after his father. His father's name was Akaki, so let his son's name be Akaki too." In this manner he became Akaki Akakiyevich. They christened the child, whereat he wept, and made a grimace, as though he foresaw that he was to be a titular councillor.

In this manner did it all come about. We have mentioned it in order that the reader might see for himself that it was a case of necessity, and that it was utterly impossible to give him any other name.

When and how he entered the department, and who appointed him, no one could remember. However much the directors and chiefs of all kinds were changed, he was always to be seen in the same place, the same attitude, the same occupation—always the letter copying clerk—so that it was afterwards affirmed that he had been born in uniform with a bald head. No respect was shown him in the department. The porter not only did not rise from his seat when he passed, but never even glanced at him, any more than if a fly had flown through the reception room. His superiors treated him in coolly despotic fashion. Some insignificant assistant to the head clerk would thrust a paper under his nose without so much as saying, "Copy," or, "Here's an interesting little case," or anything else agreeable, as is customary amongst well-bred officials. And he took it, looking only at the paper, and not observing who handed it to him, or whether he had the right to do so; simply took it, and set about copying it.

The young officials laughed at and made fun of him, so far as their official wit permitted; told in his presence various stories concocted about him, and about his landlady, an old woman of seventy; declared that she beat him; asked when the wedding was to be; and strewed bits of paper over his head, calling them snow. But Akaki Akakiyevich answered not a word, any more than if there had been no one there besides himself. It even had no effect upon his work. Amid all these annoyances he never made a single mistake in a letter. But if the joking became wholly unbearable, as when they jogged his head, and prevented his attending to his work, he would exclaim:

"Leave me alone! Why do you insult me?"

And there was something strange in the words and the voice in which they were uttered. There was in it something which moved to pity; so much so that one young man, a newcomer, who, taking pattern by the others, had permitted himself to make sport of Akaki, suddenly stopped short, as though all about him had undergone a transformation, and presented itself in a different aspect. Some unseen force repelled him from the comrades whose acquaintance he had made, on the supposition that they were decent, well-bred men. Long afterwards, in his gayest moments, there recurred to his mind the little official with the bald forehead, with his heart-rending words, "Leave me alone! Why do you insult me?" In these moving words, other words resounded— "I am thy brother." And the young man covered his face with his hand; and many a time afterwards, in the course of his life, shuddered at seeing how much inhumanity there is in man, how much savage coarseness is concealed beneath refined, cultured, worldly refinement, and even, O God! in that man whom the world acknowledges as honorable and upright.

It would be difficult to find another man who lived so entirely for his duties. It is not enough to say that Akaki labored with zeal; no, he labored with love. In his copying, he found a varied and agreeable employment. Enjoyment was written on his face; some letters were even favorites with him; and when he encountered these, he smiled, winked, and worked with his lips, till it seemed as though each letter might be read in his face, as his pen traced it. If his pay had been in proportion to his zeal, he would, perhaps, to his great surprise, have been made even a councillor of state. But he worked, as his companions, the wits, put it, like a horse in a mill.

However, it would be untrue to say that no attention was paid to him. One director being a kindly man, and desirous of rewarding him for his long service, ordered him to be given something more important than mere copying. So he was ordered to make a report of an already concluded affair, to another department; the duty consisting simply in changing the heading and altering a few words from the first to the third person. This caused him so much toil, that he broke into a perspiration, rubbed his forehead, and finally said, "No, give me rather something to copy." After that they let him copy on forever.

Outside this copying, it appeared that nothing existed for him. He gave no thought to his clothes. His uniform was not green, but a sort of rusty meal color. The collar was low, so that his neck, in spite of the fact that it was not long, seemed inordinately so as it emerged from it, like the necks of the plaster cats which pedlars carry about on their heads. And something was always sticking to his uniform, either a bit of hay or some trifle. Moreover, he had a peculiar knack, as he walked along the street, of arriving beneath a window just as all sorts of rubbish was being flung out of it; hence he always bore about on his hat scraps of melon rinds, and other such articles. Never once in his life did he give heed to what was going on every day in the street; while it is well known that his young brother officials trained the range of their glances till they could see when any one's trouser straps came undone upon the opposite sidewalk, which always brought a malicious smile to their faces. But Akaki Akakiyevich saw in all things the clean, even strokes of his written lines; and only when a horse thrust his nose, from some unknown quarter, over his shoulder, and sent a whole gust of wind down his neck from his nostrils, did he observe that he was not in the middle of a line, but in the middle of the street.

On reaching home, he sat down at once at the table, sipped his cabbage soup up quickly, and swallowed a bit of beef with onions, never noticing their taste, and gulping down everything with flies and anything else which the Lord happened to send at the moment. When he saw that his stomach was beginning to swell, he rose from the table and copied papers which he had brought home. If there happened to be none, he took copies for himself, for his own gratification, especially if the document was noteworthy, not on account of its style, but of its being addressed to some distinguished person.

Even at the hour when the grey St. Petersburg sky had quite disappeared, and all the official world had eaten or dined, each as he could, in accordance with the salary he received and his own fancy; when all were resting from the department jar of pens, running to and fro, for their own and other people's indispensable occupations, and from all the work that an uneasy man makes willingly for himself, rather than what is necessary; when officials hasten to dedicate to pleasure the time which is left to them, one bolder than the rest going to the theatre; another, into the street looking under the bonnets; another wasting his evening in compliments to some pretty girl, the star of a small official circle; another—and this is the common case of all—visiting his comrades on the third or fourth floor, in two small rooms with an anteroom or kitchen, and some pretensions to fashion, such as a lamp or some other trifle which has cost many a sacrifice of dinner or pleasure trip; in a word, at the hour when all officials disperse among the contracted quarters of their friends, to play whist, as they sip their tea from glasses with a kopek's worth of sugar, smoke long pipes, relate at time some bits of gossip which a Russian man can never, under any circumstances, refrain from, and when there is nothing else to talk of, repeat eternal anecdotes about the commandant to whom they had sent word that the tails of the horses on the Falonet Monument had been cut off;

when all strive to divert themselves, Akaki Akakiyevich indulged in no kind of diversion. No one could even say that he had seen him at any kind of evening party. Having written to his heart's content, he lay down to sleep, smiling at the thought of the coming day—of what God might send him to copy on the morrow.

Thus flowed on the peaceful life of the man, who, with a salary of four hundred rubles, understood how to be content with his lot; and thus it would have continued to flow on, perhaps, to extreme old age, were it not that there are various ills strewn along the path of life for titular councillors as well as for private, actual, court, and every other species of councillor, even to those who never give any advice or take any themselves.

There exists in St. Petersburg a powerful foe of all who receive a salary of four hundred rubles a year, or thereabouts. This foe is no other than the Northern cold, although it is said to be very healthy. At nine o'clock in the morning, at the very hour when the streets are filled with men bound for the various official departments, it begins to bestow such powerful and piercing nips on all noses impartially, that the poor officials really do not know what to do with them. At an hour when the foreheads of even those who occupy exalted positions ache with the cold, and tears start to their eyes, the poor titular councillors are sometimes quite unprotected. Their only salvation lies in traversing as quickly as possible, in their thin little cloaks, five or six streets, and then warming their feet in the porter's room, and so thawing all their talents and qualifications for official service, which had become frozen on the way.

Akaki Akakiyevich had felt for some time that his back and shoulders were paining with peculiar poignancy, in spite of the fact that he tried to traverse the distance with all possible speed. He began finally to wonder whether the fault did not lie in his cloak. He examined it thoroughly at home, and discovered that in two places, namely, on the back and shoulders, it had become thin as gauze. The cloth was worn to such a degree that he could see through it, and the lining had fallen into pieces. You must know that Akaki Akakiyevich's cloak served as an object of ridicule to the officials. They even refused it the noble name of cloak, and called it a cape. In fact, it was of singular make, its collar diminishing year by year to serve to patch its other parts.

The patching did not exhibit great skill on the part of the tailor, and was, in fact, baggy and ugly. Seeing how the matter stood, Akaki Akakiyevich decided that it would be necessary to take the cloak to Petrovich, the tailor, who lived somewhere on the fourth floor up a dark staircase, and who, in spite of his having but one eye and pockmarks all over his face, busied himself with considerable success in repairing the trousers and coats of officials and others; that is to say, when he was sober and not nursing some other scheme in his head.

It is not necessary to say much about this tailor, but as it is the custom to have the character of each personage in a novel clearly defined there is no help for it, so here is Petrovich the tailor. At first he was called only Grigori, and was some gentleman's serf. He commenced calling himself Petrovich from the time when he received his free papers, and further began to drink heavily on all holidays, at first on the great ones, and then on all church festivals without discrimination, wherever a cross stood in the calendar. On this point he was faithful to ancestral custom; and when quarrelling with his wife, he called her a low female and a German. As we have mentioned his wife, it will be necessary to say a word or two about her. Unfortunately, little is known of her, beyond the fact that Petrovich had a wife, who wore a cap and a dress, but could not lay claim to beauty, at least, no one but the soldiers of the guard even looked under her cap when they met her.

Ascending the staircase which led to Petrovich's room—which staircase was all soaked with dishwater and reeked with the smell of spirits which affects the eyes, and is an inevitable adjunct to all dark stairways in St. Petersburg houses—ascending the stairs, Akaki Akakiyevich pondered how much Petrovich would ask, and mentally resolved not to give more than two rubles. The door was open, for the mistress, in cooking some fish, had raised such a smoke in the kitchen that not even the beetles were visible. Akaki Akakiyevich passed through the kitchen unperceived, even by the housewife, and at length reached a room where he beheld Petrovich seated on a large unpainted table, with his legs tucked under him like a Turkish pasha. His feet were bare, after the fashion of tailors as they sit at work; and the first thing which caught the eye was his thumb, with a deformed nail thick and strong as a turtle's shell. About Petrovich's neck hung a skein of silk and thread, and upon his knees lay some old garment. He had been trying unsuccessfully for three minutes to thread his needle, and was enraged at the darkness and even at the thread, growling in a low voice, "It won't go through, the barbarian! You pricked me, you rascal!"

Akaki Akakiyevich was vexed at arriving at the precise moment when Petrovich was angry. He liked to order something of Petrovich when he was a little downhearted, or, as his wife expressed it, "when he had settled himself with brandy, the one-eyed devil!" Under such circumstances Petrovich generally came down in his price very readily, and even bowed and returned thanks. Afterwards, to be sure, his wife would come, complaining that her husband had been drunk, and so had fixed the price too low; but, if only a ten-kopek piece were added then the matter would be settled. But now it appeared that Petrovich was in a sober condition, and therefore rough, taciturn, and inclined to demand, Satan only knows what price. Akaki Akakiyevich felt this, and would gladly have beat a retreat, but he was in for it. Petrovich screwed up his one eye very intently at him, and Akaki Akakiyevich involuntarily said, "How do you do, Petrovich?"

"I wish you a good morning, sir," said Petrovich squinting at Akaki Akakiyevich's hands, to see what sort of booty he had brought.

"Ah! I—to you, Petrovich, this——" It must be known that Akaki Akakiyevich expressed himself chiefly by prepositions, adverbs, and scraps of phrases which had no meaning whatever. If the matter was a very difficult one, he had a habit of never completing his sentences, so that frequently, having begun a phrase with the words, "This, in fact, is quite——" he forgot to go on, thinking he had already finished it.

"What is it?" asked Petrovich, and with his one eye scanned Akaki Akakiyevich's whole uniform from the collar down to the cuffs, the back, the tails and the buttonholes, all of which were well known to him, since they were his own handiwork. Such is the habit of tailors; it is the first thing they do on meeting one.

"But I, here, this—Petrovich—a cloak, cloth—here you see,

everywhere, in different places, it is quite strong—it is a little dusty and looks old, but it is new, only here in one place it is a little—on the back, and here on one of the shoulders, it is a little worn, yes, here on this shoulder it is a little—do you see? That is all. And a little work——"

Petrovich took the cloak, spread it out, to begin with, on the table, looked at it hard, shook his head, reached out his hand to the window sill for his snuffbox, adorned with the portrait of some general, though what general is unknown for the place where the face should have been had been rubbed through by the finger and a square bit of paper had been pasted over it. Having taken a pinch of snuff, Petrovich held up the cloak, and inspected it against the light, and again shook his head. Then he turned it, lining upwards, and shook his head once more. After which he again lifted the general-adorned lid with its bit of pasted paper, and having stuffed his nose with snuff, closed and put away the snuffbox, and said finally, "No, it is impossible to mend it. It is a wretched garment!"

Akaki Akakiyevich's heart sank at these words.

"Why is it impossible, Petrovich?" he said, almost in the pleading voice of a child. "All that ails it is, that it is worn on the shoulders. You must have some pieces——"

"Yes, patches could be found, patches are easily found," said Petrovich, "but there's nothing to sew them to. The thing is completely rotten. If you put a needle to it—see, it will give way."

"Let it give way, and you can put on another patch at once."

"But there is nothing to put the patches on to. There's no use in strengthening it. It is too far gone. It's lucky that it's cloth, for, if the wind were to blow, it would fly away."

"Well, strengthen it again. How this, in fact——"

"No," said Petrovich decisively, "there is nothing to be done with it. It's a thoroughly bad job. You'd better, when the cold winter weather comes on, make yourself some gaiters out of it, because stockings are not warm. The Germans invented them in order to make more money." Petrovich loved on all occasions to have a fling at the Germans. "But it is plain you must have a new cloak."

At the word "new" all grew dark before Akaki Akakiyevich's eyes, and everything in the room began to whirl round. The only thing he saw clearly was the general with the paper face on the lid of Petrovich's snuffbox. "A new one?" said he, as if still in a dream. "Why, I have no money for that."

"Yes, a new one," said Petrovich, with barbarous composure.

"Well, if it came to a new one, how—it——"

"You mean how much would it cost?"

"Yes."

"Well, you would have to lay out a hundred and fifty or more," said Petrovich, and pursed up his lips significantly. He liked to produce powerful effects, liked to stun utterly and suddenly, and then to glance sideways to see what face the stunned person would put on the matter.

"A hundred and fifty rubles for a cloak!" shrieked poor Akaki Akakiyevich, perhaps for the first time in his life, for his voice had always been distinguished for softness.

"Yes, sir," said Petrovich, "for any kind of cloak. If you have a marten fur on the collar, or a silk-lined hood, it will mount up to two hundred."

"Petrovich, please," said Akaki Akakiyevich in a beseeching tone, not hearing, and not trying to hear, Petrovich's words, and disregarding all his "effects," "some repairs, in order that it may wear yet a little longer."

"No, it would only be a waste of time and money," said Petrovich. And Akaki Akakiyevich went away after these words, utterly discouraged. But Petrovich stood for some time after his departure, with significantly compressed lips, and without betaking himself to his work, satisfied that he would not be dropped, and an artistic tailor employed.

Akaki Akakiyevich went out into the street as if in a dream. "Such an affair!" he said to himself. "I did not think it had come to——" and then after a pause, he added, "Well, so it is! see what it has come to at last! and I never imagined that it was so!" Then followed a long silence, after which he exclaimed, "Well, so it is! see what already—nothing unexpected that—it would be nothing—what a strange circumstance!" So saying, instead of going home, he went in exactly the opposite direction without suspecting it. On the way, a chimney sweep bumped up against him, and blackened his shoulder, and a whole hatful of rubbish landed on him from the top of a house which was building. He did not notice it, and only when he ran against a watchman, who, having planted his halberd beside him, was shaking some snuff from his box into his horny hand, did he recover himself a little, and that because the watchman said, "Why are you poking yourself into a man's very face? Haven't you the pavement?" This caused him to look about him, and turn towards home.

There only, he finally began to collect his thoughts, and to survey his position in its clear and actual light, and to argue with himself, sensibly and frankly, as with a reasonable friend, with whom one can discuss private and personal matters. "No," said Akaki Akakiyevich, "it is impossible to reason with Petrovich now. He is that—evidently, his wife has been beating him. I'd better go to him on Sunday morning. After Saturday night he will be a little cross-eyed and sleepy, for he will want to get drunk, and his wife won't give him any money, and at such a time, a ten-kopeck piece in his hand will—he will become more fit to reason with, and then the cloak and that——" Thus argued Akaki Akakiyevich with himself, regained his courage, and waited until the first Sunday, when, seeing from afar that Petrovich's wife had left the house, he went straight to him.

Petrovich's eye was indeed very much askew after Saturday. His head drooped, and he was very sleepy; but for all that, as soon as he knew what it was a question of, it seemed as though Satan jogged his memory. "Impossible," said he. "Please to order a new one." Thereupon Akaki Akakiyevich handed over the ten-kopek piece. "Thank you, sir. I will drink your good health," said Petrovich. "But as for the cloak, don't trouble yourself about it; it is good for nothing. I will make you a capital new one, so let us settle about it now."

Akaki Akakiyevich was still for mending it, but Petrovich would not hear of it, and said, "I shall certainly have to make you a new one, and you may depend upon it that I shall do my best. It may even be, as the fashion goes, that the collar can be fastened by silver hooks under a flap."

Then Akaki Akakiyevich saw that it was impossible to get along without a new cloak, and his spirit sank utterly. How, in fact, was it to be done? Where was the money to come from? He must have some new trousers, and pay a debt of long standing to the shoemaker for putting new tops to his old boots, and he must order three shirts from the seamstress, and a couple of pieces of linen. In short, all his money must be spent. And even if the director should be so kind as to order him to receive forty-five or even fifty rubles instead of forty, it would be a mere nothing, a mere drop in the ocean towards the funds necessary for a cloak, although he knew that Petrovich was often wrong-headed enough to blurt out some outrageous price, so that even his own wife could not refrain from exclaiming, "Have you lost your senses, you fool?" At one time he would not work at any price, and now it was quite likely that he had named a higher sum than the cloak would cost.

But although he knew that Petrovich would undertake to make a cloak for eighty rubles, still, where was he to get the eighty rubles from? He might possibly manage half. Yes, half might be procured, but where was the other half to come from? But the reader must first be told where the first half came from.

Akaki Akakiyevich had a habit of putting, for every ruble he spent, a groschen into a small box, fastened with lock and key, and with a slit in the top for the reception of money. At the end of every half-year he counted over the heap of coppers, and changed it for silver. This he had done for a long time, and in the course of years, the sum had mounted up to over forty rubles. Thus he had one half on hand. But where was he to find the other half? Where was he to get another forty rubles from? Akaki Akakiyevich thought and thought, and decided that it would be necessary to curtail his ordinary expenses, for the space of one year at least, to dispense with tea in the evening, to burn no candles, and, if there was anything which he must do, to go into his landlady's room, and work by her light. When he went into the street, he must walk as lightly as he could, and as cautiously, upon the stones, almost upon tiptoe, in order not to wear his heels down in too short a time. He must give the laundress as little to wash as possible; and, in order not to wear out his clothes, he must take them off as soon as he got home, and wear only his cotton dressing gown, which had been long and carefully saved.

To tell the truth, it was a little hard for him at first to accustom himself to these deprivations. But he got used to them at length, after a fashion, and all went smoothly. He even got used to being hungry in the evening, but he made up for it by treating himself, so to say, in spirit, by bearing ever in mind the idea of his future cloak. From that time forth, his existence seemed to become, in some way, fuller, as if he were married, or as if some other man lived in him, as if, in fact, he were not alone, and some pleasant friend had consented to travel along life's path with him, the friend being no other than the cloak, with thick wadding and a strong lining incapable of wearing out. He became more lively, and even his character grew firmer, like that of a man who has made up his mind, and set himself a goal. From his face and gait, doubt and indecision, all hesitating and wavering disappeared of themselves. Fire gleamed in his eyes, and occasionally the boldest and most daring ideas flitted through his mind. Why not, for instance, have marten fur on the collar? The thought of this almost made him absent-minded. Once, in copying a letter, he nearly made a mistake, so that he exclaimed almost aloud, "Ugh!" and crossed himself. Once, in the course of every month, he had a conference with Petrovich on the subject of the cloak, where it would be better to buy the cloth, and the colour, and the price. He always returned home satisfied, though troubled, reflecting that the time would come at last when it could all be bought, and then the cloak made.

The affair progressed more briskly than he had expected. For beyond all his hopes, the director awarded neither forty nor forty-five rubles for Akaki Akakiyevich's share, but sixty. Whether he suspected that Akaki Akakiyevich needed a cloak, or whether it was merely chance, at all events, twenty extra rubles were by this means provided. This circumstance hastened matters. Two or three months more of hunger and Akaki Akakiyevich had accumulated about eighty rubles. His heart, generally so quiet, began to throb. On the first possible day, he went shopping in company with Petrovich. They bought some very good cloth, and at a reasonable rate too, for they had been considering the matter for six months, and rarely let a month pass without their visiting the shops to inquire prices. Petrovich himself said that no better cloth could be had. For lining, they selected a cotton stuff, but so firm and thick, that Petrovich declared it to be better than silk, and even prettier and more glossy. They did not buy the marten fur, because it was, in fact, dear, but in its stead, they picked out the very best of catskin, which could be found in the shop, and which might, indeed, be taken for marten at a distance.

Petrovich worked at the cloak two whole weeks, for there was a great deal of quilting; otherwise it would have been finished sooner. He charged twelve rubles for the job, it could not possibly have been done for less. It was all sewed with silk, in small, double seams, and Petrovich went over each seam afterwards with his own teeth, stamping in various patterns.

It was—it is difficult to say precisely on what day, but probably the most glorious one in Akaki Akakiyevich's life, when Petrovich at length brought home the cloak. He brought it in the morning, before the hour when it was necessary to start for the department. Never did a cloak arrive so exactly in the nick of time, for the severe cold had set in, and it seemed to threaten to increase. Petrovich brought the cloak himself as befits a good tailor. On his countenance was a significant expression, such as Akaki Akakiyevich had never beheld there. He seemed fully sensible that he had done no small deed, and crossed a gulf separating tailors who put in linings, and execute repairs, from those who make new things. He took the cloak out of the pocket handkerchief in which he had brought it. The handkerchief was fresh from the laundress, and he put it in his pocket for use. Taking out the cloak, he gazed proudly at it, held it up with both hands, and flung it skilfully over the shoulders of Akaki Akakiyevich. Then he pulled it and fitted it down behind with his hand, and he draped it around Akaki Akakiyevich without buttoning it. Akaki Akakiyevich, like an experienced man, wished to try the sleeves. Petrovich helped him on with them, and it turned out that the sleeves were satisfactory also. In short, the cloak appeared to be perfect, and most seasonable. Petrovich did not neglect to observe that it was only because he lived in a narrow street, and had no signboard, and had known Akaki Akakiyevich so long, that he had made it so cheaply; but that if he had been in business on the Nevski Prospect, he would have charged seventy-five rubles for the making alone. Akaki Akakiyevich did not care to argue this point with Petrovich. He paid him, thanked him, and set out at once in his new cloak for the department. Petrovich followed him, and pausing in the street, gazed long at the cloak in the distance, after which he went to one side expressly to run through a crooked alley, and emerge again into the street beyond to gaze once more upon the cloak from another point, namely, directly in front.

Meantime Akaki Akakiyevich went on in holiday mood. He was conscious every second of the time that he had a new cloak on his shoulders, and several times he laughed with internal satisfaction. In fact, there were two advantages, one was its warmth, the other its beauty. He saw nothing of the road, but suddenly found himself at the department. He took off his cloak in the anteroom, looked it over carefully, and confided it to the special care of the attendant. It is impossible to say precisely how it was that every one in the department knew at once that Akaki Akakiyevich had a new cloak, and that the "cape" no longer existed. All rushed at the same moment into the anteroom to inspect it. They congratulated him, and said pleasant things to him, so that he began at first to smile and then to grow ashamed. When all surrounded him, and said that the new cloak must be "christened," and that he must at least give them all a party, Akaki Akakiyevich lost his head completely, and did not know where he stood, what to answer, or how to get out of it. He stood blushing all over for several minutes, trying to assure them with great simplicity that it was not a new cloak, that it was in fact the old "cape."

At length one of the officials, assistant to the head clerk, in order to show that he was not at all proud, and on good terms with his inferiors, said:

"So be it, only I will give the party instead of Akaki Akakiyevich; I invite you all to tea with me tonight. It just happens to be my nameday too."

The officials naturally at once offered the assistant clerk their congratulations, and accepted the invitation with pleasure. Akaki Akakiyevich would have declined; but all declared that it was discourteous, that it was simply a sin and a shame, and that he could not possibly refuse. Besides, the notion became pleasant to him when he recollected that he should thereby have a chance of wearing his new cloak in the evening also.

That whole day was truly a most triumphant festival for Akaki Akakiyevich. He returned home in the most happy frame of mind, took off his cloak, and hung it carefully on the wall, admiring afresh the cloth and the lining. Then he brought out his old, worn-out cloak, for comparison. He looked at it, and laughed, so vast was the difference. And long after dinner he laughed again when the condition of the "cape" recurred to his mind. He dined cheerfully, and after dinner wrote nothing, but took his ease for a while on the bed, until it got dark. Then he dressed himself leisurely, put on his cloak, and stepped out into the street.

Where the host lived, unfortunately we cannot say. Our memory begins to fail us badly. The houses and streets in St. Petersburg have become so mixed up in our head that it is very difficult to get anything out of it again in proper form. This much is certain, that the official lived in the best part of the city; and therefore it must have been anything but near to Akaki Akakiyevich's residence. Akaki Akakiyevich was first obliged to traverse a kind of wilderness of deserted, dimly-lighted streets. But in proportion as he approached the official's quarter of the city, the streets became more lively, more populous, and more brilliantly illuminated. Pedestrians began to appear; handsomely dressed ladies were more frequently encountered; the men had otter skin collars to their coats; shabby sleighmen with their wooden, railed sledges stuck over with brass-headed nails, became rarer; whilst on the other hand, more and more drivers in red velvet caps, lacquered sledges and bearskin coats began to appear, and carriages with rich hammer-cloths flew swiftly through the streets, their wheels scrunching the snow.

Akaki Akakiyevich gazed upon all this as upon a novel sight. He had not been in the streets during the evening for years. He halted out of curiosity before a shopwindow, to look at a picture representing a handsome woman, who had thrown off her shoe, thereby baring her whole foot in a very pretty way; whilst behind her the head of a man with whiskers and a handsome mustache peeped through the doorway of another room. Akaki Akakiyevich shook his head, and laughed, and then went on his way. Why did he laugh? Either because he had met with a thing utterly unknown, but for which every one cherishes, nevertheless, some sort of feeling, or else he thought, like many officials, "Well, those French! What is to be said? If they do go in for anything of that sort, why——" But possibly he did not think at all.

Akaki Akakiyevich at length reached the house in which the head clerk's assistant lodged. He lived in fine style. The staircase was lit by a lamp, his apartment being on the second floor. On entering the vestibule, Akaki Akakiyevich beheld a whole row of goloshes on the floor. Among them, in the center of the room, stood a samovar, humming and emitting clouds of steam. On the walls hung all sorts of coats and cloaks, among which there were even some with beaver collars, or velvet facing. Beyond, the buzz of conversation was audible, and became clear and loud, when the servant came out with a trayful of empty glasses, cream jugs and sugar bowls. It was evident that the officials had arrived long before, and had already finished their first glass of tea.

Akaki Akakiyevich, having hung up his own cloak, entered the inner room. Before him all at once appeared lights, officials, pipes, and card tables, and he was bewildered by a sound of rapid conversation rising from all the tables, and the noise of moving chairs. He halted very awkwardly in the middle of the room, wondering what he ought to do. But they had seen him. They received him with a shout, and all thronged at once into the ante-room, and there took another look at his cloak. Akaki Akakiye-vich, although somewhat confused, was frank-hearted, and could not refrain from rejoicing when he saw how they praised his cloak. Then, of course, they all dropped him and his cloak, and returned, as was proper, to the tables set out for whist.

All this, the noise, the talk, and the throng of people, was rather overwhelming to Akaki Akakiyevich. He simply did not know where he stood, or where to put his hands, his feet, and his whole body. Finally he sat down by the players, looked at the cards, gazed at the face of one and another, and after a while began to gape, and to feel that it was wearisome, the more so, as the hour was already long past when he usually went to bed. He wanted to take leave of the host, but they would not let him go, saying that he must not fail to drink a glass of champagne, in honor of his new garment. In the course of an hour, supper, consisting of vegetable salad, cold veal, pastry, confectioner's pies, and champagne, was served. They made Akaki Akakiyevich drink two glasses of champagne, after which he felt things grow livelier.

Still, he could not forget that it was twelve o'clock, and that he should have been at home long ago. In order that the host might not think of some excuse for detaining him, he stole out of the room quickly, sought out, in the anteroom, his cloak, which, to his sorrow, he found lying on the floor, brushed it, picked off every speck upon it, put it on his shoulders, and descended the stairs to the street.

In the street all was still bright. Some petty shops, those permanent clubs of servants and all sorts of folks, were open. Others were shut, but, nevertheless, showed a streak of light the whole length of the door crack, indicating that they were not yet free of company, and that probably some domestics, male and female, were finishing their stories and conversations, while leaving their masters in complete ignorance as to their whereabouts. Akaki Akakiyevich went on in a happy frame of mind. He even started to run, without knowing why, after some lady, who flew past like a flash of lightning. But he stopped short, and went on very quietly as before, wondering why he had quickened his pace. Soon there spread before him those deserted streets which are not cheerful in the daytime, to say nothing of the evening. Now they were even more dim and lonely. The lanterns began to grow rarer, oil, evidently, had been less liberally supplied. Then came wooden houses and fences. Not a soul anywhere; only the snow sparkled in the streets, and mournfully veiled the low-roofed cabins with their closed shutters. He approached the spot where the street crossed a vast square with houses barely visible on its farther side, a square which seemed a fearful desert.

Afar, a tiny spark glimmered from some watchman's box, which seemed to stand on the edge of the world. Akaki Akakiyevich's cheerfulness diminished at this point in a marked degree. He entered the square, not without an involuntary sensation of fear, as though his heart warned him of some evil. He glanced back, and on both sides it was like a sea about him. "No, it is better not to look," he thought, and went on, closing his eyes. When he opened them, to see whether he was near the end of the square, he suddenly beheld, standing just before his very nose, some bearded individuals of precisely what sort, he could not make out. All grew dark before his eyes, and his heart throbbed.

"Of course, the cloak is mine!" said one of them in a loud voice, seizing hold of his collar. Akaki Akakiyevich was about to shout

"Help!" when the second man thrust a fist, about the size of an official's head, at his very mouth, muttering, "Just you dare to scream!"

Akaki Akakiyevich felt them strip off his cloak, and give him a kick. He fell headlong upon the snow, and felt no more.

In a few minutes he recovered consciousness, and rose to his feet, but no one was there. He felt that it was cold in the square, and that his cloak was gone. He began to shout, but his voice did not appear to reach the outskirts of the square. In despair, but without ceasing to shout, he started at a run across the square, straight towards the watchbox, beside which stood the watchman, leaning on his halberd, and apparently curious to know what kind of a customer was running towards him shouting. Akaki Akakiyevich ran up to him, and began in a sobbing voice to shout that he was asleep, and attended to nothing, and did not see when a man was robbed. The watchman replied that he had seen two men stop him in the middle of the square, but supposed that they were friends of his, and that, instead of scolding vainly, he had better go to the police on the morrow, so that they might make a search for whoever had stolen the cloak.

Akaki Akakiyevich ran home and arrived in a state of complete disorder, his hair which grew very thinly upon his temples and the back of his head all tousled, his body, arms and legs, covered with snow. The old woman, who was mistress of his lodgings, on hearing a terrible knocking, sprang hastily from her bed, and, with only one shoe on, ran to open the door, pressing the sleeve of her chemise to her bosom out of modesty. But when she had opened it, she fell back on beholding Akaki Akakiyevich in such a condition. When he told her about the affair, she clasped her hands, and said that he must go straight to the district chief of police, for his subordinate would turn up his nose, promise well, and drop the matter there. The very best thing to do, therefore, would be to go to the district chief, whom she knew, because Finnish Anna, her former cook, was now nurse at his house. She often saw him passing the house, and he was at church every Sunday, praying, but at the same time gazing cheerfully at everybody; so that he must be a good man, judging from all appearances. Having listened to this opinion, Akaki Akakiyevich betook himself sadly to his room. And how he spent the night there, any one who can put himself in another's place may readily imagine.

Early in the morning, he presented himself at the district chief's, but was told the official was asleep. He went again at ten and was again informed that he was asleep. At eleven, and they said, "The superintendent is not at home." At dinner time, and the clerks in the anteroom would not admit him on any terms, and insisted upon knowing his business. So that at last, for once in his life, Akaki Akakiyevich felt an inclination to show some spirit, and said curtly that he must see the chief in person, that they ought not to presume to refuse him entrance, that he came from the department of justice, and that when he complained to them, they would see.

The clerks dared make no reply to this, and one of them went to call the chief, who listened to the strange story of the theft of the coat. Instead of directing his attention to the principal points of the matter, he began to question Akaki Akakiyevich. Why was he going home so late? Was he in the habit of doing so, or had he been to some disorderly house? So that Akaki Akakiyevich got thoroughly confused, and left him, without knowing whether the affair of his cloak was in proper train or not.

All that day, for the first time in his life, he never went near the department. The next day he made his appearance, very pale, and in his old cape, which had become even more shabby. The news of the robbery of the cloak touched many, although there were some officials present who never lost an opportunity, even such a one as the present, of ridiculing Akaki Akakiyevich. They decided to make a collection for him on the spot, but the officials had already spent a great deal in subscribing for the director's portrait and for some book, at the suggestion of the head of that division, who was a friend of the author; and so the sum was trifling.

One of them, moved by pity, resolved to help Akaki Akakiyevich with some good advice, at least, and told him that he ought not to go to the police, for although it might happen that a police officer, wishing to win the approval of his superiors, might hunt up the cloak by some means, still, his cloak would remain in the possession of the police if he did not offer legal proof that it belonged to him. The best thing for him, therefore, would be to apply to a certain prominent personage; since this prominent personage, by entering into relation with the proper persons, could greatly expedite the matter.

As there was nothing else to be done, Akaki Akakiyevich decided to go to the prominent personage. What was the exact official position of the prominent personage, remains unknown to this day. The reader must know that the prominent personage had but recently become a prominent personage, having up to that time been only an insignificant person. Moreover, his present position was not considered prominent in comparison with others still more so. But there is always a circle of people to whom what is insignificant in the eyes of others, is important enough. Moreover, he strove to increase his importance by sundry devices. For instance, he managed to have the inferior officials meet him on the staircase when he entered upon his service; no one was to presume to come directly to him, but the strictest etiquette must be observed; the collegiate recorder must make a report to the government secretary, the government secretary to the titular councillor, or whatever other man was proper, and all business must come before him in this manner. In Holy Russia, all is thus contaminated with the love of imitation; every man imitates and copies his superior. They even say that a certain titular councillor, when promoted to the head of some small separate office, immediately partitioned off a private room for himself, called it the audience chamber, and posted at the door, a lackey with red collar and braid, who grasped the handle of the door, and opened to all comers, though the audience chamber would hardly hold an ordinary writing table.

The manners and customs of the prominent personage were grand and imposing, but rather exaggerated. The main foundation of his system were strictness. "Strictness, strictness, and always strictness!" he generally said; and at the last word he looked significantly into the face of the person to whom he spoke. But there was no necessity for this, for the halfscore of subordinates, who formed the entire force of the office, were properly afraid. On catching sight of him afar off, they left their work, and waited, drawn up in line, until he had passed through the room. His ordinary converse with his inferiors smacked of sternness, and consisted chiefly of three phrases: "How dare you?" "Do you know whom you are speaking to?" "Do you realise who is standing before you?"

Otherwise he was a very kindhearted man, good to his comrades, and ready to oblige. But the rank of general threw him completely off his balance. On receiving any one of that rank, he became confused, lost his way, as it were, and never knew what to do. If he chanced to be amongst his equals, he was still a very nice kind of man, a very good fellow in many respects, and not stupid, but the very moment that he found himself in the society of people but one rank lower than himself, he became silent. And his situation aroused sympathy, the more so, as he felt himself that he might have been making an incomparably better use of his time. In his eyes, there was sometimes visible a desire to join some interesting conversation or group, but he was kept back by the thought, "Would it not be a very great condescension on his part? Would it not be familiar? And would he not thereby lose his importance?" And in consequence of such reflections, he always remained in the same dumb state, uttering from time to time a few monosyllabic sounds, and thereby earning the name of the most wearisome of men.

To this prominent personage Akaki Akakiyevich presented himself, and this at the most unfavourable time for himself, though opportune for the prominent personage. The prominent personage was in his cabinet, conversing very gaily with an old acquaintance and companion of his childhood, whom he had not seen for several years, and who had just arrived, when it was announced to him that a person named Bashmachkin had come. He asked abruptly, "Who is he?"—"Some official," he was informed. "Ah, he can wait! This is no time for him to call," said the important man.

It must be remarked here that the important man lied outrageously. He had said all he had to say to his friend long before, and the conversation had been interspersed for some time with very long pauses, during which they merely slapped each other on the leg, and said, "You think so, Ivan Abramovich!" "Just so, Stepan Varlamovich!" Nevertheless, he ordered that the official should be kept waiting, in order to show his friend, a man who had not been in the service for a long time, but had lived at home in the country, how long officials had to wait in his ante-room.

At length, having talked himself completely out, and more than that, having had his fill of pauses, and smoked a cigar in a very comfortable armchair with reclining back, he suddenly seemed to recollect, and said to his secretary, who stood by the door with papers of reports, "So it seems that there is an official waiting to see me. Tell him that he may come in." On perceiving Akaki Akakiyevich's modest mien and his worn uniform, he turned abruptly to him, and said, "What do you want?" in a curt hard voice, which he had practised in his room in private, and before the looking glass, for a whole week before being raised to his present rank.

Akaki Akakiyevich, who was already imbued with a due amount of fear, became somewhat confused, and as well as his tongue would permit, explained, with a rather more frequent addition than usual of the word "that" that his cloak was quite new, and had been stolen in the most inhuman manner; that he had applied to him, in order that he might, in some way, by his intermediation—that he might enter into correspondence with the chief of police, and find the cloak.

For some inexplicable reason, this conduct seemed familiar to the prominent personage.

"What, my dear sir!" he said abruptly, "are you not acquainted with etiquette? To whom have you come? Don't you know how such matters are managed? You should first have presented a petition to the office. It would have gone to the head of the department, then to the chief of the division, then it would have been handed over to the secretary, and the secretary would have given it to me."

"But your excellency," said Akaki Akakiyevich, trying to collect his small handful of wits, and conscious at the same time that he was perspiring terribly, "I, your excellency, presumed to trouble you because secretaries—are an untrustworthy race."

"What, what, what!" said the important personage. "Where did you get such courage? Where did you get such ideas? What impudence towards their chiefs and superiors has spread among the young generation!" The prominent personage apparently had not observed that Akaki Akakiyevich was already in the neighborhood of fifty. If he could be called a young man, it must have been in comparison with some one who was seventy. "Do you know to whom you are speaking? Do you realise who is standing before you? Do you realise it? Do you realise it, I ask you!" Then he stamped his foot, and raised his voice to such a pitch that it would have frightened even a different man from Akaki Akakiyevich.

Akaki Akakiyevich's senses failed him. He staggered, trembled in every limb, and, if the porters had not run in to support him, would have fallen to the floor. They carried him out insensible. But the prominent personage, gratified that the effect should have surpassed his expectations, and quite intoxicated with the thought that his word could even deprive a man of his senses, glanced sideways at his friend in order to see how he looked upon this, and perceived, not without satisfaction, that his friend was in a most uneasy frame of mind, and even beginning on his part, to feel a trifle frightened.

Akaki Akakiyevich could not remember how he descended the stairs, and got into the street. He felt neither his hands nor feet. Never in his life had he been so rated by any high official, let alone a strange one. He went staggering on through the snow-storm, which was blowing in the streets, with his mouth wide open. The wind, in St. Petersburg fashion, darted upon him from all quarters, and down every cross street. In a twinkling it had blown a quinsy into his throat, and he reached home unable to utter a word. His throat was swollen, and he lay down on his bed. So powerful is sometimes a good scolding!

The next day a violent fever developed. Thanks to the generous assistance of the St. Petersburg climate, the malady progressed more rapidly than could have been expected, and when the doctor arrived, he found, on feeling the sick man's pulse, that there was nothing to be done, except to prescribe a poultice, so that the patient might not be left entirely without the beneficent aid of medicine. But at the same time, he predicted his end in thirty-six hours. After this he turned to the landlady, and said, "And as for you, don't waste your time on him. Order his pine coffin now, for an oak one will be too expensive for him."

Did Akaki Akakiyevich hear these fatal words? And if he heard them, did they produce any overwhelming effect upon him? Did he lament the bitterness of his life?—We know not, for he continued in a delirious condition. Visions incessantly appeared to him, each stranger than the other. Now he saw Petrovich, and ordered him to make a cloak, with some traps for robbers, who seemed to him to be always under the bed; and he cried every moment to the landlady to pull one of them from under his coverlet. Then he inquired why his old mantle hung before him when he had a new cloak. Next he fancied that he was standing before the prominent person, listening to a thorough setting-down and saying, "Forgive me, your excellency!" but at last he began to curse, uttering the most horrible words, so that his aged landlady crossed herself, never in her life having heard anything of the kind from him, and more so, as these words followed directly after the words "your excellency." Later on he talked utter nonsense, of which nothing could be made, all that was evident being that these incoherent words and thoughts hovered ever about one thing, his cloak.

At length poor Akaki Akakiyevich breathed his last. They sealed up neither his room nor his effects, because, in the first place, there were no heirs, and, in the second, there was very little to inherit beyond a bundle of goose quills, a quire of white official paper, three pairs of socks, two or three buttons which had burst off his trousers, and the mantle already known to the reader. To whom all this fell, God knows. I confess that the person who told me this tale took no interest in the matter. They carried Akaki Akakiyevich out, and buried him.

And St. Petersburg was left without Akaki Akakiyevich, as though he had never lived there. A being disappeared, who was protected by none, dear to none, interesting to none, and who never even attracted to himself the attention of those students of human nature who omit no opportunity of thrusting a pin through a common fly and examining it under the microscope. A being who bore meekly the jibes of the department, and went to his grave without having done one unusual deed, but to whom, nevertheless, at the close of his life, appeared a bright visitant in the form of a cloak, which momentarily cheered his poor life, and upon him, thereafter, an intolerable misfortune descended, just as it descends upon the heads of the mighty of this world!

Several days after his death, the porter was sent from the department to his lodgings, with an order for him to present himself there immediately, the chief commanding it. But the porter had to return unsuccessful, with the answer that he could not come; and to the question, "Why?" replied, "Well, because he is dead! he was buried four days ago." In this manner did they hear of Akaki Akakiyevich's death at the department. And the next day a new official sat in his place, with a handwriting by no means so upright, but more inclined and slanting.

But who could have imagined that this was not really the end of Akaki Akakiyevich, that he was destined to raise a commotion after death, as if in compensation for his utterly insignificant life? But so it happened, and our poor story unexpectedly gains a fantastic ending.

A rumor suddenly spread through St. Petersburg, that a dead man had taken to appearing on the Kalinkin Bridge, and its vicinity, at night in the form of an official seeking a stolen cloak, and that, under the pretext of its being the stolen cloak, he dragged, without regard to rank or calling, every one's cloak from his shoulders, be it catskin, beaver, fox, bear, sable, in a word, every sort of fur and skin which men adopted for their covering. One of the department officials saw the dead man with his own eyes, and immediately recognised in him Akaki Akakiyevich. This, however, inspired him with such terror, that he ran off with all his might, and therefore did not scan the dead man closely, but only saw how the latter threatened him from afar with his finger. Constant complaints poured in from all quarters, that the backs and shoulders, not only of titular but even of court councillors, were exposed to the danger of a cold, on account of the frequent dragging off of their cloaks.

Arrangements were made by the police to catch the corpse, alive or dead, at any cost, and punish him as an example to others, in the most severe manner. In this they nearly succeeded, for a watchman, on guard in Kiryushkin Lane, caught the corpse by the collar on the very scene of his evil deeds, when attempting to pull off the frieze cloak of a retired musician. Having seized him by the collar, he summoned, with a shout, two of his com-rades, whom he enjoined to hold him fast, while he himself felt for a moment in his boot, in order to draw out his snuffbox, and refresh his frozen nose. But the snuff was of a sort which even a corpse could not endure. The watchman having closed his right nostril with his finger, had no sooner succeeded in holding half a handful up to the left, than the corpse sneezed so violently that he completely filled the eyes of all three. While they raised their hands to wipe them, the dead man vanished completely, so that they positively did not know whether they had actually had him in their grip at all. Thereafter the watchmen conceived such a terror of dead men that they were afraid even to seize the living, and only screamed from a distance. "Hey, there! go your way!" So the dead official began to appear even beyond the Kalinkin Bridge causing no little terror to all timid people.

But we have totally neglected that certain prominent personage who may really be considered as the cause of the fantastic turn taken by this true history. First of all, justice compels us to say, that after the departure of poor, annihilated Akaki Akakiyevich, he felt something like remorse. Suffering was unpleasant to him, for his heart was accessible to many good impulses, in spite of the fact that his rank often prevented his showing his true self. As soon as his friend had left his cabinet, he began to think about poor Akaki Akakiyevich. And from that day forth, poor Akaki Akakiyevich, who could not bear up under an official reprimand, recurred to his mind almost every day. The thought troubled him to such an extent, that a week later he even resolved to send an official to him, to learn whether he really could assist him. And when it was reported to him that Akaki Akakiyevich had died suddenly of fever, he was startled, hearkened to the reproaches of his conscience, and was out of sorts for the whole day.

Wishing to divert his mind in some way and drive away the disagreeable impression, he set out that evening for one of his friends' houses, where he found quite a large party assembled. What was better, nearly every one was of the same rank as himself, so that he need not feel in the least constrained. This had a marvellous effect upon his mental state. He grew expansive, made himself agreeable in conversation, in short, he passed a delightful evening. After supper he drank a couple of glasses of champagne— not a bad recipe for cheerfulness, as every one knows. The champagne inclined him to various adventures, and he determined not to return home, but to go and see a certain well-known lady, of German extraction, Karolina Ivanovna, a lady, it appears, with whom he was on a very friendly footing.

It must be mentioned that the prominent personage was no longer a young man, but a good husband and respected father of a family. Two sons, one of whom was already in the service, and a good-looking, sixteen year old daughter, with a slightly arched but pretty little nose, came every morning to kiss his hand and say, "*Bonjour, papa.*" His wife, a still fresh and good-looking woman, first gave him her hand to kiss, and then, reversing the procedure, kissed his. But the prominent personage, though perfectly satisfied in his domestic relations, considered it stylish to have a friend in another quarter of the city. This friend was scarcely prettier or younger than his wife; but there are such puzzles in the world, and it is not our place to judge them. So the important personage descended the stairs, stepped into his sledge, said to the coachman, "To Karolina Ivanovna's," and, wrapping himself luxuriously in his warm cloak, found himself in that delightful frame of mind than which a Russian can conceive nothing better, namely, when you think of nothing yourself, yet when the thoughts creep into your mind of their own accord, each more agreeable than the other, giving you no trouble either to drive them away, or seek them. Fully satisfied, he recalled all the gay features of the evening just passed and all the mots which had made the little circle laugh. Many of them he repeated in a low voice, and found them quite as funny as before; so it is not surprising that he should laugh heartily at them. Occasionally, however, he was interrupted by gusts of wind, which, coming suddenly, God knows whence or why, cut his face, drove masses of snow into it, filled out his cloak collar like a sail, or suddenly blew it over his head with supernatural force, and thus caused him constant trouble to disentangle himself.

Suddenly the important personage felt some one clutch him firmly by the collar. Turning around, he perceived a man of short stature, in an old, worn uniform, and recognised, not without terror, Akaki Akakiyevich. The official's face was white as snow, and looked just like a corpse's. But the horror of the important personage transcended all bounds when he saw the dead man's mouth open, and heard it utter the following remarks, while it breathed upon him the terrible odor of the grave: "Ah, here you are at last! I have you, that—by the collar! I need your cloak. You took no trouble about mine, but reprimanded me. So now give up your own."

The pallid prominent personage almost died of fright. Brave as he was in the office and in the presence of inferiors generally, and although, at the sight of his manly form and appearance, every one said, "Ugh! how much character he has!" at this crisis, he, like many possessed of an heroic exterior, experienced such terror, that, not without cause, he began to fear an attack of illness. He flung his cloak hastily from his shoulders and shouted to his coachman in an unnatural voice, "Home at full speed!" The coachman, hearing the tone which is generally employed at critical moments, and even accompanied by something much more tangible, drew his head down between his shoulders in case of an emergency, flourished his whip, and flew on like an arrow. In a little more than six minutes the prominent personage was at the entrance of his own house. Pale, thoroughly scared, and cloakless, he went home instead of to Karolina Ivanovna's, reached his room somehow or other, and passed the night in the direst distress; so that the next morning over their tea, his daughter said, "You are very pale today, papa." But papa remained silent, and said not a word to any one of what had happened to him, where he had been, or where he had intended to go.

This occurrence made a deep impression upon him. He even began to say, "How dare you? Do you realize who is standing before you?" less frequently to the underofficials, and, if he did utter the words, it was only after first having learned the bearings of the matter. But the most noteworthy point was, that from that day forward the apparition of the dead official ceased to be seen. Evidently the prominent personage's cloak just fitted his shoulders. At all events, no more instances of his dragging cloaks from people's shoulders were heard of. But many active and solicitous persons could by no means reassure themselves, and asserted that the dead official still showed himself in distant parts of the city.

In fact, one watchman in Kolomen saw with his own eyes the apparition come from behind a house. But the watchman was not a strong man, so he was afraid to arrest him, and followed him in the dark, until, at length, the apparition looked around, paused, and inquired, "What do you want?" at the same time showing such a fist as is never seen on living men. The watchman said, "Nothing," and turned back instantly. But the apparition was much too tall, wore hugh mustaches, and, directing its steps apparently towards the Obukhov Bridge, disappeared in the darkness of the night.

The Old-World Landowners

I am very fond of the modest life led by those solitary owners of remote estates in the Ukraine who are usually known as old-world landowners and who are like picturesque tumbledown houses, charming in their patches of different colour and their complete contrast to the smooth new houses, whose walls have not yet been discoloured by the rain, whose roofs have not yet been covered by green mould, and whose front steps do not yet show their red bricks through the peeling stucco. I sometimes like to descend for a moment into that extraordinarily secluded life, in which not a single desire strays beyond the palisade surrounding the small courtyard, beyond the wattle fence of the orchard, full of plum and apple trees, beyond the lopsided peasant cottages spaced round it under the shade of the willows, elders and pear-trees. The life of their modest owners is so quiet that for a moment you are lost to the world of reality and you imagine that the passions, desires and restless inventions of the evil spirit that trouble the world do not exist at all and that you have only seen them in some dazzling, garish dream. I can see, as though I were there at this moment, the little low-pitched house with its gallery of little blackened wooden pillars running all round it, so that in a thunderstorm one can close the shutters without getting drenched by the rain. Behind it a sweet-scented bird-cherry, whole rows of low-growing fruit trees, drowned in the crimson of the cherries and the sapphire sea of the plums covered with a dark bluish bloom; a spreading maple in the shade of which a rug is laid to

Reprinted from *Mirgorod* by Nikolai Gogol, by permission of Farrar, Straus & Giroux, Inc. Copyright © 1962 by David Magarshack.

lie down on for a rest; in front of the house, a spacious courtyard covered with short fresh grass and with a little path running from the storehouse to the kitchen and from the kitchen to the manor-house; a long-necked goose with young goslings, as soft as down, drinking water; a palisade hung with strings of dried pears and apples and rugs hung out to air; a cartful of melons standing near the storehouse; an unyoked ox lying lazily beside it—all this is full of inexplicable charm for me, perhaps because I no longer see them before me and because everything from which we are parted is dear to us. Be that as it may, even as my carriage used to drive up to the steps of such a little house I would feel in a wonderfully pleasant and peaceful mood; the horses would trot merrily up to the steps, the coachman would alight imperturbably from the box and fill his pipe, as though he had arrived at his own house; even the barking set up by the phlegmatic watchdogs of every breed and colour was pleasant to my ears. But most of all I liked the owners of those modest little nooks, old men and old ladies who came out solicitously to meet me. Even now amid the noisy crowds of fashionable dress-coats, I can sometimes see their faces, and then I suddenly fall into a reverie and catch a glimpse of my past life. There is so much kindness in these faces, so much cordiality and frankness, that you can't help passing imperceptibly with all your senses into their humble life and giving up, if only for a short time, all your ambitious dreams.

To this day I cannot forget two people of the last century who, alas, are no more, and my heart is still wrung with pity every time I imagine going back one day to their old, now deserted, dwelling, and seeing the heap of dilapidated cottages, the pond choked with weeds, and an overgrown ditch where their little low-pitched house once stood—and nothing more. I feel sad. I feel sad even before going there. But let me turn to my story.

Afanasy Ivanovich Tovstogub and his wife, Pulcheria Ivanovna Tovstogubikha, as she was known among the peasants of the neighbourhood, were the old people I was beginning to tell you about. If I were a painter and wanted to portray Philemon and Baucis on canvas, I should never have chosen any other models than those two. Afanasy Ivanovich was sixty and Pulcheria Ivanovna was fifty-five. Afanasy Ivanovich was tall and always wore a camlet covered sheepskin coat; he used to sit hunched up and was almost always smiling, even though he were telling you something or simply listening. Pulcheria Ivanovna was of a somewhat serious disposition and scarcely ever laughed; but there was so much kindness in her face and eyes, so much readiness to regale you with everything of the best they had, that, I believe, you would have found a smile a trifle too cloying for her kind face. The fine wrinkles on their faces were arranged so attractively that an artist, I am sure, would have stolen them. Their whole life could, it seemed, be read in them, their serene and tranquil life, the life led by the old, simplehearted, and yet rich Ukrainian families, who always present such a contrast to the lowborn Ukrainians, who, leaving their trades as tar-dealers and hucksters, swarm like locusts in the law-courts and government offices, fleece their own countrymen of their last penny, inundate Petersburg with pettifogging lawyers, make their pile at last and triumphantly disguise their origin by adding a "V" to their Ukrainian surnames ending in "O." No, like all the old and indigenous families of the Ukraine, they were nothing like those contemptible and miserable creatures.

It was impossible to look at them without feeling touched by their love for one another. They were never familiar but always formal in addressing each other.

"Was it you, Afanasy Ivanovich, who made the hole in that chair?"

"I am sorry, Pulcheria Ivanovna, it was I. Please don't be cross."

They had no children, and that was why all their affection was concentrated on each other. As a young man, Afanasy Ivanovich had served in the cavalry and had risen to the rank of captain, but that was a long time ago and Afanasy Ivanovich himself hardly ever recalled his past. Afanasy Ivanovich was married when he was thirty. At the time he was a strapping young fellow and wore an embroidered sleeveless jacket. He even devised a clever plan for eloping with Pulcheria Ivanovna when her relations objected to their marriage; but he hardly remembered that now, at least he never spoke of it.

All those far-away, extraordinary events had given place to a quiet life of complete seclusion, a life full of those drowsy yet harmonious dreams you indulge in sitting on a rustic balcony overlooking the garden, when a lovely rain comes streaming down with a glorious sound, pattering on the leaves and flowing in bubbling rivulets, inducing a numbness in all your limbs, and meanwhile a rainbow comes stealing from behind the trees in the shape of a half-ruined arch, shedding its band of seven soft colours across the sky. Or when you are lulled to sleep in a carriage, driving between green bushes while the quail of the steppes call loudly and the fragrant grass, mingled with ears of corn and wild flowers, thrusts itself in at the carriage door, flicking you delightfully across the hands and face.

Afanasy Ivanovich always listened with a pleasant smile to the people who came to see him; occasionally, he talked himself, but mostly he asked questions. He was not one of those old men who bore you with their everlasting praises of the good old days and denunciations of the new. On the contrary, in questioning you he showed great concern and curiosity about the circumstances of your life, your successes and failures, in which all kind-hearted old people usually show an interest, though it is somewhat like the interest of a child who examines the seal of your watch while talking to you. Then his face, one may say, was imbued with kindliness.

The rooms of the house in which our old people lived were small and low, the sort of rooms old-world people usually live in. Each room had an enormous stove, occupying almost a third of it. These little rooms were terribly hot, for both Afanasy Ivanovich and Pulcheria Ivanovna liked warmth very much. The stoves were all heated from the entrance hall, which was always filled almost to the ceiling with straw, commonly used in the Ukraine instead of firewood. The crackle of the burning straw and the light it shed in the hall made it a very pleasant place in the evening when ardent youth, chilled with chasing after some dark-faced girl, rushed in, clapping their hands. The walls of the rooms were adorned with a few pictures in old-fashioned narrow frames. I am convinced that their owners themselves had long forgotten what they were about and if some of them had been taken away I doubt if they would have noticed. Two of the portraits were large and painted in oils. One was of some bishop and the other of Peter III. A fly-blown Duchess de La Vallière looked out from the narrow frame of a third. There were a large number of small pictures round the windows and over the door, which for some reason you get so used to regarding as stains on the walls that you never bothered to examine them. The floor in almost all the rooms was of clay, but so cleanly polished and so neatly kept as, I dare swear, no parquet floor in a rich house, lazily swept by some sleepy gentleman in a livery, has ever been kept.

Pulcheria Ivanovna's room was cluttered up with chests and boxes of every conceivable size. Lots of little bags and sacks of flower-seeds, vegetable-seeds and melon-seeds hung on the walls. Lots of balls of wool of different colours, rags of old dresses, made half a century ago, were stored in and between the little chests in the corners of the room. Pulcheria Ivanovna was a great housewife and collected everything, though sometimes she could not tell herself what she was going to do with the things afterwards.

But the most remarkable thing in the house was its singing doors. As soon as morning came the singing of the doors could be heard all over the house. I cannot say why they sang; whether it was the fault of the rusty hinges or whether the mechanic who made them had concealed some secret in the doors, but what was so remarkable was that each door had its own special voice: the door leading to the bedroom sang in the thinnest treble; the dining-room door sang in a hoarse bass; while the door into the entrance hall emitted a kind of strangely jarring and also moaning sound so that as you listened to it carefully you could hear very distinctly the words: "Lord, I'm freezing cold!" I know that many people dislike this sound very much, but I am very fond of it, and if I sometimes hear a door creak here, I immediately get a whiff of the countryside—the little low room lit by a candle in an antique candlestick, the supper already on the table, the dark May night peeping in from the garden through the open window at the laid table, the nightingale filling the garden, the house and the far-away river with the peals of its song, the mysterious rustle of branches and . . . Good Lord, what a long train of memories came rushing into my head just then!

The chairs in the room were wooden and massive, as was usual in the old days; they all had high carved backs, in natural grain, unvarnished and unpainted; they were not even upholstered and were a little like the chairs on which bishops sit to this day. Little three-cornered tables between the walls, a mirror in a thin gold frame carved with leaves, which flies had covered with black spots, a rug before the sofa with birds which looked like flowers and flowers which looked like birds—that was practically all the furnishing of the unpretentious little house in which my old people lived.

The serf-maids' room was crowded with young and not-so-young girls in striped petticoats; Pulcheria Ivanovna sometimes gave them some knick-knacks to sew or made them prepare the fruit, but for the most part, they ran off to the kitchen and slept. Pulcheria Ivanovna considered it necessary to keep them in the house and she was very strict about their morals. But to her great amazement hardly a few months passed without the waist of some girl or other growing larger than usual; this was all the more surprising as there was hardly a bachelor in the house, except the houseboy who used to walk about barefoot in a grey tail coat and, when not eating, was sure to be asleep. Pulcheria Ivanovna usually scolded the erring maid and made it quite clear to her that it must not happen again. Hundreds of flies kept up a terrible buzzing on the window-pane, drowned by the deep bass of the bumble bee and occasionally accompanied by the shrill wail of the wasps; but as soon as candles were brought in the entire gang went to bed, covering the whole ceiling with a black cloud.

Afanasy Ivanovich was not very active on his farm, though he did drive out sometimes to the mowers and reapers and kept a rather sharp eye on their work. The whole burden of administration lay upon Pulcheria Ivanovna's shoulders. Pulcheria Ivanovna's housekeeping consisted of continually locking up and unlocking the storehouse, and salting, drying, and preserving countless quantities of fruit and vegetables. Her house resembled nothing so much as a chemical laboratory. There was always a fire burning under the apple tree, and a cauldron or copper pan of jam, jelly or fruit cheese made with honey, sugar, and I don't remember what else, was hardly ever taken off the iron tripod on which it stood. Under another tree the coachman was everlastingly distilling peach-leaf, bird-cherry-flower, centaury or cherry-stone liqueur in a copper alembic, and at the end of the process was quite unable to control his tongue and talked such nonsense that Pulcheria Ivanovna could make nothing of it and sent him off to the kitchen for a snooze. Such a great quantity of all this stuff was boiled, salted and dried that the whole courtyard would most certainly have been submerged in it—for Pulcheria Ivanovna always liked to keep a store over and above what was necessary for use—had not more than half of it been eaten up by the serf-girls who, getting into the store-room, would overeat themselves so horribly that they kept moaning and complaining of stomach-ache all day.

Pulcheria Ivanovna had little opportunity of keeping an eye on the work in the fields or any other work on the farm. The steward and the village elder combined in robbing them mercilessly. They had made it their custom to deal with their master's woods as if they were their own; they made a large number of sledges and sold them at the nearest fair; moreover, all the thick oak-trees they sold to the neighbouring Cossacks to be cut down for building flour mills. Only once did Pulcheria Ivanovna express a desire to inspect her woods. For this purpose a four-wheeler with enormous leather aprons was harnessed; as soon as the coachman shook the reins and the horses, who had served in the militia, set off, the leather apron filled the air with strange sounds, and all of a sudden, a flute, a tambourine, and a drum could all be heard clearly; every nail and iron bolt made such a din that they could hear the lady of the manor driving out of the courtyard even as far as the mill, though the distance was almost two miles. Pulcheria Ivanovna could not help noticing the terrible devastation in the woods and the loss of the oak-trees which even as a child she had known to be over a hundred years old.

"Why is it, Nichipor," she said, addressing herself to the steward who was there at the time, "why is it that there are so few oaks about? Take care you are not left with as few hairs on your head."

"Why so few?" the steward, as usual, replied. "Because they got lost! Yes, ma'am, got lost: struck by lightning, eaten away by worms,—got lost, ma'am! Got lost."

Pulcheria Ivanovna was completely satisfied with this answer and, on her return home, merely gave orders to double the watch in the orchard near the Spanish cherry-trees and the big winter pears.

These worthy administrators, the steward and the village elder, found it quite unnecessary to take all the flour to their master's barns, thinking that half would be quite sufficient; in the end, they took to the barns the half which had gone mouldy or got wet and been rejected at the fair. But however much the steward and the village elder stole; however much all of them in the house gorged themselves, from the housekeeper to the pigs, who destroyed an immense number of plums and apples, and often pushed the trees with their snouts to bring a veritable rain of fruit down from them; however many presents the servants carried to their relations and friends in other villages, even dragging off old linen and yarn from the storerooms, all of which found its own way to the universal source, that is, the pothouse; however much was stolen by visitors, phlegmatic coachmen and footmen—the blessed earth produced everything in such abundance and Afanasy Ivanovich and Pulcheria Ivanovna wanted so little, that all these terrible robberies were scarcely noticed in their household.

Both the old people, as was the long-standing custom among old-world landowners, were very fond of a good meal. As soon as day dawned (they always got up early) and as soon as the doors set up their discordant concert, they would be sitting down at a little table and drinking coffee. Having finished his coffee, Afanasy Ivanovich would go into the entrance hall and, shaking his handkerchief, exclaim: "Shoo, shoo! Come on, geese, get off the front steps!" In the courtyard he usually came across the steward. As usual he entered into conversation with him, questioned him closely about the work in the fields, and gave orders which would have impressed anyone with his extraordinary knowledge of farming; indeed, it would never have occurred to anyone new to farming that one could steal from so sharp-eyed a master. But the steward was a man of great experience; he knew what answers to give and, what's more, how best to feather his own nest.

After this Afanasy Ivanovich would go back into the house and, going up to Pulcheria Ivanovna, say:

"Well, my dear, don't you think it's time we had a bite of something?"

"What could we have now, Afanasy Ivanovich? Lard cakes, or poppy-seed patties, or, perhaps, salted mushrooms?"

"Oh, I don't mind mushrooms or patties," replied Afanasy Ivanovich, and in a twinkling patties and red-brown mushrooms appeared on the table.

An hour before dinner, Afanasy Ivanovich had another snack, drinking an old silver goblet of vodka, and eating mushrooms, all sorts of dried fruit and other delicacies. They sat down to dinner at twelve o'clock. In addition to the dishes and sauce-boats, there were lots of little pots on the table, their lids most carefully sealed so that no concoction of old Ukrainian cuisine should lose its flavour. The conversation at dinner usually concerned subjects most closely related to the meal.

"I'm afraid," Afanasy Ivanovich would say, "this porridge is a little bit burnt. What do you think, Pulcheria Ivanovna?"

"I don't think so, Afanasy Ivanovich. Put in a little more dripping and then it won't taste burnt, or pour some of this mushroom sauce over it."

"Oh, well," Afanasy Ivanovich would say, passing his plate, "let's try it."

After dinner Afanasy Ivanovich would go to lie down for an hour, after which Pulcheria Ivanovna would bring him a sliced watermelon and say:

"Have a piece of this delicious melon, Afanasy Ivanovich."

"Don't be deceived by its appearance, Pulcheria Ivanovna," said Afanasy Ivanovich, taking a large slice. "Even if it is red in the middle, it may not be nice at all."

But the melon would disappear in no time. After that Afanasy Ivanovich would eat a few pears and then go for a walk in the garden with Pulcheria Ivanovna. On returning home, Pulcheria Ivanovna went about her business, while her husband sat under a lean-to facing the yard and watched the storehouse constantly displaying and concealing its interior, and the serf-girls pushing one another, bringing in or taking out various kinds of comestibles in wooden boxes, sieves, small troughs, and other receptacles for fruit storage. A little later, he would send for Pulcheria Ivanovna, or go to see her himself.

"Can you suggest anything for me to eat, Pulcheria Ivanovna?" he would say.

"Well, what will you have?" Pulcheria Ivanovna asked. "Would you like me to go and tell them to bring you the fruit dumplings I ordered to be kept especially for you?"

"Yes, I think that will do nicely," replied Afanasy Ivanovich.

"You wouldn't rather have some fruit jelly, would you?"

"I don't mind if I do," replied Afanasy Ivanovich, after which both were brought and, as usual consumed at once.

Before supper Afanasy Ivanovich would have another bite of

something. At half-past nine they sat down to supper. After supper they went to bed at once and a dead silence fell upon this active, though quiet, little homestead.

The room in which Afanasy Ivanovich and Pulcheria Ivanovna slept was so hot that very few people indeed would have been able to stay there for several hours. But, to be even warmer, Afanasy Ivanovich would sleep on the stove-couch, though the intense heat often made him get up a few times in the middle of the night and take a turn round the room. Sometimes as he paced the room Afanasy Ivanovich would moan.

Then Pulcheria Ivanovna would ask:

"Why do you moan, Afanasy Ivanovich?"

"Goodness only knows, Pulcheria Ivanovna," replied Afanasy Ivanovich. "I seem to have a little stomach upset."

"Don't you think you'd better have a bite of something, Afanasy Ivanovich?"

"I'm sure I don't know, Pulcheria Ivanovna. But tell me what is there?"

"Some sour milk or some compote of stewed pears."

"Oh, well, I might as well try it," said Afanasy Ivanovich.

A sleepy serf-girl went off to rummage in the cupboards and Afanasy Ivanovich would have a plateful, after which he usually said,

"I seem to be feeling a little better now."

Sometimes, if the sun was shining and it was comfortably warm indoors, Afanasy Ivanovich, being in a merry mood, liked to pull Pulcheria Ivanovna's leg by talking of something else.

"Now," he would say, "what if our house suddenly caught fire, Pulcheria Ivanovna? Where should we go?"

"Goodness gracious, the things you say, Afanasy Ivanovitch! How could our house burn down? God would never permit it."

"Well, but what if it did?"

"Well, we'd move into the kitchen then. You'd take over the housekeeper's room for a time."

"But what if the kitchen burnt down too?"

"What will you be thinking next? The Lord will preserve us from such a calamity. House and kitchen to be burnt down all at once! Why, if that should happen, we'd move into the storehouse and live there until a new house was built."

"And what if the storehouse burnt down too?"

"Goodness, what are you saying? I don't want to listen to you. It's a sin to talk like that and God will punish you for saying such things."

Satisfied with having pulled Pulcheria Ivanovna's leg, Afanasy Ivanovich just smiled as he sat down on his chair.

But I found the old couple interesting when they had visitors. Then everything in their house looked different. These kindly people could be said to have lived for visitors. The best they had of everything was all brought out. They vied with each other in trying to treat you to everything their farm produced. But what appealed to me most of all was that there was not a trace of gush in the way they entreated you to eat. This hospitality, this readiness to please you, was gently expressed in their faces and was so characteristic of them that you could not help giving in to their entreaties. For this was indeed what you would have expected from the pure and serene simplicity of their kindly, artless souls. This hospitality was not at all like that dispensed to you by some clerk in a provincial office, whom you have helped in his career and who calls you his benefactor and crawls at your feet. The visitor was never allowed to depart on the same day: he simply had to stay the night.

"You can't possibly set off on such a long journey at so late an hour!" Pulcheria Ivanovna always said (their visitor usually lived two or three miles away).

"Why, of course not," Afanasy Ivanovich said. "You never know what might happen: you may be attacked by a highwayman or some other evil person."

"God preserve us from highwaymen," Pulcheria Ivanovna exclaimed. "One shouldn't talk of such things at night. It isn't a question of highwayman at all. It's dark and it isn't the right time for travelling. Besides your coachman—and I know your coachman—is so frail, and he's such a little man too—why, an old mare could get the better of him! Anyway, I expect he must be dead drunk by now and fast asleep somewhere."

And the visitor had to stay the night there. Still, an evening spent in the low, warm room, friendly, warming, soporific conversation, steam rising from the served meal on the table, a meal always nourishing and prepared in quite a masterly fashion, was sufficient compensation for him. I can see, just as though I were there now, Afanasy Ivanovich listening to his guest with attention and even delight. The talk often turned on politics. The visitor, who also very rarely left his village, would often make all sorts of conjectures with an important air and a mysterious expression about a secret agreement between the French and the English to let Bonaparte loose in Russia again, or would simply speak of a war that was bound to break out shortly, and then Afanasy Ivanovich would say, pretending not to look at Pulcheria Ivanovna:

"I think I shall go to the war myself. Indeed, why shouldn't I go to the war?"

"Off to the war, are you?" Pulcheria Ivanovna would interrupt. "Don't you believe him," she would say, turning to the visitor. "An old man like him go to the war! Why, the first soldier he met would shoot him dead. Indeed, he would. He'd just take aim and shoot him."

"Well," Afanasy Ivanovich would say, "and what about me shooting him?"

"Just listen to him!" Pulcheria Ivanovna would exclaim. "Can you imagine him going to the war? Why, his pistols have been lying rusty and unloaded for years. You should see them: they'd explode with the gunpowder before they'd fire a shot. He'd blow off his hands and injure his face and remain a cripple for the rest of his life."

"Well," Afanasy Ivanovich would say, "I'd buy myself new weapons. Get myself a sabre or a Cossack lance."

"He's just romancing! Gets an idea into his head and starts spinning a yarn," Pulcheria Ivanovna would declare with vexation. "I know he's only joking, but I don't like hearing it all the same. He always talks like that. Sometimes you keep listening to him till you get frightened."

But Afanasy Ivanovich, pleased at having frightened Pulcheria Ivanovna a little, would laugh as he sat back in his chair.

I found Pulcheria Ivanovna most entertaining when she was inviting a visitor to help himself to some snacks before a meal.

"This," she usually said, taking a stopper out of a decanter, "this is a milfoil-and-sage brandy. It's an excellent remedy for a pain between the shoulder-blades or the small of the back. This one here is centaury brandy, an excellent remedy for ringing in the ears or a rash on the face. And this one here is distilled with peach-stones. Have a glass. It smells lovely, doesn't it? If you knock your head against the corner of the cupboard or table when getting up in the morning and a lump comes up on your forehead, all you have to do is drink one glass of this before dinner and it will go away, pass off in a minute, just as though it had never been there at all."

After which similar accounts followed about the contents of the other decanters, which all seemed to have some medicinal proper-ties. Having loaded her visitor with all that pharmacopaea, she next led him to a table laid with countless plates full of all sorts of comestibles.

"These are mushrooms with wild thyme! These are mushrooms with cloves and hazelnuts. A Turkish woman taught me to pickle them when we still had Turkish prisoners of war here. She was ever such a kind woman, you wouldn't believe she was of the Turkish religion. She was just like any of us, except that she wouldn't eat pork. She told me that in her country there was some law against it. Now, these are mushrooms pickled with black-currant leaves and nutmeg. And these are large dace. It's the first time I have boiled them in vinegar. I'm afraid I don't know what they're like. I learnt the secret from Father Ivan. First of all you spread a few oak-leaves in a small tub and then sprinkle them with pepper and saltpetre, then put in the flowers of mouse-eared hawk weed, which must be laid with stalks uppermost. And here are the pasties: These are stuffed with cheese, these with poppy-seeds, and those are the ones Afanasy Ivanovich likes so much—they're stuffed with cabbage and buckwheat."

"Yes, indeed," Afanasy Ivanovich used to add, "I like them very much. They're soft and sourish."

Pulcheria Ivanovna was, as a rule, in the best of spirits when entertaining visitors. Such a kindly old woman! She was simply devoted to her guests. I liked visiting them and though I gorged myself terribly, as anyone else who stayed with them did, and though it was very bad for me, I was always glad to go see them. As a matter of fact, I am inclined to believe that the very air of the Ukraine possesses a special kind of property which aids digestion, for if anyone took it into his head to eat like that here, he'd without a doubt find himself lying in his coffin instead of in his bed.

Dear old people! But I've now come to a very melancholy event in my story, an event that changed forever the life of this peaceful little corner of the world. This event is all the more striking since it was caused by a most unimportant incident. But such is the strange order of things that insignificant causes give rise to great events while, on the other hand, the consequences of great enterprises are often quite insignificant.

Some conqueror rallies all his country's forces, wages war for several years, his generals cover themselves with glory, and it all ends with the acquisition of a patch of land on which there is barely room to plant potatoes; while sometimes two sausage-makers have a fight over some trifle and in the end their quarrel spreads over cities, big and small villages and finally, the whole kingdom. But let us leave aside these reflections; they are out of place here. Besides, I am not fond of reflections when they merely remain reflections.

Pulcheria Ivanovna had a pretty little grey cat which almost always lay curled up at her feet. Pulcheria Ivanovna sometimes used to stroke her or scratch her neck with a finger while the pampered cat stretched as high as she could. I don't think Pulcheria Ivanovna was excessively fond of her cat; she was simply attached to her, being used to seeing her about. Afanasy Ivanovich, though, often teased her about her affection for the cat.

"I can't imagine what you can see in that cat, Pulcheria Ivanovna. What use is she? Now, if you had a dog, it would be different: a dog can be taken out shooting, but what's the use of a cat?"

"Oh, do be quiet, Afanasy Ivanovich," Pulcheria Ivanovna would say in reply. "You just like to talk and nothing else. A dog is not clean, a dog will make a mess, a dog will break everything, while a cat is a quiet creature, she does no harm to anyone."

Not that Afanasy Ivanovich cared more for dogs than for cats; he only said it to tease Pulcheria Ivanovna a little.

Behind their orchard was a large wood which had been completely spared by their enterprising steward, perhaps because the sound of the axe would have reached the ears of Pulcheria Ivanovna. It was overgrown and neglected: the old tree-trunks were covered with dense nut bushes and looked like the feathered legs of pigeons. In this wood lived wild cats. Now wild woodland cats must not be confused with those daredevils who run about on roofs of houses which living in towns are, in spite of their violent tempers, far more civilized than the inhabitants of the forest. The woodland cats are for the most part wild and gloomy creatures; they are gaunt and lean and they miaow in coarse uncultivated voices. They sometimes tunnel their way under storehouses and steal lard. They even appear in the kitchen, jumping suddenly through an open window, when they see that the cook has gone off into the tall weeds. As a rule, they have no trace of honourable feelings; they live a predatory life and smother little sparrows in their nests. These tomcats and Pulcheria Ivanovna's gentle little cat had for a long time been sniffing at each other through a hole under the storehouse and at last they enticed her away as a company of soldiers entice a silly country girl. Pulcheria Ivanovna noticed the disappearance of her cat and went to look for her, but she was nowhere to be found. Three days passed; Pulcheria Ivanovna was very sorry for her cat, but at last forgot about her. One day she had been inspecting her vegetable garden, and as she was returning with fresh green cucumbers picked by her own hand for Afanasy Ivanovich, she was struck by the sound of pitiful miaowing. As though by instinct she called: "Puss, puss!"—and suddenly her little grey cat, lean, skinny, came out of the thicket of tall weeds; it was clear that she had not tasted food for several days. Pulcheria Ivanovna went on calling her, but the cat stood miaowing and dared not come near her; it was clear that she had grown wild since her disappearance. Pulcheria Ivanovna walked on, still calling the cat, who followed her timidly as far as the fence. At last, catching sight of the old familiar places, she went indoors. Pulcheria Ivanovna at once ordered milk and meat to be brought for her. Sitting down before her cat, she enjoyed the avidity with which her poor little favourite swallowed bit after bit all the food and lapped up the milk. The grey little runaway was growing fat almost before Pulcheria Ivanovna's very eyes and was no longer eating so greedily. Pulcheria Ivanovna stretched out her hand to stroke her, but the ungrateful creature, who had evidently grown too used to the ways of the predatory cats or had adopted the romantic rule that poverty with love is better than life in a palace (for the wild tomcats were as poor as churchmice), jumped out of the window and none of the house-serfs could catch her.

The old lady sank into thought. "It was my death who came for me," she said to herself, and she could not get the idea out of her head. All day she was sad. In vain did Afanasy Ivanovich crack jokes and try to find out what made her so sad all at once: Pulcheria Ivanovna refused to say anything or said something that could not possibly satisfy Afanasy Ivanovich. Next day she grew perceptibly thinner.

"What's the matter, Pulcheria Ivanovna? You are not ill, are you?"

"No I'm not ill, Afanasy Ivanovich. I'd like to tell you something extraordinary that happened to me: I know that I shall die this summer: my death has already come for me."

Afanasy Ivanovich's lips twisted in a rather painful fashion. He tried, however, to banish the feeling of sadness from his heart and said with a smile: "Goodness me, what are you saying, Pulcheria Ivanovna? I expect you must have drunk some peach brandy instead of your usual decoction."

"No, Afanasy Ivanovich," said Pulcheria Ivanovna, "I have not drunk any peach brandy."

Afanasy Ivanovich felt sorry that he had made fun of her like that, and he looked at her and a tear hung on his eyelash.

"I beg you, Afanasy Ivanovich," said Pulcheria Ivanovna, "to carry out my last wish. When I die, bury me by the church fence. Put my grey dress on me, the one with the little flowers on a brown ground. Don't put on me my satin dress with the raspberry coloured stripes: a dead woman needs no dress. What use is it to her? It will be of use to you: have a fine dressing-gown made of it so that if visitors come to see you, you can look decent when you come out to welcome them."

"What are you saying, Pulcheria Ivanovna?" asked Afanasy Ivanovich. "One day we shall all die, but you are frightening me already by talking like this."

"No, no, Afanasy Ivanovich. I know very well when my death will come. You should not grieve for me though: I am an old woman and have lived long enough. And you're old, too. We shall soon meet in the other world."

But Afanasy Ivanovich was sobbing like a child.

"It's a sin to weep, Afanasy Ivanovich. Do not sin and anger God by your sorrow. I am not sorry to be dying. There's only one thing I'm sorry about" (a heavy sigh interrupted her speech): "I am sorry I do not know in whose care to leave you, who is going to look after you when I am dead. You're like a little child: you need someone who loves you to take care of you."

As she said this there was an expression of such deep, such shattering heartfelt pity on her face that I don't know anyone who could have looked at her that moment unmoved.

"Mind, Yavdokha," she said, turning to the housekeeper whom she had purposely sent for, "when I die you take good care of your master. Look after him as if he were the apple of your eye, like your own child. Make sure that what he likes is cooked for him in the kitchen, that you always give him clean clothes and clean linen, that when visitors come you put decent clothes on him, otherwise he may sometimes come out in his old dressing-gown, for even now he often forgets when it's a holiday and when it's not. Don't take your eyes off him, Yavdokha. I'll pray for you in the next world and God will reward you. See you don't forget, Yavdokha. You, too, are old and have not long to live, do not take a sin upon your soul. If you don't look after him properly, you will have no happiness in this world. I shall beseech God myself not to give you a peaceful death. And you'll be unhappy yourself and your children will be unhappy and all your family will have God's blessing in nothing."

Poor old woman! Just then she was not thinking of the great moment awaiting her, nor of her soul, nor of her own future life; she was thinking only of her poor companion with whom she had spent her life and whom she was leaving helpless and forsaken. With quite extraordinary efficiency she took all the necessary steps to make sure that Afanasy Ivanovitch did not notice her absence when she was gone. Her conviction that her death was near at hand was so strong and her mind was so attuned to it that a few days later she really took to her bed and was not able to eat anything. Afanasy Ivanovich was all solicitude and did not leave her bedside for a moment. "Won't you have a little something, Pulcheria Ivanovna?" he asked, looking anxiously into her eyes. But Pulcheria Ivanovna said nothing. At last, after a long silence, she seemed to wish to say something, her lips stirred and—her breathing stopped.

Afanasy Ivanovich was struck all of a heap. What had happened seemed to him so absolutely outrageous that he did not even burst into tears. He looked at her with dull eyes, as though not grasping the significance of the corpse.

The dead woman was laid on the table, wearing the dress she had herself chosen to be buried in, her arms crossed and a wax candle put in her hand—he gazed at all this without betraying any feeling. A great number of people of every station in life filled the courtyard; a great number of guests came to the funeral; long tables were laid out in the courtyard; groaning under the weight of home-made brandies, pies and barley and rice puddings with honey and raisins; the guests talked, wept, gazed at the dead woman, discussed her qualities, looked at him—but he himself regarded it all strangely. The coffin with the dead woman was carried out at last, the people thronged after it, and he followed it; the priests wore their full vestments, the sun was shining, babies were crying in their mothers' arms, larks were singing, half naked children were running about and playing in the road. At last the coffin was put down over the grave, he was told to walk up to it and kiss his dead wife for the last time; he walked up, kissed her, and tears started to his eyes—but unfeeling tears they somehow seemed. The coffin was lowered, the priest took the spade and was the first to throw in a handful of earth, the deacon and the two sacristans intoned the last prayer for the dead in deep, drawn-out voices, under a clear, cloudless sky. The sextons took up their spades and in no time the earth covered the grave and made it level.

At that moment he struggled forward, the crowd stepped aside and made way for him, curious to know what he was going to do. He raised his eyes, looked round him vaguely and said: "So you've already buried her, have you? Why?" He stopped short and did not finish what he was going to say.

But when he returned home, when he saw that his room was empty, that even the chair Pulcheria Ivanovna used to sit on had been taken away, he burst into sobs and he sobbed violently, he sobbed disconsolately, and tears, like a flood, flowed from his lacklustre eyes.

Five years have passed since then. What grief does not time carry away? What passion can remain inviolate in the unequal struggle with it? I knew a man in the prime of his life, full of true nobility of character. I knew him in love, tenderly, passionately, madly, boldly, modestly, and almost in my presence, before my very eyes, the woman he loved so passionately—adorable and beautiful as an angel—was struck down by insatiable death. I have never seen such terrible outbursts of deep suffering, such frenzied, fierce anguish, such devouring despair as overwhelmed the unhappy lover. I had never imagined that a man could create for himself such a hell with no shadow, no shape of hope—nothing that remotely resembled hope . . . . He was not let out of sight, all weapons with which he might have killed himself were hidden from him. Two weeks later he suddenly mastered himself: he began laughing and jesting; he was given his freedom and the first thing he did was to buy himself a pistol. One day his family was terrified by the sudden sound of a shot. They ran into his room and found him stretched out on the floor with a shattered skull. A doctor, who happened to be there at the time and who was famous throughout the land for his skill, saw signs of life in him, discovered that his wound was not altogether fatal and, to everyone's surprise, he recovered. He was placed under even stricter supervision. Even at table a knife was not laid for him and they tried to remove everything with which he could have hurt himself; but in a short time he found another opportunity and threw himself under the wheels of a passing carriage. His arms and leg were broken, but he again recovered. A year later I saw him at a crowded party; he was sitting at a table, saying gaily "*petite ouverte*" as he covered a card, and behind him, leaning on the back of his chair, his young wife was turning over his counters.

At the end of the five years after Pulcheria Ivanovna's death I happened to be in those parts again and I drove to Afanasy Ivanovich's little farm to visit my old neighbour at whose house I used to spend a pleasant day and invariably to overeat myself on the most wonderful dishes of its hospitable mistress. When I drove up to the courtyard the house seemed to me twice as old as it had been, the peasant's cottage were lying completely on one side, as their owners no doubt were too; the palisade and the wattle fence round the courtyard were completely broken down, and I myself saw the cook pull stakes out of the fence to heat the stove when she had only to take a couple of steps to reach the pile of firewood. Sadly I drove up to the front steps; the same old watchdogs, by now blind or lame, started barking, raising their wavy tails covered with burdock. An old man came out to greet me. So it was he! I recognized him at once, but he was bent twice as much as before. He recognized me and welcomed me with the smile I knew so well. I followed him into the house. Everything seemed to be unchanged; but I noticed a strange disorder in everything, a sort of palpable absence of something; in short, I experienced the strange feelings which overwhelm us when we enter for the first time the house of a widower whom we have known before inseparable from the wife who had been at his side all his life. The feelings are like those we experience when we meet a cripple whom we have always known to be in good health. The absence of solicitous Pulcheria Ivanovna could be detected in everything; at table a knife was laid without a handle, the dishes were no longer prepared with the same skill. I did not want to ask about the farm, I was afraid even to look at the farm buildings.

When we sat down to dinner, a maid tied a napkin round Afanasy Ivanovich, and it was a good thing she did so, for without it he would have spilt sauce all over his coat. I tried to interest him in something and told him various bits of news; he listened with the same smile, but at times his eyes were completely vacant and his thoughts did not wander, but vanished. He often raised a spoonful of porridge and instead of putting it to his mouth put it to his nose; instead of sticking his fork into a piece of chicken, he poked it at the decanter, and then the maid took his hand and directed it towards the chicken. We sometimes had to wait for several minutes for the next course. Afanasy Ivanovich became aware of it himself and kept saying: "Why does it take them so long to bring the food?" But I could see through the crack of the door that the boy who was serving us was not thinking of it at all, but was asleep with his head drooping on a bench.

"This," said Afanasy Ivanovich, when we were served cheese pancakes with sour cream, "this," he repeated, and I noticed that his voice began to tremble and a tear was about to start in his leaden eyes, but he did his utmost not to let it, "this is the dish my dear de—depart——" and suddenly the tears gushed from his eyes. His hand fell on the plate, the plate tipped over, flew into the air and was smashed, and the sauce was spilt all over him; he sat there dead to everything around him, not realising that he was still holding the spoon in his hand, and tears, like a stream, like a ceaselessly flowing fountain, poured, poured uncontrollably, on the napkin that covered him.

"Good Lord," I thought to myself, looking at him, "five years of all destroying time, an old man who seems to be incapable of any feeling, an old man who had apparently never been troubled by any strong emotions, whose whole life seemed to consist of sitting in a high chair, of eating dried fish and pears, of telling goodnatured tales—and such long, such consuming grief! What exercises a stronger hold over us—passion or habit? Or are all the violent impulses, the whole vortex of our desires and burning passions merely the result of our bright-eyed youth and do they seem so deep and shattering only because of that alone." Be that as it may, at that moment all our passions seemed childish to me compared with this long, and slow—almost insensible habit. Several times he tried to utter his late wife's name, but, half way through it, his quiet and ordinary face twitched convulsively, and his child-like weeping cut me to the very heart. No, those were not the tears doddering old men are so lavish with, when they complain about their miserable position and troubles to you, nor the kind of tears they drop over a glass of punch: No! They were tears which flowed by themselves, uninvited, accumulated from the searing pain of a heart already turning cold.

He did not live long after that. I heard of his death a few days ago. The strange thing about it is that the circumstances of his end had a certain resemblance to those of Pulcheria Ivanovna's death. One day Afanasy Ivanovich decided to go for a little walk in the garden. As he was walking slowly along a path without showing, as was his wont, any interest in anything, without a thought of any kind, a strange thing happened to him. He suddenly heard someone behind him say in a rather distinct voice: "Afanasy Ivanovich!" He turned round, but no one at all was there; he looked in all directions, glanced into the bushes—there was no one anywhere. It was a calm day and the sun was shining. He pondered for a moment, then seemed to grow animated and, at last, murmured: "It's Pulcheria Ivanovna calling me!"

I have no doubt that some time or other you, too, happen to hear a voice calling you by your name, which the common people believe to indicate that a soul is pining for a human being and calling him, after which death follows inevitably. I confess I was always terrified by that mysterious call. I remember hearing it often as a child: sometimes someone suddenly distinctly uttered my name. The day, as a rule, was bright and sunny at the time; not a leaf stirred on the trees in the garden; there was a dead hush all around, even the grass-hoppers ceased churring just then; there was not a soul in the garden; but, to be quite frank, even if the wildest and stormiest night with all the fury of the elements had overtaken me alone in the middle of an impenetrable forest, I should not have been so frightened as by that awful stillness amid a cloudless day. Whenever this happened, I usually ran panting in a great panic out of the garden and only calmed down when I came across some person, the sight of whom dispelled this terrible feeling of emptiness in my heart.

Afanasy Ivanovich gave in entirely to his profound conviction that Pulcheria Ivanovna was calling him; he gave in with the willingness of an obedient child, wasted away, coughed, melted like a candle and, at last, snuffed out as it does when there is nothing left to feed its feeble flame. "Lay me beside Pulcheria Ivanovna," was all he said before he died.

His wish was carried out and he was buried near the church beside Pulcheria Ivanovna's grave. There were fewer guests at his funeral than at hers, but there were just as many peasants and beggars. The little manor house was now completely empty. The enterprising steward and the village elder dragged over to their cottages all that was left of the ancient furniture and the other things the housekeeper had not been able to carry off. Soon some distant relative arrived from goodness only knows where, the heir to the estate, who had been a lieutenant of I don't remember what regiment and who was a terrible reformer. He immediately noticed the awful disorder and neglect into which the estate had fallen and he decided to put a stop to it, to get it right and to bring order into everything. He bought six excellent English sickles, nailed a special number to each cottage, and arranged everything so beautifully that within six months the estate was taken over by a board of trustees. The wise trustees (consisting of a ex-assessor and a first lieutenant in a faded uniform) had within a very short time made short shrift of all the hens and eggs. The cottages, which were almost lying on the ground, fell to pieces completely; the peasants took to drink and most of them were soon registered as runaway serfs. The real owner himself, who was on the most amiable terms with the trustees and used to drink punch with them, visited his estate very rarely and did not stay there long. He still drives about to all the fairs in the Ukraine, carefully inquires the prices of all sorts of goods sold wholesale, such as flour, hemp, honey and so on, but only buys small trifles, such as flints, a nail to clean his pipe with and generally everything which at most does not exceed one rouble in price.

Selected Readings

BAUMGARTEN, MURRAY. "Gogol's *The Overcoat* as a Picaresque Epic." *Dalhousie Review*, XLVI (1966), 186–99.

BRODIANSKY, NINA. "Gogol and His Characters." *Slavonic and East European Review*, XXXI (1953), 36–57.

ERLICH, VICTOR. "Gogol and Kafka: Note on 'Realism' and 'Surrealism,' " *For Roman Jakobson: Essays on the Occasion of His Sixtieth Birthday, 11 October, 1956*, ed. Morris Halle et al., pp. 100–08. The Hague: Mouton and Company, 1956.

LAVRIN, JANKO. *Gogol*. London: Routledge and Sons, 1926.

————. *Nikolai Gogol (1809–1852): A Centenary Survey*. London: Sylvan Press, 1951.

MAGARSHACK, DAVID. *Gogol: A Life*. New York: Grove Press, 1957.

NABOKOV, VLADIMIR. *Nikolai Gogol*. Norfolk, Conn.: New Directions Books, 1944.

POGGIOLI, RENATO. "Gogol's 'Old-fashioned Land-owners': An Inverted Eclogue." *Indiana Slavic Studies*, III (1963), 54–72.

SETCHKAVEV, VSEVOLOD. *Gogol: His Life and Works*. Trans. Robert Kramer. London: Peter Owen, 1965.

STILMAN, LEON. "Gogol's *Overcoat*—Thematic Pattern and Origins." *American Slavic and East European Review*, XI (1952), 138–48.

FYODOR DOSTOEVSKY

(1821–1881)

Fyodor Dostoevsky is the poet of guilt. Given this rationale, Dostoevsky's long aesthetic trip need no longer be described as "shocking," "daemonic," "ecstatic," "mystical," "criminal," or "divine." Because the truth is, Dostoevsky defies labeling. He must be experienced at first hand. Frequently a hasty craftsman, Dostoevsky makes his primary appeal as writer directly to the unconscious experience of the reader.

Dostoevsky's father, an army doctor, was a harsh—possibly a brutal—disciplinarian. Caught between hatred for his father and love for his gentle mother, Dostoevsky experienced eighteen impressionable years of emotional ambivalence. The murder of his father by angry serfs in 1839, no doubt a traumatic experience for the son, transformed his feelings of hatred to those of guilt, and the rest of his life seems to be a literary expurgation of that guilt. If one might say that psychology is the study of conscience and guilt, then Dostoevsky is the master of psychoanalytic literature. In it, the reader experiences psychological identification with the most exquisitely criminal and saintly personalities. Dostoevsky allows every man to realize for himself that, as Goethe suggested, there is no crime which he could not be capable of committing.

Many other traumatic experiences followed in Dostoevsky's life: in 1849 a last-second reprieve from a firing squad for socialist conspiracy; beginning in 1849, ten years in Siberia; beginning in 1857, seven years of an unhappy marriage; throughout his ten years in Siberia, recurrent epileptic seizures. According to Dostoevsky's own descriptions of these attacks, the euphoric moments prior to unconsciousness were rapturous, harmonious, ecstatic;

these experiences were followed by feelings of profound guilt, depression, and desolation.

In spite of this bizarre background, or because of it, Dostoevsky emerged in 1864, after his second marriage, a more powerful, universal artist. Some of the works that followed his second marriage were: *Notes From Underground* (1864); *Crime and Punishment* (1866); *The Idiot* (1868–69); *The Possessed* (1871–72); *The Brothers Karamazov* (1879–80). These works are marked by his great psychological portraits of colossal characters of conflicting extremes who respond ambivalently to the human condition. They portray, many of them simultaneously, the extremes of guilt and innocence, love and hate, spirituality and rationality, reason and absurdity, cruelty and compassion. They are some of the great anti-heroes of modern literature.

The Peasant Marey

It was the second day in Easter week. The air was warm, the sky was blue, the sun was high, warm, bright, but my soul was very gloomy. I sauntered behind the prison barracks. I stared at the palings of the stout prison fence, counting them over; but I had no inclination to count them, though it was my habit to do so. This was the second day of the "holidays" in the prison; the convicts were not taken out to work, there were numbers of men drunk, loud abuse and quarrelling was springing up continually in every corner. There were hideous, disgusting songs and card-parties installed beside the platform-beds. Several of the convicts who had been sentenced by their comrades, for special violence, to be beaten till they were half dead, were lying on the platform-bed, covered with sheepskins till they should recover and come to themselves again; knives had already been drawn several times. For these two days of holiday all this had been torturing me till it made me ill. And indeed I could never endure without repulsion the noise and disorder of drunken people, and especially in this place. On these days even the prison officials did not look into the prison, made no searches, did not look for vodka, understanding that they must allow even these outcasts to enjoy themselves once a year, and that things would be even worse if they did not. At last a sudden fury flamed up in my heart. A political prisoner called M. met me; he looked at me gloomily, his eyes flashed and his lips quivered. "*Je haïs ces brigands!*" he hissed to

Reprinted with permission of The Macmillan Company from *An Honest Thief* by Fyodor Dostoevsky, translated by Constance Garnett. First printed in Great Britain.

me through his teeth, and walked on. I returned to the prison ward, though only a quarter of an hour before I had rushed out of it, as though I were crazy, when six stalwart fellows had all together flung themselves upon the drunken Tatar Gazin to suppress him and had begun beating him; they beat him stupidly, a camel might have been killed by such blows, but they knew that this Hercules was not easy to kill, and so they beat him without uneasiness. Now on returning I noticed on the bed in the furthest corner of the room Gazin lying unconscious, almost without sign of life. He lay covered with a sheepskin, and every one walked round him, without speaking; though they confidently hoped that he would come to himself next morning, yet if luck was against him, maybe from a beating like that, the man would die. I made my way to my own place opposite the window with the iron grating, and lay on my back with my hands behind my head and my eyes shut. I liked to lie like that; a sleeping man is not molested, and meanwhile one can dream and think. But I could not dream, my heart was beating uneasily, and M.'s words, "*Je haïs ces brigands!*" were echoing in my ears. But why describe my impressions; I sometimes dream even now of those times at night, and I have no dreams more agonising. Perhaps it will be noticed that even to this day I have scarcely once spoken in print of my life in prison. *The House of the Dead* I wrote fifteen years ago in the character of an imaginary person, a criminal who had killed his wife. I may add by the way that since then, very many persons have supposed, and even now maintain, that I was sent to penal servitude for the murder of my wife.

Gradually I sank into forgetfulness and by degrees was lost in memories. During the whole course of my four years in prison I was continually recalling all my past, and seemed to live over again the whole of my life in recollection. These memories rose up of themselves, it was not often that of my own will I summoned them. It would begin from some point, some little thing, at times unnoticed, and then by degrees there would rise up a complete picture, some vivid and complete impression. I used to analyse these impressions, give new features to what had happened long ago, and best of all, I used to correct it, correct it continually, that was my great amusement. On this occasion, I suddenly for some reason remembered an unnoticed moment in my early childhood when

I was only nine years old—a moment which I should have thought I had utterly forgotten; but at that time I was particularly fond of memories of my early childhood. I remembered the month of August in our country house: a dry bright day but rather cold and windy; summer was waning and soon we should have to go to Moscow to be bored all the winter over French lessons, and I was so sorry to leave the country. I walked past the threshing-floor and, going down the ravine, I went up to the dense thicket of bushes that covered the further side of the ravine as far as the copse. And I plunged right into the midst of the bushes, and heard a peasant ploughing alone on the clearing about thirty paces away. I knew that he was ploughing up the steep hill and the horse was moving with effort, and from time to time the peasant's call "come up!" floated upwards to me. I knew almost all our peasants, but I did not know which it was ploughing now, and I did not care who it was, I was absorbed in my own affairs. I was busy, too; I was breaking off switches from the nut trees to whip the frogs with. Nut sticks make such fine whips, but they do not last; while birch twigs are just the opposite. I was interested, too, in beetles and other insects; I used to collect them, some were very ornamental. I was very fond, too, of the little nimble red and yellow lizards with black spots on them, but I was afraid of snakes. Snakes, however, were much more rare than lizards. There were not many mushrooms there. To get mushrooms one had to go to the birch wood, and I was about to set off there. And there was nothing in the world that I loved so much as the wood with its mushrooms and wild berries, with its beetles and its birds, its hedgehogs and squirrels, with its damp smell of dead leaves which I loved so much, and even as I write I smell the fragrance of our birch wood: these impressions will remain for my whole life. Suddenly in the midst of the profound stillness I heard a clear and distinct shout, "Wolf!" I shrieked and, beside myself with terror, calling out at the top of my voice, ran out into the clearing and straight to the peasant who was ploughing.

It was our peasant Marey. I don't know if there is such a name, but every one called him Marey—a thick-set, rather well-grown peasant of fifty, with a good many grey hairs in his dark brown, spreading beard. I knew him, but had scarcely ever happened to speak to him till then. He stopped his horse on hearing my cry, and when, breathless, I caught with one hand at his plough and with the other at his sleeve, he saw how frightened I was.

"There is a wolf!" I cried, panting.

He flung up his head, and could not help looking round for an instant, almost believing me.

"Where is the wolf?"

"A shout . . . some one shouted: 'wolf' . . . " I faltered out.

"Nonsense, nonsense! A wolf? Why, it was your fancy! How could there be a wolf?" he muttered, reassuring me. But I was trembling all over, and still kept tight hold of his smock frock, and I must have been quite pale. He looked at me with an uneasy smile, evidently anxious and troubled over me.

"Why, you have had a fright, *aïe, aïe!*" He shook his head. "There, dear . . . . Come, little one, *aïe!*"

He stretched out his hand, and all at once stroked my cheek.

"Come, come, there; Christ be with you! Cross yourself!" But I did not cross myself. The corners of my mouth were twitching, and I think that struck him particularly. He put out his thick, black-nailed, earth-stained finger and softly touched my twitching lips.

"*Aïe*, there, there," he said to me with a slow, almost motherly smile. "Dear, dear, what is the matter? There; come, come!"

I grasped at last that there was no wolf, and that the shout that I had heard was my fancy. Yet that shout had been so clear and distinct, but such shouts (not about wolves) I had imagined once or twice before, and I was aware of that. (These hallucinations passed away later as I grew older.)

"Well, I will go then," I said, looking at him timidly and inquiringly.

"Well, do, and I'll keep watch on you as you go. I won't let the wolf get at you," he added, still smiling at me with the same motherly expression. "Well, Christ be with you! Come, run along then," and he made the sign of the cross over me and then over himself. I walked away, looking back almost at every tenth step. Marey stood still with his mare as I walked away, and looked after me and nodded to me every time I looked round. I must own I felt a little ashamed at having let him see me so frightened, but I was still very much afraid of the wolf as I walked away, until I reached the first barn half-way up the slope of the ravine; there my fright vanished completely, and all at once our yard-dog Voltchok flew to meet me. With Voltchok I felt quite safe, and I turned round to Marey for the last time; I could not see his face distinctly, but I felt that he was still nodding and smiling affectionately to me. I waved to him; he waved back to me and started his little mare. "Come up!" I heard his call in the distance again, and the little mare pulled at the plough again.

All this I recalled all at once, I don't know why, but with extraordinary minuteness of detail. I suddenly roused myself and sat up on the platform-bed, and, I remember, found myself still smiling quietly at my memories. I brooded over them for another minute.

When I got home that day I told no one of my "adventure" with Marey. And indeed it was hardly an adventure. And in fact I soon forgot Marey. When I met him now and then afterwards, I never even spoke to him about the wolf or anything else; and all at once now, twenty years afterwards in Siberia, I remembered this meeting with such distinctness to the smallest detail. So it must have lain hidden in my soul, though I knew nothing of it, and rose suddenly to my memory when it was wanted; I remembered the soft motherly smile of the poor serf, the way he signed me with the cross and shook his head. "There, there, you have had a fright, little one!" And I remembered particularly the thick earth-stained finger with which he softly and with timid tenderness touched my quivering lips. Of course any one would have reassured a child, but something quite different seemed to have happened in that solitary meeting; and if I had been his own son, he could not have looked at me with eyes shining with greater love. And what made him like that? He was our serf and I was his little master, after all. No one would know that he had been kind to me and reward him for it. Was he, perhaps, very fond of little children? Some people are. It was a solitary meeting in the deserted fields, and only God, perhaps, may have seen from above with what deep and humane civilised feeling, and with what delicate, almost feminine tenderness, the heart of a coarse, brutally ignorant Russian serf, who had as yet no expectation, no idea even of his freedom, may be filled. Was not this, perhaps, what Konstantin Aksakov meant when he spoke of the high degree of culture of our peasantry?

And when I got down off the bed and looked around me, I remember I suddenly felt that I could look at these unhappy creatures with quite different eyes, and that suddenly by some miracle all hatred and anger had vanished utterly from my heart. I walked about, looking into the faces that I met. That shaven peasant, branded on his face as a criminal, bawling his hoarse, drunken song, may be that very Marey; I cannot look into his heart.

I met M. again that evening. Poor fellow! he could have no memories of Russian peasants, and no other view of these people but: "*Je haïs ces brigands!*" Yes, the Polish prisoners had more to bear than I.

An Honest Thief

One morning, just as I was about to leave for my place of employment, Agrafena (my cook, laundress, and housekeeper all in one person) entered my room, and, to my great astonishment, started a conversation.

She was a quiet, simple-minded woman, who during the whole six years of her stay with me had never spoken more than two or three words daily, and that in reference to my dinner—at least, I had never heard her.

"I have come to you, sir," she suddenly began, "about the renting out of the little spare room."

"What spare room?"

"The one that is near the kitchen, of course; which should it be?"

"Why?"

"Why do people generally take lodgers? Because."

"But who will take it?"

"Who will take it! A lodger, of course! Who should take it?"

"But there is hardly room in there, mother mine, for a bed; it will be too cramped. How can one live in it?"

"But why live in it! He only wants a place to sleep in; he will live on the window-seat."

"What window-seat?"

"How is that? What window-seat? As if you did not know! The one in the hall. He will sit on it and sew, or do something else. But maybe he will sit on a chair; he has a chair of his own—and a table also, and everything."

"But who is he?"

"A nice, worldy-wise man. I will cook for him and will charge him only three rubles in silver a month for room and board——"

At last, after long endeavor, I found out that some elderly man had talked Agrafena into taking him into the kitchen as lodger. When Agrafena once got a thing into her head that thing had to be done; otherwise I knew I would have no peace. On those occasions when things did go against her wishes, she immediately fell into a sort of brooding, became exceedingly melancholy, and continued in that state for two or three weeks. During this time the food was invariably spoiled, the linen was missing, the floors unscrubbed; in a word, a lot of unpleasant things happened. I had long ago become aware of the fact that this woman of very few words was incapable of forming a decision, or of coming to any conclusion based on her own thoughts; and yet when it happened that by some means there had formed in her weak brain a sort of idea or wish to undertake a thing, to refuse her permission to carry out this idea or wish meant simply to kill her morally for some time. And so, acting in the sole interest of my peace of mind, I immediately agreed to this new proposition of hers.

"Has he at least the necessary papers, a passport, or anything of the kind?"

"How then? Of course he has. A fine man like him—who has seen the world—— He promised to pay three rubles a month."

On the very next day the new lodger appeared in my modest bachelor quarters; but I did not feel annoyed in the least—on the contrary, in a way I was glad of it. I live a very solitary, hermit-like life. I have almost no acquaintance and seldom go out. Having led the existence of a moor-cock for ten years, I was naturally used to solitude. But ten, fifteen years or more of the same seclusion in company with a person like Agrafena, and in the same bachelor dwelling, was indeed a joyless prospect. Therefore, the presence of another quiet, unobtrusive man in the house was, under these circumstances, a real blessing.

Agrafena had spoken the truth: the lodger was a man who had seen much in his life. From his passport it appeared that he was a retired soldier, which I noticed even before I looked at the passport.

As soon as I glanced at him in fact.

Astafi Ivanich, my lodger, belonged to the better sort of soldiers, another thing I noticed as soon as I saw him. We liked each other from the first, and our life flowed on peacefully and comfortably. The best thing was that Astafi Ivanich could at times tell a good story, incidents of his own life. In the general tediousness of my humdrum existence, such a narrator was a veritable treasure. Once he told me a story which has made a lasting impression upon me; but first the incident which led to the story.

Once I happened to be left alone in the house, Astafi and Agrafena having gone out on business. Suddenly I heard some one enter, and I felt that it must be a stranger; I went out into the corridor and found a man of short stature, and notwithstanding the cold weather, dressed very thinly and without an overcoat.

"What is it you want?"

"The Government clerk Alexandrov? Does he live here?"

"There is no one here by that name, little brother; good day."

"The porter told me he lived here," said the visitor, cautiously retreating toward the door.

"Go on, go on, little brother; be off!"

Soon after dinner the next day, when Astafi brought in my coat, which he had repaired for me, I once more heard a strange step in the corridor. I opened the door.

The visitor of the day before, calmly and before my very eyes, took my short coat from the rack, put it under his arm, and ran out.

Agrafena, who had all the time been looking at him in open-mouthed surprise through the kitchen door, was seemingly unable to stir from her place and rescue the coat. But Astafi Ivanich rushed after the rascal, and, out of breath and panting, returned empty-handed. The man had vanished as if the earth had swallowed him.

"It is too bad, really, Astafi Ivanich," I said. "It is well that I have my cloak left. Otherwise the scoundrel would have put me out of service altogether."

But Astafi seemed so much affected by what had happened that as I gazed at him I forgot all about the theft. He could not regain his composure, and every once in a while threw down the work which occupied him, and began once more to recount how it had all happened, where he had been standing, while only two steps away my coat had been stolen before his very eyes, and how he could not even catch the thief. Then once more he resumed his work, only to throw it away again, and I saw him go down to the porter, tell him what had happened, and reproach him with not taking sufficient care of the house, that such a theft could be perpetrated in it. When he returned he began to upbraid Agrafena. Then he again resumed his work, muttering to himself for a long time—how this is the way it all was—how he stood here, and I there, and how before our very eyes, no farther than two steps away, the coat was taken off its hanger, and so on. In a word, Astafi Ivanich, though he knew how to do certain things, worried a great deal over trifles.

"We have been fooled, Astafi Ivanich," I said to him that evening, handing him a glass of tea, and hoping from sheer ennui to call forth the story of the lost coat again, which by dint of much repetition had begun to sound extremely comical.

"Yes, we were fooled, sir. It angers me very much, though the loss is not mine, and I think there is nothing so despicably low in this world as a thief. They steal what you buy by working in the sweat of your brow—— Your time and labor—— The loathsome creature! It sickens me to talk of it—pfui! It makes me angry to think of it. How is it, sir, that you do not seem to be at all sorry about it?"

"To be sure, Astafi Ivanich, one would much sooner see his things burn up than see a thief take them. It is exasperating——"

"Yes, it is annoying to have anything stolen from you. But of course there are thieves and thieves—I, for instance, met an honest thief through an accident."

"How is that? An honest thief? How can a thief be honest, Astafi Ivanich?"

"You speak truth, sir. A thief can not be an honest man. There never was such. I only wanted to say that he was an honest man, it seems to me, even though he stole. I was very sorry for him."

"And how did it happen, Astafi Ivanich?"

"It happened just two years ago. I was serving as house steward at the time, and the baron whom I served expected shortly to leave for his estate, so that I knew I would soon be out of a job, and then God only knew how I would be able to get along; and just then it was that I happened to meet in a tavern a poor forlorn creature, Emelian by name. Once upon a time he had served somewhere or other, but had been driven out of service on account of tippling. Such an unworthy creature as he was! He wore whatever came along. At times I even wondered if he wore a shirt under his shabby cloak; everything he could put his hands on was sold for drink. But he was not a rowdy. Oh, no; he was of a sweet, gentle nature, very kind and tender to every one; he never asked for anything, was, if anything, too conscientious—— Well, you could see without asking when the poor fellow was dying for a drink, and of course you treated him to one. Well, we became friendly, that is, he attached himself to me like a little dog—you go this way, he follows—and all this after our very first meeting.

"Of course he remained with me that night; his passport was in order and the man seemed all right. On the second night also. On the third he did not leave the house, sitting on the window-seat of the corridor the whole day, and of course he remained over that night too. Well, I thought, just see how he has forced himself upon you. You have to give him to eat and to drink and to shelter him. All a poor man needs is some one to sponge upon him. I soon found out that once before he had attached himself to a man just as he had now attached himself to me; they drank together, but the other one soon died of some deep-seated sorrow. I thought and thought: What shall I do with him? Drive him out—my conscience would not allow it—I felt very sorry for him: he was such a wretched, forlorn creature, terrible! And so dumb he did not ask for anything, only sat quietly and looked you straight in the eyes, just like a faithful little dog. That is how drink can ruin a man. And I thought to myself: Well, suppose I say to him: 'Get out of here, Emelian; you have nothing to do in here, you come to the wrong person; I will soon have nothing to eat myself, so how do you expect me to feed *you*?' And I tried to imagine what he would do after I'd told him all this. And I could see how he would look at me for a long time after he had heard me, without understanding a word; how at last he would understand what I was driving at, and, rising from the window-seat, take his little bundle—I see it before me now—a red-checked little bundle full of holes, in which he kept God knows what, and which he carted along with him wherever he went; how he would brush and fix up his worn cloak a little, so that it would look a bit more decent and not show so much the holes and patches—he was a man of very fine feelings! How he would have opened the door afterward and would have gone forth with tears in his eyes.

"Well, should a man be allowed to perish altogether? I all at once felt heartily sorry for him; but at the same time I thought: And what about me, am I any better off? And I said to myself: Well, Emelian, you will not feast overlong at my expense; soon I shall have to move from here myself, and then you will not find me again. Well, sir, my baron soon left for his estate with all his household, telling me before he went that he was very well satisfied with my services, and would gladly employ me again on his return to the capital. A fine man my baron was, but he died the same year.

"Well, after I had escorted my baron and his family a little way, I took my things and the little money I had saved up, and went to live with an old woman I knew, who rented out a corner of the room she occupied by herself. She used to be a nurse in some well-to-do family, and now, in her old age, they had pensioned her off. Well, I thought to myself, now it is good-by to you, Emelian, dear man, you will not find me now! And what do you think, sir? When I returned in the evening—I had paid a visit to an acquaintance of mine—whom should I see but Emelian sitting quietly upon my trunk with his red-checked bundle by his side. He was wrapped up in his poor little cloak, and was awaiting my home-coming. He must have been quite lonesome, because he had borrowed a prayer-book of the old woman and held it upside down. He had found me after all! My hands fell helplessly at my sides. Well, I thought, there is nothing to be done, why did I not drive him away first off? And I only asked him: 'Have you taken your passport along, Emelian?' Then I sat down, sir, and began to turn the matter over in my mind: Well, could he, a roving man, be much in my way? And after I had considered it well, I decided that he would not, and besides, he would be of very little expense to me. Of course, he would have to be fed, but what does that amount to? Some bread in the morning and, to make it a little more appetizing, a little onion or so. For the midday meal again some bread and onion, and for the evening again onion and bread, and some kvass, and, if some cabbage-soup should happen to come our way, then we could both fill up to the throat. I ate little, and Emelian, who was a drinking man, surely ate almost nothing: all he wanted was vodka. He would be the undoing of me with his drinking; but at the same time I felt a curious feeling creep over me. It seemed as if life would be a burden to me if Emelian went away. And so I decided then and there to be his father-bene-factor. I would put him on his legs, I thought, save him from per-ishing, and gradually wean him from drink. Just you wait, I thought. Stay with me, Emelian, but stand pat now. Obey the word of command!

"Well, I thought to myself, I will begin by teaching him some work, but not at once; let him first enjoy himself a bit, and I will in the mean while look around and discover what he finds easiest, and would be capable of doing, because you must know, sir, a man must have a calling and a capacity for a certain work to be able to do it properly. And I began stealthily to observe him. And a hard subject he was, that Emelian! At first I tried to get at him with a kind word. Thus and thus I would speak to him: 'Emelian, you had better take more care of yourself and try to fix yourself up a little.

" 'Give up drinking. Just look at yourself, man, you are all ragged, your cloak looks more like a sieve than anything else. It is not nice. It is about time for you to come to your senses and know when you have had enough.'

"He listened to me, my Emelian did, with lowered head; he had already reached that state, poor fellow, when the drink affected his tongue and he could not utter a sensible word. You talk to him about cucumbers, and he answers beans. He listened, listened to me for a long time, and then he would sigh deeply.

" 'What are you sighing for, Emelian?' I ask him.

" 'Oh, it is nothing, Astafi Ivanich, do not worry. Only what I saw to-day, Astafi Ivanich—two women fighting about a basket of huckleberries that one of them had upset by accident.'

" 'Well, what of that?'

" 'And the woman whose berries were scattered snatched a like basket of huckleberries from the other woman's hand, and not only threw them on the ground, but stamped all over them.'

" 'Well, but what of that, Emelian?'

" 'Ech!' I think to myself, 'Emelian! You have lost your poor wits through the cursed drink!'

" 'And again,' Emelian says, 'a baron lost a bill on the Gorok-hova Street—or was it on the Sadova? A muzhik saw him drop it, and says, "My luck," but here another one interfered and says, "No, it is my luck! I saw it first . . . . " '

" 'Well, Emelian?'

" 'And the two muzhiks started a fight, Astafi Ivanich, and the upshot was that a policeman came, picked up the money, handed it back to the baron, and threatened to put the muzhiks under lock for raising a disturbance.'

" 'But what of that? What is there wonderful or edifying in that, Emelian?'

" 'Well, nothing, but the people laughed, Astafi Ivanich.'

" 'E-ch, Emelian! What have the people to do with it?' I said. 'You have sold your immortal soul for a copper. But do you know what I will tell you, Emelian?'

" 'What, Astafi Ivanich?'

" 'You'd better take up some work, really you should. I am telling you for the hundredth time that you should have pity on yourself!'

" 'But what shall I do, Astafi Ivanich? I do not know where to begin and no one would employ me, Astafi Ivanich.'

" 'That is why they drove you out of service, Emelian; it is all on account of drink!'

" 'And to-day,' said Emelian, 'they called Vlass the barkeeper into the office.'

" 'What did they call him for, Emelian?' I asked.

" 'I don't know why, Astafi Ivanich. I suppose it was needed, so they called him.'

" 'Ech,' I thought to myself, 'no good will come of either of us, Emelian! It is for our sins that God is punishing us!'

"Well, what could a body do with such a man, sir!

"But he was sly, the fellow was, I tell you! He listened to me, listened, and at last it seems it began to tire him, and as quick as he would notice that I was growing angry he would take his cloak and slip out—and that was the last to be seen of him! He would not show up the whole day, and only in the evening would he return, as drunk as a lord. Who treated him to drinks, or where he got the money for it, God only knows; not from me, surely! . . .

" 'Well,' I say to him, 'Emelian, you will have to give up drink, do you hear? you will have to give it up! The next time you return tipsy, you will have to sleep on the stairs. I'll not let you in!'

"After this Emelian kept to the house for two days; on the third he once more sneaked out. I wait and wait for him; he does not come! I must confess that I was kind of frightened; besides, I felt terribly sorry for him. What had I done to the poor devil! I thought. I must have frightened him off. Where could he have gone to now, the wretched creature? Great God, he may perish yet! The night passed and he did not return. In the morning I went out into the hall, and he was lying there with his head on the lower step, almost stiff with cold.

" 'What is the matter with you, Emelian? The Lord save you! Why are you here?'

" 'But you know, Astafi Ivanich,' he replied, 'you were angry with me the other day; I aggravated you, and you promised to make me sleep in the hall, and I—so I—did not dare—to come in —and lay down here.'

" 'It would be better for you, Emelian,' I said, filled with anger and pity, 'to find a better employment than needlessly watching the stairs!'

" 'But what other employment, Astafi Ivanich?'

" 'Well, wretched creature that you are,' here anger had flamed up in me, 'if you would try to learn the tailoring art. Just look at the cloak you are wearing! Not only is it full of holes, but you are sweeping the stairs with it! You should at least take a needle and mend it a little, so it would look more decent. E-ch, a wretched tippler you are, and nothing more!'

"Well, sir! What do you think! He did take the needle—I had told him only for fun, and there he got scared and actually took the needle. He threw off his cloak and began to put the thread through; well, it was easy to see what would come of it; his eyes began to fill and reddened, his hands trembled! He pushed and pushed the thread—could not get it through: he wetted it, rolled it between his fingers, smoothed it out, but it would not—go! He flung it from him and looked at me.

" 'Well, Emelian!' I said, 'you served me right! If people had seen it I would have died with shame! I only told you all this for fun, and because I was angry with you. Never mind sewing; may the Lord keep you from sin! You need not do anything, only keep out of mischief, and do not sleep on the stairs and put me to shame thereby!'

" 'But what shall I do, Astafi Ivanich; I know myself that I am always tipsy and unfit for anything! I only make you, my be— benefactor, angry for nothing.'

"And suddenly his bluish lips began to tremble, and a tear

rolled down his unshaven, pale cheek, then another and another one, and he broke into a very flood of tears, my Emelian. Father in Heaven! I felt as if some one had cut me over the heart with a knife.

" 'E-ch you, sensitive man; why, I never thought! And who *could* have thought such a thing! No, I'd better give you up altogether, Emelian; do as you please.'

"Well, sir, what else is there to tell! But the whole thing is so insignificant and unimportant, it is really not worth while wasting words about it; for instance, you, sir, would not give two broken groschen for it; but I, I would give much, if I had much, that this thing had never happened! I owned, sir, a pair of breeches, blue, in checks, a first-class article, the devil take them—a rich land-owner who came here on business ordered them from me, but refused afterward to take them, saying that they were too tight, and left them with me.

"Well, I thought, the cloth is of first-rate quality! I can get five rubles for them in the old-clothes market-place, and, if not, I can cut a fine pair of pantaloons out of them for some St. Petersburg gent, and have a piece left over for a vest for myself. Everything counts with a poor man! And Emelian was at that time in sore straits. I saw that he had given up drinking, first one day, then a second, and a third, and looked so downhearted and sad.

"Well, I thought, it is either that the poor fellow lacks the necessary coin or maybe he has entered on the right path, and has at last listened to good sense.

"Well, to make a long story short, an important holiday came just at that time, and I went to vespers. When I came back I saw Emelian sitting on the window-seat as drunk as a lord. Eh! I thought, so that is what you are about! And I go to my trunk to get out something I needed. I look! The breeches are not there. I rummage about in this place and that place: gone! Well, after I had searched all over and saw that they were missing for fair, I felt as if something had gone through me! I went after the old woman—as to Emelian, though there was evidence against him in his being drunk, I somehow never thought of him!

" 'No,' says my old woman; 'the good Lord keep you, gentleman, what do I need breeches for? can I wear them? I myself missed a skirt the other day. I know nothing at all about it.'

" 'Well,' I asked, 'has any one called here?'

" 'No one called,' she said. 'I was in all the time; your friend here went out for a short while and then came back; here he sits! Why don't you ask him?'

" 'Did you happen, for some reason or other, Emelian, to take the breeches out of the trunk? The ones, you remember, which were made for the landowner?'

" 'No,' he says, 'I have not taken them, Astafi Ivanich.'

" 'What *could* have happened to them?' Again I began to search, but nothing came of it! And Emelian sat and swayed to and fro on the window-seat.

"I was on my knees before the open trunk, just in front of him. Suddenly I threw a sidelong glance at him. Ech, I thought, and felt very hot round the heart, and my face grew very red. Suddenly my eyes encountered Emelian's.

" 'No,' he says, 'Astafi Ivanich. You perhaps think that I— you know what I mean—but I have not taken them.'

" 'But where have they gone, Emelian?'

" 'No,' he says, 'Astafi Ivanich, I have not seen them at all.'

" 'Well, then, you think they simply went and got lost by themselves, Emelian?'

" 'Maybe they did, Astafi Ivanich.'

"After this I would not waste another word on him. I rose from my knees, locked the trunk, and after I had lighted the lamp I sat down to work. I was remaking a vest for a government clerk, who lived on the floor below. But I was terribly rattled, just the same. It would have been much easier to bear, I thought, if all my wardrobe had burned to ashes. Emelian, it seems, felt that I was deeply angered. It is always so, sir, when a man is guilty; he always feels beforehand when trouble approaches, as a bird feels the coming storm.

" 'And do you know, Astafi Ivanich,' he suddenly began, 'the leach married the coachman's widow to-day.'

"I just looked at him; but, it seems, looked at him so angrily that he understood: I saw him rise from his seat, approach the bed, and begin to rummage in it, continually repeating: 'Where could they have gone, vanished, as if the devil had taken them!'

"I waited to see what was coming; I saw that my Emelian had crawled under the bed. I could contain myself no longer.

" 'Look here,' I said. 'What makes you crawl under the bed?'

" 'I am looking for the breeches, Astafi Ivanich,' said Emelian from under the bed. 'Maybe they got here somehow or other.'

" 'But what makes you, sir (in my anger I addressed him as if he was—somebody), what makes you trouble yourself on account of such a plain man as I am; dirtying your knees for nothing!'

" 'But, Astafi Ivanich—I did not mean anything—I only thought maybe if we look for them here we may find them yet.'

" 'Mm! Just listen to me a moment, Emelian!'

" 'What, Astafi Ivanich?'

" 'Have you not simply stolen them from me like a rascally thief, serving me so for my bread and salt?' I said to him, beside myself with wrath at the sight of him crawling under the bed for something he knew was not there.

" 'No, Astafi Ivanich.' For a long time he remained lying flat under the bed. Suddenly he crawled out and stood before me— I seem to see him even now—as terrible a sight as sin itself.

" 'No,' he says to me in a trembling voice, shivering through all his body and pointing to his breast with his finger, so that all at once I became scared and could not move from my seat on the window. 'I have not taken your breeches, Astafi Ivanich.'

" 'Well,' I answered, 'Emelian, forgive me if in my foolishness I have accused you wrongfully. As to the breeches, let them go hang; we will get along without them. We have our hands, thank God, we will not have to steal, and now, too, we will not have to sponge on another poor man; we will earn our living.'

"Emelian listened to me and remained standing before me for some time, then he sat down and sat motionless the whole evening; when I lay down to sleep he was still sitting in the same place.

"In the morning, when I awoke, I found him sleeping on the bare floor, wrapped up in his cloak; he felt his humiliation so strongly that he had no heart to go and lie down on the bed.

"Well, sir, from that day on I conceived a terrible dislike for the man; that is, rather, I hated him the first few days, feeling as if, for instance, my own son had robbed me and given me deadly offense. Ech, I thought, Emelian, Emelian! And Emelian, my dear sir, had gone on a two weeks' spree. Drunk to bestiality from morning till night. And during the whole two weeks he had not uttered a word. I suppose he was consumed the whole time by a deep-seated grief, or else he was trying in this way to make an end to himself. At last he gave up drinking. I suppose he had no longer the wherewithal to buy vodka—had drunk up every copeck —and he once more took up his old place on the window-seat. I remember that he sat there for three whole days without a word; suddenly I see him weep; sits there and cries, but what crying! The tears come from his eyes in showers, drip, drip, as if he did not know that he was shedding them. It is very painful, sir, to see a grown man weep, all the more when the man is of advanced years, like Emelian, and cries from grief and a sorrowful heart.

" 'What ails you, Emelian?' I say to him.

"He starts and shivers. This was the first time I had spoken to him since that eventful day.

" 'It is nothing—Astafi Ivanich.'

" 'God keep you, Emelian; never you mind it all. Let bygones be bygones. Don't take it to heart so, man!' I felt very sorry for him.

" 'It is only that—that I would like to do something—some kind of work, Astafi Ivanich.'

" 'But what kind of work, Emelian?'

" 'Oh, any kind. Maybe I will go into some kind of service, as before. I have already been at my former employer's asking. It will not do for me, Astafi Ivanich, to use you any longer. I, Astafi Ivanich, will perhaps obtain some employment, and then I will pay you for everything, food and all.'

" 'Don't, Emelian, don't. Well, let us say you committed a sin; well, it is over! The devil take it all! Let us live as before—as if nothing had happened!' "

" 'You, Astafi Ivanich, you are probably hinting about *that*. But I have not taken your breeches.'

" 'Well, just as you please, Emelian!'

" 'No, Astafi Ivanich, evidently I can not live with you longer. You will excuse me, Astafi Ivanich.'

" 'But God be with you, Emelian,' I said to him; 'who is it that is offending you or driving you out of the house? Is it I who am doing it?'

" 'No, but it is unseemly for me to misuse your hospitality any longer, Astafi Ivanich; 'twill be better to go.'

"I saw that he had in truth risen from his place and donned his ragged cloak—he felt offended, the man did, and had gotten it into his head to leave, and—basta.

" 'But where are you going, Emelian? Listen to sense: what are you? Where will you go?'

" 'No, it is best so, Astafi Ivanich, do not try to keep me back,' and he once more broke into tears; 'let me be, Astafi Ivanich, you are no longer what you used to be.'

" 'Why am I not? I am just the same. But you will perish when left alone—like a foolish little child, Emelian.'

" 'No, Astafi Ivanich. Lately, before you leave the house, you have taken to locking your trunk, and I, Astafi Ivanich, see it and weep—No, it is better you should let me go, Astafi Ivanich, and forgive me if I have offended you in any way during the time we have lived together.'

"Well, sir! And so he did go away. I waited a day and thought: Oh, he will be back toward evening. But a day passes, then another, and he does not return. On the third—he does not return. I grew frightened, and a terrible sadness gripped at my heart. I stopped eating and drinking, and lay whole nights without closing my eyes. The man had wholly disarmed me! On the fourth day I went to look for him; I looked in all the taverns and pot-houses in the vicinity, and asked if any one had seen him. No, Emelian had wholly disappeared! Maybe he has done away with his miserable existence, I thought. Maybe, when in his cups, he has perished like a dog, somewhere under a fence. I came home half dead with fatigue and despair, and decided to go out the next day again to look for him, cursing myself bitterly for letting the foolish, helpless man go away from me. But at dawn of the fifth day (it was a holiday) I heard the door creak. And whom should I see but Emelian! But in what a state! His face was bluish and his hair was full of mud, as if he had slept in the street; and he had grown thin, the poor fellow had, as thin as a rail. He took off his poor cloak, sat down on my trunk, and began to look at me. Well, sir, I was overjoyed, but at the same time felt a greater sadness than ever pulling at my heart-strings. This is how it was, sir: I felt that if a thing like that had happened to me, that is—I would sooner have perished like a dog, but would not have returned. And Emelian did. Well, naturally, it is hard to see a man in such a state. I began to coddle and to comfort him in every way.

" 'Well,' I said, 'Emelian, I am very glad you have returned; if you had not come so soon, you would not have found me in, as

I intended to go hunting for you. Have you had anything to eat?'

" 'I have eaten, Astafi Ivanich.'

" 'I doubt it. Well, here is some cabbage soup—left over from yesterday; a nice soup with some meat in it—not the meagre kind. And here you have some bread and a little onion. Go ahead and eat; it will do you good.'

"I served it to him; and immediately realized that he must have been starving for the last three days—such an appetite as he showed! So it was hunger that had driven him back to me. Looking at the poor fellow, I was deeply touched, and decided to run into the nearby dram-shop. I will get him some vodka, I thought, to liven him up a bit and make peace with him. It is enough. I have nothing against the poor devil any longer. And so I brought the vodka and said to him: 'Here, Emelian, let us drink to each other's health in honor of the holiday. Come, take a drink. It will do you good.'

"He stretched out his hand, greedily stretched it out, you know, and stopped; then, after a while, he lifted the glass, carried it to his mouth, spilling the liquor on his sleeve; at last he did carry it to his mouth, but immediately put it back on the table.

" 'Well, why don't you drink, Emelian?'

" 'But no, I'll not, Astafi Ivanich.'

" 'You'll not drink it!'

" 'But I, Astafi Ivanich, I think—I'll not drink any more, Astafi Ivanich.'

" 'Is it for good you have decided to give it up, Emelian, or only for to-day?'

"He did not reply, and after a while I saw him lean his head on his hand, and I asked him: 'Are you not feeling well, Emelian?'

" 'Yes, pretty well, Astafi Ivanich.'

"I made him go to bed, and saw that he was truly in a bad way. His head was burning hot and he was shivering with ague. I sat by him the whole day; toward evening he grew worse. I prepared a meal for him of kvass, butter, and some onion, and threw in it a few bits of bread, and said to him: 'Go ahead and take some food; maybe you will feel better!'

"But he only shook his head: 'No, Astafi Ivanich, I shall not have any dinner to-day.'

"I had some tea prepared for him, giving a lot of trouble to the poor old woman from whom I rented a part of the room—but he would not take even a little tea.

"Well, I thought to myself, it is a bad case. On the third morning, I went to see the doctor, an acquaintance of mine, Dr. Kostopravov, who had treated me when I still lived in my last place. The doctor came, examined the poor fellow, and only said: 'There was no need of sending for me, he is already too far gone, but you can give him some powders which I will prescribe.'

"Well, I didn't give him the powders at all, as I understood that the doctor was only doing it for form's sake; and in the mean while came the fifth day.

"He lay dying before me, sir. I sat on the window-seat with some work I had on hand lying on my lap. The old woman was raking the stove. We were all silent, and my heart was breaking over this poor, shiftless creature, as if he were my own son whom I was losing. I knew that Emelian was gazing at me all the time; I noticed for the earliest morning that he longed to tell me something, but seemingly dared not. At last I looked at him, and saw that he did not take his eyes from me, but that whenever his eyes met mine, he immediately lowered his own.

" 'Astafi Ivanich!'

" 'What, Emelian?'

" 'What if my cloak should be carried over to the old clothes market, would they give much for it, Astafi Ivanich?'

" 'Well, I said, 'I do not know for certain, but three rubles they would probably give for it, Emelian.' I said it only to comfort the simple-minded creature; in reality they would have laughed in my face for even thinking to sell such a miserable, ragged thing.

" 'And I thought that they might give a little more, Astafi Ivanich. It is made of cloth, so how is it that they would not wish to pay more than three rubles for it?'

" 'Well, Emelian, if you wish to sell it, then of course you may ask more for it at first.'

"Emelian was silent for a moment, then he once more called to me.

" 'Astafi Ivanich!'

" 'What is it, Emelian?'

" 'You will sell the cloak after I am no more; no need of burying me in it, I can well get along without it; it is worth something, and may come in handy to you.'

"Here I felt such a painful gripping at my heart as I can not even express, sir. I saw that the sadness of approaching death had already come upon the man. Again we were silent for some time. About an hour passed in this way. I looked at him again and saw that he was still gazing at me, and when his eyes met mine he immediately lowered his.

" 'Would you like a drink of cold water?' I asked him.

" 'Give me some, and may God repay you, Astafi Ivanich.'

" 'Would you like anything else, Emelian?'

" 'No, Astafi Ivanich, I do not want anything, but I——'

" 'What?'

" 'You know that——'

" 'What is it you want, Emelian?'

" 'The breeches—— You know—— It was I who took them—Astafi Ivanich——'

" 'Well,' I said, 'the great God will forgive you, Emelian, poor, unfortunate fellow that you are! Depart in peace.'

"And I had to turn away my head for a moment because grief for the poor devil took my breath away and the tears came in torrents from my eyes.

" 'Astafi Ivanich!——'

"I looked at him, saw that he wished to tell me something more, tried to raise himself, and was moving his lips—— He reddened and looked at me—— Suddenly I saw that he began to grow paler and paler; in a moment he fell with his head thrown back, breathed once, and gave his soul into God's keeping."

The Dream of
a Ridiculous Man

I

I am a ridiculous person. Now they call me a madman. That would be a promotion if it were not that I remain as ridiculous in their eyes as before. But now I do not resent it, they are all dear to me now, even when they laugh at me—and, indeed, it is just then that they are particularly dear to me. I could join in their laughter—not exactly at myself, but through affection for them, if I did not feel so sad as I look at them. Sad because they do not know the truth and I do know it. Oh, how hard it is to be the only one who knows the truth! But they won't understand that. No, they won't understand it.

In old days I used to be miserable at seeming ridiculous. Not seeming, but being. I have always been ridiculous, and I have known it, perhaps, from the hour I was born. Perhaps from the time I was seven years old I knew I was ridiculous. Afterwards I went to school, studied at the university, and, do you know, the more I learned, the more thoroughly I understood that I was ridiculous. So that it seemed in the end as though all the sciences I studied at the university existed only to prove and make evident to me as I went more deeply into them that I was ridiculous. It was the same with life as it was with science. With every year the same consciousness of the ridiculous figure I cut in every relation grew and strengthened. Every one always laughed at me.

Reprinted with permission of The Macmillan Company from *An Honest Thief* by Fyodor Dostoevsky, translated by Constance Garnett. First printed in Great Britain.

But not one of them knew or guessed that if there were one man on earth who knew better than anybody else that I was absurd, it was myself, and what I resented most of all was that they did not know that. But that was my own fault; I was so proud that nothing would have ever induced me to tell it to any one. This pride grew in me with the years; and if it had happened that I allowed myself to confess to any one that I was ridiculous, I believe that I should have blown out my brains the same evening. Oh, how I suffered in my early youth from the fear that I might give way and confess it to my schoolfellows. But since I grew to manhood, I have for some unknown reason become calmer, though I realised my awful characteristic more fully every year. I say "unknown," for to this day I cannot tell why it was. Perhaps it was owing to the terrible misery that was growing in my soul through something which was of more consequence than anything else about me: that something was the conviction that had come upon me that *nothing in the world mattered.* I had long had an inkling of it, but the full realisation came last year almost suddenly. I suddenly felt that it was all the same to me whether the world existed or whether there had never been anything at all: I began to feel with all my being that there was *nothing existing.* At first I fancied that many things had existed in the past, but afterwards I guessed that there never had been anything in the past either, but that it had only seemed so for some reason. Little by little I guessed that there would be nothing in the future either. Then I left off being angry with people and almost ceased to notice them. Indeed this showed itself even in the pettiest trifles: I used, for instance, to knock against people in the street. And not so much from being lost in thought: what had I to think about? I had almost given up thinking by that time; nothing mattered to me. If at least I had solved my problems! Oh, I had not settled one of them, and how many they were! But I gave up caring about anything, and all the problems disappeared.

And it was after that that I found out the truth. I learnt the truth last November—on the third of November, to be precise—and I remember every instant since. It was a gloomy evening, one of the gloomiest possible evenings. I was going home at about eleven o'clock, and I remember that I thought that the evening could not be gloomier. Even physically. Rain had been falling all day, and it had been a cold, gloomy, almost menacing rain, with, I remember, an unmistakable spite against mankind. Suddenly between ten and eleven it had stopped, and was followed by a horrible dampness, colder and damper than the rain, and a sort of steam was rising from everything, from every stone in the street, and from every by-lane if one looked down it as far as one could. A thought suddenly occurred to me, that if all the street lamps had been put out it would have been less cheerless, that the gas made one's heart sadder because it lighted it all up. I had had scarcely any dinner that day, and had been spending the evening with an engineer, and two other friends had been there also. I sat silent—I fancy I bored them. They talked of something rousing and suddenly they got excited over it. But they did not really care, I could see that, and only made a show of being excited. I suddenly said as much to them. "My friends," I said, "you really do not care one way or the other." They were not offended, but they all laughed at me. That was because I spoke without any note of reproach, simply because it did not matter to me. They saw it did not, and it amused them.

As I was thinking about the gas lamps in the street I looked up at the sky. The sky was horribly dark, but one could distinctly see tattered clouds, and between them fathomless black patches. Suddenly I noticed in one of these patches a star, and began watching it intently. That was because that star gave me an idea: I decided to kill myself that night. I had firmly determined to do so two months before, and poor as I was, I bought a splendid revolver that very day, and loaded it. But two months had passed and it was still lying in my drawer; I was so utterly indifferent that I wanted to seize a moment when I would not be so indifferent—why, I don't know. And so for two months every night that I came home I thought I would shoot myself. I kept waiting for the right moment. And so now this star gave me a thought. I made up my mind that it should certainly be that night. And why the star gave me the thought I don't know.

And just as I was looking at the sky, this little girl took me by the elbow. The street was empty, and there was scarcely any one to be seen. A cabman was sleeping in the distance in his cab. It was a child of eight with a kerchief on her head, wearing nothing but a wretched little dress all soaked with rain, but I noticed particularly her wet broken shoes and I recall them now. They caught my eye particularly. She suddenly pulled me by the elbow and called me. She was not weeping, but was spasmodically crying out some words which she could not utter properly, because she was shivering and shuddering all over. She was in terror about something, and kept crying, "Mamma, mamma!" I turned facing her, I did not say a word and went on; but she ran, pulling at me, and there was that note in her voice which in frightened children means despair. I know that sound. Though she did not articulate the words, I understood that her mother was dying, or that something of the sort was happening to them, and that she had run out to call some one, to find something to help her mother. I did not go with her; on the contrary, I had an impulse to drive her away. I told her first to go to a policeman. But clasping her hands, she ran beside me sobbing and gasping, and would not leave me. Then I stamped my foot, and shouted at her. She called out "Sir! sir!..." but suddenly abandoned me and rushed headlong across the road. Some other passer-by appeared there, and she evidently flew from me to him.

I mounted up to my fifth storey. I have a room in a flat where there are other lodgers. My room is small and poor, with a garret window in the shape of a semicircle. I have a sofa covered with American leather, a table with books on it, two chairs and a comfortable arm-chair, as old as old can be, but of the good old-fashioned shape. I sat down, lighted the candle, and began thinking. In the room next to mine, through the partition wall, a perfect Bedlam was going on. It had been going on for the last three days. A retired captain lived there, and he had half a dozen visitors, gentlemen of doubtful reputation, drinking vodka and playing *stoss* with old cards. The night before there had been a fight, and I know that two of them had been for a long time engaged in dragging each other about by the hair. The landlady wanted to complain, but she was in abject terror of the captain. There was only one other lodger in the flat, a thin little regimental lady, on a visit to Petersburg, with three little children who had been taken ill since they came into the lodgings. Both she and her children were in mortal fear of the captain, and lay trembling and crossing themselves all night, and the youngest child had a sort of fit from fright. That captain, I know for a fact, sometimes stops people in the Nevsky Prospect and begs. They won't take him into the service, but strange to say (that's why I am telling this), all this month that the captain has been here his behaviour has caused me no annoyance. I have, of course, tried to avoid his acquaintance from the very beginning, and he, too, was bored with me from the first; but I never care how much they shout the other side of the partition nor how many of them there are in there: I sit up all night and forget them so completely that I do not even hear them. I stay awake till daybreak, and have been going on like that for the last year. I sit up all night in my arm-chair at the table, doing nothing. I only read by day. I sit— don't even think; ideas of a sort wander through my mind and I let them come and go as they will. A whole candle is burnt every night. I sat down quietly at the table, took out the revolver and put it down before me. When I had put it down I asked myself, I remember, "Is that so?" and answered with complete conviction, "It is." That is, I shall shoot myself. I knew that I should shoot myself that night for certain, but how much longer I should go on sitting at the table I did not know. And no doubt I should have shot myself if it had not been for that little girl.

II

You see, though nothing mattered to me, I could feel pain, for instance. If any one had struck me it would have hurt me. It was the same morally: if anything very pathetic happened, I should have felt pity just as I used to do in old days when there were things in life that did matter to me. I had felt pity that evening. I should have certainly helped a child. Why, then, had I not helped the little girl? Because of an idea that occurred to me at the time: when she was calling and pulling at me, a question suddenly arose before me and I could not settle it. The question was an idle one, but I was vexed. I was vexed at the reflection that if I were going to make an end of myself that night, nothing in life ought to have mattered to me. Why was it that all at once I did not feel that nothing mattered and was sorry for the little girl? I remember that I was very sorry for her, so much so that I felt a strange pang, quite incongruous in my position. Really I do not know better how to convey my fleeting sensation at the moment, but the sensation persisted at home when I was sitting at the table, and I was very much irritated as I had not been for a long time past. One reflection followed another. I saw clearly that so long as I was still a human being and not nothingness, I was alive and so could suffer, be angry and feel shame at my actions. So be it. But if I am going to kill myself, in two hours, say, what is the little girl to me and what have I to do with shame or with anything else in the world? I shall turn into nothing, absolutely nothing. And can it really be true that the consciousness that I shall *completely* cease to exist immediately and so everything else will cease to exist, does not in the least affect my feeling of pity for the child nor the feeling of shame after a contemptible action? I stamped and shouted at the unhappy child as though to say—not only I feel no pity, but even if I behave inhumanly and contemptibly, I am free to, for in another two hours everything will be extinguished. Do you believe that that was why I shouted that? I am almost convinced of it now. It seemed clear to me that life and the world somehow depended upon me now. I may almost say that the world now seemed created for me alone: if I shot myself the world would cease to be at least for me. I say nothing of its being likely that nothing will exist for any one when I am gone, and that as soon as my consciousness is extinguished the whole world will vanish too and become void like a phantom, as a mere appurtenance of my consciousness, for possibly all this world and all these people are only me myself. I remember that as I sat and reflected, I turned all these new questions that swarmed one after another quite the other way, and thought of something quite new. For instance, a strange reflection suddenly occurred to me, that if I had lived before on the moon or on Mars and there had committed the most disgraceful and dishonourable action and had there been put to such shame and ignominy as one can only conceive and realise in dreams, in nightmares, and if, finding myself afterwards on earth, I were able to retain the memory of what I had done on the other planet and at the same time knew that I should never, under any circumstances, return there, then looking from the earth to the moon—*should I care or not?* Should I feel shame for that action or not? These were idle and superfluous questions for the revolver was already lying before me, and I knew in every fibre of my being that *it* would happen for certain, but they excited me and I raged. I could not die now without having first settled something. In short, the child had saved me, for I put off my pistol shot for the sake of these questions. Meanwhile the clamour had begun to subside in the captain's room: they had finished their game, were settling down to sleep, and meanwhile were grumbling and languidly winding up their quarrels. At that point I suddenly fell asleep in my chair at the table—a thing which had never happened to me before. I dropped asleep quite unawares.

Dreams, as we all know, are very queer things: some parts are presented with appalling vividness, with details worked up with the elaborate finish of jewellery, while others one gallops through, as it were, without noticing them at all, as, for instance, through space and time. Dreams seem to be spurred on not by reason but by desire, not by the head but by the heart, and yet what complicated tricks my reason has played sometimes in dreams, what utterly incomprehensible things happen to it! My brother died five years ago, for instance. I sometimes dream of him; he takes part in my affairs, we are very much interested, and yet all through my dream I quite know and remember that my brother is dead and buried. How is it that I am not surprised that, though he is dead, he is here beside me and working with me? Why is it that my reason fully accepts it? But enough. I will begin about my dream. Yes, I dreamed a dream, my dream of the third of November. They tease me now, telling me it was only a dream. But does it matter whether it was a dream or reality, if the dream made known to me the truth? If once one has recognised the truth and seen it, you know that it is the truth and that there is no other and there cannot be, whether you are asleep or awake. Let it be a dream, so be it, but that real life of which you make so much I had meant to extinguish by suicide, and my dream, my dream—oh, it revealed to me a different life, renewed, grand and full of power!

Listen.

III

I have mentioned that I dropped asleep unawares and even seemed to be still reflecting on the same subjects. I suddenly dreamt that I picked up the revolver and aimed it straight at my heart—my heart, and not my head; and I had determined beforehand to fire at my head, at my right temple. After aiming at my chest I waited a second or two, and suddenly my candle, my table, and the wall in front of me began moving and heaving. I made haste to pull the trigger.

In dreams you sometimes fall from a height, or are stabbed, or beaten, but you never feel pain unless, perhaps, you really bruise yourself against the bedstead, then you feel pain and almost always wake up from it. It was the same in my dream. I did not feel any pain, but it seemed as though with my shot everything within me was shaken and everything was suddenly dimmed, and it grew horribly black around me. I seemed to be blinded and benumbed, and I was lying on something hard, stretched on my back; I saw nothing, and could not make the slightest movement. People were walking and shouting around me, the captain bawled, the landlady shrieked—and suddenly another break and I was being carried in a closed coffin. And I felt how the coffin was shaking and reflected upon it, and for the first time the idea struck me that I was dead, utterly dead, I knew it and had no doubt of it, I could neither see nor move and yet I was feeling and reflecting. But I was soon reconciled to the position, and as one usually does in a dream, accepted the facts without disputing them.

And now I was buried in the earth. They all went away, I was left alone, utterly alone. I did not move. Whenever before I had imagined being buried the one sensation I associated with the grave was that of damp and cold. So now I felt that I was very cold, especially the tips of my toes, but I felt nothing else.

I lay still, strange to say I expected nothing, accepting without dispute that a dead man had nothing to expect. But it was damp. I don't know how long a time passed—whether an hour, or several days, or many days. But all at once a drop of water fell on my closed left eye, making its way through a coffin lid; it was followed a minute later by a second, then a minute later by a third—and so on, regularly every minute. There was a sudden glow of profound indignation in my heart, and I suddenly felt in it a pang of physical pain. "That's my wound," I thought; "that's the bullet ...." And drop after drop every minute kept falling on my closed eyelid. And all at once, not with my voice, but with my whole being, I called upon the power that was responsible for all that was happening to me:

"Whoever you may be, if you exist, and if anything more rational than what is happening here is possible, suffer it to be here now. But if you are revenging yourself upon me for my senseless suicide by the hideousness and absurdity of this subsequent existence, then let me tell you that no torture could ever equal the contempt which I shall go on dumbly feeling, though my martyrdom may last a million years!"

I made this appeal and held my peace. There was a full minute of unbroken silence and again another drop fell, but I knew with infinite unshakable certainty that everything would change immediately. And behold my grave suddenly was rent asunder, that is, I don't know whether it was opened or dug up, but I was caught up by some dark and unknown being and we found ourselves in space. I suddenly regained my sight. It was the dead of night, and never, never had there been such darkness. We were flying through space far away from the earth. I did not question the being who was taking me; I was proud and waited. I assured myself that I was not afraid, and was thrilled with ecstasy at the thought that I was not afraid. I do not know how long we were flying, I cannot imagine; it happened as it always does in dreams when you skip over space and time, and the laws of thought and existence, and only pause upon the points for which the heart yearns. I remember that I suddenly saw in the darkness a star. "Is that Sirius?" I asked impulsively, though I had not meant to ask any questions.

"No, that is the star you saw between the clouds when you were coming home," the being who was carrying me replied.

I knew that it had something like a human face. Strange to say, I did not like that being, in fact I felt an intense aversion for it. I had expected complete non-existence, and that was why I had put a bullet through my heart. And here I was in the hands of a creature not human, of course, but yet living, existing. "And so there is life beyond the grave," I thought with the strange frivolity one has in dreams. But in its inmost depth my heart remained unchanged. "And if I have got to exist again," I thought, "and live once more under the control of some irresistible power, I won't be vanquished and humiliated."

"You know that I am afraid of you and despise me for that," I said suddenly to my companion, unable to refrain from the humiliating question which implied a confession, and feeling my humiliation stab my heart as with a pin. He did not answer my question, but all at once I felt that he was not even despising me, but was laughing at me and had no compassion for me, and that our journey had an unknown and mysterious object that concerned me only. Fear was growing in my heart. Something was mutely and painfully communicated to me from my silent companion, and permeated my whole being. We were flying through dark, unknown space. I had for some time lost sight of the constellations familiar to my eyes. I knew that there were stars in the heavenly spaces the light of which took thousands or millions of years to reach the earth. Perhaps we were already flying through those spaces. I expected something with a terrible anguish that tortured my heart. And suddenly I was thrilled by a familiar feeling that stirred me to the depths: I suddenly caught sight of our sun! I knew that it could not be *our* sun, that gave life to *our* earth, and that we were an infinite distance from our sun, but for some reason I knew in my whole being that it was a sun exactly like ours, a duplicate of it. A sweet, thrilling feeling resounded with ecstasy in my heart: the kindred power of the same light which had given me light stirred an echo in my heart and awakened it, and I had a sensation of life, the old life of the past for the first time since I had been in the grave.

"But if that is the sun, if that is exactly the same as our sun," I cried, "where is the earth?"

And my companion pointed to a star twinkling in the distance with an emerald light. We were flying straight towards it.

"And are such repetitions possible in the universe? Can that be the law of Nature? . . . And if that is an earth there, can it be just the same earth as ours . . . just the same, as poor, as unhappy, but precious and beloved for ever, arousing in the most ungrateful of her children the same poignant love for her that we feel for our earth?" I cried out, shaken by irresistible, ecstatic love for the old familiar earth which I had left. The image of the poor child whom I had repulsed flashed through my mind.

"You shall see it all," answered my companion, and there was a note of sorrow in his voice.

But we were rapidly approaching the planet. It was growing before my eyes; I could already distinguish the ocean, the outline of Europe; and suddenly a feeling of a great and holy jealousy glowed in my heart.

"How can it be repeated and what for? I love and can love only that earth which I have left, stained with my blood, when, in my ingratitude, I quenched my life with a bullet in my heart. But I have never, never ceased to love that earth, and perhaps on the very night I parted from it I loved it more than ever. Is there suffering upon this new earth? On our earth we can only love with suffering and through suffering. We cannot love otherwise, and we know of no other sort of love. I want suffering in order to love. I long, I thirst, this very instant, to kiss with tears the earth that I have left, and I don't want, I won't accept life on any other!"

But my companion had already left me. I suddenly, quite without noticing how, found myself on this other earth, in the bright light of a sunny day, fair as paradise. I believe I was standing on one of the islands that make up on our globe the Greek archipelago, or on the coast of the mainland facing that archipelago. Oh, everything was exactly as it is with us, only everything seemed to have a festive radiance, the splendour of some great, holy triumph attained at last. The caressing sea, green as emerald, splashed softly upon the shore and kissed it with manifest, almost conscious love. The tall, lovely trees stood in all the glory of their blossom, and their innumerable leaves greeted me, I am certain, with their soft, caressing rustle and seemed to articulate words of love. The grass glowed with bright and fragrant flowers. Birds were flying in flocks in the air, and perched fearlessly on my shoulders and arms and joyfully struck me with their darling, fluttering wings. And at last I saw and knew the people of this happy land. They came to me of themselves, they surrounded me, kissed me. The children of the sun, the children of their sun —oh, how beautiful they were! Never had I seen on our own earth such beauty in mankind. Only perhaps in our children, in their earliest years, one might find some remote, faint reflection of this beauty. The eyes of these happy people shone with a clear brightness. Their faces were radiant with the light of reason and fulness of a serenity that comes of perfect understanding, but those faces were gay; in their words and voices there was a note of childlike joy. Oh, from the first moment, from the first glance at them, I understood it all! It was the earth untarnished by the Fall; on it lived people who had not sinned. They lived just in such a paradise as that in which, according to all the legends of mankind, our first parents lived before they sinned; the only difference was that all this earth was the same paradise. These people, laughing joyfully, thronged round me and caressed me; they took me home with them, and each of them tried to reassure me. Oh, they asked me no questions, but they seemed, I fancied, to know everything without asking, and they wanted to make haste and smoothe away the signs of suffering from my face.

IV

And do you know what? Well, granted that it was only a dream, yet the sensation of the love of those innocent and beautiful people has remained with me for ever, and I feel as though their love is still flowing out to me from over there. I have seen them myself, have known them and been convinced; I loved them, I suffered for them afterwards. Oh, I understood at once even at the time that in many things I could not understand them at all; as an up-to-date Russian progressive and contemptible Petersburger, it struck me as inexplicable that, knowing so much, they had, for instance, no science like ours. But I soon realised that their knowledge was gained and fostered by intuitions different from those of us on earth, and that their aspirations, too, were quite different. They desired nothing and were at peace; they did not aspire to knowledge of life as we aspire to understand it, because their lives were full. But their knowledge was higher and deeper than ours; for our science seeks to explain what life is, aspires to understand it in order to teach others how to live, while they without science knew how to live; and that I understood, but I could not understand their knowledge. They showed me their trees, and I could not understand the intense love with which they looked at them; it was as though they were talking with creatures like themselves. And perhaps I shall not be mistaken if I say that they conversed with them. Yes, they had found their language, and I am convinced that the trees understood them. They looked at all Nature like that—at the animals who lived in peace with them and did not attack them, but loved them, conquered by their love. They pointed to the stars and told me something about them which I could not understand, but I am convinced that they were somehow in touch with the stars, not only in thought, but by some living channel. Oh, these people did not persist in trying to make me understand them, they loved me without that, but I knew that they would never understand me, and so I hardly spoke to them about our earth. I only kissed in their presence the earth on which they lived and mutely worshipped them themselves. And they saw that and let me worship them without being abashed at my adoration, for they themselves loved much. They were not unhappy on my account when at times I kissed their feet with tears, joyfully conscious of the love with which they would respond to mine. At times I asked myself with wonder how it was they were able never to offend a creature like me, and never once to arouse a feeling of jealousy or envy in me? Often I wondered how it could be that, boastful and untruthful as I was, I never talked to them of what I knew—of which, of course, they had no notion—that I was never tempted to do so by a desire to astonish or even to benefit them.

They were as gay and sportive as children. They wandered about their lovely woods and copses, they sang their lovely songs; their fare was light—the fruits of their trees, the honey from their woods, and the milk of the animals who loved them. The work they did for food and raiment was brief and not laborious. They loved and begot children, but I never noticed in them the impulse of that *cruel* sensuality which overcomes almost every man on this earth, all and each, and is the source of almost every sin of mankind on earth. They rejoiced at the arrival of children as new beings to share their happiness. There was no quarrelling, no jealousy among them, and they did not even know what the words meant. Their children were the children of all, for they all made up one family. There was scarcely any illness among them, though there was death; but their old people died peacefully, as though falling asleep, giving blessings and smiles to those who surrounded them to take their last farewell with bright and loving smiles. I never saw grief or tears on those occasions, but only love, which reached the point of ecstasy, but a calm ecstasy, made perfect and contemplative. One might think that they were still in contact with the departed after death, and that their earthly union was not cut short by death. They scarcely understood me when I questioned them about immortality, but evidently they were so convinced of it without reasoning that it was not for them a question at all. They had no temples, but they had a real living and uninterrupted sense of oneness with the whole of the universe; they had no creed, but they had a certain knowledge that when their earthly joy had reached the limits of earthly nature, then there would come for them, for the living and for the dead, a still greater fulness of contact with the whole of the universe. They looked forward to that moment with joy, but without haste, not pining for it, but seeming to have a foretaste of it in their hearts, of which they talked to one another.

In the evening before going to sleep they liked singing in musical and harmonious chorus. In those songs they expressed all the sensations that the parting day had given them, sang its glories and took leave of it. They sang the praises of nature, of the sea, of the woods. They liked making songs about one another, and praised each other like children; they were the simplest songs, but they sprang from their hearts and went to one's heart. And not only in their songs but in all their lives they seemed to do nothing but admire one another. It was like being in love with each other, but an all-embracing, universal feeling.

Some of their songs, solemn and rapturous, I scarcely understood at all. Though I understood the words I could never fathom their full significance. It remained, as it were, beyond the grasp of my mind, yet my heart unconsciously absorbed it more and more. I often told them that I had had a presentiment of it long before, that this joy and glory had come to me on our earth in the form of a yearning melancholy that at times approached insufferable sorrow; that I had had a foreknowledge of them all and of their glory in the dreams of my heart and the visions of my mind; that often on our earth I could not look at the setting sun without tears . . . that in my hatred for the men of our earth there was always a yearning anguish: why could I not hate them without loving them? why could I not help forgiving them? and in my love for them there was a yearning grief: why could I not love them without hating them? They listened to me, and I saw they could not conceive what I was saying, but I did not regret that I had spoken to them of it: I knew that they understood the intensity of my yearning anguish over those whom I had left. But when they looked at me with their sweet eyes full of love, when I felt that in their presence my heart, too, became as innocent and just as theirs, the feeling of the fulness of life took my breath away, and I worshipped them in silence.

Oh, every one laughs in my face now, and assures me that one cannot dream of such details as I am telling now, that I only dreamed or felt one sensation that arose in my heart in delirium and made up the details myself when I woke up. And when I told them that perhaps it really was so, my God, how they shouted with laughter in my face, and what mirth I caused! Oh, yes, of course I was overcome by the mere sensation of my dream, and that was all that was preserved in my cruelly wounded heart; but the actual forms and images of my dream, that is, the very ones I really saw at the very time of my dream, were filled with such harmony, were so lovely and enchanting and were so actual, that on awakening I was, of course, incapable of clothing them in our poor language, so that they were bound to become blurred in my mind; and so perhaps I really was forced afterwards to make up the details, and so of course to distort them in my passionate desire to convey some at least of them as quickly as I could. But on the other hand, how can I help believing that it was all true? It was perhaps a thousand times brighter, happier and more joyful than I describe it. Granted that I dreamed it, yet it must have been real. You know, I will tell you a secret: perhaps it was not a dream at all! For then something happened so awful, something so horribly true, that it could not have been imagined in a dream. My heart may have originated the dream, but would my heart alone have been capable of originating the awful event which happened to me afterwards? How could I alone have invented it or imagined it in my dream? Could my petty heart and my fickle, trivial mind have risen to such a revelation of truth? Oh, judge for yourselves: hitherto I have concealed it, but now I will tell the truth. The fact is that I . . . corrupted them all!

V

Yes, yes, it ended in my corrupting them all! How it could come to pass I do not know, but I remember it clearly. The dream embraced thousands of years and left in me only a sense of the whole. I only know that I was the cause of their sin and downfall. Like a vile trichina, like a germ of the plague infecting whole kingdoms, so I contaminated all this earth, so happy and sinless before my coming. They learnt to lie, grew fond of lying, and discovered the charm of falsehood. Oh, at first perhaps it began innocently, with a jest, coquetry, with amorous play, perhaps indeed with a germ, but that germ of falsity made its way into their hearts and pleased them.   Then sensuality was soon begotten, sensuality begot jealousy, jealousy—cruelty . . . . Oh, I don't know, I don't remember; but soon, very soon the first blood was shed. They marvelled and were horrified, and began to be split up and divided. They formed into unions, but it was against one another. Reproaches, upbraidings followed. They came to know shame, and shame brought them to virtue. The conception of honour sprang up, and every union began waving its flags. They began torturing animals, and the animals withdrew from them into the forests and became hostile to them. They began to struggle for separation, for isolation, for individuality, for mine and thine. They began to talk in different languages. They became acquainted with sorrow and loved sorrow; they thirsted for suffering, and said that truth could only be attained through suffering. Then science appeared. As they became wicked they began talking of brotherhood and humanitarianism, and understood those ideas. As they became criminal, they invented justice and drew up whole legal codes in order to observe it, and to ensure their being kept, set up a guillotine. They hardly remembered what they had lost, in fact refused to believe that they had ever been happy and innocent. They even laughed at the possibility of this happiness in the past, and called it a dream. They could not even imagine it in definite form and shape, but, strange and wonderful to relate, though they lost all faith in their past happiness and called it a legend, they so longed to be happy and innocent once more that they succumbed to this desire like children, made an idol of it, set up temples and worshipped their own idea, their own desire; though at the same time they fully believed that it was unattainable and could not be realised, yet they bowed down to it and adored it with tears! Nevertheless, if it could have happened that they had returned to the innocent and happy condition which they had lost, and if some one had shown it to them again and had asked them whether they wanted to go back to it, they would certainly have refused. They answered me:

"We may be deceitful, wicked and unjust, we *know* it and weep over it, we grieve over it; we torment and punish ourselves more perhaps than that merciful Judge Who will judge us and whose Name we know not. But we have science, and by means of it we shall find the truth and we shall arrive at it consciously. Knowledge is higher than feeling, the consciousness of life is higher than life. Science will give us wisdom, wisdom will reveal the laws, and the knowledge of the laws of happiness is higher than happiness."

That is what they said, and after saying such things every one began to love himself better than any one else, and indeed they could not do otherwise. All because so jealous of the rights of their own personality that they did their very utmost to curtail and destroy them in others, and made that the chief thing in their lives. Slavery followed, even voluntary slavery; the weak eagerly submitted to the strong, on condition that the latter aided them to subdue the still weaker. Then there were saints who came to these people, weeping, and talked to them of their pride, of their loss of harmony and due proportion, of their loss of shame. They were laughed at or pelted with stones. Holy blood was shed on the threshold of the temples. Then there arose men who began to think how to bring all people together again, so that everybody, while still loving himself best of all, might not interfere with others, and all might live together in something like a harmonious society. Regular wars sprang up over this idea. All the combatants at the same time firmly believed that science, wisdom and the instinct of self-preservation would force men at last to unite into a harmonious and rational society; and so, meanwhile, to hasten matters, "the wise" endeavoured to exterminate as rapidly as possible all who were "not wise" and did not understand their idea, that the latter might not hinder its triumph. But the instinct of self-preservation grew rapidly weaker; there arose men, haughty and sensual, who demanded all or nothing. In order to obtain everything they resorted to crime, and if they did not succeed—to suicide. There arose religions with a cult of non-existence and self-destruction for the sake of the everlasting peace of annihilation. At last these people grew weary of their meaningless toil, and signs of suffering came into their faces, and then they proclaimed that suffering was a beauty, for in suffering alone was there meaning. They glorified suffering in their songs. I moved about among them, wringing my hands and weeping over them, but I loved them perhaps more than in old days when there was no suffering in their faces and when they were innocent and so lovely. I loved the earth they had polluted even more than when it had been a paradise, if only because sorrow had come to it. Alas! I always loved sorrow and tribulation, but only for myself, for myself; but I wept over them, pitying them. I stretched out my hands to them in despair, blaming, cursing and despising myself. I told them that all this was my doing, mine alone; that it was I had brought them corruption, contamination and falsity. I besought them to crucify me, I taught them how to make a cross. I could not kill myself, I had not the strength, but I wanted to suffer at their hands. I yearned for suffering, I longed that my blood should be drained to the last drop in these agonies. But they only laughed at me, and began at last to look upon me as crazy. They justified me, they delcared that they had only got what they wanted themselves, and that all that now was could not have been otherwise. At last they declared to me that I was becoming dangerous and that they should lock me up in a mad-house if I did not hold my tongue. Then such grief took possession of my soul that my heart was wrung, and I felt as though I were dying; and then . . . then I awoke.

It was morning, that is, it was not yet daylight, but about six o'clock. I woke up in the same arm-chair; my candle had burnt out; every one was asleep in the captain's room, and there was a stillness all round, rare in our flat. First of all I leapt up in great amazement: nothing like this had ever happened to me before, not even in the most trivial detail; I had never, for instance, fallen asleep like this in my arm-chair. While I was standing and coming to myself I suddenly caught sight of my revolver lying loaded, ready—but instantly I thrust it away! Oh, now, life, life! I lifted up my hands and called upon eternal truth, not with words but with tears; ecstasy, immeasurable ecstasy flooded my soul. Yes, life and spreading the good tidings! Oh, I at that moment resolved to spread the tidings, and resolved it, of course, for my whole life. I go to spread the tidings, I want to spread the tidings—of what? Of the truth, for I have seen it, have seen it with my own eyes, have seen it in all its glory.

And since then I have been preaching! Moreover I love all

those who laugh at me more than any of the rest. Why that is so I do not know and cannot explain, but so be it. I am told that I am vague and confused, and if I am vague and confused now, what shall I be later on? It is true indeed: I am vague and confused, and perhaps as time goes on I shall be more so. And of course I shall make many blunders before I find out how to preach, that is, find out what words to say, what things to do, for it is a very difficult task. I see all that as clear as daylight, but, listen, who does not make mistakes? And yet, you know, all are making for the same goal, all are striving in the same direction anyway, from the sage to the lowest robber, only by different roads. It is an old truth, but this is what is new: I cannot go far wrong. For I have seen the truth; I have seen and I know that people can be beautiful and happy without losing the power of living on earth. I will not and cannot believe that evil is the normal condition of mankind. And it is just this faith of mine that they laugh at. But how can I help believing it? I have seen the truth—it is not as though I had invented it with my mind, I have seen it, seen it, and *the living image* of it has filled my soul for ever. I have seen it in such full perfection that I cannot believe that it is impossible for people to have it. And so how can I go wrong? I shall make some slips no doubt, and shall perhaps talk in second-hand language, but not for long: the living image of what I saw will always be with me and will always correct and guide me. Oh, I am full of courage and freshness, and I will go on and on if it were for a thousand years! Do you know, at first I meant to conceal the fact that I corrupted them, but that was a mistake—that was my first mistake! But truth whispered to me that I was *lying*, and preserved me and corrected me. But how establish paradise—I don't know, because I do not know how to put it into words. After my dream I lost command of words. All the chief words, anyway, the most necessary ones. But never mind, I shall go and I shall keep talking, I won't leave off, for anyway I have seen it with my own eyes, though I cannot describe what I saw. But the scoffers do not understand that. It was a dream, they say, delirium, hallucination. Oh! As though that meant so much! And they are so proud! A dream! What is a dream? And is not our life a dream? I will say more. Suppose that this paradise will never come to pass (that I understand), yet I shall go on preaching it. And yet how simple it is: in one day, *in one hour* everything could be arranged at once! The chief thing is to love others like yourself, that's the great thing, and that's everything; nothing else is wanted—you will find out at once how to arrange it all. And yet it's an old truth which has been told and retold a billion times—but it has not formed part of our lives! The consciousness of life is higher than life, the knowledge of the laws of happiness is higher than happiness—that is what one must contend against. And I shall. If only every one wants it, it can all be arranged at once.

And I tracked out that little girl . . . and I shall go on and on!

Selected Readings

BERDYAEV, NIKOLAI. *Dostoevsky: An Interpretation.* Trans. Donald Atwater. London: Sheed and Ward Ltd., Publishers, 1934.

FANGER, DONALD. *Dostoevsky and Romantic Realism: A Study of Dostoevsky in Relation to Balzac, Dickens, and Gogol.* Cambridge, Mass.: Harvard University Press, 1965.

GIDE, ANDRÉ. *Dostoevsky.* 2nd ed. Norfolk, Conn.: New Directions Books, 1961.

JACKSON, ROBERT LOUIS. *Dostoevsky's Quest for Form: A Study of His Philosophy of Art.* New Haven, Conn.: Yale University Press, 1966.

MAGARSHACK, DAVID. *Dostoevsky.* New York: Harcourt, Brace & World, Inc., 1962.

MARTIN, MILDRED A. "The Last Shall Be First: A Study of Three Russian Short Stories." *Bucknell Review,* VI (1956), 13–23.

MORTIMER, RUTH. "Dostoevski and the Dream." *Modern Philology,* LIV (1956), 106–16.

PAYNE, ROBERT. *Dostoyevsky.* New York: Alfred A. Knopf, 1961.

SIMMONS, ERNEST J. *Dostoevsky: The Making of a Novelist.* New York: Vintage Books, 1940.

TRAHAN, ELIZABETH WELT. "The Golden Age—Dream of a Ridiculous Man?" *Slavic and East European Journal*, XVII (1959), 349–71.

WELLEK, RENÉ (ed.). *Dostoevsky: A Collection of Critical Essays.* Englewood Cliffs, N.J.: Prentice-Hall, Inc., 1962.

YARMOLINSKY, AVRAHM. *Dostoevsky: His Life and Art.* 2nd ed. New York: Criterion Books, 1957.

ANTON CHEKHOV
(1860-1904)

Anton Chekhov was born in Taganrog, Russia, in 1860. His father, a shopkeeper, fled his creditors in 1876, so that Chekhov early assumed responsibility for his brothers and sister. He graduated medical school in 1884 and by 1886 had something of a reputation as a journalist and a writer of anecdotes, fragments, and jokes. By the early '90's, however, he had gradually moved away from comic fragments and short stories of heavy plot-line emphasis to the more typically Chekhovian short story: a taut, microcosmic world within a world in which sharply delineated characters conflict psychologically.

Chekhov became the consummate artist, the careful stylist. He achieved the macrocosmic through his microscopic selection of details. His revelation of psychological themes through character, descriptive detail, and symbol has influenced a great deal of twentieth-century literature.

Unlike Dostoevsky, Chekhov was not interested in politics nor in grand themes of moral and religious significance. He always began with the man, the character himself, and explored his every day frustrations, hopes, and pathetic failures. In short stories and plays he examined man's ennui, apathy, and boredom in the hope of rousing him to personal commitment, responsibility, and freedom. Although apolitical, Chekhov seemed to sense the direction and destiny of prerevolutionary Mother Russia and was prophetic in his revolt against conservatism and the inverse and stupid pride of the declining landed nobility, apologetically and sentimentally clinging to a dying world. And in spite of the brooding pessimism hanging over his work, Chekhov could still write in one of his notebooks, "Man will become better when you show him what he is like."

In 1890 Chekhov took a long (6,000 mile) trip to Sakhalin, a Russian prison island. The experiences and observations of this trip found their way into many of his short stories. Upon his return, Chekhov settled down on a small estate outside Moscow. His disease of long standing, tuberculosis, steadily worsened. But while living and resting in the country, Chekhov had ample opportunity to observe the desultory, useless, listless lives of the women of his day. Many of them appeared in his dramas produced between 1897 and 1901: *The Sea Gull, Uncle Vanya,* and *The Three Sisters.* He said he hoped his dramas would change the condition of some lives. He attended the opening of his play *The Cherry Orchard,* but died several months later, on July 3, 1904, still believing the human condition capable of improvement.

A Joke

It was noon of a bright winter's day. The air was crisp with frost, and Nadia, who was walking beside me, found her curls and the delicate down on her upper lip silvered with her own breath. We stood at the summit of a high hill. The ground fell away at our feet in a steep incline which reflected the sun's rays like a mirror. Near us lay a little sled brightly upholstered with red.

"Let us coast down, Nadia!" I begged. "Just once! I promise you nothing will happen."

But Nadia was timid. The long slope, from where her little overshoes were planted to the foot of the ice-clad hill, looked to her like the wall of a terrible, yawning chasm. Her heart stopped beating, and she held her breath as she gazed into that abyss while I urged her to take her seat on the sled. What might not happen were she to risk a flight over that precipice! She would die, she would go mad!

"Come, I implore you!" I urged her again. "Don't be afraid! It is cowardly to fear, to be timid."

At last Nadia consented to go, but I could see from her face that she did so, she thought, at the peril of her life. I seated her, all pale and trembling, in the little sled, put my arm around her, and together we plunged into the abyss.

The sled flew like a shot out of a gun. The river wind lashed our faces; it howled and whistled in our ears, and plucked furiously at us, trying to wrench our heads from our shoulders; its pressure stifled us; we felt as if the devil himself had seized us

"A Joke" is reprinted with the permission of Charles Scribner's Sons from *Russian Silhouettes* by Anton Chekhov, translated by Marian Fell. Copyright 1915 Charles Scribner's Sons; renewal copyright 1943 Olivia Fell Vans Agnew.

in his talons, and were snatching us with a shriek down into the infernal regions. The objects on either hand melted into a long and madly flying streak. Another second, and it seemed we must be lost!

"I love you, Nadia!" I whispered.

And now the sled began to slacken its pace, the howling of the wind and the swish of the runners sounded less terrible, we breathed again, and found ourselves at the foot of the mountain at last. Nadia, more dead than alive, was breathless and pale. I helped her to her feet.

"Not for anything in the world would I do that again!" she said, gazing at me with wide, terror-stricken eyes. "Not for anything on earth. I nearly died!"

In a few minutes, however, she was herself again, and already her inquiring eyes were asking the question of mine:

"Had I really uttered those four words, or had she only fancied she heard them in the tumult of the wind?"

I stood beside her smoking a cigarette and looking attentively at my glove.

She took my arm and we strolled about for a long time at the foot of the hill. It was obvious that the riddle gave her no peace. Had I spoken those words or not? It was for her a question of pride, of honour, of happiness, of life itself, a very important question, the most important one in the whole world. Nadia looked at me now impatiently, now sorrowfully, now searchingly; she answered my questions at random and waited for me to speak. Oh, what a pretty play of expression flitted across her sweet face! I saw that she was struggling with herself; she longed to say something, to ask some question, but the words would not come; she was terrified and embarrassed and happy.

"Let me tell you something," she said, without looking at me.

"What?" I asked.

"Let us—let us slide down the hill again!"

We mounted the steps that led to the top of the hill. Once more I seated Nadia, pale and trembling, in the little sled, once more we plunged into that terrible abyss; once more the wind howled, and the runners hissed, and once more, at the wildest and most tumultuous moment of our descent, I whispered:

"I love you, Nadia!"

When the sleigh had come to a standstill, Nadia threw a backward look at the hill down which we had just sped, and then gazed for a long time into my face, listening to the calm, even tones of my voice. Every inch of her, even her muff and her hood, every line of her little frame expressed the utmost uncertainty. On her face was written the question:

"What can it have been? Who spoke those words? Was it he, or was it only my fancy?"

The uncertainty of it was troubling her, and her patience was becoming exhausted. The poor girl had stopped answering my questions, she was pouting and ready to cry.

"Had we not better go home?" I asked.

"I—I love coasting!" she answered with a blush. "Shall we not slide down once more?"

She "loved" coasting, and yet, as she took her seat on the sled, she was as trembling and pale as before and scarcely could breathe for terror!

We coasted down for the third time and I saw her watching my face and following the movements of my lips with her eyes. But I put my handkerchief to my mouth and coughed, and when we were half-way down I managed to say:

"I love you, Nadia!"

So the riddle remained unsolved! Nadia was left pensive and silent. I escorted her home, and as she walked she shortened her steps and tried to go slowly, waiting for me to say those words. I was aware of the struggle going on in her breast, and of how she was forcing herself not to exclaim:

"The wind could not have said those words! I don't want to think that it said them!"

Next day I received the following note:

"If you are going coasting, to-day, call for me. N."

Thenceforth Nadia and I went coasting every day, and each time that we sped down the hill on our little sled I whispered the words:

"I love you, Nadia!"

Nadia soon grew to crave this phrase as some people crave morphine or wine. She could no longer live without hearing it! Though to fly down the hill was as terrible to her as ever, danger and fear lent a strange fascination to those words of love, words which remained a riddle to torture her heart. Both the wind and I were suspected; which of us two was confessing our love for her now seemed not to matter; let the draught but be hers, and she cared not for the goblet that held it!

One day, at noon, I went to our hill alone. There I perceived Nadia. She approached the hill, seeking me with her eyes, and at last I saw her timidly mounting the steps that led to the summit. Oh, how fearful, how terrifying she found it to make that journey alone! Her face was as white as the snow, and she shook as if she were going to her doom, but up she climbed, firmly, without one backward look. Clearly she had determined to discover once for all whether those wondrously sweet words would reach her ears if I were not there. I saw her seat herself on the sled with a pale face and lips parted with horror, saw her shut her eyes and push off, bidding farewell for ever to this world. "zzzzzzz!" hissed the runners. What did she hear? I know not—I only saw her rise tired and trembling from the sled, and it was clear from her expression that she could not herself have said what she had heard; on her downward rush terror had robbed her of the power of distinguishing the sounds that came to her ears.

And now, with March, came the spring. The sun's rays grew warmer and brighter. Our snowy hillside grew darker and duller, and the ice crust finally melted away. Our coasting came to an end.

Nowhere could poor Nadia now hear the beautiful words, for there was no one to say them; the wind was silent and I was preparing to go to St. Petersburg for a long time, perhaps for ever.

One evening, two days before my departure, I sat in the twilight in a little garden separated from the garden where Nadia lived by a high fence surmounted by iron spikes. It was cold and the snow was still on the ground, the trees were lifeless, but the scent of spring was in the air, and the rooks were cawing noisily as they settled themselves for the night. I approached the fence, and for a long time peered through a chink in the boards. I saw Nadia come out of the house and stand on the door-step, gazing with anguish and longing at the sky. The spring wind was blowing directly into her pale, sorrowful face. It reminded her of the wind that had howled for us on the hillside when she had heard those four words, and with that recollection her face grew very sad indeed, and the tears rolled down her cheeks. The poor child held out her arms as if to implore the wind to bring those words to her ears once more. And I, waiting for a gust to carry them to her, said softly:

"I love you, Nadia!"

Heavens, what an effect my words had on Nadia! She cried out and stretched forth her arms to the wind, blissful, radiant, beautiful . . . .

And I went to pack up my things. All this happened a long time ago. Nadia married, whether for love or not matters little. Her husband is an official of the nobility, and she now has three children. But she has not forgotten how we coasted together and how the wind whispered to her:

"I love you, Nadia!"

That memory is for her the happiest, the most touching, the most beautiful one of her life.

But as for me, now that I have grown older, I can no longer understand why I said those words and why I jested with Nadia.

The Man in a Case

At the furthest end of the village of Mironositskoe some belated
sportsmen lodged for the night in the elder Prokofy's barn.
There were two of them, the veterinary surgeon Ivan Ivanovitch
and the schoolmaster Burkin. Ivan Ivanovitch had a rather
strange double-barrelled surname—Tchimsha-Himalaisky— which
did not suit him at all, and he was called simply Ivan Ivanovitch
all over the province. He lived at a stud-farm near the town, and
had come out shooting now to get a breath of fresh air. Burkin,
the high-school teacher, stayed every summer at Count P——'s,
and had been thoroughly at home in this district for years.

They did not sleep. Ivan Ivanovitch, a tall, lean old fellow
with long moustaches, was sitting outside the door, smoking a
pipe in the moonlight. Burkin was lying within on the hay,
and could not be seen in the darkness.

They were telling each other all sorts of stories. Among other
things, they spoke of the fact that the elder's wife, Mavra, a
healthy and by no means stupid woman, had never been beyond
her native village, had never seen a town nor a railway in her
life, and had spent the last ten years sitting behind the stove,
and only at night going out into the street.

"What is there wonderful in that!" said Burkin. "There are
plenty of people in the world, solitary by temperament, who try
to retreat into their shell like a hermit crab or a snail. Perhaps

it is an instance of atavism, a return to the period when the ancestor of man was not yet a social animal and lived alone in his den, or perhaps it is only one of the diversities of human character—who knows? I am not a natural science man, and it is not my business to settle such questions; I only mean to say that people like Mavra are not uncommon. There is no need to look far; two months ago a man called Byelikov, a colleague of mine, the Greek master, died in our town. You have heard of him, no doubt. He was remarkable for always wearing goloshes and a warm wadded coat, and carrying an umbrella even in the very finest weather. And his umbrella was in a case, and his watch was in a case made of grey chamois leather, and when he took out his penknife to sharpen his pencil, his penknife, too, was in a little case; and his face seemed to be in a case too, because he always hid it in his turned-up collar. He wore dark spectacles and flannel vests, stuffed up his ears with cotton-wool, and when he got into a cab always told the driver to put up the hood. In short, the man displayed a constant and insurmountable impulse to wrap himself in a covering, to make himself, so to speak, a case which would isolate him and protect him from external influences. Reality irritated him, frightened him, kept him in continual agitation, and, perhaps to justify his timidity, his aversion for the actual, he always praised the past and what had never existed; and even the classical languages which he taught were in reality for him goloshes and umbrellas in which he sheltered himself from real life.

" 'Oh, how sonorous, how beautiful is the Greek language!' he would say, with a sugary expression; and as though to prove his words he would screw up his eyes and, raising his finger, would pronounce 'Anthropos!'

"And Byelikov tried to hide his thoughts also in a case. The only things that were clear to his mind were government circulars and newspaper articles in which something was forbidden. When some proclamation prohibited the boys from going out in the streets after nine o'clock in the evening, or some article declared carnal love unlawful, it was to his mind clear and definite; it was forbidden, and that was enough. For him there was always a doubtful element, something vague and not fully expressed, in any sanction or permission. When a dramatic club or a reading-room or a tea-shop was licensed in the town, he would shake his head and say softly:

" 'It is all right, of course; it is all very nice, but I hope it won't lead to anything!'

"Every sort of breach of order, deviation or departure from rule, depressed him, though one would have thought it was no business of his. If one of his colleagues was late for church or if rumours reached him of some prank of the high-school boys, or one of the mistresses was seen late in the evening in the company of an officer, he was much disturbed, and said he hoped that nothing would come of it. At the teachers' meetings he simply oppressed us with his caution, his circumspection, and his characteristic reflection on the ill-behaviour of the young people in both male and female high-schools, the uproar in the classes . . . .

"Oh, he hoped it would not reach the ears of the authorities; oh, he hoped nothing would come of it; and he thought it would be a very good thing if Petrov were expelled from the second class and Yegorov from the fourth. And, do you know, by his sighs, his despondency, his black spectacles on his pale little face, a little face like a pole-cat's, you know, he crushed us all, and we gave way, reduced Petrov's and Yegorov's marks for conduct, kept them in, and in the end expelled them both. He had a strange habit of visiting our lodgings. He would come to a teacher's, would sit down, and remain silent, as though he were carefully inspecting something. He would sit like this in silence for an hour or two and then go away. This he called 'maintaining good relations with his colleagues'; and it was obvious that coming to see us and sitting there was tiresome to him, and that he came to see us simply because he considered it his duty as our colleague. We teachers were afraid of him. And even the headmaster was afraid of him. Would you believe it, our teachers were all intellectual, right-minded people, brought up on Turgenev and Shtchedrin, yet this little chap, who always went about with goloshes and an umbrella, had the whole high-school under his thumb for fifteen long years! High-school, indeed—he had the whole town under his thumb! Our ladies did not get up private theatricals on Saturdays for fear he should hear of it, and the clergy dared not eat meat or play cards in his presence. Under the influence of people like Byelikov we have got into the way of being afraid of everything in our town for the last ten or fifteen years. They are afraid to speak aloud, afraid to send letters, afraid to make acquaintances, afraid to read books, afraid to help the poor, to teach people to read and write . . . . "

Ivan Ivanovitch cleared his throat, meaning to say something, but first lighted his pipe, gazed at the moon, and then said, with pauses:

"Yes, intellectual, right-minded people read Shtchedrin and Turgenev, Buckle, and all the rest of them, yet they knocked under and put up with it . . . that's just how it is."

"Byelikov lived in the same house as I did," Burkin went on, "on the same storey, his door facing mine; we often saw each other, and I knew how he lived when he was at home. And at home it was the same story: dressing-gown, nightcap, blinds, bolts, a perfect succession of prohibitions and restrictions of all sorts, and—'Oh, I hope nothing will come of it!' Lenten fare was bad for him, yet he could not eat meat, as people might perhaps say Byelikov did not keep the fasts, and he ate fresh-water fish with butter—not a Lenten dish, yet one could not say that it was meat. He did not keep a female servant for fear people might think evil of him, but had as cook an old man of sixty, called Afanasy, half-witted and given to tippling, who had once been an officer's servant and could cook after a fashion. This Afanasy was usually standing at the door with his arms folded; with a deep sigh, he would mutter always the same thing:

" 'There are plenty of *them* about nowadays!'

"Byelikov had a little bedroom like a box; his bed had curtains. When he went to bed he covered his head over; it was hot and stuffy; the wind battered on the closed doors; there was a droning noise in the stove and a sound of sighs from the kitchen—ominous sighs . . . . And he felt frightened under the bed-clothes. He was afraid that something might happen, that Afanasy might murder him, that thieves might break in, and so he had troubled dreams all night, and in the morning, when we went together to the high-school, he was depressed and pale, and it was evident that the high-school full of people excited dread and aversion in his whole being, and that to walk beside me was irksome to a man of his solitary temperament.

" 'They make a great noise in our classes,' he used to say, as though trying to find an explanation for his depression. 'It's beyond anything.'

"And the Greek master, this man in a case—would you believe it?—almost got married."

Ivan Ivanovitch glanced quickly into the barn, and said: "You are joking!"

"Yes, strange as it seems, he almost got married. A new teacher of history and geography, Mihail Savvitch Kovalenko, a Little Russian, was appointed. He came, not alone, but with his sister Varinka. He was a tall, dark young man with huge hands, and one could see from his face that he had a bass voice, and, in fact, he had a voice that seemed to come out of a barrel—'boom, boom, boom!' And she was not so young, about thirty, but she, too, was tall, well-made, with black eyebrows and red cheeks—in fact, she was a regular sugar-plum, and so sprightly, so noisy; she was always singing Little Russian songs and laughing. For the least thing she would go off into a ringing laugh—'Ha-ha-ha!' We made our first thorough acquaintance with the Kovalenkos at the headmaster's name-day party. Among the glum and intensely bored teachers who came even to the name-day party as a duty we suddenly saw a new Aphrodite risen from the waves; she walked with her arms akimbo, laughed, sang, danced . . . . She sang with feeling 'The Winds do Blow,' then another song, and another, and she fascinated us all—all, even Byelikov. He sat down by her and said with a honeyed smile:

" 'The Little Russian reminds one of the ancient Greek in its softness and agreeable resonance.'

"That flattered her, and she began telling him with feeling and earnestness that they had a farm in the Gadyatchsky district, and that her mamma lived at the farm, and that they had such pears, such melons, such *kabaks!* The Little Russians call pumpkins *kabaks* (i.e., pothouses), while their pothouses they call *shinki,* and they make a beetroot soup with tomatoes and aubergines in it, 'which was so nice—awfully nice!'

"We listened and listened, and suddenly the same idea dawned upon us all:

" 'It would be a good thing to make a match of it,' the headmaster's wife said to me softly.

"We all for some reason recalled the fact that our friend Byelikov was not married, and it now seemed to us strange that we had hitherto failed to observe, and had in fact completely lost sight of, a detail so important in his life. What was his attitude to woman? How had he settled this vital question for himself? This had not interested us in the least till then; perhaps we had not even admitted the idea that a man who went out in all weathers in goloshes and slept under curtains could be in love.

" 'He is a good deal over forty and she is thirty,' the head-master's wife went on, developing her idea. 'I believe she would marry him.'

"All sorts of things are done in the provinces through boredom, all sorts of unnecessary and nonsensical things! And that is because what is necessary is not done at all. What need was there, for instance, for us to make a match for this Byelikov, whom one could not even imagine married? The headmaster's wife, the in-spector's wife, and all our high-school ladies, grew livelier and even better-looking, as though they had suddenly found a new object in life. The headmaster's wife would take a box at the theatre, and we beheld sitting in her box Varinka, with such a fan, beaming and happy, and beside her Byelikov, a little bent figure, looking as though he had been extracted from his house by pincers. I would give an evening party, and the ladies would insist on my inviting Byelikov and Varinka. In short, the machine was set in motion. It appeared that Varinka was not averse to matrimony. She had not a very cheerful life with her brother; they could do nothing but quarrel and scold one another from morning till night. Here is a scene, for instance. Kovalenko would be coming along the street, a tall, sturdy young ruffian, in an embroidered shirt, his love-locks falling on his forehead under his cap, in one hand a bundle of books, in the other a thick knotted stick, followed by his sister, also with books in her hand.

" 'But you haven't read it, Mihalik!' she would be arguing loudly. 'I tell you, I swear you have not read it at all!'

" 'And I tell you I have read it,' cries Kovalenko, thumping his stick on the pavement.

" 'Oh, my goodness, Mihalik! why are you so cross? We are arguing about principles.'

" 'I tell you that I have read it!' Kovalenko would shout, more loudly than ever.

"And at home, if there was an outsider present, there was sure to be a skirmish. Such a life must have been wearisome, and of course she must have longed for a home of her own. Besides, there was her age to be considered; there was no time left to pick and choose; it was a case of marrying anybody, even a Greek master. And, indeed, most of our young ladies don't mind whom they marry as long as they do get married. However that may be, Varinka began to show an unmistakable partiality for Byelikov.

"And Byelikov? He used to visit Kovalenko just as he did us. He would arrive, sit down, and remain silent. He would sit quiet, and Varinka would sing to him 'The Winds do Blow,' or would look pensively at him with her dark eyes, or would suddenly go off into a peal—'Ha-ha-ha!'

"Suggestion plays a great part in love affairs, and still more in getting married. Everybody—both his colleagues and the ladies—began assuring Byelikov that he ought to get married, that there was nothing left for him in life but to get married; we all congratulated him, with solemn countenances delivered ourselves of various platitudes, such as 'Marriage is a serious step.' Besides, Varinka was good-looking and interesting; she was the daughter of a civil councillor, and had a farm; and what was more, she was the first woman who had been warm and friendly in her manner to him. His head was turned, and he decided that he really ought to get married."

"Well, at that point you ought to have taken away his goloshes and umbrella," said Ivan Ivanovitch.

"Only fancy! that turned out to be impossible. He put Varinka's portrait on his table, kept coming to see me and talking about Varinka, and home life, saying marriage was a serious step. He was frequently at Kovalenko's but he did not alter his manner of life in the least; on the contrary, indeed, his determination to get married seemed to have a depressing effect on him. He grew thinner and paler, and seemed to retreat further and further into his case.

" 'I like Varvara Savvishna,' he used to say to me, with a faint and wry smile, 'and I know that every one ought to get married, but . . . you know all this has happened so suddenly . . . . One must think a little.'

" 'What is there to think over?' I used to say to him. 'Get married—that is all.'

" 'No; marriage is a serious step. One must first weigh the duties before one, the responsibilities . . . that nothing may go wrong afterwards. It worries me so much that I don't sleep at night. And

I must confess I am afraid: her brother and she have a strange way of thinking; they look at things strangely, you know, and her disposition is very impetuous. One may get married, and then, there is no knowing, one may find oneself in an unpleasant position.'

"And he did not make an offer; he kept putting it off, to the great vexation of the headmaster's wife and all our ladies; he went on weighing his future duties and responsibilities, and meanwhile he went for a walk with Varinka almost every day—possibly he thought that this was necessary in his position—and came to see me to talk about family life. And in all probability in the end he would have proposed to her, and would have made one of those unnecessary, stupid marriages such as are made by thousands among us from being bored and having nothing to do, if it had not been for a *kolossalische scandal*. I must mention that Varinka's brother, Kovalenko, detested Byelikov from the first day of their acquaintance, and could not endure him.

" 'I don't understand,' he used to say to us, shrugging his shoulders—'I don't understand how you can put up with that sneak, that nasty phiz. Ugh! how can you live here! The atmosphere is stifling and unclean! Do you call yourselves schoolmasters, teachers? You are paltry government clerks. You keep, not a temple of science, but a department for red tape and loyal behaviour, and it smells as sour as a police-station. No, my friends; I will stay with you for a while, and then I will go to my farm and there catch crabs and teach the Little Russians. I shall go, and you can stay here with your Judas—damm his soul!'

"Or he would laugh till he cried, first in a loud bass, then in a shrill, thin laugh, and ask me, waving his hands:

" 'What does he sit here for? What does he want? He sits and stares.'

"He even gave Byelikov a nickname, 'The Spider.' And it will readily be understood that we avoided talking to him of his sister's being about to marry 'The Spider.'

"And on one occasion, when the headmaster's wife hinted to him what a good thing it would be to secure his sister's future with such a reliable, universally respected man as Byelikov, he frowned and muttered:

" 'It's not my business; let her marry a reptile if she likes. I don't like meddling in other people's affairs.'

"Now hear what happened next. Some mischievous person

drew a caricature of Byelikov walking along in his goloshes with his trousers tucked up, under his umbrella, with Varinka on his arm; below, the inscription 'Anthropos in love.' The expression was caught to a marvel, you know. The artist must have worked for more than one night, for the teachers of both the boys' and girls' high-schools, the teachers of the seminary, the government officials, all received a copy. Byelikov received one, too. The caricature made a very painful impression on him.

"We went out together; it was the first of May, a Sunday, and all of us, the boys and the teachers, had agreed to meet at the high-school and then to go for a walk together to a wood beyond the town. We set off, and he was green in the face and gloomier than a storm-cloud.

" 'What wicked, ill-natured people there are!' he said, and his lips quivered.

"I felt really sorry for him. We were walking along, and all of a sudden—would you believe it?—Kovalenko came bowling along on a bicycle, and after him, also on a bicycle, Varinka, flushed and exhausted, but good-humoured and gay.

" 'We are going on ahead,' she called. 'What lovely weather! Awfully lovely!'

"And they both disappeared from our sight. Byelikov turned white instead of green, and seemed petrified. He stopped short and stared at me . . . .

" 'What is the meaning of it? Tell me, please!' he asked. 'Can my eyes have deceived me? Is it the proper thing for high-school masters and ladies to ride bicycles?'

" 'What is there improper about it?' I said. 'Let them ride and enjoy themselves.'

" 'But how can that be?' he cried, amazed at my calm. 'What are you saying?'

"And he was so shocked that he was unwilling to go on, and returned home.

"Next day he was continually twitching and nervously rubbing his hands, and it was evident from his face that he was unwell. And he left before his work was over, for the first time in his life. And he ate no dinner. Towards evening he wrapped himself up warmly, though it was quite warm weather, and sallied out to the Kovalenkos'. Varinka was out; he found her brother, however.

" 'Pray sit down,' Kovalenko said coldly, with a frown. His face looked sleepy; he had just had a nap after dinner, and was in a very bad humour.

"Byelikov sat in silence for ten minutes, and then began:

" 'I have come to see you to relieve my mind. I am very, very much troubled. Some scurrilous fellow has drawn an absurd caricature of me and another person, in whom we are both deeply interested. I regard it as a duty to assure you that I have had no hand in it . . . . I have given no sort of ground for such ridicule—on the contrary, I have always behaved in every way like a gentleman.'

"Kovalenko sat sulky and silent. Byelikov waited a little, and went on slowly in a mournful voice:

" 'And I have something else to say to you. I have been in the service for years, while you have only lately entered it, and I consider it my duty as an older colleague to give you a warning. You ride on a bicycle, and that pastime is utterly unsuitable for an educator of youth.'

" 'Why so?' asked Kovalenko in his bass.

" 'Surely that needs no explanation, Mihail Savvitch—surely you can understand that? If the teacher rides a bicycle, what can you expect the pupils to do? You will have them walking on their heads next! And so long as there is no formal permission to do so, it is out of the question. I was horrified yesterday! When I saw your sister everything seemed dancing before my eyes. A lady or a young girl on a bicycle—it's awful!'

" 'What is it you want exactly?'

" 'All I want is to warn you, Mihail Savvitch. You are a young man, you have a future before you, you must be very, very careful in your behaviour, and you are so careless—oh, so careless! You go about in an embroidered shirt, are constantly seen in the street carrying books, and now the bicycle, too. The headmaster will learn that you and your sister ride the bicycle, and then it will reach the higher authorities . . . . Will that be a good thing?'

" 'It's no business of anybody else if my sister and I do bicycle!' said Kovalenko, and he turned crimson. 'And damnation take any one who meddles in my private affairs!'

"Byelikov turned pale and got up.

" 'If you speak to me in that tone I cannot continue,' he said. 'And I beg you never to express yourself like that about our superiors in my presence; you ought to be respectful to the authorities.'

" 'Why, have I said any harm of the authorities?' asked Kovalenko, looking at him wrathfully. 'Please leave me alone. I am an
honest man, and do not care to talk to a gentleman like you. I
don't like sneaks!'

"Byelikov flew into a nervous flutter, and began hurriedly putting on his coat, with an expression of horror on his face. It was
the first time in his life he had been spoken to so rudely.

" 'You can say what you please,' he said, as he went out from
the entry to the landing on the staircase. 'I ought only to warn
you: possibly some one may have overheard us, and that our conversation may not be misunderstood and harm come of it, I shall
be compelled to inform our headmaster of our conversation . . . in
its main features. I am bound to do so.'

" 'Inform him? You can go and make your report!'

"Kovalenko seized him from behind by the collar and gave him
a push, and Byelikov rolled downstairs, thudding with his goloshes.
The staircase was high and steep, but he rolled to the bottom un-
hurt, got up, and touched his nose to see whether his spectacles
were all right. But just as he was falling down the stairs Varinka
came in, and with her two ladies; they stood below staring, and to
Byelikov this was more terrible than anything. I believe he would
rather have broken his neck or both legs than have been an object
of ridicule. Why, now the whole town would hear of it; it would
come to the headmaster's ears, would reach the higher authorities
—oh, it might lead to something! There would be another caricature, and it would all end in his being asked to resign his post . . . .

"When he got up, Varinka recognized him, and, looking at his
ridiculous face, his crumpled overcoat, and his goloshes, not understanding what had happened and supposing that he had slipped
down by accident, could not restrain herself, and laughed loud
enough to be heard by all the flats:

" 'Ha-ha-ha!'

"And this pealing, ringing 'Ha-ha-ha!' was the last straw that
put an end to everything: to the proposed match and to Byelikov's
earthly existence. He did not hear what Varinka said to him; he
saw nothing. On reaching home, the first thing he did was to remove her portrait from the table; then he went to bed, and he
never got up again.

"Three days later Afanasy came to me and asked whether we
should not send for the doctor, as there was something wrong with

his master. I went in to Byelikov. He lay silent behind the curtain, covered with a quilt; if one asked him a question, he said 'Yes' or 'No' and not another sound. He lay there while Afanasy, gloomy and scowling, hovered about him, sighing heavily, and smelling like a pothouse.

"A month later Byelikov died. We all went to his funeral—that is, both the high-schools and the seminary. Now when he was lying in his coffin his expression was mild, agreeable, even cheerful, as though he were glad that he had at last been put into a case which he would never leave again. Yes, he had attained his ideal! And, as though in his honour, it was dull, rainy weather on the day of his funeral, and we all wore goloshes and took our umbrellas. Varinka, too, was at the funeral, and when the coffin was lowered into the grave she burst into tears. I have noticed that Little Russian women are always laughing or crying—no intermediate mood.

"One must confess that to bury people like Byelikov is a great pleasure. As we were returning from the cemetery we wore discreet Lenten faces; no one wanted to display this feeling of pleasure—a feeling like that we had experienced long, long ago as children when our elders had gone out and we ran about the garden for an hour or two, enjoying complete freedom. Ah, freedom, freedom! The merest hint, the faintest hope of its possibility gives wings to the soul, does it not?

"We returned from the cemetery in good humour. But not more than a week had passed before life went on as in the past, as gloomy oppressive, and senseless—a life not forbidden by government prohibition, but not fully permitted, either: it was no better. And, indeed, though we had buried Byelikov, how many such men in cases were left, how many more of them will there be!"

"That's just how it is," said Ivan Ivanovitch, and he lighted his pipe.

"How many more of them there will be!" repeated Burkin.

The schoolmaster came out of the barn. He was a short, stout man, completely bald, with a black beard down to his waist. The two dogs came out with him.

"What a moon!" he said, looking upwards.

It was midnight. On the right could be seen the whole village, a long street stretching far away for four miles. All was buried in deep silent slumber; not a movement, not a sound; one could hardly believe that nature could be so still. When on a moonlight night you see a broad village street, with its cottages, haystacks, and slumbering willows, a feeling of calm comes over the soul; in this peace, wrapped away from care, toil, and sorrow in the darkness of night, it is mild, melancholy, beautiful, and it seems as though the stars look down upon it kindly and with tenderness, and as though there were no evil on earth and all were well. On the left the open country began from the end of the village; it could be seen stretching far away to the horizon, and there was no movement, no sound in that whole expanse bathed in moonlight.

"Yes, that is just how it is," repeated Ivan Ivanovitch; "and isn't our living in town, airless and crowded, our writing useless papers, our playing *vint*—isn't that all a sort of case for us? And our spending our whole lives among trivial, fussy men and silly, idle women, our talking and our listening to all sorts of nonsense—isn't that a case for us, too? If you like, I will tell you a very edifying story."

"No; it's time we were asleep," said Burkin.

"Tell it tomorrow."

They went into the barn and lay down on the hay. And they were both covered up and beginning to doze when they suddenly heard light footsteps—patter, patter . . . . Some one was walking not far from the barn, walking a little and stopping, and a minute later, patter, patter again . . . . The dogs began growling.

"That's Mavra," said Burkin.

The footsteps died away.

"You see and hear that they lie," said Ivan Ivanovitch, turning over on the other side, "and they call you a fool for putting up with their lying. You endure insult and humiliation, and dare not openly say that you are on the side of the honest and the free, and you lie and smile yourself; and all that for the sake of a crust of bread, for the sake of a warm corner, for the sake of a wretched little worthless rank in the service. No, one can't go on living like this."

"Well, you are off on another tack now, Ivan Ivanovitch," said the schoolmaster. "Let us go to sleep!"

And ten minutes later Burkin was asleep. But Ivan Ivanovitch kept sighing and turning over from side to side; then he got up, went outside again, and, sitting in the doorway, lighted his pipe.

A Visit to Friends

The morning mail brought this note:

Kuzminki, July 7

Dear Misha!

You have completely forgotten us, come to see us, we want to have a glimpse of you. Both of us entreat you on our knees, come today, show us your fair countenance. We are waiting for you impatiently.

Ta and Va

The letter was from Tatyana Alexeyevna Loseva, whom they had called Ta for short a dozen years previously, when Podgorin was staying at Kuzminki. But who was Va? Oh, yes, it was Varya, or Varvara Pavlovna, a friend of Tatyana's. Podgorin recalled the long talks, the gay laughter, the flirtations, the evenings walks, and the flower garden of girls and young women who were then staying at Kuzminki, and he also recalled the plain, animated, intelligent face and the freckles that went so well with Varya's dark-red hair. Since then she had graduated from medical school, taken a position as a doctor in a factory somewhere near Tula, and now was apparently visiting Kuzminki.

"Dear Va!" thought Podgorin, giving himself up to reminiscences. "How nice she is!"

Tatyana, Varya and he were almost of the same age. But at the

time he had been only a student, and they marriageable girls. He
had been considered a mere boy. And now, although he was already an established lawyer and his hair was beginning to turn
gray, they still called him Misha, thought of him as a young man
and declared that he had not lived.

He loved them dearly, but it would seem rather as memories
than in actuality. The present was scarcely real to him, was incomprehensible and alien. Alien also was this short, playful letter.
Much time and effort must have gone to composing it, and as
Tatyana was writing it, her husband, Sergey Sergeich, must have
been standing behind her. The Kuzminki estate had become Tatyana's property six years ago when she was married, but this
Sergey Sergeich had already succeeded in ruining it, and now every
time payment to the bank or on a mortgage fell due, they turned
to Podgorin, as a lawyer, for advice. Besides, they had already tried
to borrow from him twice. Apparently, now too they wanted
money or advice from him.

He was no longer drawn to Kuzminki, as he used to be. There
was something melancholy about the place. The laughter, the
clamor, the bright carefree faces, trysts on still moonlit nights—
all that was gone, above all, youth was gone; and, furthermore, all
this was probably fascinating only in retrospect . . . . In addition
to Ta and Va, there had then been Na, Tatyana's sister Nadezhda.
Half in jest, half in earnest they had called her his fiancée. She had
grown up before his eyes, everyone thought that he would marry
her, and indeed at one time he had been in love with her and was
ready to propose to her. Yet she was already in her twenty-fourth
year, and he hadn't proposed to her.

"Strange, how it all turned out," he reflected, rereading the note
with embarrassment. "But I can't *not* go, they'll be offended . . . ."

The fact that he hadn't been to see the Losevs for a long time
lay like a weight on his conscience. And after he had paced the
room for a while and turned the matter over in his mind, he over-
came his reluctance and decided to go to Kuzminki for a stay of
two or three days, and then be free from any sense of obligation at
least until the following summer. And as he was getting ready to
drive to the Brest Station after breakfast he told the servants that
he would return in three days.

There was a two hours' train ride from Moscow to Kuzminki

and a twenty minutes' drive from the station to the estate. When one got off the train, Tatyana's forest came into view, as well as three summer cottages, which Losev had started building but had not completed—during the first years of his marriage he had had all kinds of schemes. He was ruined by these summer cottages and other money-making enterprises, and by frequent trips to Moscow, where he lunched at the Slavyansky Bazar, dined at the Hermitage and at the close of the day wound up on Malaya Bronnaya Street or at the Gypsy place known as The Slaughterhouse (he called this "getting shaken up"). Podgorin himself drank, sometimes rather heavily, took up with all kinds of women, but indolently, coldly, without enjoyment, and he was disgusted when in his presence others gave themselves over to that sort of thing passionately; he did not understand men who were more at ease at The Slaughterhouse than at home, in the company of decent women, and he disliked such men. It seemed to him that all kinds of dirt clung to them like burrs. He disliked Losev and considered him a dull fellow, lazy and without ability, and more than once he felt a sense of distaste for his company . . .

Sergey Sergeich and Nadezhda were waiting for him just beyond the forest.

"My dear fellow, why have you been completely neglecting us?" asked Sergey Sergeich, kissing him three times and putting both arms around his waist. "You don't love us any more, old man."

He had massive features, a fleshy nose, a rather thin blond beard, and he combed his hair to one side, like a merchant, to give himself a simple, typically Russian appearance. He had a way of breathing in the face of the person he was speaking to, and when he was silent he breathed heavily, through his nose. His obesity and his habit of overeating made it hard for him to fill his lungs, and in consequence he kept thrusting out his chest, which gave him an air of haughtiness. Beside him, Nadezhda, his sister-in-law, seemed ethereal. She was a pale, slim blonde with kindly eyes that seemed to caress you. Whether she was beautiful or not Podgorin could not tell, for he had known her since childhood and he took her for granted. She wore a white dress, open at the neck, and the sight of her long, white, naked throat was strange to him and affected him disagreeably.

"Sister and I have been waiting for you since morning," she

said. "Varya is with us, and she has been waiting for you, too."

She took his arm, laughed abruptly without any reason, and gave a light, joyous cry, as though suddenly struck by some pleasant thought. The field of flowering rye, motionless in the still air, the forest lit by the sun, were beautiful, and it seemed as though Nadezhda had noticed it just now, as she walked beside Podgorin.

"I can stay three days," he said. "Forgive me, I couldn't get away from Moscow any sooner.'

"It's wrong, wrong, you've completely neglected us," said Sergey Sergeich, in good-natured reproach. "*Jamais de ma vie!*" he said suddenly and snapped his fingers.

He had a way of astonishing the person to whom he was speaking by an exclamation that had no bearing whatever on the talk, at the same time snapping his fingers. And he was always aping someone. If he rolled his eyes, or nonchalantly tossed back his hair, or turned bathetic, it meant that the previous evening he had been to the theatre or had attended a banquet with speeches. He was now walking mincingly like a victim of gout without bending his knees—apparently imitating someone.

"You know, Tanya didn't think that you would come," said Nadezhda. "But I had a premonition that you would, and so did Varya; for some reason I knew that you would come on this train."

"*Jamais de ma vie!*" repeated Sergey Sergeich.

The ladies were waiting on the terrace in the garden. Ten years back Podgorin, then a needy student, had tutored Nadezhda in mathematics and history for room and board. He had also given Latin lessons to Varya, a medical student. As for Tanya, at the time already a grown girl and a beauty, she had thought of nothing but love, and had wanted only love and happiness, passionately wanted and hoped for a husband, of whom she dreamed day and night. And now when she was over thirty and just as beautiful as ever, in a loose tea gown, with her full, white arms, she had thoughts for nothing but her husband and her two little girls. She wore an expression which seemed to say that although there she was talking and smiling so casually, she was nevertheless on guard, she stood prepared to defend her love and her right to this love, and at a moment's notice she was ready to pounce on an enemy who wanted to take away her husband and her children. She loved devotedly and she believed that she was loved in the same way, but jealousy and fear for her children constantly tormented her and interfered with her happiness.

After a clamorous reunion on the terrace, everyone went off to Tatyana's room, with the exception of Sergey Sergeich.

The lowered blinds kept out the sun and created a twilight in the room, so that all the roses in a large bouquet seemed to be of the same color. They made Podgorin sit down in an old armchair at the window. Nadezhda sat on a low stool at his feet. He knew that in addition to friendly reproaches, jokes, laughter, which so keenly reminded him of the past, there would also be an unpleasant conversation on the subject of promissory notes and mortgages —that was unavoidable—and it occurred to him that it would be best to have the business talk at once, without delay, to put it behind them and then go out into the open, to the garden . . . .

"Shouldn't we first talk about business?" he said. "What's new at Kuzminki? There's nothing rotten in the state of Denmark?"

"Things are out of joint at Kuzminki," replied Tatyana, sighing sadly. "Oh, the situation there is bad, so bad that I don't think it could be worse," she said, agitatedly pacing the room. "The estate is to be sold, August 7th is the date of the auction; the announcement had already been published, and buyers have started coming here, they walk through the house, they stare . . . Anyone has the right to come into my room now, and look. Perhaps according to law this is as it should be, but it humiliates me, it offends me deeply. We have no money and there is no one we can borrow from. It's simply terrible, terrible! I swear to you by all that's holy," she continued, halting in the middle of the room, her voice breaking and her eyes filling with tears, "I swear to you by the happiness of my children, I cannot live without Kuzminki! I was born here, it's my home, and if it's taken from me, I shan't be able to go on, I shall die of despair."

"It seems to me you are taking too black a view of the matter," said Podgorin. "Things will arrange themselves. Your husband will find a position, you will adjust yourself to a new setting and live a new life."

"How can you say such a thing?" cried Tatyana. As she spoke, she looked very beautiful and strong, and her readiness to pounce instantly on the enemy who would take her husband, her children, her home away from her was very evident in her face and in her whole bearing. "A new life, indeed! Sergey is busy trying to make connections, he has been promised the post of tax collector somewhere in the province of Ufa or Perm. I am prepared to go anywhere, even to Siberia, I am ready to live there ten years, twenty, but I must know that sooner or later I'll return to Kuzminki. Without Kuzminki I cannot live. I can't and I don't want to. I don't want to!" she cried, and stamped her foot.

"You are a lawyer, Misha," said Varya, "you know how to turn a trick, and it's your business to advise us what to do."

There was only one piece of sensible advice that he could offer: "Nothing can be done," but Podgorin did not have the heart to blurt it out, and he mumbled hesitantly:

"I'll have to give the matter some thought . . . . I'll think it over."

There were two men in him. As a lawyer he occasionally had to deal with pretty ugly affairs. At court and with clients he behaved haughtily and spoke his mind bluntly. With casual acquaintances he could be rather cutting. But with intimates or friends of long standing he was exceedingly delicate, shy and sensitive, and could not speak harshly. A tear, a sidelong glance, a lie, or even an unseemly gesture was sufficient to make him flinch and lose his self-possession. Nadezhda was still sitting at his feet, and her bare throat offended him. This was a source of distress, so that he even thought of going home. The previous year he had happened to run into Sergey Sergeich in the flat of a certain lady on Bronnaya Street, and now he felt embarrassed in Tatyana's presence, as if he himself had been party to her husband's infidelity. And this conversation about the estate placed him in a very awkward position. He was used to having all thorny and unpleasant questions settled by judges or jurymen, or simply by some statute. But when a matter was put up to him personally for decision, he was lost.

"Misha, you're our friend, we all love you as one of our own," continued Tatyana, "and I'll be frank with you: you are our only hope. For God's sake, tell us what to do. Maybe an appeal is possible? Perhaps it isn't too late to put the estate in Nadya's name, or Varya's? What shall we do?"

"Come to our rescue, Misha, do," said Varya, lighting up. "You were always so clever. You haven't really lived, you've had no experience, but you've a good head on your shoulders. You'll help Tanya, you know you will."

"I must think it over . . . . Maybe, I'll come up with some scheme."

They all went out for a walk in the garden, and then they wandered off into the fields. Sergey Sergeich went along. He took Podgorin by the arm and tried to walk ahead of the rest, apparently intending to broach the subject of his financial straits. To walk beside him and talk to him was torment. Now and then he would kiss his guest, always three times, put his arms around his waist, breathe in his face, and it seemed as though he were covered with a sweet glue and would actually stick to his companion. And that expression of his eyes, which showed that he wanted something from Podgorin, that he was going to ask him for something, had a painful effect, as if he were aiming a gun at his guest.

The sun set, it was getting dark. Here and there along the railway line lights appeared, green, red . . . . Varya halted, and looking at the signals, recited:

> "There is a straight and shining road,
> With rails and posts, a bridge afar,
> On either side lie Russian bones,
> Oh, what huge heaps of them there are! . . .

How does it go on? Oh, good Lord, I can't remember any of it!

> We labored in the heat, the cold,
> Our heads were bowed, our backs were bent . . . "

She recited with deep feeling, in a magnificent chest-voice. Her face grew flushed and tears came into her eyes. It was the old Varya, Varya the student, and as he listened to her Podgorin thought of the past and recalled that as a student himself he had known many fine poems by heart and had liked to recite them.

> "And even now his back is bent,
> His silence stolid as before . . . "

Varya could not remember any more. She fell silent and smiled uncertainly and faintly, and the green and red signals had a melancholy look.

"Oh, I've forgotten it!"

But Podgorin recalled the way it went on—somehow the lines had remained in his memory from his student days, and he recited quietly, under his breath:

> "*The Russian folk have borne enough,*
> *This road-building—a fearful load—*
> *They've borne and more will they endure,*
> *And build themselves a glorious road.*
> *The pity is . . .* "

" 'The pity is,' " Varya broke in, having remembered:

> "*The pity is that neither you nor I*
> *Will be alive to greet that glorious time.*"

She laughed and slapped him on the back.

They returned to the house and sat down to supper. Aping someone, Sergey Serveich carelessly stuck a corner of his napkin into his collar.

"Let's have a drink," he said, pouring some vodka for himself and Podgorin. "In our student days we knew how to drink, how to make a speech, how to work seriously. I drink your health, friend, and you drink the health of an old fool of an idealist and wish him this: that he die an idealist."

All during supper Tatyana kept looking tenderly at her husband, fretting lest he eat or drink something that might disagree with him. It seemed to her that he was weary, that he was spoiled by women—she liked this in him, but at the same time she suffered from jealousy. Varya and Nadya, too, were tender with him and looked at him anxiously, as though afraid that he would suddenly get up and leave them. When he wanted to pour himself a second glass of vodka, Varya made an angry face and said:

"You're poisoning yourself, Sergey Serveich. You're a nervous, impressionable sort, and you can easily become an alcoholic. Tanya, tell them to remove the vodka."

Sergey Sergeich was generally very successful with women. They loved his stature, his build, his massive features, his idleness, his misfortunes. They said that he was very kind and therefore a spendthrift, an idealist and therefore impractical, that he was honest, pure of heart, that he could not adjust himself to people and circumstances, and so owned nothing and could find no definite occupation. They believed him implicitly, adored him, and so spoiled him by their admiration that he himself became convinced that he was idealistic, impractical, honest, pure of heart, and that he was superior to these women and that they should look up to him.

"Why don't you say a word of praise about my little girls?" asked Tatyana, feasting her eyes on her two little daughters and piling high with rice the plates of these healthy-looking, well-nourished children, who made one think of dinner rolls. "Just look at them! They say that all mothers dote on their children, but I assure you I'm unbiased, my little girls are extraordinary. Particularly the elder."

Podgorin smiled at her and at the little girls, but he found it odd that this young, healthy, rather intelligent woman—a big complex organism—should spend all her energy, all her vital forces on such a simple, petty job as the building of this nest, that in any case was complete.

"Perhaps that's as it should be," he reflected, "but it's dull and stupid."

> "Before the clumsy churl could gasp,
>   Old Bruin had him in his grasp,"

said Sergey Sergeich, and snapped his fingers.

Supper was over. Tatyana and Varya made Podgorin sit down on a divan in the drawing room and again started talking to him about business matters.

"You must rescue Sergey Serveich," said Varya. "It is your moral duty. He has his weaknesses, he's not thrifty, he doesn't plan for a rainy day, but that's because he is kind and generous. He has the soul of a child. Present him with a million, and in a month there'll be nothing left of it, he will have given it all away."

"It's true, it's true," said Tatyana, and tears streamed down her cheeks. "He has made me suffer very much, but I must admit, he's a wonderful human being."

And neither of them, Tatyana or Varya, could refrain from the little cruelty of saying to Podgorin reproachfully:

"Your generation, Misha, is different!"

"What has my generation to do with it?" thought Podgorin. "Losev isn't more than half a dozen years older than I . . . ."

"Life is not easy," said Varya, and sighed. "You are always threatened by a loss. They want to take your property away, or someone close to you falls ill and you fear for his life—and so on, day after day. But what's to be done, my dears? One must submit to the higher Will without a murmur, one must remember that in this world nothing is accidental, everything has its purpose, no matter how remote. You haven't really lived, Misha, and you haven't suffered much, and you will laugh at me; laugh, but I will say this, nevertheless: during the period when I was most anxious, I had several experiences of clairvoyance, and the result has been a spiritual revolution within me, and now I know that nothing is accidental, and that everything that happens to us is necessary."

How different she was, this Varya, already gray-haired, corseted, wearing a fashionable dress with puffed sleeves, rolling a cigarette in long, thin fingers, that trembled for some reason, this Varya, easily falling prey to mysticism, speaking in such a weak, monotonous voice, how different she was from Varya, the medical student, the gay, noisy, bold red-head . . . .

"What has time done to them?" Podgorin wondered, listening to her with boredom.

"Sing us something, Va," he said, to put an end to the talk about clairvoyance. "You used to sing beautifully."

"Oh, Misha, That's all past and gone."

"Or recite something by Nekrasov."

"I don't remember any of it. It was just an accident that I recalled those lines earlier in the evening."

In spite of the corset and the fashionable sleeves, it was plain that she was far from prosperous and that she lived meagerly at the factory beyond Tula. It was noticeable, too, that she was overworked. Heavy, monotonous work and the constant concern with other people's affairs, her fretting about other people had been a strain on her, and had aged her prematurely, and Podgorin, looking now at her sad face, already faded, thought that not Kuzminki, not Sergey Serveich, but she herself who was so concerned about them, was in need of help.

Higher education and the fact that she was a physician did not seem to have affected the woman in her. Like Tatyana, she took pleasure in weddings, births, baptisms, lengthy conversations about children, she liked terrifying novels with happy endings; when she took up a newspaper it was to read only about fires, floods and public ceremonies. She was dying to have Podgorin propose to Nadezhda, and were it to happen, she would burst into tears.

He did not know whether it was by chance or whether Varya

had arranged it, but he found himself alone with Nadezhda. The mere suspicion that he was being watched and that something was wanted of him constrained and embarrassed him, and sitting beside Nadezhda, he felt as though the two of them had been placed in a cage.

"Let us go down to the garden," she said.

They went off to the garden: he, disgruntled, vexed, not knowing what to talk to her about, she—joyous, proud of having him at her side, obviously happy that he would stay there another three days, and perhaps full of sweet reveries and hopes. He did not know if she was in love with him, but he was aware that she had long since grown used to him and was attached to him, that she still saw her tutor in him, and that she was just the way Tatyana used to be, that is, she thought of nothing but love, of how to get married as soon as possible, to have a husband, children, a nook of her own. She had preserved that feeling about friendship which is so intense in children, and it was possible that she merely respected Podgorin and was fond of him as of a friend, that she was in love not with him, but with her dreams of a husband and children.

"It's getting dark," said he.

"Yes. The moon rises late now."

They kept strolling along one alley, near the house. Podgorin was loath to go far into the garden: it was dark there, he would have to take her by the arm, be very close to her. Shadows were moving on the terrace, and it seemed to him that Tatyana and Varya were watching them.

"I must ask your advice," said Nadezhda, halting. "If Kuzminki is sold, then Sergey Sergeich will take a position, and our life will be completely changed. I'm not going to stay with sister, we shall separate, because I don't want to be a burden on the family. One must work. I'll find some employment in Moscow, I'll earn money and be able to help sister and her husband. You'll advise me, won't you?"

Knowing nothing at all about it, she was now animated by the idea of working and of independence, she was making plans for the future—this was written on her face, and the prospect of working and helping others seemed to her beautiful, poetical. He saw her pallid face and dark eyebrows at close range and recalled what an intelligent, keen, capable pupil she had been, and how pleasant it had been to tutor her. And it might well be that now she was not simply a young lady who wanted a husband, but a high-minded girl, of extraordinary kindness, with a gentle, pliable soul, which could be molded into any shape, like wax, a girl who, given proper surroundings, could grow into an admirable woman.

"Why not marry her, really?" thought Podgorin, but was immediately frightened by the thought and began walking in the direction of the house.

When they entered the drawing room, they found Tatyana sitting at the piano, and her playing vividly brought back the past, when in this very drawing room there was playing, singing and dancing late into the night, with the windows open, and the birds in the garden and on the river singing, too. Podgorin brightened, grew playful, danced with Nadezhda and with Varya, and afterwards he sang. A corn on his foot annoyed him, so he asked if he might wear Sergey Sergeich's slippers, and, strange to say, in slippers he felt like one of the family, a relative ("like a brother-in-law" flashed through his mind) and he grew even gayer. This made all of them come to life, they brightened, were rejuvenated, as it were; hope shone in everyone's face: Kuzminki was saved! It was a simple matter: all that was needed was to think up something, dig up a law, or if Podgorin were to marry Nadya . . . And, obviously, the affair was under way. Nadya, pink-cheeked, happy, her eyes shining with tears in the expectation of something extraordinary, circled in the dance, her white dress billowing and showing glimpses of her slim, pretty legs in their flesh-tinted stockings. Varya, thoroughly contented, took Podgorin by the arm and said to him under her breath with a significant expression:

"Misha, don't run away from your happiness. Take it while it offers itself to you freely, later you will be running after it, but you won't overtake it."

Podgorin wanted to promise, to be encouraging, and he himself believed that Kuzminki was saved, and that it could all be arranged very simply.

"And thou shalt be queen of the world," he broke into song, striking a pose, but suddenly remembering that he could do nothing for these people, nothing at all, he fell silent like one stricken with guilt.

And there he sat in a corner, mute, cross-legged, with his feet in another man's slippers.

At the sight of him, the others understood that nothing could be done, and fell silent, too. The piano was closed. Everyone noticed that it was late, time to go to bed, and Tatyana put out the big lamp in the drawing room.

A bed was made up for Podgorin in the same wing in which he used to live years back. Sergey Sergeich went to see him settled, holding the candle high above his head, although the moon had risen and it was light. They walked between lilac bushes, and the gravel of the path crunched under their feet.

> "Before the clumsy churl could gasp,
> Old Bruin had him in his grasp."

said Sergey Sergeich.

It seemed to Podgorin as if he had heard these lines a thousand times. He was fed up with them. When they reached the wing, Sergey Sergeich produced a bottle and two glasses from the pocket of his ample jacket and put them on the table.

"It's cognac," he said. "Number zero-zero. Varya's in the house, you can't drink in her presence, she'll start squawking about alcoholism, but here we're free. It's excellent cognac."

They sat down. The cognac was indeed excellent.

"This time we must finish the bottle," continued Sergey Sergeich, biting into a lemon. "I haven't forgotten my student days, sometimes I like to let myself go. One has to."

But there was that look in his eyes that said he needed something from Podgorin and was about to ask for something.

"Let's drink, old chap," he continued, sighing, "life is getting too hard for me. My kind is finished, for good. Idealism is out of fashion. The ruble is king nowadays, and you have to kneel down and worship it if you don't want to be kicked out, left nowhere. I can't do it. It's disgusting!"

"When is the auction?" asked Podgorin, to change the subject.

"The seventh of August. But I have no hope of being able to save Kuzminki, my dear friend. The arrears are enormous, and the estate brings in nothing, there are only losses every year. The game isn't worth the candle . . . . Of course, Tanya is cut up, it's her patrimony, but as for me, to be frank, I'm rather glad. I don't care for the country. Give me the big, bustling city, with its struggle— then I'm in my element!"

He kept on talking, but he didn't say what he wanted to say, and he watched Podgorin intently, as though looking for an opportune moment. And suddenly Podgorin felt the man's eyes peering closely into his and the man's breath on his face.

"My dear fellow, save me!" Sergey Sergeich brought out, breathing heavily. "Give me two hundred rubles! I implore you!"

Podgorin wanted to say that he was short of funds, and it flashed through his mind that it would be better to give the two hundred rubles to some poor devil or even lose them at cards, but he became terribly embarrassed, and feeling himself trapped in this little room with the one candle, and wishing to rid himself as soon as possible of this breath on his face, these soft, sticky arms which clasped his waist and already seemed glued to him, he began to rummage hastily in his pockets for his wallet.

"Here . . ." he mumbled, taking out a hundred rubles. "The rest later. I don't have any more on me. As you see, I can't refuse," he went on with irritation, beginning to get angry. "I have an insufferably flabby character. Only, please, consider this a loan. I'm hard up myself."

"Thank you! Thank you, old chap!"

"And please, stop imagining that you're a idealist. You are as much of an idealist as I am a turkey. You are just an unthinking loafer and nothing else."

Sergey Sergeich drew a deep sigh and sat down on the couch.

"You're angry, my dear fellow," he said, "but if you knew what I'm going through! I'm having a hellish time. My dear fellow, I swear to you—it's not myself I'm sorry for, not a bit of it! I'm only sorry for my wife and the children. If it weren't for my wife and the children, I'd have committed suicide long ago."

And suddenly his head and shoulders began to shake, and he burst into sobs.

"That's all that was wanting," said Podgorin, dreadfully vexed, pacing the room in agitation. "Well, what am I to do with a man who has behaved like a rascal and then starts to sob? Your tears disarm me, I can't say anything to you. You sob, therefore you are right."

"I behaved like a rascal?" asked Sergey Sergeich, getting up, and looking at Podgorin in amazement. "My dear fellow, how can you say such a thing? I behaved like a rascal? Oh, how little you know me! How little you understand me!"

"Very well, I don't understand you, only please stop blubbering. It's disgusting."

"Oh, how little you know me!" Losev repeated, quite sincerely. "How little you know me!"

"Look at yourself in the mirror," Podgorin continued, "you're no longer young, soon you will be an old man, it's high time for you to come to your senses, to realize who you are and what you are. All your life you've done nothing, all your life—this idle, puerile chatter, these airs, these affectations—aren't you fed up with all this, aren't you sick of it all? It's painful to be with you! And so dreadfully boring!"

With this, Podgorin left the room, banging the door. Almost for the first time in his life he had been completely sincere and had said what he wanted to say.

A little later he was sorry that he had been so harsh. What good was it to speak seriously to or argue with a man who lied constantly, ate a lot, drank a lot, spent a lot of money belonging to other people and at the same time was convinced that he was an idealist and a martyr? You were dealing with stupidity or with inveterate bad habits, which are as firmly lodged in the organism as an incurable disease. At any rate, indignation and severe reproaches were useless. It would have been better to laugh at it all; one good gibe could do more than ten sermons!

"Still better, pay no attention," thought Podgorin, "and, above all, don't lend him money."

A little later, Sergey Sergeich and his hundred rubles were far from his thoughts. There was something pensive about the night, which was still and brilliant. When Podgorin looked at the sky on moonlit nights, it seemed to him that only he and the moon were awake, while everything else was either asleep or drowsing; he didn't think of people or of money, and gradually a quiet, peaceful mood possessed him; he felt alone in the world, and in the nocturnal silence the sound of his own footsteps seemed melancholy to him.

The garden was enclosed by a white stone wall. In the right corner of the side facing the fields there was a tower, built a long time back, in the days of serfdom. The lower part of the tower was of stone, the upper was built of wood, and had a balcony; from the conical roof rose a tall spire topped by a black weathervane.

Below there were two doors, so that one could either pass from the garden into the fields or reach the balcony by a stairway that creaked underfoot. Under the stairs old broken armchairs were lying about; the moonlight, coming through the door, made them gleam, so that with their crooked legs sticking up they seemed to have come to life in the night and to be lying in wait for someone there in the stillness.

Podgorin walked up the stairs and sat down on the balcony. Just beyond the wall there was a ditch with an embankment marking the boundary of the property. Farther off, were the broad fields, flooded with moonlight. Podgorin knew that there was a forest straight ahead, about two miles from the house, and it seemed to him that he saw a dark stripe in the distance. Quails and corn crakes were calling, and from time to time the voice of the cuckoo, which was also still wakeful, came from the direction of the woods.

There was the sound of footsteps. Someone was walking in the garden, approaching the tower.

A dog barked.

"Beetle!" a woman's voice called gently. "Beetle, come back!"

One could hear below someone entering the tower, and after a moment a black dog, an old friend of Podgorin's, appeared on the embankment. It stood still and, looking up to where Podgorin was sitting, wagged its tail in a friendly fashion. A little later a white figure rose like a shadow from the black ditch and also stood still on the embankment. It was Nadezhda.

"What do you see up there?" she asked the dog, as she too looked up.

She did not see Podgorin, but apparently felt his presence: she was smiling, and her pale face, lighted by the moon, seemed happy. The black shadow of the tower that stretched far out over the field, the motionless white figure and the pale face smiling happily, the black dog, the shadows cast by the two—it was all like a dream.

"There is someone there . . ." said Nadezhda softly.

She stood and waited, hoping that he would either come down or call her to him, and that he would finally propose to her, and they would be happy in this still, beautiful night. White, pale, slim, very lovely in the moonlight, she was longing for caresses. Her continual dreams of happiness and love had wearied her, she could no longer hide her feelings, and her whole posture, the brilliance of her eyes, her fixed, blissful smile, betrayed her sweet thoughts. As for him, he was ill at ease, he shrank together, he froze, not knowing whether to say something so as to turn it all into a joke, or to remain silent, and he was vexed, and could only reflect that here in the country, on a moonlit night, with a beautiful, enamored, dreamy girl so near, his emotions were as little involved as on Malaya Bronskaya Street—clearly this fine poetry meant no more to him than that crude prose. All this was dead: trysts on moonlit nights, slimwaisted figures in white, mysterious shadows, towers and country houses, and "types" like Sergey Sergeich, and like himself, Podgorin, with his chilly boredom, constant vexation, his inability to adjust himself to real life, inability to take from it what it had to offer, and with an aching, wearying thirst for what was not and could not be on earth. And now, sitting here in this tower, he would have preferred a good display of fireworks or a procession in the moonlight, or to have Varya recite Nekrasov's "Railroad" again, or some other woman, who, standing there on the embankment where Nadezhda was standing, would speak of something absorbing, novel, having no relation to love or happiness, or if she did speak of love, it would be a call to a new kind of life, exalted and yet reasonable, a life on the threshold of which we live and of which we sometimes have a premonition....

"No one there," said Nadezhda.

And, after waiting another moment, she walked off slowly with lowered head in the direction of the woods. The dog ran in front of her. For quite a long while Podgorin could see a white spot moving in the distance.

"Strange, how it all turned out," he kept repeating to himself, as he went back to his room.

He could not picture what he would talk about to Sergey Sergeich, to Tatyana, the next day, and the day after that, how he would behave toward Nadezhda—and in anticipation he felt embarrassment, fear and boredom. How was he going to fill the interminable three days that he had promised to stay on? He recalled the talk about clairvoyance, Sergey Sergeich's phrase:

> "Before the clumsy churl could gasp,
>   Old Bruin had him in his grasp."

He recalled that the next day, to please Tatyana, he would have to smile at her plump, well-fed little girls—and he decided to leave.

At half past five Sergey Sergeich, wearing a Bokharan dressing-gown and a fez with a tassel, appeared on the terrace of the big house. Without losing a moment's time, Podgorin went up to him and began his farewells.

"I have to be in Moscow at ten," he said, without looking at his host. "I had completely forgotten that they would be waiting for me at the notary public's. Please, don't detain me. When the family is up, give them my apologies, I am terribly sorry . . ."

He did not hear what Sergey Sergeich was saying to him, and hurried off, and kept looking back at the windows of the big house, afraid that the ladies would wake up and try to detain him. He was ashamed of his nervousness. He felt that this was his last visit to Kuzminki, that he would not come there again. Several times, as he was driving off, he looked back at the wing in which he had spent so many happy days, but his heart was unmoved and he did not grow melancholy.

When he reached home, the first thing he noticed on his table was the note he had received the previous day. "Dear Misha," he read, "you have completely forgotten us, come as soon as possible . . . ." And for some reason he recalled how Nadezhda had circled in the dance, how her dress billowed, showing her legs in the flesh tinted stockings.

Ten minutes later he was at his desk, working, and without a thought of Kuzminki.

A Fragment

Having retired from the service, Actual State Councilor Kozerogov bought himself a modest property and settled down in the country. Here, in imitation partly of Cincinnatus, partly of the distinguished professor of natural history, Kaigorodov, he toiled in the sweat of his face and noted in his diary his observations of Nature. After his death the diary, together with his other effects, by his testament came into the possession of his housekeeper, Marfa Yevlampievna. As everyone knows, that estimable old soul tore down the manór house and on its site erected a wonderful eating-house which was licensed to serve spirituous liquors. In this tavern there was a "better" room set aside for traveling landowners and functionaries, and there the diary of the deceased lay on a table for the convenience of such guests as might be in need of paper. I chanced to get hold of one sheet. Apparently it related to the very beginning of the agricultural activities of the deceased and contained the following entries:

"March 3. The spring migration of birds has started: yesterday I saw sparrows. I greet you, feathered children of the south! In your sweet warbling I seem to hear the wish: 'Be happy, your Excellency!'

"March 14. Today I asked Marfa Yevlampievna; 'Why does the cock crow so often?' She replied: 'Because he has a throat.' My retort was: 'I too have a throat, yet I do not crow!' How many mysteries does Nature harbor! During my service in St. Petersburg I

Reprinted with permission of Farrar, Straus & Giroux, Inc. from *The Unknown Chekhov,* translated and with an Introduction by Avrahm Yarmolinsky. Copyright © 1954 by Avrahm Yarmolinsky.

ate turkey more than once, but live turkeys I saw only yesterday. A very remarkable bird.

"March 22. The local police officer called. For a long time we discussed virtue—I sitting down, he standing up. Among other things, he asked me: 'Would you wish, your Excellency, to be young again?' To this I replied: 'No, I would not wish it, for, were I young, I would not have my present high rank.' He saw eye to eye with me, and drove off visibly moved.

"April 16. With my own hands I dug up two beds in the kitchen garden and planted buckwheat grits in them. I said nothing about it to anyone, in order to have a surprise for my Marfa Yevlampievna, to whom I owe so many happy moments of my life. Yesterday at tea she complained bitterly of her corpulence, saying that already her increasing girth was preventing her from passing through the doorway of the storeroom. I observed to her in reply: 'On the contrary, darling, the fullness of your figure is an adornment to you and serves to dispose me toward you even more favorably.' She blushed, and I arose and embraced her, placing both arms around her, for with one arm alone you cannot embrace her.

"May 28. An old man, seeing me at the riverside near the women's bathing huts, asked me why I was sitting there. My answer was: 'I am staying to see to it that young men don't come and loiter here.' To this the old man replied: 'Let us see to it together.' Having said this, he sat down beside me, and we began to talk of virtue."

Selected Readings

BRUFORD, WALTER H. *Anton Chekhov*. New Haven, Conn.: Yale University Press, 1957.

GORDON, CAROLINE. "Notes on Chekhov and Maugham." *Sewanee Review*, LVII (1949), 401–10.

HAGAN, JOHN. "Chekhov's Fiction and the Ideal of 'Objectivity.'" *PMLA*, LXXXI (1966), 409–17.

HINGLEY, RONALD. *Chekhov: A Biographical and Critical Study.* New York: The Macmillan Company, 1950.

MAGARSHACK, DAVID. *Chekhov: A Life.* London: Faber and Faber, Ltd., 1952.

SAUNDERS, BEATRICE. *Tchekov, The Man.* London: Centaur Press, 1960.

SIMMONS, ERNEST J. *Chekhov: A Biography.* Boston: Little, Brown and Company, 1962.

WINNER, THOMAS G. *Chekhov and His Prose.* New York: Holt, Rinehart and Winston, Inc., 1966.

MIGUEL DE UNAMUNO

(1864-1936)

Miguel de Unamuno—philosopher, teacher, short story writer, novelist, essayist, poet, dramatist—was born in Bilbao, a port town in the Basque country of Spain. He taught in Bilbao prior to becoming a professor of languages at the University of Salamanca in 1891. By 1901 he was Rector of the University. A man of anarchic ideas, tempermental, outspoken, he had by 1924 totally alienated the dictator, Primo de Rivera. He was banished to the Canary Islands and after that spent six years in self-exile in France. The troubled times that followed in Spain resulted in many reversals of fortune for Unamuno. When the Spanish Republic took over in 1931, Unamuno was reinstated as Rector at Salamanca; when the Spanish Civil War commenced in 1936, he was re-relieved of his post. Unamuno ultimately renounced both sides and remained until his death a foe of Franco.

If the political life of Unamuno was turbulent, his philosophical, speculative life was equally active. Written in 1912 his *Tragic Sense of Life* dealt with his monumental theme—the tragic sense of life is Death, an impossible possibility. "Some day we shall all die," he said, "even the dead." Life, death, and immortality formed his literary trinity. His *Tragic Sense of Life*, a study in existential thought, defines man as a creature of flesh and bones who dies. Man's existence precedes his essence, so in the face of his own concrete, physical existence and subsequent death, it becomes man's chief struggle and obligation to transcend death. "If I am not all and for ever," he writes, "it is as though I were nothing." Man's struggle against nothingness becomes the thematic correlative linking together Unamuno's philosophy and his *oeuvre*.

Stylistically, Unamuno's work is reminiscent of the medieval *exempla*, debate, parable, and allegory. His stories are frequently developed through dialectic, an elemental exchange of dialogue. While his characters are unique creations and well developed, he does not employ the specific settings, descriptions, and psychological details of writers like Chekhov. Some of Unamuno's important works are *The Life of Don Quixote* (1905); *The Mirror of Death* (1913); *Abel Sanchez* (1917); and *Three Exemplary Novels* (1920).

The Marquis of Lumbría

The manorial house of the Marquis of Lumbría, "the palace" as it was called in the gloomy city of Lorenza, was like a chest of silent, mysterious memories. Although it was inhabited, its windows and balconies that faced the street were almost always closed. Its façade, which boldly displayed the great coat-of-arms of the Lumbría family, faced south toward the spacious square of the Cathedral and stood opposite this imposing edifice; but since the sun shone upon it almost all day long, and there are scarcely any cloudy days in Lorenza, all its windows and doors remained closed. And this happened because the most excellent Marquis of Lumbría, Don Rodrigo Suárez de Tejada, abhorred sunlight and fresh air. "Street dust and sunlight," he used to say, "do nothing but dull the furniture and spoil the rooms—and then the flies . . ." The Marquis had a veritable horror of the flies which might come from a ragged, or perhaps a scurvy beggar. The Marquis trembled at the possibility of contracting any of the plebeian diseases. The people of Lorenza and its environs were so filthy . . .

The rear of the mansion faced an enormous rugged cliff that overlooked the river. A blanket of ivy covered the wide walls of the palace on this side. And though the ivy sheltered mice and other vermin, the Marquis respected it. It was a family tradition. And on a balcony, built here on the shady side, free from the sun and its accompanying flies, the Marquis used to sit down to read while the murmur of the river soothed him, as it rushed down the

Reprinted with permission of A. and C. Boni, from *Three Exemplary Novels,* translated by Angel Flores. Copyright 1930 by A. and C. Boni.

narrow channel of its bed, surging with foam to force its way through the rocks of the cliff.

The most excellent Marquis of Lumbría lived with his two daughters, Carolina, the elder, and Luisa, and with his second wife, Doña Vicenta, a woman with a foggy brain, who, when she was not sleeping, was complaining of everything, expecially of the noise. For, just as the Marquis feared sunshine, the Marquise feared noise; and while the former went on summer afternoons to read in the shade of the ivy-covered balcony to the sound of the river's ageless song, his wife stayed in the front parlor and took her siesta in an old satin arm-chair which the sun had not touched, lulled by the silence of the cathedral square.

The Marquis of Lumbría had no male children, and this was the most painful thorn in his existence. It was in order to have them that, shortly after having become a widower, he had married Doña Vicenta, his present wife, but she had proved sterile.

The Marquis' life was as monotonous and quotidian, as un-changing and regular, as the murmur of the river below the cliff or as the liturgic services in the cathedral. He managed his estate and pasture lands, to which he paid short visits from time to time, and at night he used to play *ombre* with the priest, the intimate advisor of his family, a curate, and the clerk of records. They all arrived at the same hour, went through the great door above which was ex-hibited a plaque of the Sacred Heart of Jesus with its inscription: "I shall reign in Spain, more reverenced there than elsewhere," seated themselves around the little table already arranged for them, and on the stroke of ten, they parted until the following day, even though there might still be open stakes. Meanwhile the Marquise dozed off and the Marquis' daughters did their needlework, read edifying books—perhaps some others obtained on the sly—or quarreled with each other.

For in order to break the tedium which was everywhere, from the parlor closed tight against the sun and flies to the ivy-clad walls, Carolina and Luisa had to quarrel. Carolina, the elder, hated the sun, like her father, and kept herself rigorously observant of all the family traditions; while Luisa liked to sing, to lean out the win-dows and over balconies and even to grow flowers there in flower-pots—a vulgar custom according to the Marquis. "What about the garden?" he would say to his daughter, referring to a tiny garden which adjoined the palace, but was seldom visited by any of the latter's inhabitants. But Luisa wanted to have flower-pots on the balcony of her bedroom, which faced a side street of the cathedral square; she wanted to water them, and with this as a pretext, to lean out and see who was passing by. "What bad taste to pry into what does not concern us . . ." her father would say; and her older sister, Carolina, would add: "No, but to go hunting!" And then the fun would begin.

And the appearances on the bedroom balcony and the watering of the potted flowers yielded their fruit. Tristan Ibáñez del Gamonal, of a titled family, one of the oldest in the city of Lorenza, remarked the second daughter of the Marquis of Lumbría; he saw her smiling, with her violet-like eyes and geranium-like mouth, among the flowers on the balcony of her bedroom. And it happened one day as Tristan was passing through the narrow street, the water overflowing from the flower-pots came down on him, and when Luisa exclaimed: "O, excuse me, Tristan!" he felt as if the voice of a suffering princess imprisoned in an enchanted castle were calling him to her aid.

"Such things, my daughter," said her father, "are done formally and seriously. I will have no foolishness!"

"But what do you mean by that, father?" exclaimed Luisa. "Carolina will tell you."

Luisa stood looking at her older sister and the latter said:

"It does seem to me, sister, that we, the daughters of the Marquis of Lumbría, should not carry on flirtations and strut about like peacocks on the balcony as women of the working class do. Is that what the flowers were for?"

"Let that young man ask to be admitted," pronounced her father, "and as I have nothing against him, everything will be arranged. How about you, Carolina?"

"I," said the latter, "do not object either."

And so Tristan entered the house as a formal suitor for the hand of Luisa.

The Marquise did not perceive this at once. And as the *ombre* session passed, the lady dozed in a corner of the drawing-room; and near her Carolina and Luisa, knitting or making lace, whis-

pered with Tristan, whom they were careful never to leave alone
with Luisa but always with both sisters. In this respect the father
was most vigilant. He did not mind, on the other hand, if Carolina
sometimes received her future brother-in-law alone, for thus she
could better instruct him in the customs and traditions of the
household.

*   *   *

The card players, the domestics and even the townspeople who
were intrigued by the mystery of the mansion, noticed that shortly
after Tristan's admission into the house as the sweetheart of the
second daughter of the Marquis, the spiritual atmosphere of the
hieratic family seemed to grow more dense and shadowy. The
Marquis grew more taciturn, and his wife complained more than
ever about the noise and the noise was greater than ever. For the
quarrels and disputes of the two sisters were more violent and bitter than before, but more silent. When one of them insulted or
perhaps pinched the other, as they met in the hall, it would be an
affair of whispers and smothered complaints. Only once did Mariana, the old chambermaid, hear Luisa shouting: "Well, the whole
city shall know it! Yes, the whole city shall know it! I shall go out
on the balcony overlooking the cathedral square and shout it to
everyone!" "Be quiet," roared the voice of the Marquis, and then
followed an expression, so unheard in that house, that Mariana
fled in terror from the door at which she had been listening.

A few days later the Marquis went away from Lorenza and took
his eldest daughter, Carolina, with him. And during the time he
was gone Tristan did not appear at the house. When the Marquis
returned, he felt obliged one night to give some explanation at the
card party. "The poor girl is not feeling well," he said, looking
fixedly at the priest, "it's a case of nerves that comes from constant quarrels, trivial, of course, with her sister whom she really
adores, and so I took her away to recuperate." Nobody answered
a word.

A few days later, the marriage of Tristan Ibáñez del Gamonal to
the second daughter of the most excellent Marquis de Lumbría
was celebrated en famille —decidedly en famille. No outsiders attended it except the mother of the groom and the card players.

Tristan came to live with his father-in-law and the atmosphere in the mansion grew denser and still more tenebrous. The flowers on the bedroom balcony of the new bride withered for lack of care. The Marquise slept more than ever and the Marquis, like a ghost, taciturn and crestfallen, roamed about the living-room sealed against the light from the street. He felt that his life was ebbing away, and he was clutching at it. He gave up *ombre*, and this act seemed like a farewell to the world—if he ever lived in the world. "I have not the head for the game now," he told his confidant, the priest, "I am distracted every minute and the game no longer a-muses me. The only thing left is to prepare myself to die well."

One day he awoke with a paralytic stroke. He hardly remem-bered anything. But as he recovered, he seemed to clutch at life with a more desperate tenacity. "No, I can't die until I see how things turn out." And of his daughter, who brought him his dinner in bed, he inquired anxiously: "How's it going? Will it be long?"

"Not much longer, father."

"Well, I am not going away, I cannot go until I see the new Mar-quis; because it must be a male, a male! We need a man here and if it is not a Suárez de Tejada, it will be a Rodrigo and a Marquis de Lumbría."

"That does not depend on me, father . . ."

"Well, that would be the last straw, my daughter," and his voice trembled as he said it, "that after taking that madcap into our house, he should not give us a Marquis . . . Why I would . . . "

Poor Luisa wept and Tristan seemed a criminal and a servant at the same time.

The excitement of the poor man reached its height when he learned that his daughter was about to deliver. He trembled all over with a feverish expectancy. "You require more care than the expectant mother," said the doctor.

"When Luisa gives birth to the child," said the Marquis to his son-in-law, "if it is a son, a Marquis, bring him to me at once that I may see him and then die in peace; bring him to me yourself."

When the Marquis heard the cry, he sat up in bed and stared at the door. Shortly afterwards Tristan entered, looking remorseful and carrying the child well wrapped up. "Marquis?" the old man shouted.

"Yes!"

He leaned forward a little to examine the new-born babe; he

gave it a shaky tremulous kiss, the kiss of death, and without even looking at his son-in-law, he fell back heavily upon the pillow, senseless. Without regaining consciousness he died two days later.

With black cloth, they draped the coat-of-arms on the façade of house in mourning, and the black of the cloth soon began to fade in the sun which shone full force upon it all day long. An air of mourning seemed to descend upon the whole house to which the child brought no happiness.

Poor Luisa, his mother, was left so weak after childbirth that though she insisted on nursing her child at the beginning, she had to give it up. "A hired breast . . . ," she sighed. "Now, Tristan, a wet nurse will nurse the Marquis," she repeated to her husband.

Tristan had fallen into an indefinable sadness; he felt himself growing old. "I am like an appurtenance of the house, almost a piece of furniture," he would say to himself. And from the narrow street he would gaze at the balcony of Luisa's bedroom, a balcony with no more flower-pots.

"Couldn't we put some flowers on your balcony again, Luisa?" he once ventured to ask his wife.

"Here there is no other flower but the Marquis," she answered.

The poor man suffered because they called his son nothing but the Marquis. Shunning his home, he took to seeking refuge in the cathedral. Other times he would go out without anyone knowing where he went. And what hurt him most was that his wife did not even try to discover where he went.

Luisa felt that she was dying, for life was melting away from her drop by drop. "My life is leaving me like a fine stream of water," she said, "I feel my blood grow thinner; my head is buzzing, and if I'm still alive, it's because I am dying very slowly . . . And if I regret it, it is for his sake, for my little Marquis, only for him . . . How sad life is in this sunless house! I thought that you, Tristan, would bring sunshine, freedom and happiness; but no, you have brought me nothing but the little Marquis . . . Bring him to me!" And she covered him with long, tremulous, feverish kisses. And although they spoke to each other, between husband and wife there fell a curtain of frozen silence. They said nothing of what most tormented their minds and hearts.

When Luisa felt that the thread of her life was about to break, she placed her cold hand on her son Rodrigo's forehead and said to his father: "Take care of the Marquis! Sacrifice yourself for the Marquis! Oh, and tell her that I forgive her!"

"And me?" moaned Tristan.

"You? You don't have to be pardoned!" The words fell like a fearful sentence upon the poor man. And shortly after hearing them, he was left a widower.

* * *

A young widower, master of a considerable fortune, that of his son the Marquis, and imprisoned in that gloomy mansion shut against the sun, with memories which, even though they were only a few years old, already seemed incredibly old to him. He passed the dreary hours on the balcony at the rear of the house, among the ivy, listening to the droning of the river. Soon he resumed the card parties. He spent long hours alone with the priest, going over, so it was said, the papers of the late Marquis and arranging his will.

But what gave the whole city of Lorenza something to talk about one day was the fact that after an absence of some days, Tristan returned to the mansion with Carolina, his sister-in-law, now his new wife. But didn't people say that she had become a nun? Where and how had she lived during those four years?

Carolina returned proudly, with an air of insolent defiance on her face. The first thing she did on returning was to order that the mourning draperies be removed from the family coat-of-arms. "Let the sun shine on it," she exclaimed, "let the sun shine on it and I have a mind to have it daubed with honey so that it will fill with flies." Then she ordered the ivy to be removed. "But Carolina," begged Tristan, "forget about these relics of the past!"

The child, the little Marquis, immediately perceived an enemy in his new mother. He would not consent to call her "mama" in spite of his father's requests; he always called her aunt.

"But who told him I am his aunt?" she asked. "Perhaps Mariana?"

"I don't know, I don't know," answered Tristan, "I don't see how, but around here people know everything."

"Everything?"

"Yes, everything. It seems that this house tells everything . . ."

"Well, we shall keep quiet."

Life in the mansion seemed to acquire a bitter, concentrated intensity. The married couple seldom left their room, in which Carolina kept Tristan. And so the little Marquis was left to the mercy of servants, of a tutor who came every day to teach him his ABC's and of the priest who undertook to instruct him in religion.

The card parties were renewed; but during them, Carolina, seated next to her husband, followed his plays and even coached him in them. They all noticed that she did nothing but look for opportunities to put her hand on his and that she was continually leaning on his arm. When the clock was about to strike ten, she said, "Tristan, the time is up." He did not venture out of the house without her, holding his arm and sweeping the street with a look of defiance.

*   *   *

Carolina's pregnancy was very painful. It seemed that she did not desire the child that was coming. When it was born, she did not wish to see it. And when she was told that it was a girl born ill-formed and weak, she only answered dryly: "Yes, our punishment!" And a little later when the poor creature was beginning to die, the mother said: "For the life she would have led . . ."

"You are very much alone," Carolina said one day, years afterwards, to her nephew, the little Marquis, "you need a companion, some one to stimulate you to study; and so your father and I have decided to bring home a nephew, one who was left an orphan . . ."

The boy, who was then already ten years old, and precocious in a sickly, sad way, remained pensive.

When the other one came, the intruder, the orphan, the little Marquis was on his guard and all of Lorenza did nothing but comment on the extraordinary occurrence. Everyone thought that since Carolina had not been successful in having children of her own, she had brought the adopted son, this intruder, to annoy and oppress the other, her sister's child . . .

From the very beginning the two children regarded each other as enemies, for if the one was haughty, the other was no less so.

"Well, what do you think," said Pedrito to Rodriguín, "that because you are a marquis you are going to give me orders? . . . If you annoy me much more I'll go away and leave you alone."

"Leave me alone, that's how I want to be. Go back to where your own folks are."

But Carolina would come in and with a "Children!" make them look at each other in silence.

"Uncle," Pedrito would say to Tristan (for this is what he called him), "I'm going away. I want to go away. I want to go back to my aunts. I can't stand Rodriguín; he is always throwing it up to my face that I am here to serve you and as if out of charity."

"Have patience, Pedrín, have patience. Haven't I?" And caressing the child's little head, he pressed it to his lips and shed tears over it—copious, long, silent tears.

Those tears were for the child like a rain of pity. He felt a profound sorrow for the poor man, for the poor father of the little Marquis.

The one who never wept was Carolina.

*   *   *

It happened one day, while husband and wife were sitting close together on the sofa, their hands clasped, staring at the gloomy emptiness of the sitting room, that they heard the noise of a quarrel and suddenly the children burst in, sweating and breathless.

"I'm going away! I'm going away!" cried Pedrito.

"Go! Go! And don't come back to my house!" answered Rodriguín.

But when Carolina saw the blood on Pedrito's nostrils, she leaped towards him like a lioness shouting: "My son! My son!" And then, turning to the little Marquis, she spat out this word: "Cain!"

"Cain? Is he my brother?" asked the little Marquis, opening his eyes widely.

Carolina hesitated a moment. And then, as if clenching her heart, she said in a hoarse voice: "Pedro is my son!"

"Carolina!" groaned her husband.

"Yes," continued the little Marquis, "I suspected that he was your son, and they say so around here . . . But what we don't know is who his father is . . . if he has any."

Carolina stiffened suddenly. Her eyes flashed, her lips trembled. She seized Pedrillo, her son, pressed him between her knees and looking fixedly at her husband exclaimed:

"His father? You tell him, you the father of the little Marquis, you tell the son of Luisa, of my sister, you tell the grandson of Don Rodrigo Suárez de Tejada, Marquis of Lumbría, tell him who his father is! Tell him! Tell him! If you don't, I will! Tell him!"

"Carolina!" begged Tristan weeping.

"Tell him. Tell him who is the true Marquis of Lumbría!"

"You do not need to tell me," said the child.

"Well then, I shall! The Marquis is this one, this one and not you; he who was born before you and is my son, I who am the rightful heiress, and your father's son . . . yes, your father's . . . But I shall remove the coat-of-arms and open all the balconies to the sun and I shall make everyone recognize my son for what he is: the Marquis."

Then she began to shout, calling all the servants and the old Marquise, who now almost in the imbecility of second childhood, was dozing. And when she had them all before her, she ordered the balconies opened wide and in a loud voice she began calmly saying:

"This, this is the Marquis; this is the true Marquis of Lumbría; this is the rightful heir. This is the son I had by Tristan, of this very Tristan who now hides and weeps, just after he had married my sister, a month after they were married. My father, the most excellent Marquis de Lumbría, sacrificed me to his principles— perhaps my sister was as much compromised as I myself . . ."

"Carolina!" groaned her husband.

"Be silent you—today everything must be revealed. Your son, yours and hers, has drawn blood, blue blood! no, just red blood, very red blood from our son, from my son, from the Marquis . . ."

"What a noise, good Heavens!" complained the old lady, huddling in an arm-chair in a corner.

"And now," continued Carolina, addressing herself to the servants, "go and shout the news throughout the city: repeat what you have heard me say in the squares, in the courtyards and at the fountains. Let everyone know of it—let everyone know of the blot on the escutcheon."

"Why all the city knew it already," mumbled Mariana.

"What?" shouted Carolina.

"Yes, madam, yes; everyone said so . . ."

"Was it to keep an open secret, to conceal an enigma that was clear to everyone, to cover up appearances that we have lived like this, Tristan? Misery, nothing but misery! Open those balconies, let the light enter, all the light and dust and flies of the street, and tomorrow the escutcheon will be taken down. Flower-pots will be placed on all the balconies and a party will be given for the people of the city, the real people. But, no, the party will be given on the day when my son, your son, whom the priest calls a child of sin, when the real sin was the one which made the other one your son, shall be recognized for what he is—the Marquis of Lumbría."

They had to carry poor Rodriguín from a corner in the room— he was pale and feverish. Afterwards he refused to see either his father or brother.

"We shall put him in a school," Carolina decided.

*   *   *

Afterwards all Lorenza people spoke of nothing except the masculine firmness with which Carolina executed her plans. She went out daily, holding her husband by the arm as if he were her prisoner and holding the hand of the child of their indiscretion. She kept all the balconies of the mansion wide open, and the sun faded the satin of the arm-chairs and even fell upon the ancestral portraits. She entertained every night at the card games, for no one dared to refuse her invitations and she stayed at Tristan's side playing his cards. She caressed him before the guests and patting him on the cheek she would say to him: "My, what a poor man you are, Tristan!" And then to the others: "My poor, dear husband doesn't know how to play alone!" And when they had gone, she would say to him: "It's a pity, Tristan, that we haven't more children . . . after that poor little girl . . . she was a daughter of sin, she, not our Pedrín; but now to bring up this one, the Marquis!"

She made her husband recognize him as his own, begotten before his father had married, and she began to prepare for her son, her Pedrín, the succession to the title. The other one, Rodriguín, in the meantime, away at school was being consumed with anger and sadness.

"The best thing that could happen," said Carolina, "would be for him to be inspired to a religious vocation. Haven't you ever felt such an inspiration, Tristan? For it seems to me that you were born more to be a monk than anything else . . ."

"And *you* say that, Carolina! . . ." her husband ventured to say in a supplicating tone.

"Yes, I really think so, Tristan! And don't pretend to be proud of what happened, what the priest called our sin and my father, the Marquis, called the blot on our escutcheon. Our sin? Not yours, Tristan, no. I was the one who seduced you! I! She, the girl of the geraniums, who watered your hat—your hat and not your head—with the water from her flower-pots, brought you to the mansion, but it was I who won you. Remember that! I wanted to be the mother of the Marquis. Only I didn't count on the other one. And the other one, he was strong, stronger than I. I wanted you to rebel and you did not know how, you could not rebel . . ."

"But Carolina . . ."

"Yes, yes, I know well enough what happened; I know. Your flesh has always been weak. The sin was your letting yourself get married to her: that was your sin. And what you made me suffer! But I knew that my sister, that Luisa, couldn't endure her betrayal and your infamy. And I waited. I waited patiently and reared my son. What a task it was to bring him up when a terrible secret divided us! I have brought him up for revenge! And as for you, his father . . ."

"Yes, he must despise me . . ."

"No, he doesn't despise you, no! Do you think I despise you?"

"Well, what else?"

"I pity you! You awoke my flesh and with it my pride as heiress. Since nobody could meet me except formally and through my father . . . since I wasn't going to lean out over the balcony like my sister and smile on the people in the street . . . since no men come here except country rustics . . . When you came here I made you feel that *I* was the woman, *I*, and not my sister . . . Do you want me to remind you of our sin?"

"No, for God's sake, Carolina, no!"

"Yes, it's better that I shouldn't remind you of it. You're the fallen one. Do you see why I said that you were born to be a monk? But no, no, you were born that I might be the mother of the Marquis of Lumbría, of Don Pedro Ibáñez del Gamonal y Suárez de Tejada. Him I shall make a man. And I will order him to carve a new escutcheon, of bronze and not of stone. That's why I had the stone one removed to make room for a bronze one. On it will be a red stain, the red of blood, blood-red, blood-red like the blood which his brother, his half brother, your other son, son of betrayal and sin, drew from him, red as my blood, red as the blood which you too made me shed . . . Don't grieve," and as she said this she put her hand on his head, "don't feel depressed, Tristan, my husband . . . Look here, look at my father's portrait and tell me, you who saw him die, what he would say if he saw his other grandson, the Marquis . . . So he made you carry your son, Luisa's son, to him! I shall place a ruby on the bronze escutcheon, and the ruby will sparkle in the sun. Well, did you think that there was no blood, red blood, red and not blue, in this house? And now, Tristan, as soon as we see our son, the red-blooded Marquis, asleep, let us go to bed."

Tristan bowed his head under a weight of centuries.

Every Inch a Man

Julia's beauty was famed throughout the countryside that bordered the ancient town of Renada; Julia was, one might say, its official beauty, one more monument—but a living and fresh one—amid all the architectural treasures of the capital. "I'm going to Renada," people would say, "to see the cathedral and to see Julia Yáñez." An omen of impending tragedy seemed to dwell in the eyes of this beauty. Her conduct disquieted all who knew or saw her. Old men grew sad when she passed by, compelling all eyes to follow in her wake, and young men would be long in falling asleep on those nights. And she, fully conscious of her power, sensed the weight of a fatal future hanging over her. A secret voice from the depths of her conscience seemed to be saying: "Your beauty will undo you!" And she tried not to hear it.

The father of this local beauty, Don Victorino Yáñez, an individual with a very shady record, had placed his last and final hopes of economic salvation in his daughter. He was now engaged in business, but things were going from bad to worse. His last and supreme financial hope, the last card left for him to play, was his daughter. He also had a son; but he was a good-for-nothing and for some time they had had no news of his whereabouts.

"Julia is all that is left to us now," he used to say to his wife. "Everything depends upon the kind of a marriage she makes or we make for her. If she makes one foolish mistake, and I'm afraid she will, we're lost."

"And what do you call making a foolish mistake?"

Reprinted with permission of A. and C. Boni, from *Three Exemplary Novels*, translated by Angel Flores. Copyright 1930 by A. and C. Boni.

"There you go again! I tell you, Anacleta, you haven't a bit of common sense . . . ."

"Well, what would you do, Victorino? You're the only sensible person around here, so tell me."

"Well, what's needed here, as I've told you a hundred times, is for you to watch over Julia and prevent her from getting into those idiotic love affairs that make all the girls around here lose their time, lose their chances and even their health. I want no little love chats at the window, no sentimental stuff; no two-bit students for lovers."

"But what can I do with her?"

"What can you *do* with her? Make her understand that our future, our mutual welfare, even our honor perhaps—you understand? . . ."

"Yes, I understand."

"No, you don't understand! Our honor—you hear me?—the family honor depends upon her marriage. She must keep herself desirable."

"Poor little child!"

"Poor little child? She absolutely must not throw herself into the arms of silly lovers, and she must not read those crazy novels, which only turn her head and fill it with air."

"But what do you want her to do?"

"Think wisely, realize what she can do with her beauty, and learn how to profit by it."

"Well, when I was her age . . ."

"Come now, Anacleta, that's enough foolishness! You never open your mouth but out comes nonsense. You, at her age . . . You, at her age . . . Indeed! Don't forget that I knew you then . . . . "

"Yes, unfortunately . . ."

And the parents of the beauty would leave each other only to begin a similar conversation the following day.

Poor Julia, fully comprehending the horrible purpose behind her father's calculations, suffered in consequence. "He wants to sell me," she would say to herself, "to save his bankrupt business; possibly to keep himself out of jail." And it was so.

Instinctively rebellious, Julia accepted the advances of the first admirer that came along.

"For heaven's sake be careful, my child," said her mother. "I'm well aware of what's going on. I have seen him strolling near the the house and making signs to you. I know he wrote you a letter, and that you answered it . . . ."

"What of it, mama? Must I live like a captive slave, till the day when some Sultan appears to buy me from my father?"

"Don't say such things, my child . . . ."

"Can't I have a sweetheart like other girls?"

"Of course, but he must be a serious one . . . ."

"How is one to know if he is serious or not? One must begin somewhere. You have to get to know a person before you can love him."

"Love him . . . love him . . . ."

"Why no, I suppose I must wait for my purchaser."

"You just can't reason with you or with your father. That's the way you Yáñezes are! Ah! I rue the day I was married . . . ."

"That's just what I don't want to have to say some day."

And then her mother would let her alone.

Determined to risk everything Julia found the courage to go down to the first floor and speak to her lover from the window of a sort of little store. "If my father discovers us here," she thought to herself, "he would do something terrible to me. But it might be better so: people will then know that I am a victim whose beauty he wishes to barter." She came down to the window and, in this first interview, she confided to Enrique, a budding provincial Don Juan, all the miserable, gloomy details of her home life. He had come to save her, to redeem her.

But Enrique, in spite of his infatuation with the beautiful girl, felt his enthusiasm waning. "This little wench," he said to himself, "puts on tragic airs; she reads sentimental novels." And once all Renada had been informed of how this famous local beauty had permitted him to approach her window, he began to seek a way out of his compromising situation. He found one soon enough. One morning Julia came downstairs all upset, with her brilliant eyes red from weeping and said to him: "Enrique, I can't bear this any longer. This is no home nor family: this is hell. My father has found out about our affair. He beat me last night just because I was trying to defend myself—think of that!"

"What a brute!"

"You can't imagine what he is! And he said that you would have him to deal with."

"We'll see—let him come! That's the last straw!" But, at the same time, he was saying to himself: "This really must stop; this ogre is quite capable of any atrocity if he sees his treasure being carried off, and since I can't get him out of debt . . ."

"Tell me, Enrique, do you love me?"

"What a question to ask me now!"

"Answer me; do you love me?"

"With all my heart and soul, darling!"

"But do you really?"

"Really and truly!"

"Are you ready to do anything for me?"

"Yes, anything!"

"Well then, abduct me, take me away. We must escape, but far, very far away, where my father won't be able to reach us."

"Compose yourself, little girl!"

"No, no, abduct me; if you love me, take me away. Steal this treasure from my father so that he won't be able to sell it! I don't want to be sold—I want to be abducted!"

And so they set about arranging their escape.

But on the following day—the one which they had appointed for the elopment—while Julia was ready with her bundle of clothes impatiently awaiting the arrival of the carriage which had been secretly ordered, Enrique failed to appear. "Coward! Worse than a coward! Despicable! Worse than despicable!" cried poor Julia, as she flung herself down on the bed and bit the pillow in her rage. "And he said he loved me! No, no, he did not love me; he loved my beauty. Indeed, not even that! What he wanted was to be able to boast before all Renada that I, Julia Yáñez—no less than I—had accepted him as a suitor. And now he'll go telling everyone how I offered to run away with him. Oh! Despicable, despicable, despicable! He is as mean as my father; despicable as all men are!" And she fell into an inconsolable despair.

"My child," said her mother. "I see that this affair is now over with and I thank God for it. But look here, your father is right; if you continue like this you will only bring discredit upon yourself."

"If I continue how?"

"Like this—accepting the advances of the first man who comes along. You'll become known as a coquette and . . ."

"So much the better, mother, so much the better! That way more men will present themselves. Especially so long as I have not lost what God gave me."

"Alas, alas! You are indeed your father's daughter, my child."

In fact, shortly after this, Julia accepted another suitor. She confided exactly the same things to him, and alarmed him just as she had Enrique. But Pedro was of stouter heart.

And after the same preliminary steps, she finally proposed that they elope.

"Look here, Julia," replied Pedro, "I don't object to our running off together. Why, you know I would be delighted. But after we have fled, where shall we go and what shall we do?"

"We shall see about that later!"

"No, we can't put it off. We must decide that now. As for me, at the present time and for some time to come, I won't be able to support you. I know that they won't admit us at my house and as for your father . . ."

"What! You don't mean to retreat, do you?"

"But what are we going to do?"

"You're not going to be a coward, are you?"

"What shall we do, pray tell me?"

"Well . . . commit suicide!"

"Julia, you're crazy!"

"Yes, I am crazy; crazy with despair, crazy with disgust, mad with horror at this father of mine who wants to sell me. . . . And if you were crazy and madly in love with me, you would commit suicide with me."

"But, Julia, remember that you want me to be so madly in love with you as to commit suicide with you; you do not say that you would kill yourself with me because you are madly in love with me, but rather because you are crazed by your disgust for your father and your home. It's not the same thing."

"Ah! how well you reason! Love doesn't reason!"

They, too, broke off their relations. And Julia would say to herself, "He didn't love me either, he didn't either. They fall in love with my beauty, not me. I defy them all!" Then she would weep bitterly.

"You see, my child," said her mother, "didn't I tell you there goes another!"

"And there'll be a hundred, mama, a hundred, until at last I find my own, the one who will deliver me from you both. Oh, to want to sell me!"

"Tell that to your father."

And Doña Anacleta would go to her room alone, and cry.

Finally, Julia's father said to her, "Look here, my child, I have overlooked these two love affairs of yours, I have not resorted to the measures I should have taken. But I warn you now that I will not tolerate any more foolishness. Now then, you know my stand."

"Well, there's still more!" cried Julia in a tone of bitter irony, with a challenging look into her father's eyes.

"What is it?" he asked menacingly.

"It's that I have another sweetheart."

"Another one! Who?"

"Who? I'll bet you can't guess!"

"Come now, don't joke, answer me, or you'll make me lose patience."

"Well, no less a personage than Don Alberto Menéndez de Cabuérniga."

"What an outrage!" exclaimed her mother.

Don Victorino turned pale without uttering a word. Don Alberto Menéndez de Cabuérniga was an exceedingly wealthy landowner, dissolute, very capricious as regards women, and it was said of him that he did not spare any expense to win them. He was married but separated from his wife. He had already married off two of his mistresses and had given splendid dowers to both women.

"What do you say to this father? Are you silent?"

"You're crazy!"

"No, I'm not crazy and I don't see visions. He walks up and down our street constantly and watches our house. Shall I tell him that he is to arrange matters with you?"

"I'm going. If I don't this interview will end badly."

Her father got up and left the house.

"But my child! My child!" her mother remonstrated.

"Mother, I can assure you that this proposition doesn't strike him as being so very bad; I tell you that he is capable of selling me to Don Alberto."

The poor girl's will power was breaking. She realized that even a sale would be a redemption. The essential thing was to leave home and get away from her father any way she could.

About this time an "Indiano"—that is a Spaniard who made his fortune in America—by the name of Alejandro Gómez, purchased one of the richest and largest estates on the outskirts of Renada. No one was certain about his origin or his past life, for no one had ever heard him speak of his parents, his relatives, his home, or his childhood. The only thing they knew about him was that his parents had taken him first to Cuba when he was very young and later to Mexico, where (and no one knew just how) he amassed an enormous, a fabulous fortune—it was said to run into several million dollars—before he had reached the age of thirty-four, at which time he had returned to Spain with the intention of settling there. People said that he was a childless widower and told the most fantastic legends about him. Those who had dealings with him thought him ambitious, filled with vast projects, strong willed, obstinate and self-centered. He boasted that he was a plebeian.

"One can do everything with money," he would say.

"Not always, and not everyone can," people would reply.

"Not everyone, no; but those who have known how to make money can. Of course one of these would-be *senore* who inherits his money—a sugar paste count or duke—can't do anything, in spite of the millions he may have. But I! I! I who have known how to make my fortune myself by the strength of my arm? I?"

And you ought to have heard him pronounce the word "I." The whole man was concentrated in this personal affirmation.

"Nothing that I have really wanted to have I ever failed to obtain. If I wanted to I could become Prime Minister. But the fact is that I don't desire it."

People spoke to Alejandro of Julia, the monumental beauty of Renada. "We must see her," he said to himself. And as soon as he had seen her he exclaimed, "We must have her!"

One day Julia said to her father, "This fabulous Alejandro—you know the man; for a long time now they've talked of nothing else—the man who purchased the Carbajedo estate? . . ."

"Yes, yes, I know who he is. Well, what about him?"

"Do you know that he, too, has his eye on me?"

"Julia, are you trying to make fun of me?"

"I'm not joking. I'm quite serious about it; he's courting me."

"Don't joke, I tell you . . . . "

"Well, here's his letter!"

She took one from her bosom and thrust it into her father's face.

"And what do you intend to do?" he asked her.

"Indeed! What should I do? I'll tell him to see you and that you will fix the price."

Don Victorino looked sharply at his daughter and left the room without a word. For a few days an ominous silence and an atmosphere of mute anger reigned through the house. Julia had written her latest suitor a sarcastic and disdainful answer. Shortly after she received a reply containing the following words heavily underlined and written in large, clear, angular characters: "You will eventually be mine. Alejandro Gómez knows how to get what he wants." As she read this, Julia thought, "Here is a real man. Will he save me? Will I save him?" A few days after the arrival of the second letter Don Victorino closeted himself with his daughter and said to her with tears in his eyes and almost upon his knees:

"Listen, my child, now everything depends upon your decision: our future and my honor. If you refuse to accept Alejandro it will not be long before I shall be unable to conceal my ruin, my frauds and even my . . ."

"Don't tell me."

"No, I will no longer be able to hide anything. My terms are expiring. They will throw me into prison. Until now I have been able to ward off the blow because of you, by bringing in your name! Your beauty has been my protection. 'Poor little girl,' they say."

"And if I accept him?"

"Well, then, I'll tell you the entire truth now. He has learned all about my situation, he has been informed of everything. And now, thanks to him, I breathe freely. He has settled all my bad debts and he has paid my . . ."

"Yes, I know, don't tell me. But what now?"

"I am utterly dependent upon him—we all are; I am living upon his generosity and you, yourself, are dependent upon him."

"In other words you have already sold me to him?"

"No, he has bought us all."

"Therefore, I belong to him already whether I want to or not?"

"He does not demand that. He asks for nothing, demands nothing."

"How generous!"

"Julia!"

"Yes, yes, I understand! Tell him that so far as I'm concerned he can come whenever he pleases."

She began to tremble as she spoke. Who was it that had really said that? Was it she? No, rather another being concealed within her who tyrannized over her.

"Thank you, my child, thank you!"

The father rose to embrace his daughter; but she, pushing him aside, cried out:

"No, don't soil me!"

"But, my dear child . . ."

"Go and kiss your mortgages! Or rather the ashes of those that would have cast you into prison."

"Julia, didn't I tell you that Alejandro Gómez knows how to get what he wants? To say such things to me! To me!"

These were the first words which the young "Indiano" addressed to Victorino's daughter. The young girl trembled at them; for the first time in her life she sensed that she was standing before a real man. And it seemed to her that this man was more docile and less uncouth than she had expected.

At the third visit the parents left them alone. Julia trembled. Alejandro remained silent. For a time this trembling and this silence persisted.

"Julia, you seem to be ill," he said.

"No, no, I'm all right."

"Then, why do you tremble so?"

"Perhaps because of the cold."

"No, because you're afraid."

"Afraid! Afraid of what?"

"Afraid of me."

"Why should I be afraid of you?"

"Yes, you're afraid of me."

And she gave vent to her fear by bursting into tears. Julia wept from the very depths of her being—wept with all her heart. Her sobs choked her, she could not breathe.

"Am I an ogre?" whispered Alejandro.

"They have sold me! They have sold me! They have bartered my beauty! They have sold me!"

"Who says so?"

"I, I say so! But no—I'll never be yours, not unless I'm dead."

"You will be mine, Julia; you will give yourself to me and you will love me . . . . Do you mean that you're not going to love me? Me? Well, that's the last straw!"

There was something in the tone of that "me" that shut off the fountain of Julia's tears: her heart seemed to stop beating. Then, as she looked at this man, a voice seemed to say: "This is a *man*."

"You can do with me whatever you please," she said.

"What do you mean by that?" he asked, continuing to address her with the familiar "tu" (thou).

"I don't know . . . I don't know what I mean . . . ."

"Why do you say that I can do whatever I want with you?"

"Because you can . . . ."

"What I want," and his *I* sounded clear and triumphant, "is to make you my wife."

Julia was unable to suppress a cry; her large beautiful eyes shone in surprise as she gazed at the man who was smiling and thinking to himself: "I shall have the most beautiful wife in all Spain."

"But what did you think I wanted?" he asked her.

"I thought . . . I thought . . ."

Again her breast heaved with stifled sobs. Presently she felt lips pressing upon hers and heard a voice that was saying to her:

"Yes, my wife . . . mine . . . my own . . . my legitimate wife of course. The law will sanction my will . . . or my will the law!"

"Yes, yours."

She was conquered. And so the wedding was arranged.

What was there about this crude and secretive man that frightened her while compelling her respect? And the most terrible thing about it was that he inspired in her a sort of strange love. For Julia did not want to love this adventurer, who had made up his mind to have one of the most beautiful women for his wife simply to make her show off his millions. But, unwilling to love him, she felt herself yielding to a submission that bore some resemblance to passion. It was akin to that form of love that an arrogant conqueror must inspire in the heart of a captive slave-girl. He had not purchased her, no! but he had conquered her.

"But," said Julia to herself, "does he really love me? Does he love me, really me, as he says he does—and how he says it! Does he love me, or does he seek only to display my beauty? Can I mean nothing more to him than a rare and costly piece of furniture? Is he truly in love with me? Won't he soon become tired of my charms? At any rate he's going to be my husband and I'll be free of this accursed home, free from my father. For my father shall certainly not live with us! We will give him an allowance and let him continue insulting my poor mother and carrying on with the servant girls. We shall avoid his getting into business difficulties again. And I shall be wealthy, enormously wealthy!"

But this did not satisfy her completely. She knew that she was envied by the townspeople; she knew that her wonderful good fortune was the favorite topic of conversation and that it was said that her beauty had won for her all that it possibly could. But did this man love her? Did he truly love her?

"I must win his love," she would say to herself. "I must have him really love me—I cannot become his wife if he does not, for that would be a transaction of the worst possible kind. But, do I really love him?" In his presence, she felt herself grow timid, as a mysterious voice, issuing from the depths of her being, said to her: "This is a real man." Every time Alejandro said *I* she would tremble. And she trembled with love though she thought it was for some other reason, or could not imagine why.

They were married and went to live in the capital. Thanks to his large fortune Alejandro had numerous acquaintances and friends but they were somewhat curious. Julia imagined that most of the people who frequented their home, and there were many aristocrats among them, were debtors of her husband who loaned them money on solid mortgages. But she knew nothing concerning his affairs, and he never spoke to her about them. She had everything she wanted; she could gratify her slightest whim, but she wanted something which it was only natural for her to want most. It was no longer the love of this man whom she felt had conquered and even bewitched her, but rather the absolute certainty

of that love. "Does he love me or doesn't he?" she would ask herself. "He showers me with attentions, he treats me with the greatest
respect, but a trifle as if I were only a capricious child; he even
spoils me. But does he love me?" It was quite useless to speak of
love and affection to this man.

"Only fools talk about such things," he would say. "My charming one ... my beauty ... my beloved ... I? I talking of such things?
Sentiment belongs in novels. I know that you used to enjoy reading them ...."

"I still like to."

"Then read all you want. Why look here, if it pleases you, I will
erect a pavilion on the grounds next door, which you can use as a
library and I will stock it with all the novels that have been written
since the time of Adam."

"How you talk!"

Alejandro dressed as modestly and carelessly as possible. It was
not so much that he sought to pass unnoticed because of his attire,
but he affected a certain plebeian vulgarity. It was hard for him to
change his clothes, since he had grown fond of those he was accustomed to wearing. One would have said that whenever he donned
a new suit he purposely rubbed himself against the walls to make
it appear shabby. On the other hand, he insisted that his wife
should dress herself most elegantly, in a manner that would show
her natural beauty off to best advantage. He paid all his bills
promptly but those he paid most cheerfully were dressmakers' and
milliners' bills for pretty things for his Julia.

He took pleasure in going out with her and in emphasizing the
difference in dress and bearing that existed between them. He enjoyed seeing men stop to glance at his wife, and if she in turn co-
quettishly provoked their glances, he never noticed or pretended
not to. He seemed to be saying to those who looked at her with
sensual desire: "She pleases you? Well, I'm most delighted, but
she's mine, mine only, so you can covet all you want!" She guessed
this sentiment and thought: "Does this man love me or doesn't
he?" For always she thought of him as *this man*—as *her man* or
rather, as the man whose mistress she had become. Little by little
she developed the soul of a slave-girl in a harem; a favorite, unique
slave, but a slave-girl just the same.

No intimacy existed between them. She could not imagine what might interest her husband. Once she ventured to ask him about his family.

"My family?" Alejandro replied. "I have no family but you. I am my family. I and you who are mine."

"But what of your parents?"

"You must realize that I never had any. My family begins with me. I made myself."

"I wanted to ask you something else, Alejandro, but I don't dare."

"What do you mean you don't dare? Am I going to devour you? Have I ever taken offense at anything you have said to me?"

"No, never, I have no complaint to make . . . ."

"Well, that's the last straw!"

"I have no complaint to make, but . . ."

"Good, ask and let's be done with it!"

"No, I'm not going to ask you."

"Ask me!"

And he said it in such a tone and with such supreme egoism that she answered him in a voice trembling with fear and love—the submissive love of a favorite slave:

"Well, then, tell me, are you a widower?"

"Yes, I am a widower."

"And your first wife."

"People have been telling you something."

"Why, no, but . . ."

"People have been telling you something; what is it?"

"Well, yes, I heard something . . . ."

"And you believed it."

"No . . . No, I didn't believe it."

"Of course. You couldn't have—you shouldn't have believed it."

"And I didn't believe it."

"That's quite natural. Anyone who loves me as you love me and who belongs to me as you do, could not believe such fantastic lies."

"It's evident that I love you," and as she said this she hoped to excite a similar avowal of affection on his part.

"I have already told you that I don't like phrases from sentimental novels. The less one confesses one's love for another, the better."

After a short pause he continued:

"You've been told that I was married in Mexico, when I was very young, to an immensely wealthy woman, much older than I—an old heiress—and that I forced her to make me her heir, and then killed her. That's what they told you, didn't they?"

"Yes, that's what they told me."

"And you believed it?"

"No, I didn't believe it. I couldn't believe that you killed your wife."

"I see that you have more sense than I gave you credit for. How could I have killed my own wife—something belonging to me?"

What was it that made poor Julia tremble when she heard this? She did not realize the cause of her trembling—but it was the word *thing* applied to his former wife by her husband.

"It would have been absolutely foolish," Alejandro went on. "What for? To be her heir? Why, I enjoyed her fortune as much then as I do today! To kill one's own wife! There's no reason in the world for killing one's own wife."

"Nevertheless, there have been husbands who have killed their wives," Julia ventured to say.

"Why?"

"Out of jealousy or because they were being betrayed . . ."

"Nonsense! Only fools are jealous. Only fools can be jealous because fools alone permit their wives to betray them. But I! My wife can't possibly betray me. My first one couldn't and neither can you!"

"Don't talk like that. Let's change the subject."

"Why?"

"It pains me to hear you say such things. As if the thought of deceiving you could enter my mind, even in dreams . . . ."

"I know; I know, you don't have to tell me: I know that you will never be untrue to me! Deceive me! My own wife? Impossible. As for her, the other one, she died without my having killed her."

This was one of the times when Alejandro spoke at greatest length to his wife. She had remained pensive and trembling. Did this man love her or didn't he?

Poor Julia! This new home of hers was terrible; as terrible as her father's. She was free, absolutely free. She was able to do whatever she fancied there, go and come at will, receive her women-friends and even men as she pleased. But her lord and master—did he love her? This uncertainty of his love held her a captive in this magnificent prison with wide-open doors.

A beam of the rising sun filtered through the tempestuous shadows of her captive soul when she realized that she was pregnant by her husband. "Now," she said, "I shall know if he loves me or not."

When she announced the good news to her husband he exclaimed:

"I expected it. Now I have an heir and I will make a man of him —a man like me. I expected him."

"And what if he hadn't come?" she inquired.

"Impossible! He had to come. I had to have a child—I."

"Well, there are many who get married and don't have any."

"Maybe others don't. But not I! I had to have a child."

"Why?"

"Because you couldn't do otherwise than bear one."

The child was born, but the father remained as uncommunicative as ever. Only he forbade his wife to nurse the boy.

"I don't doubt that you are healthy and strong, but nursing mothers lose their strength, and I don't want you to. I want you to keep yourself young as long as possible."

He relinquished the idea only after the doctor had assured him that Julia, far from being hurt, would be benefited by nursing her child, and that her beauty would thereby reach its plenitude.

The father refused to kiss his child. "One only annoys them with such tender foolishness," he would explain. Occasionally he would take him up in his arms and examine him attentively for a long time.

"Didn't you once question me about my family?" said Alejandro one day to his wife. "Well, here it is. Now I have a family and someone who will be my heir and continue my work."

Julia was tempted to ask her husband what his work was, but she did not dare. "My work!" Indeed, what could the work of this man be? She had heard him use this same expression before.

Among the people who came most frequently to the house were the Count and Countess of Bordaviella and, especially the Count who had business relations with Alejandro and to whom the latter had loaned considerable sums on interest. Often the Count would play a game of chess with Julia, who liked it, and unburden his mind by confiding to his friend—his creditor's wife—his unfortunate domestic affairs. For the home of the Count of Bordaviella was a miniature hell, though with very few flames. The Count and Countess neither got along nor loved each other. They both devoted themselves to their own interests and she, the Countess, made herself liable to outrageous gossip. People had invented for her benefit this little riddle: "Who is Count of Bordaveilla's assistant husband?" So it was that the Count went to the home of the beautiful Julia, to play chess with her and to contrive another's misfortune to console him for his own.

"What? Has that Count been here today, too?" demanded Alejandro of his wife.

"That Count . . . that Count . . . why, what Count do you mean?"

"What one! The Count! There is only one Count, one Marquis and one Duke . . . . To me they're all the same, as if they were one and the same thing."

"Well, yes; he has been here."

"I'm glad, if it amuses you. That's the only thing he's good for—the poor fool."

"Well, I think that he's an intelligent man, cultured, well brought up and very attractive."

"Yes, like the ones you read about in novels. But if that interests you . . ."

"And he's so very miserable."

"Bah! That's his own fault."

"Why?"

"Because he's such an idiot. What happens to him is perfectly natural. It is quite natural that a wife should deceive a little bungler like this Count. Why, he's not a man! I don't know how anyone could have married such a thing as that. Of course, she didn't marry him but his title. I would like to see a woman treat me as his woman treats that miserable creature!"

Julia looked at her husband and suddenly exclaimed, without realizing what she was saying:

"And what if she should? What if your wife turned out to be like his?"

"Nonsense!" and Alejandro burst into laughter. "You are trying to season our domestic life with the salt extracted from books. But if you want to test me by making me jealous you're making a mistake. I'm not of that kind. Amuse yourself playing with the poor fool."

"Is it possible that this man is entirely free from jealousy?" Julia asked herself. "Doesn't it trouble him to see the Count coming to my home and courting me as he does? Is it his confidence in my fidelity and my love? Or is it his confidence in his power over me? Is it mere indifference? Does he or does he not love me?" She began to grow exasperated. Her lord and master was torturing her heart.

The unfortunate woman persisted in trying to provoke her husband's jealousy as if it were the touchstone of his love; but she did not succeed.

"Do you want to accompany me to the Count's?" she would ask.

"What for?"

"For tea."

"For tea? I have no bellyache. In my time, where I come from, nobody drank that bilgewater except when he had a bellyache. May it agree with you! And do your best to console the poor Count a little. I suppose the Countess will be there with her latest flame. That's fine society!"

Meanwhile, the Count continued to beseige Julia. He pretended to suffer from his domestic misfortunes in order to arouse his friend's compassion and, through her compassion, to lead her into love, into illegitimate love. At the same time he sought to make her understand that he was also somewhat aware of the little troubles in her own household.

"Yes, Julia, it's true; my house is hell, a real hell!—you do right to pity me as you do. Ah! if we had only known each other sooner! Before I had joined myself to my misfortune. And before you . . ."

"And I to mine, you mean to say?"

"No, no, that's not what I meant . . ."

"Well, what was it that you intended to say, Count?"

"Before you had given yourself to this other man, to your husband . . . ."

"And are you so certain then that I would have given myself to you?"

"Oh, of course, beyond a doubt."

"How insolent you men are!"

"Insolent?"

"Yes, insolent. I suppose you think you're irresistible?"

"I?"

"Well who then?"

"Will you allow me to say something to you, Julia?"

"You may say anything you wish."

"Well, then, it is not I who would have been irresistible, but my love. Yes, my love!"

"But is this a formal proposal, Count? Don't forget that I am a married woman, virtuous and in love with my husband . . . ."

"Oh! as to that . . ."

"Do you presume to doubt it? Yes, I am in love, just what you hear—sincerely in love with my husband . . . ."

"But, as for him . . ."

"What do you mean? Who has told you he doesn't love me?"

"You yourself."

"I? When did I tell you that Alejandro does not love me? When?"

"You have told me so with your eyes, with your gestures, with your bearing."

"Now I see that I have been encouraging you to make love to me. Take care, Count, this visit is the last one you will pay me."

"For God's sake, Julia!"

"Yes, that's final, the very last one!"

"For God's sake, Julia! Let me come to see you in silence. Just let me look at you and let me dry, as I behold you, the tears I shed within me . . . ."

"How nice!"

"And as for what I said to you that seemed to offend you so . . ."

"That seemed to? It did offend me . . . ."

"Could I offend you?"

"Why, sir!"

"What I said to you that offended you so was only this: That if we had only met—I, before I had delivered myself into my wife's hands and you into your husband's—I should have loved you as madly as I love you now. Let me bare my heart to you! I should have loved you as madly as I love you now. My love would have won your love. Julia, I am not one of those men who seek to conquer and dominate a woman by their own worth—for what they are—who demand that they be loved without giving their affection in turn. You won't find such pride in my make-up."

Julia was absorbing the poison drop by drop.

"There are some men," continued the Count, "who are incapable of loving but who demand that they be loved and who think they have the right to the affection and absolute fidelity of the poor woman who has yielded herself to them. They select a woman who is famous for her beauty in order to glorify themselves and lead her along beside them like a tame lioness. 'Look at my lioness,' they exclaim: 'you see how she has been conquered by me'! And that's why they love their lionesses."

"Count, Count! You are entering upon a subject . . ."

The Count of Bordaviella drew still nearer, almost to her ear. He made her feel the tremor of his gasping breath against the lovely shell of pink flesh that lay among those shimmering locks of auburn hair, as he whispered:

"Julia, it is your soul I am entering."

His familiar "thou" made the guilty ear blush.

Julia's bosom rose and fell like the ocean at the approach of a storm.

"Yes, Julia, I'm entering your soul!"

"Leave me alone, for Heaven's sake leave me alone! What if he should come in!"

"He won't come in. He is not interested in anything you do. He leaves us here alone like this because he doesn't love you . . . . No, no, he doesn't love you, he doesn't love you, Julia, he doesn't love you!"

"It is because he has absolute confidence in me . . . ."

"In you? No, in himself. He has an absolute, blind faith in himself! He thinks that he, because he is what he is—Alejandro Gómez, the man who made his own fortune, I won't say how—he thinks that he could not be deceived by a woman. He despises me—I know!"

"Yes, he despises you . . . ."

"I knew it! But he despises you just as much as he despises me."

"For Heaven's sake keep quiet. You are killing me . . . ."

"He is the one who will kill you—he, your husband. And you won't be the first one, either!"

"That is an infamy, Count, an infamy! My husband did not

kill his wife! Go away from here; go away and don't ever return!"

"I'll go, but I shall come back. You will send for me."

With this he took his departure, leaving her wounded to the very heart.

"Can this man have spoken the truth?" she asked herself. "Can it be so? He revealed to me what I did not wish to confess even to myself. Can it be true that Alejandro despises me? Can it be true that he does not love me?"

Rumors were beginning to be spread among the scandalmongers of the capital concerning Julia's relations with the Count of Bordaviella. Alejandro didn't hear anything of them, or else he pretended not to. He cut short the veiled insinuations which a friend had begun to make to him by saying: "I know what you are going to tell me. But stop; these tales are but idle gossip. One must let romantic women interest themselves." Could he—could he be a coward?

But one day at the Casino when someone in front of him had taken the liberty of making an ambiguous jest with a double meaning about horns, he picked up a bottle and hurled it at the man's head. A terrible scandal had resulted.

"To me—to me he comes with such jokes!" he exclaimed in his most restrained tone of voice. "As if I did not understand him! As if I didn't know the idiotic things that are passed around, among busy-bodies, concerning my poor wife's romantic whims! I am determined to tear these unfounded stories up by the roots . . . ."

"But not like that, Don Alejandro," someone ventured to tell him.

"How then? Tell me how."

"You would do better to destroy the cause of the tales."

"Oh! indeed. By closing my door to the Count?"

"That would be the wiser course."

"But that would be justifying the slanderers. Besides I am not a tyrant. If this puppet of a Count amuses my poor wife, am I going to deprive her of the distraction afforded by this idiot who is—I swear—a thorough simpleton, an inoffensive nonentity who's trying to play the role of a Don Juan—merely because the other idiots will say this or that about it? Well, that's the last straw! Fancy my wife deceiving me! Me! You don't know me."

"But Don Alejandro . . . . ?"

"I live by realities and not appearances!"

The following day two very serious looking gentlemen presented themselves at Alejandro's home to demand satisfaction of him in the name of the insulted man.

"Tell him," he said to them, "to send me his doctor's or his surgeon's bill; I will pay it as well as whatever other damages there may have been."

"But Don Alejandro . . ."

"Well, what do you want?"

"We ask nothing. But the offended party demands reparation . . . some satisfaction . . . an honorable explanation . . . ."

"I don't understand you. . . or rather I don't care to understand."

"And if not, then he demands a duel."

"Very well. Whenever he wishes. But it is quite unneccessary for you to bother about arrangements. We have no need of seconds. Just tell him that he can notify me when his head is better—I mean when he has recovered from the bottle-blow; we will go anywhere he wishes, lock ourselves in a room and settle this affair properly with our bare fists. I agree to no other weapons. He'll see who Alejandro Gómez is."

"But you are making fun of us, Don Alejandro," cried one of the seconds.

"Not at all. You are of one world, I of another. You come from illustrious fathers—from aristocratic families . . . . As for me I have only the one family I have made for myself. I come from nothing at all and I don't want to hear about such hypocrisies as a code of honor. So there, you know my stand."

The seconds rose to their feet and one of them, very gravely and with a certain emphasis, but not wholly disrespectfully (for after all this person was an influential millionaire and a man of mysterious birth), exclaimed:

"In this case, Senor Don Alejandro Gómez, allow me to tell you . . ."

"Say anything you want, but be careful of your words, for I have another bottle handy."

"Then, Senor Don Alejandro Gómez," he said raising his voice, "you are not a gentleman."

"Why, of course not; of course I'm not a gentleman. I, a gentleman? Since when? How? I was brought up an asskeeper and not a gentleman! And I didn't even bring lunch to the man who called himself my father, riding upon a donkey, but walking on foot. Of course I'm no gentleman. Gentlemanliness and me—come now, how absurd!"

"Let's leave," said the other witness, "we have nothing further to do here. And as for you, Senor Don Alejandro, you will have to stand the consequences of your unspeakable conduct."

"Certainly, I await them. And as for that—that gentleman with a loose tongue whose skull I have fractured—tell him, I repeat it, to send me the doctor's bill and in the future to be careful of what he says. And you two, for anything can happen, if one day you find yourselves in need of this savage and incomprehensible millionaire, a savage who has no code of honor, you can turn to me for assistance and I will serve you as I have served and still do serve other gentlemen."

"This is unbearable! Let's leave!"

With these words the seconds made their departure.

That same night Alejandro told his wife about the scene he had had with the two seconds, after having explained to her the affair of the bottle. He amused himself greatly in telling about his adventure. She listened to what he had to say with terror.

"I, a gentleman! Alejandro Gómez! Never! I am only a man, but I am a real man."

"And what about me?" she asked, in order to say something.

"You? You are a real woman. A woman who reads novels. And he, the little Count, who plays chess with you, is a nobody, less than a nobody. Why should I forbid you to amuse yourself with him as you might with a little lap-dog? If you were to purchase one of those fuzzy little dogs, or an angora cat, or a little pet monkey, and you were to pet and even kiss it, would I then take the little dog, or the cat or the pet monkey and throw it out of the window? That would be a clever thing to do, especially when it might fall on the head of some passer-by! Well, it's the same with that Count, another little puppy or kitten or monkey as he is! Amuse yourself with him as much as you please!"

"But, Alejandro, they are right about what they say; you must close your house to this man . . . ."

"Man, did you say?"

"As you like. But you should close your door to the Count of Bordaviella."

"Why don't you? As long as you don't there's precious little he has won in your heart. For if you had begun to take an interest in him you would have sent him away just to protect yourself!"

"And what if I were interested in him?"

"That's a good one! Here we are back at the same point again. You want to make me jealous! Me! When will you realize that I am not like other men?"

As time passed Julia understood her husband less and less, but he fascinated her more and more, and she felt more anxious than ever to know if he really loved her or not. On the other hand, Alejandro, although he felt fully reassured as to his wife's fidelity or rather as to the impossibility of his wife's—Alejandro's wife—deceiving him, a real man! began to say to himself: "This life here in the capital and all these novels she reads is turning my poor wife's head." He therefore decided to take her away to the country and so they departed for one of their estates.

"A short stay in the country will do you a lot of good," he said to her. "It calms one's nerves. Furthermore, if you are afraid of being bored without having your little monkey you can invite him to accompany us. Because now you know that I am not jealous. I am very sure of you, of my wife."

But poor Julia's anxiety only increased in the country. She was frightfully bored. Her husband would not allow her to read.

"I brought you here to take you away from your books and to cure you of your neurasthenia before it became worse."

"My neurasthenia?"

"Why, yes! That's all that's the matter with you. It comes from the books you read."

"Then I will never read any more of them."

"I don't ask that of you . . . I demand nothing. Am I some kind of a tyrant? Have I ever exacted anything of you?"

"No, you don't even demand that I love you."

"Naturally, when that's something it would be impossible to demand! And besides, I know that you love me and that it is impossible for you to love anyone else . . . . Since you have known me and learned, thanks to me, what a real man is like, you are quite incapable of loving another man even if you set out to. But enough of this book-talk. I have told you that I don't like novels. They're just the thing to serve as the topic of conversation with little Counts over the tea-table."

Julia's suffering increased when she discovered that her husband was involved in a common love affair with a coarse servant girl who was not even pretty. One night when they were alone together after dinner, Julia suddenly said to him:

"Don't think, Alejandro, that I have not noticed your affair with Simona."

"Nor have I tried to conceal it. But it is of no importance. Chicken every day . . . ."

"What do you mean by that?"

"That you are much too beautiful for daily use."

His wife trembled. It was the first time that her husband had ever referred to her openly as beautiful. Could he possibly love her?

"But," said Julia, "with that bundle of rags!"

"For that very reason! Her dirtiness amuses me. Don't forget that I was brought up in a sort of pig pen and that I am fairly susceptible to what one of my friends calls the voluptuousness of dirt. And now, after a taste of this little rustic appetizer I shall appreciate all the more your beauty, your elegance and your refinement."

"I hardly know whether you are flattering or insulting me."

"There now! Your neurasthenia again! And I had thought you were improving!"

"Of course, you men can gratify your every whim and deceive us . . . ."

"Who has deceived you?"

"You!"

"Do you call that deceiving you? Bah! Books . . . books! I wouldn't give a pin for Simona . . . ."

"Of course not. She is nothing more than a little puppy, a little kitten or a pet monkey to you!"

"Yes, a pet monkey, that's it. Nothing more than a pet monkey. That's what she looks like most! You certainly named her well: a monkey! But does that mean that I have ceased to be your husband?"

"You mean that I have not ceased to be your wife because of this affair . . . ."

"I see, Julia, you are getting clever . . . ."

"One acquires everything in time."

"From me, of course, and not from your little pet monkey."

"Of course, from you."

"Good, I can't believe that this little rustic incident is going to make you jealous. You, jealous! You, my wife! And of this she-monkey? As for her, I give her a dowry and that's the end!"

"Of course, when one is wealthy . . ."

"And with this dowry she'll get married in a jiffy and present her husband with a boy along with her dowry. And should the boy resemble his father, who is a real man, it will be a double gain for her sweetheart."

"Be still! Be still!" and poor Julia burst into tears.

"I thought," concluded Alejandro, "that country life had cured you of your neurasthenia. Be careful or it will get worse!"

Two days later they returned to their city residence.

Julia resumed her suffering and the Count of Bordaviella resumed his visits, although with greater prudence than before. It was finally Julia who, exasperated, began to listen to the venomous insinuations of her friend and especially to make a show of this friendship before her husband who limited himself to a single warning: "We will have to return to the country and submit you to treatment."

One day, exasperated beyond all endurance, Julia attacked her husband, saying:

"You're not a man, Alejandro, no; you're not a man!"

"What's that! I? And why not?"

"No, you're not a man, you're not!"

"Explain yourself."

"Now I know that you don't love me, that nothing that concerns me interests you, that to you I am not even the mother of your child and that you only married me out of vanity to boast of it, to exhibit me, to exalt yourself by my beauty, to . . ."

"Well, well, that's more literature. Why am I not a man?"

"Now I know that you don't love me."

"I've told you a hundred times already that all this talk about loving and not loving, about love and all that nonsense, is conversation fit for some Count's tea-table."

"Now I know that you don't love me."

"Well, what else?"

"But your consenting that the Count—the monkey, as you call him—should enter here whenever he pleases . . ."

"You are the one who consents to that."

"And why shouldn't I consent to it, if he is my lover? You heard me, my lover: that monkey is my lover!"

Alejandro remained impassive, looking at his wife. The latter expecting an outburst of rage from the man, became more excited than before and shouted at him:

"Well, what? Aren't you going to kill me now as you did the other woman?"

"It is not true that I killed the other woman and it is equally untrue that that monkey is your lover. You are lying to me in order to provoke me. You want to make an Othello out of me and my home is not a theater. Furthermore, if you continue this way, you will end by becoming insane and we shall have to lock you up."

"Insane? Me—insane?"

"Absolutely! Fancy reaching the point of believing she has a lover! That is to say, trying to make me believe it! As if my wife could deceive me! Me! Alejandro Gómez is no monkey. He's a real man! But you won't succeed in your ambition, you won't succeed in having me tickle your ears with story-book words and expressions fit for a Count's tea-table conversations. My home is not a theater."

"Coward, coward, coward that you are!" screamed Julia, quite beyond herself.

"We shall have to use special measures." retorted her husband. And he went off.

Two days after this scene, after having kept his wife under lock and key, Alejandro summoned her to his study. Poor Julia was terrified. She found her husband awaiting her in his office with the Count of Bordaviella and two other gentlemen.

"Listen, Julia," said her husband with a terrible calm, "these two gentlemen are alienists who have come here at my request to examine your case in order that we may be able to give you the proper treatment. You are not very well mentally; doubtless you are aware of this during your moments of lucidity."

"And what are you doing here, Juan?" Julia asked the Count without noticing her husband.

"You see?" exclaimed the latter, turning toward the doctors. "She persists in her hallucination. She insists on imagining that this gentleman is . . ."

"Yes, he is my lover!" she broke in. "If it is not true, then let him deny it."

The Count looked fixedly at the floor.

"You see, Count, how she persists in her madness." said Alejandro to Bordaviella. "Indeed you have never had—you could not have had any relationship of this nature with my wife . . . ."

"Of course not!" cried the Count.

"You see how it is?" continued Alejandro, addressing the doctors.

"But how do you dare, Juan, you, my darling, deny that I have belonged to you?" cried Julia.

The Count trembled beneath Alejandro's frigid gaze and he replied:

"Control yourself, Señora. You know quite well that if I frequented your house it was solely as your friend, Señora, yours and your husband's, and also that I, a Count of Bordaviella, could never have offended a friend such as . . ."

"Such a friend as I am," interrupted Alejandro. "I! I? Alejandro Gómez! No Count could offend me, any more than my wife could betray me. So you see, gentlemen, the poor woman is insane."

"And you, too, Juan, you too, my darling!" she cried. "Coward, coward that you are! My husband has threatened you and because you're afraid, you coward, you don't dare tell the truth, and so you're lending your aid to this infamous farce to declare me insane! Coward! Coward! Villain—you, yes, and my husband, too!"

"You see, gentlemen?" said Alejandro to the doctors.

Poor Julia was overcome by a nervous fit and fainted dead away.

"And now, my dear sir," said Alejandro to the Count, "we shall leave the room and allow these two excellent doctors to finish their consultation alone with my poor wife."

The Count followed him. When they were out of the room Alejandro said to him:

"So then you thoroughly understand, Count, either my wife is declared insane or I will blow out your brains and hers, too. It is up to you to decide."

"The thing for me to do is to pay you what I owe in order to have no further dealings with you."

"No! What you owe me is to keep your mouth shut. So we have decided—my wife is raving mad and you are the worst of idiots. And—beware of this!" And he showed him a revolver.

When a few minutes later, the two alienists left Alejandro's study, they were saying to each other:

"This is a horrible tragedy. What shall we do?"

"What shall we do but declare her insane? Otherwise this man will kill her and this poor Count as well."

"But what of our professional duty?"

"Our duty in this instance is to prevent a greater crime."

"Would it not be better to declare Don Alejandro crazy?"

"No, he is not crazy; something else is the matter with him."

"Every inch a man, as he says."

"Poor woman! It was horrible to listen to her. What I fear is that she will end by really going crazy."

"Well, by declaring her so, perhaps we shall save her. At any rate, we shall remove her from this house."

Consequently they did declare her insane, and, on the strength of this declaration, her husband had her shut up in a madhouse.

A starless night, dense, gloomy and cold settled upon Julia's soul when she found herself locked up in the madhouse. Her only consolation was that they brought her son to see her almost every day. She would gather him in her arms and bathe his little face with her tears. And the poor little boy, although he did not understand why, would cry with her too.

"Oh, my baby, my dear little baby!" she would say to him, "if I could only drain from you all your father's blood! Because he's your father!"

And when she was alone, the poor woman, feeling herself on the verge of insanity, would say: "But won't I end up by really going mad in this place and by convincing myself that my whole affair with this infamous Count was merely a dream and an hallucination? Ah! the coward, yes, the coward that he is! To abandon me like this! To allow them to shut me up in this place! Oh! the little monkey—the little monkey! My husband was right! And why didn't Alejandro kill us both? Ah, no! This is a more terrible vengeance! Why should he kill that cowardly monkey! No, indeed, far better to humiliate him and force him to lie and abandon me. He trembled in my husband's presence, he trembled before him. It is because my husband is a man! And why didn't he kill me? Othello would have killed me! But Alejandro is not an Othello; he is not such a brute as Othello. Othello was an impetuous Moor, but not very clever. Alejandro has a powerful mind with which to serve his infernal plebeian pride. No! This man didn't have to kill his first wife, he made her die. She died of pure fright at his presence. And me . . . ? Does he really love me?"

Here, in this madhouse, she began once more to wring her heart and torture her mind with the painful dilemma: "Does he love me —or doesn't he?" Then she would say to herself: "As for me, I love him madly!"

Finally, through fear of really going crazy, she pretended to be cured by assuring them that her love affair with Bordaviella had only been an hallucination. Her husband was informed of this.

One day they summoned Julia to the sitting room, where her husband was waiting for her. She threw herself at his feet, sobbing:

"Forgive me, Alejandro, forgive me!"

"Get up, Julia," he said, assisting her to her feet.

"Forgive me!"

"Forgive you? Forgive you for what? They have told me that you are cured, that you do not have any more of these hallucinations . . . ."

Julia observed with terror her husband's cold and penetrating eyes. She was overcome by a mad and blind love, founded upon an equally blind terror.

"You are quite right, Alejandro, you are quite right. I have been quite crazy, absolutely crazy. And to make you jealous, just to make you jealous, I invented all those stories. But they were nothing but lies. Indeed, how could I have deceived you! I, you? Do you believe me now?"

"Once, Julia," said her husband in an icy voice, "you asked me if it were true that I had killed my first wife and I in turn asked you whether you could believe it. What was it that you told me?"

"That I didn't believe it; that I couldn't believe it."

"Well, then, I now say to you that I have never believed—that I could not believe, that you had given yourself to that little monkey. Does this suffice you?"

Julia was trembling, she felt herself on the brink of madness—of mad terror and love combined.

"And now," added the poor woman, kissing her husband and whispering in his ear, "now, Alejandro, do tell me, do you love me?"

Then the poor woman saw in Alejandro for the first time something that she had never seen before she discovered the depths of the terrible and reticent soul which this wealthy, self-made man had kept jealously concealed. It was as though a flash of tempestuous light had for an instant illuminated the black, tenebrous lake of that soul and had caused its surface to shimmer. It was that she saw two teardrops in this man's cold eyes as piercing as daggers. Then he burst forth:

"Do I love you, my dear child, do I love you! I love you with all my soul, with all my blood and with all my being, more than my own self! At first when we were married I didn't. But now? Now I love you blindly—wildly! I am yours more than you are mine."

And, kissing her with bestial fury, feverishly, deliriously, like a madman, he exclaimed brokenly: "Julia! Julia! my goddess, my everything!"

She thought that she would go mad again at the sight of her husband's naked soul.

"Now I should like to die, Alejandro," she murmured in his ear, letting her head fall upon his shoulder.

At these words the man seemed to arouse himself and shake himself from a dream; and, as if his eyes, which were again cold and piercing, had swallowed their tears, he said:

"This has not happened, Julia. Do you understand? Now you know everything; but I have not said what I said . . . Forget it."

"Forget it?"

"Well, remember it then, but as if you had never heard it!"

"I will be silent."

"You must not repeat it even to your own self."

"I will not, but . . ."

"That will do."

"But for your sake, Alejandro, let me continue for a moment . . . only one moment . . . . Do you love me for my own self, just for what I am, even if I belonged to another man? Or is it just because I am something that belongs to you?"

"I have told you that you must forget what I said to you. If you insist, I shall leave you here. I have come to take you away, but you must leave here entirely cured."

"And I am cured!" his wife affirmed vehemently.

Alejandro took his wife home.

A few days after Julia's return from the sanatorium the Count of Bordaviella received from Alejandro what was not only an invitation, but a command as well, to come and take dinner at his house. This was the letter:

As you must know, my dear Count, my wife has left the sanatorium completely cured; and as the poor woman offended you gravely during her delirium—though no offense was intended—by supposing you capable of committing an infamy of which, being the perfect gentleman that you are, you were, of course, utterly incapable. I invite you to take dinner with us the day after tomorrow, Thursday, for I very much desire to give to such a gentleman as you the full satisfaction that you are entitled to. My wife begs you to come and I order you to. For should you not come on that day to receive these apologies and explanations you will suffer the consequences. And you know what I am capable of.

Alejandro Gómez

The Count of Bordaviella kept the appointment. He was pale, trembling and quite overcome. The dinner was accompanied by the most depressing conversation. They spoke of the greatest frivolities, in the presence of servants, along with the most suggestive and ferocious of Alejandro's jokes. Julia followed her husband's example. After the dessert Alejandro turned to a servant and said: "Bring in the tea."

"Tea!" escaped from the Count's mouth.

"Why certainly, my dear Count," replied the master of the house. "Not that I have a bellyache, no it's merely to preserve the proper tone. Tea goes very well with explanations between gentlemen . . . ."

Then he turned to the servant and said: "You may go."

The three of them were left alone. The Count was trembling. He did not dare to taste the tea.

"Serve me first, Julia," said her husband. "I will drink first, Count, so as to show you that one can take tea in my house with perfect confidence."

"But I . . ."

"No, Count; although I am not a gentleman, or even less than that, I have not fallen so low. And now my wife wishes to offer you a few explanations."

Alejandro glanced at Julia, and she, very slowly, began to speak in a ghastly voice. She was gloriously beautiful. Her eyes scintillated like lightning flashes. Her words flowed coldly and slowly, but one could fathom that a devouring flame burned beneath them:

"I had my husband invite you here, Count," Julia began, "because I owe you an explanation for having gravely offended you."

"Me, Julia?"

"Don't call me Julia. Yes, you. When I became mad, when I fell madly in love with my husband and was constantly seeking to discover if he really loved me or not, I attempted to accuse you of having seduced me. This was a jealousy and, due to my madness, I was led to accuse you of having seduced me. This was a lie and it would have been but pure infamy on my part had I not been insane. Is this not true, Count?"

"Indeed, it is, Doña Julia . . . ."

"Señora de Gómez," corrected Alejandro.

"You must forgive us for what I accused you of when my husband and I called you the 'little monkey.' "

"You are excused."

"What I accused you of at that time was a low and infamous act, quite unworthy of such a gentleman as you."

"That's well put," added Alejandro, "very well put. 'A low and infamous act unworthy of a gentleman.' Well put!"

"I repeat again, although I can and really should be excused on account of my condition at that time, nevertheless I ask your pardon. Do you forgive me?"

"Yes, yes, I forgive you, I forgive you both." breathed the Count, more dead than alive, and anxious to escape as soon as possible from this house.

"Us both?" interrupted Alejandro. "You have nothing to forgive me for."

"That's true . . . quite true!"

"Come now, calm yourself," said the husband. "I see that you are very nervous. Take another cup of tea. Julia, serve the Count. Would you like to have a bit of linden juice in it?"

"No, no . . ."

"Well, now that my wife has told you what she had to say to you, and that you have forgiven her for her madness, there only remains for me to beg you to be kind enough to honor our house with your visits. After what has occurred you will certainly understand that it would have very bad effects were we to sever our relations. Now that my wife, thanks to the care I have given her, is completely cured, you run no further risk in coming here. And to prove to you the confidence I have in the complete recovery of my wife, I shall leave you here alone; for she might have something to say to you which she does not dare to speak of in front of me, or which delicacy does not permit me to hear."

Alejandro left the room, leaving them facing each other and equally surprised by his conduct.

"What a man!" thought the Count.

"He, indeed, is a man!" said Julia to herself.

A heavy silence followed his departure. Julia and the Count did not dare to look at each other. Bordaviella glanced at the door by which the husband had left.

"Don't look at the door that way," said Julia. "You don't know my husband. He is not hiding behind the door to eavesdrop."

"How do I know he is not? He is capable of having brought witnesses along."

"Why do you say that, Count?"

"Do you think that I have forgotten the day when he brought two doctors along to take part in that scene in which he humiliated me as much as he possibly could and committed the crime of having them declare you insane!"

"But it was the truth. If I had not been mad at the time I would never have said, as I did, that you were my lover."

"But . . ."

"But what . . . Count!"

"Do you too want to declare me insane? Do you mean to say, Julia, that you are going to deny . . . !"

"Doña Julia, or Señora de Gómez if you please!"

"Do you mean to say, Señora de Gómez, that, for one reason or another, you did not eventually accept my advances . . . not my advances, but my love?"

"Count!"

"That you finally not only accepted them but became the party who encouraged them and that . . ."

"I have told you, Count, that I was insane. Must I continue repeating this?"

"Do you deny that I was your lover?"

"I repeat to you again that I was insane."

"I cannot remain another instant in this house! Good-by!"

The Count held out his hand to Julia fearing that she would refuse it. But she took it in hers and said to him:

"Now, then, you know what my husband said. You can come here whenever you wish, now that I am, thanks to God and to Alejandro, completely cured, cured of everything, Count. It would have a bad effect were you to stop your visits."

"But, Julia!"

"What! Are you going to begin again? Haven't I told you that I was insane?"

"I am the one you and your husband are going to drive crazy . . ."

"You? Drive you crazy! That doesn't strike me as being an easy thing to do . . . ."

"That's evident, you call me 'little monkey!'"

Julia burst out laughing. Ashamed and furious, the Count left the house with the firm resolution never to return.

All these spiritual torments shattered poor Julia's life and she became seriously ill; mentally deranged. Now she seemed to be really going mad. She frequently had spells of delirium during which she would call for her husband in the most ardent and passionate words. The man would abandon himself to the painful transports of his wife endeavoring to calm her. "I am yours, yours, all yours," he would whisper in her ear while she, clinging to his neck, would fairly strangle him in her grasp.

He took her away to one of his estates, hoping that the country life would cure her. But the disease was slowly killing her. Something terrible had entered the depths of her being.

When this wealthy man finally realized that death was going to take his wife from him, he was overcome by a cold and obstinate fury. He summoned the very best doctors. "All is hopeless," they would say to him.

"Save her for me," he would answer.

"It is quite impossible, Don Alejandro, quite impossible."

"Save her, I tell you! I will sacrifice all my wealth, all my millions to have her life!"

"It is impossible, Don Alejandro."

"Then I will give my life for hers! Can't you make a blood transfusion? Take all mine and give it to her. Come now, take mine."

"It is impossible, Don Alejandro, quite impossible."

"What do you mean—impossible? I will give all my blood for her, I say!"

"Only God can save her."

"God! Where is God? I have never thought of Him."

Then to Julia, his wife, who was pale but more beautiful than ever—beautiful with the beauty of approaching death—he would say:

"Julia, where is God?" She, looking upwards with her large, blank eyes would say in a low voice:

"He is there . . . ."

Alejandro looked at the crucifix that hung at the head of his wife's bed, he took it down and crushing it in his fist he would exclaim: "Save her for me, save her for me and ask me anything, anything, my entire fortune, all my blood, all myself . . . ." Julia would look at him and smile. Her husband's blind fury filled her soul with a very sweet light. At last she was really happy! How had she ever doubted that this man loved her?

Life was ebbing from this poor woman drop by drop. She was as cold as marble. Then her husband lay down beside her and embraced her passionately. He wanted to give her all his warmth for the warmth that was leaving her body. He wanted to give her his very breath. He was half crazy. And always she smiled.

"I am dying, Alejandro, I am dying."

"No, you are not dying," he would say to her. "You can't possibly die."

"It isn't possible for your wife to die, is it?"

"No, my wife can't die. I would rather die myself. We'll see, let death come, let it come to me! Let death come to me! Let it come!"

"Oh! Alejandro, I know now that I have not suffered in vain! And to think that I doubted your love!"

"No, I did not love you, no! I have told you a thousand times, Julia, that these foolish love-words are nothing but literary rubbish. No, I did not love you! Love, love! And to think that all these wretches, these cowards who talk about love, allow their wives to die! No, that is not love. I don't love you . . . ."

"Well, what then?" she demanded in a very faint voice, seized again by her former dread.

"No, I don't love you . . . I, I, I . . . There is no word!" And he burst into long, tearless sobs like the gasps of death—the agonized moan of suffering and savage love.

"Alejandro!"

In this one feeble cry was all the sorrowful joy of triumph.

"You are not going to die! You can't die; I don't want you to die! Kill me, Julia, but you must live! Come, kill me!"

"Yes, I am dying . . . ."

"And I with you! . . ."

"What of the child, Alejandro?"

"Let him die, too! Why should I love him without you?"

"For God's sake, Alejandro, you are mad . . . ."

"Yes, I am the one who is mad. I have always been mad, mad because of you, Julia, crazy about you . . . I, the mad-man . . . . Kill me, Julia, and take me with you!"

"If I only could . . ."

"No, no! Kill me, but you must live. Belong to yourself!"

"And you?"

"Me? If I cannot belong to you, I will be death's!"

He pressed her still closer to him, as if to hold her forever.

"Won't you tell me now who you are, Alejandro?" whispered Julia in his ear.

"I? Oh, just a man—the man you have made of me."

This word sounded like a murmur from beyond death, as if come from the shores of life as the craft is sailing off into shadowy waters beyond.

Soon Alejandro felt that his strong arms were holding only a lifeless form. The deathly cold of the great final night seemed to settle upon his soul. He got up and looked at the now rigid and lifeless beauty. He had never seen her look more beautiful. She seemed to be bathed in the radiance of that light filtering down from the eternal dawn which follows after the final night. Greater even than his remembrance of this flesh now cold he sensed his whole life passing before him like an icy cloud; this life of his which he had hidden from everyone—even from himself. He even went back over the years as far as his terrible childhood, to the time when he trembled beneath the pitiless blows dealt by the man who called himself his father; back to the time when he had cursed at him, and when, one late afternoon, exasperated beyond all endurance, he had shaken his fist at a figure of the Christ in his little village church.

He finally left the room, closing the door behind him, and went in search of his child. The little boy was scarcely more than three years old. The father took him in his arms and shut himself in with him. He began kissing him frantically and the child, who was not accustomed to his father's kisses, who, indeed, had never received a single kiss from him, and who possibly guessed the savage passion flooding his breast, began to weep.

"Keep quiet, my child, keep quiet. Will you forgive me what I am about to do? Will you forgive me?"

Terrified, the child remained quiet. He looked at his father who was seeking in his eyes, mouth and curls for the eyes, mouth and curls of his lost Julia.

"Forgive me, my child, forgive me!"

He closeted himself alone for an instant in order to set down his final wishes, and then he returned to his wife—or to what had once been his wife.

"My blood for yours," Alejandro said to her as if she could have heard him. "Death has taken you away and now I am going to come and get you!" For an instant he imagined that he saw his wife smile and that she moved her eyes. He began to embrace her, to call her and to whisper terrifying words of tenderness in her ear. But she was quite cold.

When later on, they had to break down the door of the death chamber, they found him with his arms around his wife. He was pale and deathly cold and bathed in the blood that had been drained completely from him.

Juan Manso:
A Dead Man's Tale

And now for a story.

While he was on this wicked earth Juan Manso was a simple soul, a harmless fellow who during his whole life had never hurt a fly. As a child, when he played donkey with his friends, he was always the donkey. Later, his comrades confided in him about their love affairs, and when he grew to full manhood his acquaintances still used to greet him with an affectionate "Hello, little Johnny!"

His favorite maxim was from the Chinese: "Never commit yourself, and stick to the person who can help you the most."

He loathed politics, hated business, and avoided everything that might upset the even tenor of his ways.

He lived on a small income which he spent in its entirety without ever touching the capital. He was quite devout, would never contradict anyone, and as he had a bad opinion of everybody he spoke well of them.

If you mentioned politics to him he would say: "I'm nothing— neither one side nor the other: I don't care which party runs the government. I'm just a poor sinner who wants to live at peace with everyone."

His meekness, however, was of no avail against the finality of death. It was the only definite thing he ever did in his life.

Reprinted with permission of Barron's Educational Series, Inc., from *Classic Tales from Modern Spain*, translated by William E. Colford. Copyright 1964 by Barron's Educational Series, Inc.

An angel armed with a great flaming sword was sorting out souls according to the sign made upon them as they went by an enrollment desk which they had to pass as they departed from this world and went through a kind of immigration control where angels and devils were sitting side by side in friendly fashion examining documents to see if they were all in order.

The entrance to the registration room looked like the scene outside the box office on the day of a big bullfight. There were so many people milling around, pushing and shoving, with everyone in such a hurry to learn his fate, and such was the hubbub raised by the curses, entreaties, insults and excuses in the thousands of languages, dialects and jargons of this world, that Juan Manso said to himself:

"Who says I have to get mixed up in all this? There must be some very rough characters around here."

He said this *sotto voce,* so no one could hear him. The fact is that the angel with the great flaming sword paid not the slightest attention to him, so he was able to slip past and start on his way to Heaven.

He walked along very quietly all by himself. From time to time happy groups would pass by, chanting litanies; some were dancing wildly, which seemed to him not quite a proper thing for the blessed to be doing on their way up to Heaven. When he reached the heights he found a long line of people standing beside the walls of Paradise, and a few angels keeping order like policemen on earth. Juan Manso got on the very end of the line.

Shortly a humble Franciscan friar came along, and he was so clever in advancing pathetic arguments as to why he was in such a hurry to get inside right away that Juan Manso gave him his place in line, saying to himself:

"It's a good idea to make friends for yourself even in Heaven."

The next man to come along, though not a Franciscan, wanted the same privilege, and the same thing happened. In short, there wasn't a pious soul who did not trick Juan Manso out of his place; his reputation for meekness ran along the whole line, and was handed down as a continuing tradition among the constantly-changing crowd there. And Juan Manso stayed where he was, the prisoner of his own good reputation.

Centuries went by—or so it seemed to Juan Manso, for it took that much time for the meek little lamb to begin to lose his patience. Finally one day he happened to meet a wise and saintly bishop who turned out to be the great-great-grandson of one of Manso's brothers. Juan voiced his complaints to his great-great-grandnephew, and the wise and saintly bishop offered to intercede for him when he came before the Eternal Father. On the strength of this, Juan yielded his place to the wise and saintly bishop who, when he entered Heaven, quite properly went straight to the Eternal Father to pay Him his respects. He concluded his little talk with The Almighty, who listened absent-mindedly and said:

"Wasn't there something else you wanted to say?"

And with His glance He searched the depths of the bishop's heart.

"Lord, permit me to intercede for one of Thy servants who is out there at the very tip end of the line . . . . "

"Don't beat about the bush," thundered The Lord. "You mean Juan Manso."

"Yes, Lord, he is the one; Juan Manso, who . . . . "

"All right! All right! Let him look out for himself, and don't you get mixed up again in other people's affairs!" And turning to the angel who was introducing souls, He added: "Let the next one in!"

If anything is capable of marring the eternal happiness of a soul in everlasting bliss, we could say that the soul of the wise and saintly bishop was troubled. But at least, moved by pity, he went to Heaven's walls, next to which the long line was standing. He climbed up, and calling to Juan Manso he said:

"Great-great-uncle, how sad I am about this—how very sad, my dear man! The Lord told me that you should look out for yourself, and that I shouldn't get mixed up in other people's affairs again. But . . . are you still at the end of the line? Come now, my dear man! Summon up some courage and don't yield your place again."

"Now he tells me!" exclaimed Juan Manso, shedding tears as big as chick-peas. But it was too late, for the tragic tradition was now attached to him: people no longer even asked him for his place, they just took it.

Crestfallen, he abandoned the line and began to wander about the lonely wastelands beyond the grave until he came upon many people, all downcast, walking along a road. He followed their footsteps and found himself at the gates of Purgatory.

"It will be easier to get in here," he said to himself, "and once inside they will send me directly to Heaven after I have been purified."

"Hey! Where are you going, my friend?"

Juan Manso turned around and found himself face to face with an angel who was wearing an academic mortarboard and had a pen behind his ear. He looked at Juan over the top of his glasses, had him turn around, and after examining him from head to foot frowned and said:

"H-m-m! *Malorum causa*—the root of all ills! You are completely grey, and I'm afraid to put you through our procedures for fear you'll melt. You would do better to go to Limbo."

"To Limbo!"

Upon hearing this, Juan Manso became indignant for the first time, for no man is so patient and long-suffering that he will stand for having an angel treat him like a complete idiot.

In desperation, he set out for Hell. Here there was no waiting line, nor anything like one. It had a broad entrance, from which came puffs of thick smoke and an infernal din. At the door a poor devil was playing a hand-organ and shrieking at the top of his voice:

"Come inside, gentlemen, step inside . . . Here you will see the human comedy . . . Anyone may enter . . . . "

Juan Manso closed his eyes.

"Hey, young man! Stop!" the poor devil said to him.

"Didn't you say that anyone might enter?"

"Yes, but . . . Look," said the poor devil earnestly, as he stroked his tail, "we still have some slight spark of conscience . . . and, after all . . . you?"

"All right, all right!" said Juan Manso, turning away because he could not stand the smoke.

And he heard the devil mutter to himself, "Poor fellow!"

"Poor fellow? Even the devil pities me!"

Desperate now to the point of madness, he began to bob around like a cork in mid-ocean as he crossed the vast spaces beyond the grave. From time to time he would meet other legendary lost souls.

One day, attracted by the appetizing odor that was coming from Heaven, he approached its walls to see what they were cooking inside. It was about time for sunset, and he saw that The Lord was coming out to enjoy the cool air in the gardens of Paradise. Juan Manso waited for Him near the wall, and when he saw His noble head he opened his arms wide in supplication and said in a rather indignant tone:

"Lord, Lord, didst Thou not promise the Kingdom of Heaven to the meek?"

"Yes, but to the enterprising, not to the weak-kneed."

And He turned His back on Juan.

An old legend recounts that The Lord, taking pity on Juan Manso, let him return to this wicked world, and that when he got here again he began to push people around right and left. When he died a second time, he shoved his way right past the famous line and slipped boldly into Paradise.

Now inside, he keeps repeating:

"Man has to fight his way through life on earth!"

Selected Readings

ALLUNTIS, FELIX, O.F.M. "The Philosophical Mythology of Miguel de Unamuno." *The New Scholasticism*, XXIX (1955), 278–317.

ARTURO, BAREA. *Unamuno.* New Haven, Conn.: Yale University Press, 1952.

BLANCO AGUINAGA, CARLOS. "Unamuno's *Niebla:* Existence and the Game of Fiction." *Modern Language Notes*, LXXIX (1964), 188–205.

EARLE, PETER G. *Unamuno and English Literature.* New York: Hispanic Institute, 1960.

FERRATER MORA JOSÉ. *Unamuno: A Philosophy of Tragedy.* Berkeley, Calif.: University of California Press, 1962.

HUERTAS-JOURDA, JOSÉ. *The Existentialism of Miguel de Unamuno.* University of Florida Monograph, Humanities No. 13; Gainesville, Fla.: University of Florida Press, 1963.

MARIAS AGRULERA, JULIAN. *Miguel de Unamuno.* Trans. Frances M. Lopez-Morillas. Cambridge, Mass.: Harvard University Press, 1966.

PREDMORE, R. L. "Flesh and Spirit in the Works of Unamuno." *PMLA*, LXX (1955), 587–605.

RUDD, MARGARET THOMAS. *The Love Heretic.* Austin, Tex.: University of Texas Press, 1963.

SCHUSTER, EDWARD J. "Existentialist Resolution of Conflicts in Unamuno." *Kentucky Foreign Language Quarterly*, VIII (1961), 34–39.

SEDWICK, FRANK. "Maxims, Aphorisms, Epigrams, and Paradoxes of Unamuno." *Hispania*, XXXVIII (1955), 462–64.

VALDÉS, MARIO J. *Death in the Literature of Unamuno.* Urbana, Ill.: University of Illinois Press, 1964.

WARDROPPER, BRUCE. "Unamuno's Struggle with Words." *Hispanic Review*, XV (1944), 183–95.

YOUNG, HOWARD T. *The Victorious Expression.* Madison, Wisc:. University of Wisconsin Press, 1964.

LUIGI PIRANDELLO

(1867-1936)

The art of Luigi Pirandello could have appeared only in the twentieth century. As poet, short story writer, novelist, playwright, or essayist, Pirandello concerns himself with contemporary themes. Artists have always been concerned with truth; they have not always looked for it in the same place or in the same way. Pirandello dramatizes modern man's concept of truth as being subjective rather than objective, relative rather than absolute, created rather than discovered. For Pirandello's chief character is the twentieth-century man: alone, alienated, frustrated, nauseated, anguished. When existence becomes relative, subject to chance and random act, then life becomes absurd.

Pirandello was born in Girgenti, Sicily, of wealthy parents. He studied at the University of Rome and at Bonn University, where he received his Ph.D. After the loss of the family fortune, he taught Italian literature in Rome. In 1893, a year before he married, he published his first volume of short stories, *Love Without Love*. By 1915 he had completed many poems, essays, short stories, and novels and was turning his creative talent toward drama. He wrote the plays *Right You Are If You Think You Are* in 1917; *Six Characters in Search of a Play* in 1921; *Henry VI* in 1922; *As You Desire Me* in 1930.

The illusory world of the stage perfectly suited Pirandello's purpose; his mysterious and elusive characters constantly seek to define and redefine their own existence and create their own "real" world. Contradictions within a personality do not cancel out each other; rather, they exist in balanced simultaneity. Part of the sustained horror of Pirandello's world comes when one first realizes that of all the facets of a single character, no one is the "real" personality. Whether in drama, fiction, or real life, characters and men have essentially no "real" identity. All are characters seeking reality in an illusory world—hence the world's frightening quality.

In 1934, two years before he died, Luigi Pirandello received the Nobel prize for literature.

Cinci

The dog sat patiently on his hind legs before the closed door and waited for it to open. Every so often he lifted a paw and scratched; every so often he let out a low whine.

Cinci, back from school with his books, strapped together, slung over his shoulder, found the dog still sitting there in the street. The boy was annoyed by this patient waiting and gave the dog a kick. Then he kicked the door for good measure, knowing that it was locked and that no one was home. Finally, he threw his books at the door, as if he expected them to pass right through it and land on the floor inside. But they came flying back at him with the same force with which he had hurled them. Surprised, as if the door were playing with him, Cinci threw the books back again. Then, as there were already three in the game—Cinci, the door and the books—the dog wanted to play too. He jumped at every throw and barked with each rebound.

People stopped to look. A few of them smiled, almost in spite of themselves, at the silliness of the game and at the dog's delight. Others were indignant to see expensive books treated with so little regard. Cinci soon tired of the sport and dropped his books on the ground, then lowered himself to a sitting position by scraping his spine along the wall. He had planned to sit on the books, but they slipped out from under him and he found himself coming down hard on the ground. He looked around with a foolish grin while the dog jumped back, eying him.

All the mischief that passed through Cinci's head showed clearly in that thatch of straw-colored hair and in his sparkling green eyes. He was at the awkward age, gawky and bristling. Having forgotten his handkerchief when he returned to school in the afternoon, he now sat on the ground snuffling, his long legs exposed because he still wore short pants though he was too big for them, his knobby knees pulled up almost level with his face. No shoes could withstand the treatment he gave them. The ones he had on were already done for.

He was bored. Above all, he was bored. Hugging his knees, he snorted, then dragged his back up along the wall again. Fox leaped up, expectant. Where are we off to? A walk in the country, perhaps, to swipe a couple of figs or apples? Cinci was not yet sure. He listlessly tied up his books and replaced them over his shoulder.

The paved street ended beyond his house where the dirt road began, and it led deeper and deeper into the open country. What a wonderful sensation it must be, when you're riding in a carriage, to feel the horse's hoofs and the wheels pass from the hard pavement onto the soft, silent dirt road! It must be a little like when the teacher, after being provoked and flying into a rage, suddenly speaks in a quiet, gentle voice once more and the dread of punishment decreases. To get into the open country, you followed the dirt road past the last houses of their stinking suburb until it widened out into the little square on the outskirts of town. A new hospital had just been built there, its whitewashed walls still so fresh and glaring that they blinded you in the sun.

All the patients had recently been moved from the old hospital in ambulances and on stretchers. It was like a parade when they filed by, the ambulances first, their curtains fluttering at the little windows, then the bed cases carried by on beautiful hammocklike stretchers.

By the time Cinci and his dog reached the square, it was growing late. The sun had already set, and the convalescents in their gray shirts and white nightcaps no longer leaned out of the large windows to stare sadly at the old church opposite where it rose amid a cluster of dilapidated houses and a few straggling trees.

Cinci stopped, uncertain, then lounged against a paling, filled with helpless bitterness at so many things he could not understand. First there was his mother. How did she live and what did she live on? She was never at home and insisted on sending him to that school—that cursed school so far away. Every day he had to run for at least half an hour to get there on time; then at noon he came back only to rush again after bolting a couple of mouthfuls. His mother always said he was a loafer who wasted his time playing with the dog. She was forever reproaching him: he did not study, he was dirty, he always got cheated when she sent him to buy something, he brought back food that wasn't fresh . . .

Now where was Fox?

There he was, poor little dog, mutely waiting for him to make up his mind. Anyway *he* knew what was expected of him: follow your master! Cinci wanted to do something, but there was always the same problem—he didn't know what to do. His mother could at least have given him the key when she went out to sew by the day in gentlemen's houses—for that's what she gave him to understand she was doing. But no. She said he was not to be trusted and that, if she had not returned by the time he got back from school, she would not be long and he could wait. Where? In front of the door? Sometimes he had waited two hours in the cold and even in the rain. Then, instead of taking shelter, he would go to the corner and stand under the rainspout on purpose so that he would be wringing wet. Finally, she would appear, all out of breath, carrying a borrowed umbrella, her face flaming, her eyes very bright and shifty, so nervous she could never find the latch key in her purse.

"You're soaked! Now just be patient. I was kept late!"

Cinci frowned as he kept on walking uphill. There were things he didn't want to think about—his father, for instance. He had never known his father. When he was little he had been told that his father had died before he was born, but no one had ever said who his father was; now he no longer cared to ask or to find out. He might even be that cripple over there, paralyzed down the right side, who still managed to drag himself along to the saloon. Fox went up and barked at him. It was the crutch he didn't like.

All those women standing around in a circle, bulging in front but not pregnant—well, maybe one of them was, the one with the skirt hiked up in front and nearly dragging on the ground in back. That other one with the baby in her arms, reaching into her blouse —ugh! What a blob of flesh! His own mother was beautiful, still young and slender. She too had nursed him at her breast when he was a baby, perhaps in a house in the country or out in the sun on a threshing floor. He vaguely remembered a house in the country when he was little—if he had not dreamed it, or seen it somewhere. Who knows? When evening came and the oil lamps were lit, one could feel a shadow obscure those country houses as the lamp was carried from room to room and the light faded from one window only to reappear at another.

Beyond the square, the road meandered up the side of a hill and continued on into the country. He looked up and could see the whole vast expanse of the sky. The last rays of the dying sun had disappeared, and above the darkened hill there was the softest blue. Evening shadows fell across the earth, dimming the white glare of the hospital wall.

An old woman hurried toward the little church for evening prayers. Cinci suddenly made up his mind to go in too, and Fox stopped, looking up at him because he well knew he was not allowed inside churches. At the entrance, the old woman, who was already late, was panting and whimpering as she struggled to lift the heavy leather curtain. Cinci held it aside for her, but she frowned instead of thanking him, sensing he had not come there to worship. It was cold as a cave in that little church. On the main altar two candles burned fitfully, and here and there a few stray lamps glimmered. The dust of ages lay in the penetrating dampness. Echoes lurked in the gloomy silence, ready to spring out at the least noise. The pews were lined with devout old women, each in her accustomed place. Cinci felt an impulse to let out a howl to make them jump. Not a howl perhaps, but what about throwing down his heavy load of books, as if by accident! Why not? He let them drop and, like a shot, the echoes jumped out to his great delight, thundering and crashing about him. Cinci had often tried this experiment of raising echoes. There was now no further need to gall the patience of those poor scandalized old worshipers. He walked out of the church and found Fox ready to follow along the path uphill. He longed to bite into some fruit and climbed over a low wall to grope his way through the dark trees. But he could not be certain whether this impulse was prompted by hunger or by an urge just to do *something*.

The steep country road was deserted and full of little stones loosened by the hoofs of passing donkeys and sent rolling down over and over. Cinci kicked a couple into the air with the toe of his shoe. The slopes on either side were covered with long green,

plumed oats, so pleasant to chew on. The little plumes came off
and clung together like a bouquet in your hand. If they were thrown
at someone, the oats that clung were counted as future wives or
husbands. Cinci decided to try this out on Fox. Seven wives, no
less! But then, nearly all of them stuck fast in Fox's fur, so it didn't
count. Fox, the old stupid, just stood there with his eyes closed,
not understanding the joke about the seven wives on his back.

Cinci did not feel like going any farther. He was tired and as
bored as before. He went to the left of the road and sat on the wall.
From there he looked up at the new moon, its pale gold just beginning to shine in the faint green of the sky. He saw it and he
didn't see it—like things that slip through the mind, one flowing
into another, then all receding farther and farther from his young
body sitting there so still that he was no longer aware of it. If he
had put his own hand on his knee, or on his foot hanging down
in its dirty, scuffed shoe, it would have seemed like a stranger's.
He was no longer *in* his body. He had joined the things he saw and
did not see—the darkening sky, the brightening moon, that mass
of dark trees which seemed suspended in thin air, the fresh, black
earth so newly tilled, still exhaling the odor of damp rot of these
last sunny October days.

All of a sudden, absorbed as he was, he was distracted and instinctively lifted his hand to his ear. A shrill little laugh had come
from beneath the wall. A country boy about his own age had hidden himself on the side of the wall bordering the fields. He had
picked and stripped a blade of oats too and, slipping a loose knot
in one end, he was stealthily lifting up his arm to loop it over
Cinci's ear. As soon as Cinci turned, the boy quickly signaled to
him to be still. Then he moved the blade of oats along the wall
toward the head of a little lizard peeping out from between the
stones. The boy had been hoping to trap it for an hour. Cinci
leaned down anxiously to watch. Without realizing it, the lizard
had slipped its own head into the noose but not quite far enough
to be caught. The head must advance a trifle more, and even now,
if the hand holding the trap should tremble and alarm the lizard,
it might escape. Yes, yes, but wait! Easy now! He must be prepared
to give a jerk at just the right moment. It was the work of a second.
There! The lizard was flashing like a fish at the end of that long
blade of oats.

Cinci eagerly jumped down from the wall, but the other boy,

holding the noose and probably fearing he would take the lizard from him, swung his arm around several times in the air and then brought the creature down with a dull slap on a big stone which lay among the weeds.

"No!" screamed Cinci, but too late.

The lizard lay motionless on the stone, its white stomach gleaming in the light. Cinci was angry. He too had wanted to see the lizard caught, prompted by the natural instinct of the hunter in all of us. But to kill it like that, without first looking closely at those quick little eyes, watching it up to the last convulsion, those twitching legs, that all-over quiver of its green body—no, it was too stupid and shameful! Cinci went up to the boy and punched him in the chest with all his might, sending him sprawling. The boy jumped right up again, furious, and grabbed a handful of dirt from the nearest furrow which he flung in Cinci's face, blinding him. Cinci was all the more outraged and infuriated by the taste of dirt in his mouth. He took a clod of earth and threw it back. The fight grew desperate. The country boy was quicker and had a surer aim. He never missed, moving in closer and closer with those missiles of dirt which did not wound but struck with a dull thud and fell like hail on Cinci's chest, in his face and hair, in his ears and even into his shoes. Suffocated, unable to protect or defend himself, Cinci leaped up with his arm raised to snatch a stone from the wall. Something scurried away—was it Fox? He hurled the stone and, all of a sudden, where before everything had been spinning around, striking his eyes, now nothing moved—the clump of trees, the thin crescent moon. It was as if time itself had stopped in stupefied amazement at sight of the boy stretched on the ground.

Still panting, his heart pounding, terror flooding him as he leaned against the wall in the unbelieveable silken repose of the countryside under the moonlight, Cinci foundered in a backwash of man's eternal solitude from which he wanted to flee. He had not done it! He had not meant to do it! He knew nothing about it! Then, as though he were actually someone else drawing near only out of curiosity, he took a step, then another, and bent down to look. The boy's head was bashed in; blood still dripped from his gaping mouth onto the ground. Part of his leg showed between his cotton sock and his pants leg. He looked as if he had always been dead. It was like a dream. The lizard lay stomach up on the stone with the blade of oats still caught around its throat. Cinci knew he must wake up and go away. He quickly vaulted the wall, picked up his bundle of books and started off. Fox followed him, as usual.

On the way back downhill, Cinci's confidence increased as the distance lengthened so that he did not hurry at all. He reached the empty square. The moon shone here too, but it was another moon, unheeding, which lit up the white facade of the hospital.

Now once again along the road through the suburbs, back to the house—to which, of course, his mother had not yet returned. No need to give any explanation of his whereabouts; he had simply waited here for her. And this—which would be true for his mother—became the truth for him too. In fact, he stood with his shoulders against the wall beside the door just as before.

It was enough that he be found there, waiting.

The Rose

The little train moved on through the darkness of the winter evening at a pace that left little hope of its arriving on time.

Signora Lucietta Nespi, Loffredi's widow, bored and tired as she was from the long trip in that dirty second-class carriage, was in no hurry whatsoever to arrive at Peola.

She thought and thought.

Though she was being carried along in the train, her thoughts were still back there in the empty rooms of the house in Genoa. Stripped of the handsome furniture which, almost new, had had to go for a song, the rooms had suddenly seemed very small. What a disappointment! She needed so much, on that last visit, to see them as big and grand, so that when she was poor she could say proudly, "The house I had in Genoa . . ."

She would say it anyway, but the insignificance of those bare rooms would haunt her always. She thought about the good friends to whom she had not even said goodbye at the last minute because they too had let her down, though they had pretended to outdo one another in helping her. They had helped all right, by bringing around all those honest buyers whom they had tipped off to the opportunity of picking up for a pittance things that had originally cost a small fortune.

Signora Lucietta tightly closed her beautiful eyes on these unhappy thoughts, then opened them wide again as she lifted her forefinger to pass it along her pert little nose in that unconscious, pretty little way she had.

© 1959 by Gli Eredi di Luigi Pirandello. Reprinted by permission of Simon and Schuster, Inc.

She was really very tired and would have liked to sleep. Her two fatherless children, poor dears, were sleeping soundly, the older one stretched out on the seat under a coat, and the baby curled up beside his mother, his blond head on her lap. She might have slept too if only she could have found a way of resting her head on her hand without waking the child pillowed on her knees.

The seat opposite was still marked where he had propped his little feet until the man had chosen to sit in that place—with all the empty seats in the other carriages—a big man around thirty-five, dark and bearded, with light-green eyes—big intense, sad eyes.

Signora Lucietta took an immediate dislike to him. For no reason, his large eyes gave her the feeling that no matter where she would go the world would always remain alien to her. She would be lost, vainly calling for help among eyes like those now looking at her, veiled with sorrow but essentially unconcerned.

To avoid them, she kept her face turned toward the window although nothing could be seen outside. There was only the reflection of the oil lamp in the carriage, its little red flame wavering high among the shadows, smoking up the curved glass chimney. The reflection looked like another lamp suspended outside in the night, following after the train with difficulty and giving both comfort and fright.

"Faith," the genleman murmured.

Signora Lucietta turned to look at him in astonishment. "What?"

"The light that is not there."

Brightening, she looked at him and smiled, pointing to the lamp hanging from the ceiling of their compartment. "But there it *is*!"

The man nodded, then added with a little smile, "Yes, like faith . . . we kindle a light here and we also see it there, without realizing that when it is put out here, there will be no light there either."

"You are a philosopher!" exclaimed little Signora Lucietta.

He raised a hand from the knob of his cane in a vague gesture and sighed. "I observe."

The train halted for a long time at a small junction. Not a voice could be heard. When the rhythmic noise of the wheels stopped the unbroken silence seemed eternal.

"Mazzano," the gentleman murmured. "Usually there is a wait here for the through train."

Finally, they heard in the distance the plaintive whistle of the other train arriving late.

"Here it comes."

In that oncoming train, rolling over the same tracks on which she would soon pass, Signora Lucietta could hear the voice of her fate condemning her to be lost for all the rest of her days with her two little ones.

She shook off this moment of despair and asked her traveling companion, "Are we far from Peola?"

"It's more than an hour away," he replied. "Are you going to Peola, too?"

"Yes, I am the new telegraph operator. I passed the State examinations. I was fifth on the list, so they assigned me to Peola."

"Oh, yes. You were expected last night."

Signora Lucietta brightened up. "As a matter of fact," she started to say but remembered the sleeping child on her lap. She opened her arms, indicating the two children with a look. "You see how tied down I am . . . and alone, with so many things to take care of at the last minute."

"You are the widow Loffredi, aren't you?"

"Yes." Signora Lucietta lowered her eyes.

"Did they ever find out anything more about it?" he asked after a short, weighty silence.

"Nothing. But there are those who know," Signora Lucietta said, her eyes flashing. "Loffredi's real murderer was not the hired killer who struck him in the back and then fled. They tried to imply that there was a woman involved, but I know better. Reprisal! It was political vengeance, pure and simple. Loffredi had no time to think about women. The one he had already took up too much . . . What I mean is, I was all he needed. Just imagine! He married me when I was fifteen."

As she said this, Signora Lucietta's face turned bright pink and her restless eyes lit up as they darted back and forth; finally she lowered them as before. For a moment the man watched her, impressed by the rapid change from animation to sudden embarrassment.

How could anyone take this show of feeling seriously? Although the mother of two children, she looked no more than a child herself—a doll. She was ill at ease probably because she had stated so emphatically that, with a wife as young and sparkling as herself, Loffredi had no thought for other women.

She must realize that no one, seeing her and knowing the man Loffredi was, would believe her. No doubt she was influenced by him while he lived, and perhaps still was, in her memory. She could not bear anyone to think that Loffredi had not cared for her or that, for him, she had been just a doll. She wanted to be sole heir to the sensation stirred up in all the Italian newspapers about a year ago over the tragic end of this fiery, irrepressible journalist.

Silvagni felt well pleased that he had guessed her character so exactly when, after a few well-placed questions, he succeeded in getting her to talk and unconsciously to confirm everything he had surmised.

He had a tender impulse toward this little meadowlark hardly out of its nest and just learning to fly who fancied it was already free, self-reliant and confident in its knowledge of life. No, no, Signora Lucietta would never be at a loss! To think that she had not lost her head through all the horror of that tragedy! She had run here, run there, done this and that, not so much for herself as for those little ones—and, yes, a little for herself, too. After all, she was only twenty—and at times she did not even look that! Her age was another obstacle for her, perhaps the most vexing of all. Everyone seeing her first rebel and then despair laughed as though she had no right to do either. The more furious she became, the more they laughed, each one promising her one thing or another, all of them wishing their offer might be coupled with a little caress which they dared not give. Well aware of their motives, she soon grew tired of their game and, in order to get away, applied for a civil-service job as a telegraph operator.

"Poor Signora." Her fellow traveler sighed, smiling—he too!

"*Poor.* Why poor?"

"Ah . . . because . . . you'll see, it is not very amusing in Peola."

And he told her a few things about the town.

Boredom was always visible and tangible, in all the streets and squares of Peola.

"How is it visible?"

"In the endless number of sleeping dogs stretched out on the cobblestones. They do not even wake up to scratch themselves; they do it in their sleep."

Anyone opening his mouth to yawn in Peola must beware—it might stay open for five yawns at least; their ennui took that long to come out! If there was anything specific to be done, everybody in Peola closed his eyes and said with a sigh, "Tomorrow . . ."

Because today and tomorrow were one and the same—and tomorrow was as good as never.

"You will see, there is nothing to do at the post office," he concluded. "No one ever goes there. Take this little train; it moves along like a stagecoach. Well, even a stagecoach would mean progress for Peola. Life in Peola goes by at the pace of a wheelbarrow."

"Heavens, you frighten me!" said Signora Lucietta.

"Don't be frightened," he said, smiling. "Now I'll give you some good news. In a few days, we're going to have a ball at the Club."

"Ah . . ."

Signora Lucietta looked at him with the sudden suspicion that even this gentleman wanted to make fun of her.

"Do the dogs dance?" she asked.

"No, the good citizens of Peola dance. You must go. It will amuse you. The Club happens to be right on the square, near the post office. Have you found a place to live?"

The signora said she had, in the same house where her predecessor had lodged.

"And, excuse me, your name . . . ?" she asked.

"Silvagni, Signora. Fausto Silvagni. I am secretary at the Town Hall."

"Oh, really! It's a pleasure."

"Ahem . . ."

Silvagni lifted his hand in a weary gesture and smiled bitterly at her deference, a smile which reflected the melancholy of his large, light eyes.

At last the train greeted the little station of Peola with a plaintive whistle.

"Are we here?"

II

Peola lay ringed within a vast range of blue hills, cleft here and there by valleys of mist, darkened by oaks and firs, brightened by chestnut trees. The little town with its clusters of red roofs and its

four bell towers, its uneven squares and narrow streets sloping
between small old houses and a few new and larger ones, now had
the thrill of welcoming the widow of Loffredi, the journalist whose
tragic and mysterious death was still referred to in the country's
leading newspapers. It was an uncommon privilege to hear directly
from her mouth many things no one in the big cities knew, but it
was almost enough just to see her and to be able to say, "When he
was alive, Loffredi clasped that little thing there in his arms."

The good folk of Peola were very proud of her presence. As
for the dogs, they would have gone on sleeping peacefully, stretched
out in the streets and squares of the town unaware of this honor,
had the rumor not been circulated that their torpor made a bad
impression on the signora. Everyone, particularly the young men
but the older ones too, began disturbing them, chasing them off
with kicks or by stamping their feet and clapping their hands.

The poor animals got up from the ground more surprised than
frightened, and cast sidelong glances, barely cocking an ear. Some
of them, tripping off on three legs, the fourth benumbed and drawn
up, went elsewhere to stretch out. What had happened? They
might have understood had they been less dulled by sleep. They
had only to glance at that one little square where no dog was allowed
to lie, or even to run past.

The post office stood on that square!

They might have noticed—had they just a little more wit—that
all who passed there, especially the young men but the older ones
too, seemed to breathe a different air, more stimulating, which
quickened their gait and their movements. The men's heads turned
as if a sudden rush of blood made them uncomfortable in their
starched collars, and their hands busied themselves pulling down
vests and adjusting ties.

The square crossed, they behaved as if they were intoxicated,
hilarious and nervous. And at the sight of a dog:

"Get along with you!"

"Out of my way!"

"Off with you, ugly little cur!"

They even threw stones at them. Kicks were no longer enough.

Fortunately, there were those who sided with the dogs. A window would fly up and a woman, her eyes flashing, her fists raised,
would cry out furiously, "Ruffians! What do you have against
those poor animals?"

Or else: "You too, Signor Notary? With all due respect, aren't you ashamed of yourself? What a treacherous kick! Poor little beast! Here, here, doggie. Look at his little paw! You've crippled it, and off you go with a cigar in your mouth perfectly unconcerned. How shameful! And you a decent family man!"

In no time a close bond of sympathy was established between the ugly women of Peola and the dogs, mercilessly persecuted by their men: husbands, fathers, brothers, cousins, fiancés and, by contagion, all the riffraff of the town.

The women, a little more alert than the dogs—some of them at least—immediately noticed a new air about the menfolk that made their eyes shine and stare into space. The red moss-covered roofs were brightened and every corner of the sleepy old town was ex- hilarated—or so it appeared to the men, at least.

Yes, life so filled with worries, troubles, bitterness all of a sudden had smiled. God, how it smiled, for no reason at all! If, after days and days of fog and rain, a ray of sunlight shines through, doesn't it cheer the heart? Doesn't it draw a sigh of relief from every breast? No more than a ray of sunshine, and yet all life was sud- denly changed. The heaviness lifted, the darkest thoughts bright- ened, and those who had not wanted to leave the house were out of doors again. Smell the good aroma of the damp earth. As good to breathe as the odor of fresh mushrooms. Plans for the future suddenly seemed so simple and easy. Everybody shook off the memory of bad moments, realizing that they had been given too much importance. Courage! Chin up! And up with the mustache too!

That was the effect of the ray of sunlight which had abruptly pierced the clouds hanging over Peola, brightening the post office on the little square. Besides persecuting the sleeping dogs, hus- bands began to ask their wives, "Dear, why don't you arrange your hair better?"

Never, certainly not for years and years, had the citizens of Peola hummed so much without realizing it—at the Club, in their houses, or walking along the street.

Signora Lucietta saw and felt all of this. Such obvious desire flashed from burning eyes following her every move, voluptuously caressing her with a look, enveloping her with such warmth of feeling that she too became quite intoxicated.

It didn't require much doing because Signora Lucietta was already aquiver, simmering inside herself. What a nuisance they were, those little curls on her forehead, tumbling down every time she bent over to follow the ribbon of dotted paper running through its little ticking machine on the office table! She shook her head and almost jumped with surprise as her hair tickled her neck. What sudden blushes, and catchings of breath, ending in a tired little laugh. Oh, but she cried too. At times she wept without knowing why. Hot burning tears, brought on by a strange longing which ran through her whole body. She could not control those tears, and then, out of the blue, she would laugh again.

She determined to pay strict attention to her work in order not to dwell on anything else, not to let her fancy fly after every amusing or dangerous idea that came to her, not to lose herself in certain unlikely prospects. She must take hold of herself firmly with both hands, so that everything would proceed according to rules and regulations. She must always remember that her two poor little orphans were at home in the care of that stupid old bumptious servant. What a worry that was! Two children to raise all alone, by her own hard work and sacrifices. Today here, tomorrow there, adrift with them—and then, when they were grown and had a life of their own, maybe all the hardships she had suffered would be forgotten. No, now they were still very little. Why imagine such ugly things? She would be older then, her first youth past in any case, and when one is old it is easier to smile even over sad memories.

Who was talking like that? She was, but not because such gloomy ideas came to her spontaneously. *He* passed the office every morning, that gentleman she had met on the train, and sometimes in the evening too, when he came from the Town Hall. He would stand in the doorway a moment, or before her counter, talking of different things, even amusing things. For instance they laughed together about the war on the dogs, and about the ugly women rising to their defense. But she read mournful, depressing ideas there in his eyes, those large, clear eyes, and they remained with her long after he had gone.

It was he who had started her worrying about her children—who knows why?—and without even asking about them or referring to them at all.

She felt annoyed, and repeated to herself that they were still so small—why allow herself to be discouraged? She should not and would not! Courage! She was still young, very young, and then . . .

"Can I help you, sir?" Yes, count the words of the telegram and then add two cents more. Would you like a telegram blank? No? Well, I just asked. I understand. Good day, Signore. Don't mention it.

How many came into the office just to ask silly questions! It was hard not to laugh. They were so comical, those Peola gentlemen. And the delegation of young men, members of the Club who came to the post office one morning with their nice old president to invite her to the famous ball Signor Silvagni had spoken of on the train. What a sight! They looked eager, ready to eat her up, and seemed to marvel that, at close range, she had such and such a nose, with eyes and a mouth like that—to mention only her head! But the most impertinent were also the most embarrassed. None of them knew how to begin.

"Would you do us the honor . . ." "It is a yearly custom, Signora . . ." "A little *soiree dansante* . . ." "Oh, quite unpretentious, of course . . ." "A family affair." "Let me speak . . ." "What are you trying to say? If you would be so kind as to do us the honor . . ."

They fidgeted, wrung their hands, and stared at one another in an effort to get their words out, while the president, who was also mayor of the town, fumed, turning purple with rage. He had prepared a speech and they did not even give him a chance to deliver it. He had also carefully arranged the long strand of hair over his bald pate before sticking it down and had worn yellow gloves, inserting two fingers of his right hand between the buttons of his vest.

"It is our custom every year . . ." he began at last.

Although she could hardly keep from laughing, she blushed at these pressing invitations, expressed more clearly in sly looks than big, uneasy words. At first she tried to get out of it: she was still in mourning, as they knew, and then there were the children . . . she could only spend evenings with them . . . she did not see them all day . . . she always put them to bed . . . and there were so many other things she had to do . . .

"Come now, just for one evening." "You could come after they were in bed." "Isn't the servant there?" "For one evening . . ."

One of the boys, in his enthusiasm, went so far as to say, "Mourning? What nonsense!"

Someone gave him a sharp poke in the ribs and he did not dare utter another word.

Finally Signora Lucietta promised she would go, or rather that she would do her best to go. Then, when they all had left, she stood there looking at her little white hand against her black dress and at her finger on which Loffredi had placed that gold ring when he married her. Her hand had been so delicate then, the hand of a child, and now that the fingers had filled out, the ring was too tight. She could no longer take it off.

III

In the bedroom of her little furnished apartment, Signora Lucietta was telling herself that she would not go, cradling in her arms—bye-bye—her blond angel dressed in black—bye-bye—the smallest one who wanted to fall asleep in her arms every night.

The older child, undressed by the heavy-handed old servant, had gone to bed by himself, and yes, the darling was now fast asleep.

Very lightly, careful not to waken the sleeping baby in her lap, Signora Lucietta now undressed him. Very softly, first one, then the other shoe; the socks, one, two, and now the little trousers along with the underpants, and now—ah, now it was more difficult to slip the arms out of the sleeves. Up, very carefully, with the help of the servant—no, not like that; that's right . . . there! Now the other side . . .

"No, my darling . . . yes, right here with your mama. Mama is here. I will do it alone, then. Please turn down the bed? There now."

But why so slowly, all this?

Did she really want to go dancing, a short year after her husband's death? No, and perhaps she would not have gone had she not seen—all of a sudden, as she came out of the bedroom into the little hallway in front of the closed window—a miracle.

She had been in that rented apartment for days and had not noticed the old wooden flower box standing there in front of the

window. In that flower box a beautiful red rose had just opened—
a miracle at this time of year.

She stood there astonished, looking at it as it bloomed between
the drab gray hangings of that dirty little entrance, and her heart
quickened with joy. In that rose she saw her own burning desire
to enjoy herself for at least one night. Suddenly freed from the
dilemma which made her hesitate—the specter of her husband,
the thought of the children—she picked the rose and looking into
the mirror over the console, pinned it in her hair.

Yes, there! With that rose in her hair she would go to the ball—
and with her twenty years, too, and her joy, dressed in black.

IV

It was rapture, delirium, madness!

When she appeared, just as everyone had given up the hope of
seeing her, the three dark rooms of the Club, divided by large
arches and badly lit with oil lamps and candles, suddenly seemed
ablaze with light. Her face, a little drawn from inner excitement,
was flushed, her eyes shone, and that red rose in her hair proclaimed her joy for all to see.

The men lost their heads. Throwing convention to the winds
and taking no further notice of jealous wives, sweethearts, pining
spinsters, young girls, sisters, cousins, they rushed over and crowded
about her, with the excuse of welcoming their guest. The dancing had started and, without giving her time to look right or left,
they nearly came to blows squabbling over her in their wild enthusiasm. Fifteen, twenty arms were offered, elbows crooked, all
for her! But which one first? One at a time—she would take a turn
with each of them. Make way, make way! What about the music?
What were they doing, those musicians over there? Were they also
lost in a spell of admiration? Music! Music!

And she was off, stepping out for her first dance with the old
mayor and president of the Club, in full dress.

"Excellent!"

"Look at him go!"

"Oh, the tails of his coat. How they fly!"

"Great!"

"Heavens! His hair is coming unglued."

"What? Why, he's already leading her to a chair."

Again fifteen, twenty arms with elbows crooked appeared before her.

"With me! With me!"

"One moment!"

"She's promised me."

"No, I'm next."

What a sight! It was a wonder they didn't tear each other apart. While waiting their turn, the unlucky ones wandered off dejectedly to ask other ladies to dance. The uglier ones accepted sulkily, but the others, furious, refused indignantly with a curt "No, thank *you!*"

The women exchanged baleful looks and some of them abruptly made a great show of leaving, signaling to their friends to follow.

"Come, let us go. Never have I witnessed such indecent behavior!"

Some cried tears of rage; others trembled with vexation, unburdening themselves to inconspicious little men who sat stiffly in suits polished by long use and smelling of pepper and camphor. Not to be caught up in the swirl, these shy creatures clung to the wall like dried leaves sheltered by the honest silk skirts of their wives, sisters-in-law or sisters—fancy dresses indeed, puffed and flounced, in violent shades of green, yellow, red or blue, gowns which hermetically preserved their wearers' sullen provincial modesty in the musty smell of venerable wooden chests and which comforted both their nostrils and their consciences.

The heat of the rooms became stifling. A kind of haze rose from the steaming sensuality of the men. Panting, burning, their faces flushed purple, they took advantage of the brief pauses between the dances to paste down and smooth their wet and bristling hair, by slipping trembling hands over their heads, along their temples or necks. Their animal natures rebelled out of all reason against propriety. The ball came only once a year! What harm did it do? Let the women quiet down and stay put!

Fresh, light, filled with a joy that brushed aside any vulgar contact, laughing and escaping with a quick gesture, amusing herself, intact and pure in that moment of folly, an agile, flickering flame among those dark, burning, senseless logs, Signora Lucietta, triumphant, whirled like a top, dancing and dancing without seeing anything or anyone. The arches dividing the three rooms, the furniture, the yellow, green, red and bright blue dresses of the ladies, the men's black clothes and white shirt fronts—all spun around in flashing streamers. As soon as one dancer wearied and started to pant heavily, she broke from his arms to throw herself into those of another, and off she went again, swirling around and around in a frenzied confusion of lights and colors.

Seated in the last room against the wall in a dark corner, Fausto Silvagni, his hands on the knob of his cane, watched her for two hours, his large, light eyes warmed by a friendly smile. Only he understood the purity of that mad joy and delighted in it, as though his tenderness had made her a gift of this innocent exultation.

His tenderness? Still only tenderness? Wasn't this throbbing of his heart more than tenderness?

For many years Fausto Silvagni, his eyes intent and sad, had looked at everything as if from a long way off. To him all things were but fleeting shadows, even his thoughts, his feelings.

Misfortune and heavy obligations had doomed him to failure. His youthful dreams, kindled with so much spirit, had petered out and were now remembered only with bitterness. He fled reality, choosing to lose himself in painful isolation.

Now, in that exile, a feeling had come over him, an emotion he wanted to hold at bay, as yet unwilling to accept it but equally unwilling to reject it completely.

Perhaps, since they could not appear to him in any other form, this dear, mad little creature, dressed in black with a flashing rose in her hair, had brought the living incarnation of those long-lost dreams for him to clasp—living and breathing—in his arms. Could he not check her flight, hold her and, at last, return through and with her from his remoteness? If he did not stop her, who knows where and how she would end. She too needed help, guidance, advice, lost as she was in a world not of her choosing but which, alas, she wanted to enjoy. That rose said so, that red rose in her hair.

For a while, Fausto Silvagni had looked at that rose in dismay. He didn't know quite why. There it lay like a flame in her hair. She shook that foolish little head of hers so often, how was it that the rose did not fall? Was that what he feared?

Meanwhile, deep within him, his trembling heart was saying, "Tomorrow, tomorrow or one of these days, you will speak out. Meanwhile, let her dance on like a wild little sprite."

By now, most of her partners were ready to drop and breathlessly declared themselves bested as they looked about for their wives who had left. Only six or seven obstinately held out, among them two old men—who would ever believe it?—the mayor and the widower notary. Both were in a sorry state, perspiring, faces flaming and eyes popping, ties crooked and shirts rumpled, pitiful in their senile frenzy. They had been nudged aside by the younger men all evening and now came forward for a couple of turns only to collapse on chairs like empty sacks one after the other.

It was the last lap, the closing dance.

Signora Lucietta found herself surrounded by all seven of the survivors, aggressively exuberant.

"With me!" "With me!"

The sensual overexcitement in their eyes alarmed her, and the thought that her innocent gaiety could arouse such passion disgusted and shamed her. She wanted to flee, to escape from them. At a startled fawnlike movement of her head, her hair, already loose, slipped down and the rose fell to the floor.

Fausto Silvagni was pulled to his feet by a strange presentiment of danger. The men fell all over one another in an effort to pick up the flower. It was the old mayor who retrieved it, but not without having his hand scratched.

"Here!" he cried, running with the others to offer it to Signora Lucietta, who was putting up her hair in the next room. "Here it is! Now you—" he was so out of breath that his head wobbled— "now *you* must make a choice. Here . . . offer it to one of us!"

"Hurrah! Wonderful idea!"

"She must choose . . ."

"Who will it be?"

"The judgment of Paris!"

"Hush! Wait and see!"

Breathless, holding the still-lovely rose high over her head, Signora Lucietta looked around at her pursuers like an animal at bay. She knew instinctively that they wanted to compromise her at all costs.

"To one of you? My choice?" she cried unexpectedly, a light in her eyes. "Very well, I will. But first step aside. Everyone stand aside. I will offer it to . . ."

Her eyes flew from one to another, as if hesitating in her decision. The awkward men stared at her uncertainly, their hands outstretched, their coarse faces grotesquely reflecting undisguised supplication. With a quick feint, she slipped by the last two on her left and ran toward the farther room. She had found a solution! She would present the rose to one of those who had sat quietly looking on all evening, the first one she came to.

"I will give it to . . ."

Her glance met the clear eyes of Fausto Silvagni. She turned pale and hesitated, trembling and confused.

"Oh, God!" she breathed, "have pity." Quickly recovering herself, she held out the flower, "Here, for you, take it. Take it, Signor Silvagni."

Fausto Silvagni took the rose and turned with a wan smile to look at the seven men rushing after her.

"No! Why to him? Why not to one of us! You must give it to one of us!"

"That's not so!" Signora Lucietta said impatiently. "You said *to someone,* that's all. And so I offered it to Signor Silvagni!"

"But that's an out-and-out declaration of love!" they protested.

"What?" exclaimed Signora Lucietta, her face crimson. "Not at all! It would have been a declaration had I offered it to one of you. But I gave it to Signor Silvagni, who hasn't moved from here all evening and who certainly would not interpret it like that! And you mustn't see it that way either."

"We do. We certainly do. After all, you chose him deliberately."

She was completely upset by their persecution. It had long since ceased to be a jest. Resentment showed in the men's eyes and mouths, and their sly winks and knowing grunts clearly referred to the visits Silvagni had paid her at the post office and to all the attention he had shown her since she had arrived. Meanwhile his own pallor and uneasiness, heightened their malicious suspicions. Why did he blanch and fidget? Did he too think that she . . . Impossible! Why should he? Perhaps because the others chose to believe it. Why did he not protest? Why did his eyes reflect such suffering?

With a pang she suddenly understood everything. In her perplexity she was still confronted by the defiance of those insolent, thwarted men, however, as they screamed in unbridled rage around her.

"There now, you see! *You* say it doesn't mean a thing, but he doesn't utter a word!"

"What do you mean?" she cried, allowing her scorn to dominate her feelings to the contrary.

Trembling from head to foot, she turned to Silvagni. Looking him straight in the eyes, she asked, "Do you seriously think that in offering you this rose I have made a declaration of love?"

Fausto Silvagni looked at her for a moment, a pale, sad smile on his lips.

Poor little fairy, she was forced by their crude insistence to flee the magic circle of her joy, the innocent delirium in which she had whirled all evening like a little fool. Now, to safeguard the simplicity of her gift of a rose from the relentlessness of the men—all the purity of her joy in a single evening—she was asking him to give up a love which would last a lifetime and to make a reply which would wither the rose in his hand.

Looking coldly at the men, he said, "Not only I do not believe it, but you may be sure, Signora, that no one else will ever think it. Here is the rose. Throw it away yourself because I cannot."

Signora Lucietta took the flower with a not too steady hand and tossed it into a corner.

"Thank you," she said, knowing full well what it was she was throwing away forever with that rose of a moment.

The Soft Touch of Grass

They went into the next room, where he was sleeping in a big chair, to ask if he wanted to look at her for the last time before the lid was put on the coffin.

"It's dark. What time is it?" he asked.

It was nine-thirty in the morning, but the day was overcast and the light dim. The funeral had been set for ten o'clock.

Signor Pardi stared up at them with dull eyes. It hardly seemed possible that he could have slept so long and well all night. He was still numb with sleep and the sorrow of these last days. He would have liked to cover his face with his hands to shut out the faces of his neighbors grouped about his chair in the thin light; but sleep had weighted his body like lead, and although there was a tingling in his toes urging him to rise, it quickly went away. Should he still give way to his grief? He happened to say aloud. "Always . . ." but he said it like someone settling himself under the covers to go back to sleep. They all looked at him questioningly. Always what?

Always dark, even in the daytime, he had wanted to say, but it made no sense. The day after her death, the day of her funeral, he would always remember this wan light and his deep sleep, too, with her lying dead in the next room. Perhaps the windows . . .

"The windows?"

Yes, they were still closed. They had not been opened during the night, and the warm glow of those big dripping candles lingered. The bed had been taken away and she was there in her padded casket, rigid and ashen against the creamy satin.

No. Enough. He had seen her.

He closed his eyes, for they burned from all the crying he had done these past few days. Enough. He had slept and everything had been washed away with that sleep. Now he was relaxed, with a sense of sorrowful emptiness. Let the casket be closed and carried away with all it held of his past life.

But since she was still there . . .

He jumped to his feet and tottered. They caught him and, with eyes still closed, he allowed himself to be led to the open casket. When he opened his eyes and saw her, he called her by name, her name that lived for him alone, the name in which he saw her and knew her in all the fullness of the life they had shared together. He glared resentfully at the others daring to stare at her lying still in death. What did they know about her? They could not even imagine what it meant to him to be deprived of her. He felt like screaming, and it must have been apparent, for his son hurried over to take him away. He was quick to see the meaning of this and felt a chill as though he were stripped bare. For shame—those foolish ideas up to the very last, even after his night-long sleep. Now they must hurry so as not to keep the friends waiting who had come to follow the coffin to the church.

"Come on, Papa. Be reasonable."

With angry, piteous eyes, the bereaved man turned back to his big chair.

Reasonable, yes; it was useless to cry out the anguish that welled within him and that could never be expressed by words or deeds. For a husband who is left a widower at a certain age, a man still yearning for his wife, can the loss be the same as that of a son for whom—at a certain point—it is almost timely to be left an orphan? Timely, since he was on the point of getting married and would, as soon as the three months' mourning were passed, now that he had the added excuse that it was better for both of them to have a woman to look after the house.

"Pardi! Pardi!" they shouted from the entrance hall.

His chill became more intense when he understood clearly for the first time that they were not calling him but his son. From now on their surname would belong more to his son than to him. And he, like a fool, had gone in there to cry out the living name of his mate, like a profanation. For shame! Yes, useless, foolish ideas, he now realized, after that long sleep which had washed him clean of everything.

Now the one vital thing to keep him going was his curiosity as to how their new home would be arranged. Where, for example, were they going to have him sleep? The big double bed had been removed. Would he have a small bed? he wondered. Yes, probably his son's single bed. Now he would have the small bed. And his son would soon be lying in a big bed, his wife beside him within arm's reach. He, alone, in his little bed, would stretch out his arms into thin air.

He felt torpid, perplexed, with a sensation of emptiness inside and all around him. His body was numb from sitting so long. If he tried now to get up he felt sure that he would rise light as a feather in all that emptiness, now that his life was reduced to nothing. There was hardly any difference between himself and the big chair. Yet the chair appeared secure on its four legs, whereas he no longer knew where his feet and legs belonged nor what to do with his hands. What did he care about his life? He did not care particularly about the lives of others, either. Yet as he was still alive he must go on. Begin again—some sort of life which he could not yet conceive and which he certainly would never have contemplated if things had not changed in his own world. Now, deposed like this all of a sudden, not old and yet no longer young . . .

He smiled and shrugged his shoulders. For his son, all at once, he had become a child. But after all, as everyone knows, fathers are children to their grown sons who are full of worldly ambition and have successfully outdistanced them in positions of importance. They keep their fathers in idleness to repay all they have received when they themselves were small, and their fathers in turn become young again.

The single bed . . .

But they did not even give him the little room where his son had slept. Instead, they said, he would feel more independent in another, almost hidden on the courtyard; he would feel free there to do as he liked. They refurnished it with all the best pieces, so it would not occur to anyone that it had once been a servant's room. After the marriage, all the front rooms were pretentiously decorated and newly furnished, even to the luxury of carpets. Not a trace remained of the way the old house had looked. Even with his own furniture relegated to that little dark room, out of the mainstream of the young people's existence, he did not feel at home. Yet, oddly enough, he did not resent the disregard he seemed to have reaped along with the old furniture, because he admired the new rooms and was satisfied with his son's success.

But there was another deeper reason, not too clear as yet, a promise of another life, all shining and colorful, which was erasing the memory of the old one. He even drew a secret hope from it that a new life might begin for him too. Unconsciously, he sensed the luminous opening of a door at his back whence he might escape at the right moment, easy enough now that no one bothered about him, leaving him as if on holiday in the sanctuary of his little room "to do as he pleased." He felt lighter than air. His eyes had a gleam in them that colored everything, leading him from marvel to marvel, as though he really were a child again. He had the eyes of a child—lively and open wide on a world which was still new.

He took the habit of going out early in the morning to begin his holiday which was to last as long as his life lasted. Relieved of all responsibilities, he agreed to pay his son so much every month out of his pension for his maintenance. It was very little. Though he needed nothing, his son thought he should keep some money for himself to satisfy any need he might have. But need for what? He was satisfied now just to look on at life.

Having shaken off the weight of experience, he no longer knew how to get along with oldsters. He avoided them. And the younger people considered him too old, so he went to the park where the children played.

That was how he started his new life—in the meadow among the children in the grass. What an exhilerating scent the grass had, and so fresh where it grew thick and high. The children played hide-and-seek there. The constant trickle of some hidden stream outpurled the rustle of the leaves. Forgetting their game, the children pulled off their shoes and stockings. What a delicious feeling to sink into all that freshness of soft new grass with bare feet!

He took off one shoe and was stealthily removing the other when a young girl appeared before him, her face flaming. "You pig!" she cried, her eyes flashing.

Her dress was caught up in front on a bush, and she quickly pulled it down over her legs, because he was looking up at her from where he sat on the ground.

He was stunned. What had she imagined? Already she had disappeared. He had wanted to enjoy the children's innocent fun. Bending down, he put two hands over his hard, bare feet. What had she seen wrong? Was he too old to share a child's delight in going barefoot in the grass? Must one immediately think evil because he was old? Ah, he knew that he could change in a flash from being a child to becoming a man again, if he must. He was still a man, after all, but he didn't want to think about it. He refused to think about it. It was really as a child that he had taken off his shoes. How wrong it was of that wretched girl to insult him like that! He threw himself face down on the grass. All his grief, his loss, his daily loneliness had brought about this gesture, interpreted now in the light of vulgar malice. His gorge rose in disgust and bitterness. Stupid girl! If he had wanted that—even his son admitted he might have "some desires"—he had plenty of money in his pocket for such needs.

Indignant, he pulled himself upright. Shamefacedly, with trembling hands, he put on his shoes again. All the blood had gone to his head and the pulse now beat hot behind his eyes. Yes, he knew where to go for that. He knew.

Calmer now, he got up and went back to the house. In the welter of furniture which seemed to have been placed there on purpose to drive him mad, he threw himself on the bed and turned his face to the wall.

Mortal Remains

Signor Federico Biobin was the despair of his nephews. They must have loved him dearly to put up with so much after he had turned over to them everything he owned. They called him Uncle Fifo. He was a puny little man, completely bald, with a shiny pear-shaped dome and ten stiffly dyed bristles above either side of his ferretlike mouth.

He would get up at night, light in hand, and steal quietly through the house, rummaging into everything, sniffing and snorting and grimacing as if to keep his pointed nose constantly on the alert. Suddenly the whole house would be jolted out of a sound sleep by china crashing down from a kitchen shelf, or boxes hurtling pell-mell in the storeroom. Then everyone would come running, in their shirts, pajamas or nightdresses.

"Uncle, what have you done? What's happened?"

"Nothing. It fairly stinks of old furniture in here!"

He could always manage the most unexpected replies, as if he had not made any noise—in fact, as if he himself had heard nothing. With perfect calm, though somewhat testily, he would speak of the sweet silence that had reigned in the house before they had rushed in on him.

He did not let a day pass without some trick. The best of it was that he called *doing them favors* all the trouble and annoyance he gave, driving his nephews and their servants almost out of their wits. He had been known to spend whole days in the kitchen clipping and pasting strips of paper to doctor a broken pane in the door leading from it to a smelly water closet. It drove the cook to distraction.

"You talk about old furniture stinking," she said. "What about that privy?"

But apparently he didn't smell anything and went right on sniffing, snorting and grimacing in his effort to mend the pane with those strips of thin paper.

Or he would go down to the garden and get mad as a hornet because one side of the gate was embedded in the ground and refused to budge. Pale with rage, the veins bulging at his temples, he would shake the gate so violently that his arms were almost wrenched from their sockets.

"Give up, Uncle," a nephew would call from the window. "Can't you see it won't open?"

"Give up!" he'd explode. "I'll open this gate if it kills me!"

He did not open it and it did not kill him, but he came up all out of breath, inflamed and bathed in sweat, holding out his little hands in a pitiful state to be oiled and bandaged.

When pestering his relatives no longer amused him, he would go out to plague people in the streets. For example, on days when the rain came down in torrents, he would open his umbrella and deliberately plant himself under a rain spout to annoy people by blocking their way so that they were tempted to push him back under cover, close against the wall. The malicious pleasure this gave him curled the corners of his mouth so that he looked like a surly little dog gnashing its teeth.

His latest was the gray alpaca duster he had bought to wear in the house as a bathrobe. When his nephews pointed out that it was intended to be worn for traveling, he cried, "For traveling? Well, then, I'll go."

"Go? But where will you go?"

"To Bergamo," he said. "To Ernesto's. I'll go and say goodbye before he leaves for Genoa to sail for America."

There was no dissuading him from this notion of leaving immediately. That his visit would be a hindrance rather than a pleasure for poor Ernesto in all the commotion of his imminent departure was yet another reason to go. And still another lay in the fact that the doctor had ordered him to be quiet and not overexert himself because of his heart. He *wanted* to die! "But not in Bergamo in the midst of all that upheaval!" Yes, sir, right there in the topsy-turvy house in Bergamo!

Off he went, then, in his gray duster. Unfortunately the threat of death—which his nephews had used without believing in it, just to keep him at home—was fulfilled. News of his death came like a thunderbolt the very hour he reached Bergamo, shocking his nephews in Rome because they had unwittingly predicted it and, having predicted it, albeit unwittingly, had allowed him to go.

This final ordeal meted out to his distant nephews was an even more bitter blow for the nephew in Bergamo. There Uncle Fifo lay in the midst of all the confusion of moving, stone dead on the narrow iron bedstead, in his fine gray duster, from which peeped his stiffly pointed toes. More than content, he seemed blissfully happy.

Among the scattered pieces of furniture pulled away from the walls, he lay comfortably on that bed which no one would dare touch as long as he was there. Four lighted candles stood, two at the head, two at the foot. Fifo's hands lay crossed over his already slightly swollen paunch. The slyboots, he really looked as if he were smiling through half-closed eyes, with those ten little spikes bristling on either side of his ferretlike face.

Uncle Fifo having fulfilled his mission of coming to die in Bergamo for the benefit of his nephew who was leaving for America, it was now up to Ernesto to remove him, either for burial in the cemetery at Bergamo or for shipment to Rome, if the others wanted him to rest in the family vault.

Ernesto decided it was quicker to ship him to Rome and let his cousins have the worry and expense of a funeral. For him every minute was precious. As things were now, he would just about make it to Genoa in time to embark. However, as luck would have it, in making out the shipment forms he had deemed the term *mortal remains* more respectful and dignified than the word *corpse*. He had sought in this way to make amends for all the curses he had heaped on poor Uncle Fifo, who had chosen such a crucial moment to fall dead at his feet.

In Rome, Uncle Fifo's nephews came to the station to collect him, accompanied by a magnificent hearse with four horses, wreaths of flowers, scores of friends and acquaintances as well as representatives of different societies with banners and standards, a priest for the absolution, followed by two long lines of nuns and choir boys carrying lighted candles. When they came for the coffin, the customs officials presented them with a bill amounting to a fine of several thousand lire.

"A fine? What for?" they asked.

"False declaration."

"False? How?"

"Do you think you can get away with calling a coffin containing a corpse 'mortal remains'? Mortal remains: a little pile of ashes and bones in an urn is one thing—as such it's charged at a specific rate. A coffin is something else. A different rate. No matter how small, this is still a coffin and you must pay the regular coffin rates plus the fine."

The nephews protested that there could be no question of fraud on Cousin Ernesto's part. But even admitting hypothetically that such could be the case, the fine, if any, should then be paid by the sender and not by the receiver. They offered to pay the difference in rate since this was definitely a coffin and was not mortal remains—though it did seem to them like splitting hairs. But as to the fine—no, no, no! They were not at fault. Cousin Ernesto had gone to America and if there had been a mistake—mind you, not a *fraud*—it was on the part of the customs office in Bergamo, which had received and shipped out a whole coffin, accepting the declaration as "mortal remains."

To placate the station master, called in to back up the customs official, the nephews were even ready to find excuses for the customs office in Bergamo. They explained that Cousin Ernesto must have shipped who knows how many boxes and, as it was well known in town that he was leaving Italy for good, the customs official in charge of shipments could easily have thought that he was shipping the mortal remains of a relative long-buried in the cemetery at Bergamo whom he did not want to leave behind. The fault, in this case, was reduced to a mere oversight. Were *they* to be fined for that? If anyone was responsible, it was the customs official in Bergamo. They did not enter into it at all.

While this discussion was raging in the customs office, outside on the square in front of the station the funeral party, dressed in black and wearing top hats, had lined up stiffly against the wall to take shelter from the sweltering August sun. The narrow strip of shade along the wall barely covered the toes of their shoes. All else before them shimmered in the blinding heat.

They looked like pickets of a fence as they stood there staring stiffly at the enormous hearse, which loomed, a black-and-gold nightmare, in the very center of the square. The nuns, bundled in heavy brown woolen habits, all deep-bosomed under starched white bibs, with peaked black wool hoods on their heads, stood impassively, their eyes lowered, lighted candles in their hands. The sunlight was so strong that it swallowed the candle flames and only wavering wisps of smoke could be seen.

What was going on? Why didn't they bring the coffin? What were they waiting for? The more impatient went inside. Then, little by little, all the mourners sought the delicious cool of the customs office, a vast warehouse whose four walls were piled high with crates, bales and bundles. Only the driver of the hearse, the nuns and the choir boys remained in the square.

The big place re-echoed with loud voices in the hot dispute between the nephews of the dead man and the station master and his officials. Everyone's blood was boiling. The station master was adamant: pay the fine or no coffin. Infuriated, the elder nephew threatened to leave the coffin there. A corpse was hardly the kind of merchandise to resell at auction! He'd like to see what the station master could do with it! The station master scoffed; he'd get permission to have two porters carry it off and bury it, and the bailiffs would then take care of collecting costs, duties and fine. A tremor of indignation met this retort and, encouraged by the common consent of the mourners, the younger nephew now dared him to do it. The administration, he said, would be held responsible for moral and material damage: their uncle was not a dog to be carted off and buried in this fashion. Why, several hundred people had gathered here to honor him as he deserved, with banners and standards, a first-class hearse, a holy priest, nuns and choir boys with more than forty candles!

The two nephews, red as lobsters, their white shirts bulging and showing beneath their vests in all the excitement, still trembling after their violent outburst, were led away, crying tears of rage.

Empty and swaying, the nightmare hearse rolled grandly away, back to the stables; the nuns and choir boys turned their candles over and snuffed them out on the flagstones. Everyone, even the nephews, had a strange feeling of relief over the outcome, as though Uncle Fifo had dismissed his funeral and was no longer dead.

Could he really be considered dead, Uncle Fifo, when he continued to do what he had always done in life: heckle and torment everybody?

Of course a dead man has never been known to uncross his hands and shoo a fly from his nose, but Uncle Fifo, doubly protected in a zinc and walnut coffin lying at the feet of the station master, left alone there in the customs warehouse to contemplate the long box and scratch his head, could well be imagined lifting his fine little hands and rubbing them together with glee.

Selected Readings

Bishop, Thomas. *Pirandello and the French Theatre.* New York: New York University Press, 1960.

Budel, Oscar. *Pirandello.* New York: Hillary House Publishers, 1966.

Cambon, Glauco. (ed.). *Pirandello, a Collection of Critical Essays.* Englewood Cliffs, N.J.: Prentice-Hall, Inc., 1967.

Friskin, A. M. I. "Luigi Pirandello: The Tragedy of the Man Who Thinks." *Italica,* XXV (1948), 138–49.

Golina, Carlo. "Pirandello's Least Known Novel." *Italica,* XXVI (1949), 263–68.

Hughes, Merritt Y. "Pirandello's Humor." *Sewanee Review,* XXXV (1927), 175–86.

Keene, Frances. Introduction to *Short Stories by Luigi Pirandello.* Trans. Lily Duplaix. New York: Simon and Schuster, 1965.

Knowlton, E. C. "Metaphysics and Pirandello." *South Atlantic Quarterly,* XXXIV (1935), 42–59.

Lucas, Frank Laurence. *The Drama of Chekhov, Synge, Yeats and Pirandello.* London: Cassell, 1963.

MacClintock, Lander. *The Age of Pirandello.* Bloomington, Ind.: Indiana University Press, 1951.

Sedwick, Frank. "Unamuno and Pirandello Revisited." *Italica,* XXXIII (1956), 40–51.

Starkie, Walter F. *Luigi Pirandello.* 3rd ed. Berkeley, Cal.: University of California Press, 1965.

Vittorini, Domenico. *The Drama of Luigi Pirandello.* New York: Dover Publications, 1957.

ANDRÉ GIDE

(1869–1951)

André Gide was born in Paris in 1869 of well-to-do, puritanical parents. Critics and biographers make much of the fact that he carried a Bible with him continuously until a trip to Africa in 1893 and that he probably should have taken it along at that time. The theme of struggle between sensual inclinations and spiritual attainments probably dates from that trip.

The truth is that little of the biographical seems to find its way into Gide's work. This kind of material he reserved for his autobiography, published in 1926. As a writer, Gide was more cerebral in his approach to material—Greek myth or his own private mythos afforded him the necessary distance for expressing certain intellectual concepts. He employed this mythos to reject old moral, ethical, social, or religious conceptions that impinged on man's freedom to respond impulsively to chance happenings.

In Gide's literary world, man seems to be abandoned in a world that doesn't "add up," and neither the Greek nor the Christian credos work any longer for the modern man seeking to order his own concept of existence. Theseus, the Greek hero, plays the universal strings by ear, responding to whatever involvement happens his way. Gide is another typically twentieth-century writer in that he represents a further move away from the acknowledgment of objective truth as being inherent in form, merely waiting to reveal itself or to be revealed; and a move toward the realization of relative, subjective truth emanating from the conscious existence of man as a responsible individual.

In 1947 André Gide received the Nobel prize for his contribution to the world of such books as *The Immoralist*, 1902; *The Pastoral Symphony*, 1919; *The Counterfeiters*, 1926; *Theseus*, 1931; and the drama *Oedipus*, 1931.

Theseus

I wanted to tell the story of my life as a lesson for my son Hippolytus; but he is no more, and I am telling it all the same. For his sake I should not have dared to include, as I shall now do, certain passages of love; he was extraordinarily prudish, and in his company I never dared to speak of my attachments. Besides, these only mattered to me during the first part of my life; but at least they taught me to know myself, as did also the various monsters whom I subdued. For "the first thing is to know exactly who one is," I used to say to Hippolytus; "later comes the time to assess and adopt one's inheritance. Whether you wish it or not, you are, as I was myself, a king's son. Nothing to be done about it; it's a fact; it pins you down." But Hippolytus never took much notice; even less than I had taken at his age; and like myself at that time, he got on very nicely without it. Oh, early years, all innocently passed! Oh, careless growth of body and mind! I was wind; I was wave. I grew with the plant; I flew with the bird. My self knew no boundaries, every contact with an outer world did not so much teach me my own limits as awaken within me some new power of enjoyment. Fruit I caressed, and the bark of young trees, and smooth stones on the shore, and the coats of horses and dogs, before ever my hands were laid on a woman. Toward all the charming things that Pan, Zeus, or Thetis could offer, I rose.

One day my father said to me that things couldn't go on as they were. "Why not?" Because, good heavens, I was his son and must show myself worthy of the throne to which I should succeed. . . .

From *Two Legends: Theseus and Oedipus,* by André Gide and translated by John Russell. Copyright 1950 by Alfred A. Knopf, Inc. Reprinted by permission.

Just when I was feeling so happy, sprawled naked among cool grasses or on some scorching beach. Still, I can't say that he was wrong. Certainly he was right in teaching me to rebel against myself. To this I owe all that I have achieved since that day; no longer to live at random—agreeable as such license might have been. He taught me that nothing great, nothing of value, and nothing that will last can be got without effort.

My first effort was made at his invitation. It was to overturn boulders in the hope of finding the weapons which Poseidon (so he told me) had hidden beneath one of them. He laughed to see how quickly my strength grew through this training. With the toughening of my body there came also a toughening of the will. After I dislodged the heaviest rocks of the neighborhood and was about to continue my unfruitful search by attacking the flagstones of the palace gateway, my father stopped me. "Weapons," said he, "count for less than the arm that wields them, and the arm in its turn for less than the thinking will which directs it. Here are the weapons. Before giving them to you, I was waiting to see you deserve them. I can sense in you now the ambition to use them, and that longing for fame which will allow you to take up arms only in defense of noble causes and for the weal of all mankind. Your childhood is over. Be a man. Show your fellow men what one of their kind can be and what he means to become. There are great things to be done. Claim yourself."

II

Aegeus, my father, was an excellent person; all that could be wished. In point of fact, I suspect that I was his son only in name. That's what I've been told, and that great Poseidon begat me. In which case it's from this god that I inherit my inconstancy of temper. Where women are concerned, I have never known how to settle down. Aegeus sometimes stood rather in my way, but I am grateful to him for his guardianship, and for having restored the cult of Aphrodite to honor in Attica. I am sorry for the fateful slip by which I brought about his death—when I forgot, I mean, to run up white sails in place of black, on the ship that carried me home from Crete. It had been agreed that I should do this if I were to return in triumph from my rash venture. One can't think of everything. But to tell the truth, and if I cross-question myself (a thing I never much care to do) I can't swear that it was really forgetfulness. Aegeus was in my way, as I told you, and particularly when, through the potions of the witch Medea, who found him (as, indeed, he found himself), a rather elderly bed-fellow, he formed the exasperating idea that a second meridian of enjoyment was his for the asking—thus blocking my career, whereas, after all, it's every man in his turn. Anyway, when he saw those black sails . . . I learned, on returning to Athens, that he had thrown himself into the sea.

No one can deny it. I think I have performed some notable services; I've purged the earth once and for all of a host of tyrants, bandits and monsters; I've cleaned up certain dangerous by-roads on which even the bravest could not venture without a shiver; and I've cleared up the skies in such a way that man, his head less bowed, may be less fearful of their surprises.

One must own that in those days the look of the country was hardly reassuring. Between the scattered townships there were huge stretches of uncultivated waste, crossed only by unreliable tracks. There were the dense forests, the mountainous ravines. At the most dangerous points robber gangs had taken up their positions; these pillaged, killed, or at best held for ransom the traveler, and there were no police to stop them. These incidents combined with the purposeful ferocity of wild beasts and the evil power of the deceitful elements until one could hardly tell, when some foolhardy person came to grief, whether the malignity of the gods had struck him down or merely that of his fellow men. Nor, in the case of such monsters as the Sphinx or the Gorgon who fell to Oedipus or to Bellerophon, could one be sure whether the human strain or the divine was preponderant. Whatever was inexplicable was put on to the gods. Terror and religion were so nearly one that heroism often seemed an impiety. The first and principal victories that man had to win were over the gods.

In a fight, whether with man or with god, it is only by seizing one's adversary's own weapon and turning it against him (as I did with the club of Periphetes, the dark giant of Epidaurus) that one can be sure of final victory.

And as for the thunderbolts of Zeus, I can tell you that the day will come when man will possess himself of them, as Prometheus possessed himself of fire. Yes, those are decisive victories. But with women, at once my strength and my weakness, I was always having to begin again. I escaped from one, only to fall into the lap of some other; nor did I ever conquer a woman who had not first conquered me. Pirithoüs was right when he told me (ah, how we well used to get on!) that the important thing was never to be unmanned by a woman, as was Hercules in the arms of Omphale. And since I have never been able or wished to live without women, he would say to me, as I darted off on each amorous chase: "Go ahead, but don't get stuck." There was one woman who, ostensibly to safeguard my life, would have bound me to herself by a cord—a thin one, it is true, but a fixed rein none the less. This same woman . . . but of that, more in due time.

Of them all, Antiope came nearest to catching me. She was queen of the Amazons, and like all her subjects had only one breast; but this in no way impaired her beauty. An accomplished runner and wrestler, she had muscles as firm and sturdy as those of our athletes. I took her on in single combat. In my arms she struggled like a leopard. Disarmed, she brought her teeth and nails into play; enraged by my laughter (for I, too, had no weapons) and because she could not stop herself from loving me. I had never possessed anyone more virginal. And little did it matter to me that later she could only suckle my Hippolytus, her son, with one breast. It was this chaste and savage being whom I wished to make my heir. I shall speak, during the course of my story, of what has been the greatest grief of my life. For it is not enough to exist, and then to have existed: one must make one's legacy and act in such a way that one is not extinguished with oneself, so my grandfather had often told me. Pittheus and Aegeus were much more intelligent than I; so is Pirithoüs. But people give me credit for good sense; the rest is added with the determination to do well that has never left me. Mine, too, is the kind of courage that incites me to desperate enterprises. On top of all this I was ambitious. The great deeds of my cousin Hercules, which they used to report to me, exasperated my young blood, and when it was time to leave Troezen, where I had lived till then, and rejoin my so-called father in Athens, I refused altogether to accept the advice, sound though it was, to go by sea because that route was the safer. Well I knew it but it was the very hazards of the overland route, with its immense detour, that tempted me; a chance to prove my worth. Thieves of every sort were beginning once again to infest the country, and did so with impunity now that Hercules was squandering his manhood at the feet of Omphale. I was sixteen. All the cards were in my hand. My turn had come. In great leaps my heart was bounding toward the extremity of my happiness. "What have I to do with safety," I cried, "and a route that's set in order!" I despised comfort and idleness and unlaurelled ease. So it was on the road to Athens by way of the isthmus of the Peloponnesus that I first put myself to the test, and my heart and my arm together taught me their full strength, when I cut down some well-known and well-hated robbers: Sinis, Periphetes, Procrustes, Geryon (no, that was Hercules; I meant to say Cercyon). By the way I made a slight mistake at that time, when Sciron was concerned, for he turned out afterwards to have been a very worthy man, good-natured and most helpful to passing travelers. But as I had just done away with him, it was soon agreed that he had been a rascal.

Also on the road to Athens, in a thicket of asparagus, there smiled upon me the first of my conquests in love. Perigone was tall and supple. I had just killed her father, and by way of amends I got her a very handsome son: Menalippes. I have lost track of both of them—breaking free, as usual, and anxious never to lose any time. I have never allowed the past to involve or detain me; rather have I been drawn forward by what was still to be achieved; and the most important things seemed to me always to lie ahead.

So much so that I won't waste more time with these preliminary trifles which, after all, meant only too little to me. Here I was on the threshold of an admirable adventure. Hercules himself never had one like it. I must tell it at length.

III

It's very complicated, this story. I must say first that the island of Crete was a power in those days. Minos reigned there. He held Attica responsible for the death of his son Androgeus; and by way of reprisal he had exacted from us an annual tribute: seven young men and seven young girls had to be handed over to satisfy, it was said, the appetites of the Minotaur, the monstrous child which

Pasiphaë, the wife of Minos, had brought forth after intercourse with a bull. These victims were chosen by lot.

But, in the year in question, I had just returned to Greece. Though the lot would normally have spared me (princes readily escape these things), I insisted that I should figure in the list, notwithstanding the opposition of the king, my father. I care nothing for privilege, and claim that merit alone distinguishes me from the herd. My plan was, in point of fact, to vanquish the Minotaur and thus at a blow to free Greece from this abominable exaction. Also I was most anxious to visit Crete, whence beautiful, costly and unusual objects were constantly arriving in Attica. Therefore I set sail for the island; among my thirteen companions was my friend Pirithoüs.

We landed, one morning in March, at Amnisos, a little township that served as harbor to its neighbor Knossos, the capital of the island, where Minos resided and had had his palace built. We should have arrived the previous evening, but a violent storm had delayed us. As we stepped ashore we were surrounded by armed guards, who took away my sword and that of Pirithoüs. When they had searched us for other weapons, they led us off to appear before the king, who had come from Knossos, with his court, to meet us. A large crowd of the common people pressed round to have a look at us. All the men were naked to the waist except Minos, who, seated beneath a dais, wore a long robe made from a single piece of dark red cloth; this fell in majestic folds from his shoulders to his ankles. His chest, broad as that of Zeus himself, bore three tiers of necklaces. Many Cretans wear these, but of a trumpery sort. Minos had necklaces of rare stones, and plaques of wrought gold in the shape of fleurs-de-lis. The double-headed axe hung above his throne, and with his right hand he stretched before him a golden scepter, as tall as himself. In the other hand was a three-leaved flower, like those on his necklaces, and also in gold, but larger. Above his golden crown was a gigantic panache, in which were mingled the feathers of peacock, ostrich and halcyon. He looked us over for some time and then bade us welcome to the island, with a smile that may well have been ironical, since we had come there, after all, under sentence of death. By his side were standing the queen and the two princesses, her daughters. I saw at once that the elder daughter had taken a fancy to me. As our guards were making ready to take us away, I saw her lean toward her father and say to him in Greek (she whispered, but my ears are sharp): "Not that one, I beg you," and she pointed toward me with her finger. Minos smiled once again and gave orders that I should not be taken away with my companions. I was no sooner alone before him than he began to question me.

Although I had promised myself to act with all possible prudence and to let slip no hint either of my noble birth or of my audacious project, it suddenly occurred to me that it would be better to put my cards on the table, now that I had attracted the attention of the princess. Nothing would be more likely to heighten her feeling for me, or to win me the favor of the king, than to hear me say frankly that I was the grandson of Pittheus. I even hinted that the current rumor in Attica was that the great Poseidon had begot me. To this Minos replied gravely that he would presently clear up that point by submitting me to trial by water. In return I replied complacently that I had no doubt I should survive triumphantly any test that he cared to impose. The ladies of the court, if not Minos himself, were favorably affected by my self-confidence.

"And now," said Minos, "you must go and have something to eat. Your companions are already at table and will be waiting for you. After such a disturbed night you must be quite peckish, as they say here. Have a good rest. I shall expect you to be present toward the end of the day at the ceremonial games in honor of your visit. Then, Prince Theseus, we shall take you with us to Knossos. You will sleep at the palace, and tomorrow evening you will dine with us—a simple, family meal, where you will feel quite at home, and these ladies will be delighted to hear you tell of your first exploits. And now they are going to prepare themselves for the festivities. We shall meet again at the games, where you will sit, with your companions, immediately beneath the royal box. This courtesy we owe to your princely rank; and as I do not wish to distinguish you openly from your companions they shall, by contagion, rank with you."

The games were held in a vast semi-circular arena, opening on the sea. Huge crowds, both of men and of women, had come to see them, from Knossos, from Lyttos and even from Gortyn (a matter of two hundred stadia distant, I was told), from other towns and their neighboring villages, and from the thickly-populated open country. All my senses were taken by surprise, and I cannot describe how foreign the Cretans appeared to me to be. As there was not room for them all on the tiers of the amphitheater, they pushed and jostled their way up the staircases and along the aisles. The women, no less numerous than the men, were for the most part naked to the waist. A very few wore a light bodice, but even this was generously cut away, in a fashion that I could not help thinking rather immodest, and exposed both breasts to the air. Men and women alike were tightly, even absurdly laced around the hips with belts and corselets, which gave to each the figure of an hour glass. The men were nearly all brown-skinned, and at their fingers, wrists and throats wore almost as many rings, bracelets and necklaces as the women, who, for their part, were perfectly white. All the men were clean-shaven, except for the king, Rhadamanthus, his brother, and his friend Daedalus. The ladies of the court sat on a platform just above our own, which dominated the arena from a considerable height. They had indulged a prodigious extravagance of dress and ornament. Each wore a flounced skirt; billowing out oddly below the hips, this fell in embroidered furbelows to their feet, which were shod in little boots of white leather. The fastuosity of the queen, who sat in the centre of the dais, made her most conspicuous of all. Her arms and the front of her person were bare. Upon her magnificent breasts, pearls, emeralds and precious stones were embanked. Long black curls fell on either side of her face, and smaller ringlets streaked her forehead. She had the lips of a glutton, an upturned nose, and huge empty eyes, whose expression one might have called bovine. A sort of golden diadem served her as a crown. It sat, not directly on her hair, but on a ridiculous hat of some dark material, which came up through the diadem and tapered into a sharp point, like a horn, which jutted far out in front of her forehead. Her corsage uncovered her to the waist in front, but rose high at the back and ended in an enormous cutaway collar. Her skirt was spread wide around her, and one could admire, upon their creamy ground, three rows of embroidery, one above the other—purple irises at the top, saffrons in the center and below them violets with their leaves. As I was sitting immediately below, I had only to turn round to have all this, as one might say, under my very nose. I marvelled as much at the sense of color and the beauty of the design as at the delicate perfection of the work.

Ariadne, the elder daughter, sat at her mother's right hand and presided over the corrida. She was less sumptuously dressed than the queen, and she wore different colors. Her skirt, like that of her sister, had only two circles of embroidery: on the upper one, dogs and hinds; on the lower, dogs and partridges. Phaedra, perceptibly a much younger girl, sat on Pasiphaë's left. Her dress had a frieze of children running after hoops, and another of younger children squatting on their behinds and playing marbles. She took a childish pleasure in the spectacle. As for me, I could hardly follow what was going on, it was all so disconcertingly new, but I could not help being amazed by the suppleness, speed and agility of the acrobats who took their chance in the arena after the singers, the dancers, and then the wrestlers had had their turn. Myself about to encounter the Minotaur, I learned a good deal from watching the feints and passes that might help me to baffle and tire the bull.

IV

After Ariadne had rewarded the last champion with the last prize, Minos declared the games closed. Escorted by his courtiers, he bade me come to him separately.

"I am going to take you now, Prince Theseus," he said to me, "to a place by the sea where I shall put you to the test, and we shall see if you are the true son of the god Poseidon, as you claimed to be just now."

He took me to a small promontory with waves beating at its foot. "I shall now," said the king, "throw my crown into the sea, as a mark of my confidence that you will be able to retrieve it from the bottom."

The queen and the two princesses were there to see what would come of the test; and so, emboldened by their presence, I protested:

"Am I a dog, to fetch and carry for my master, even if it be a crown? Let me dive in without bait and I shall bring back to you something or other that will attest and prove my case."

In my audacity I went still further. A stiff breeze had sprung up, and it happened that a long scarf was dislodged from Ariadne's shoulders. A gust blew it toward me. I caught it with a smile, as if the princess or one of the gods had offered it to me. Then, stripping off my close-fitting corselet, I wrapped the scarf round my loins in its place, twisted it up between my thighs and made it fast. It looked as if I did this from modesty, lest I should expose my manhood before these ladies; but in fact it allowed me to hide the leather belt that I was still wearing, to which was attached a small purse. In this I had, not metal coins, but some valuable stones that I had brought with me from Greece, knowing that they would keep their full value, no matter where I went.

Then I took a deep breath and dived.

A practiced swimmer, I dived deep, and did not come up to the surface until I had removed from my purse an onyx and two chrysoprases. Once back on dry land I offered, with my most chivalrous bow, the onyx to the queen and a chrysoprase to each of her daughters. I pretended to have gathered them on the bottom, or rather (since it was hardly plausible that the stones, so rare upon dry land, should have lain promiscuously at the bottom of the sea, or that I should have had time to pick them out) that Poseidon himself had handed them to me, in order that I could offer them to the ladies. Here was proof, better than any test of my divine origin and my good standing with the god.

After this, Minos gave me back my sword.

Soon afterwards chariots bore us off on the road to Knossos.

V

I was so overwhelmed by fatigue that I could hardly feel due astonishment at the great courtyard of the palace, or at a monumental balustraded staircase and the winding corridors through which attentive servants, torch in hand, guided me to the second floor, where a room had been set apart for me. All but one of its many lamps were snuffed out after I arrived. The bed was scented and soft; when they left me, I fell at once into a heavy sleep, which lasted until the evening of the following day, although I had already slept during our long journey; for only at dawn, after traveling all night, had we arrived at Knossos.

I am by no means a cosmopolitan. At the court of Minos I realized for the first time that I was Greek, and I felt very far from home. All unfamiliar things took me by surprise—dress, customs, ways of behaving, furniture (in my father's house we were short of furniture), household objects and the manner of their use. Among so much that was exquisite, I felt like a savage, and my awkwardness was redoubled when people began smiling at my conduct. I had been used to biting my way through my food, lifting it to my mouth in my fingers, and these delicate forks of metal or wrought gold, these knives they use, for cutting meat, gave me more trouble than the heaviest weapons of war. People couldn't take their eyes off me; and when I had to talk, I appeared a still greater oaf. God! How out of place I felt! Only on my own have I ever been good for anything; now for the first time I was in society. It was no longer a question of fighting, or carrying a thing through by main force, but rather of giving pleasure; and of this I had strangely little experience.

I sat, at table, between the two princesses. A simple family meal, without formality, I was told. And in fact, apart from Minos and the queen, Rhadamanthus, the king's brother, the two princesses and their young brother Glaucus, there was nobody except the tutor of the young prince, a Greek from Corinth, who was not even presented to me.

They asked me to describe in my own tongue (which everybody at the court understood very well and spoke fluently, though with a slight accent) what they were pleased to call my exploits. I was delighted to see that the young Phaedra and Glaucus were seized with uncontrollable laughter at the story of the treatment that Procrustes imposed upon passers-by, which I made him endure in his turn—chopping off all those parts of him which exceeded his statutory measure. But they tactfully avoided any allusion to the cause of my visit to Crete, and affected to see me as merely a traveler.

Throughout the meal, Ariadne pressed her knee against mine under the table; but it was the warmth of the young Phaedra that really stirred me. Meanwhile, Pasiphaë, the queen, who sat opposite me, was fairly eating me with her enormous eyes, and Minos, by her side, wore an unvarying smile. Only Rhadamanthus, with his long, fair beard, seemed rather out of humor. Both he and the king left the room after the fourth course—"to sit on their throne," they said. Only later did I realize what this meant.

I still felt some traces of my sea-sickness. I ate a great deal, and drank still more. I was so liberally plied with wines and liqueurs of every sort that before long I didn't know where I was. I was used to drinking only water or diluted wine. With everything reeling before me, but still able to stand, I begged permission to leave the room. The queen at once led me into a small closet that adjoined her private apartments. After I had been thoroughly sick, I rejoined her on a sofa in her room, and it was then that she began to tackle me.

"My young friend—if I may call you so," she began, "we must make the most of these few moments alone together. I am not what you suppose, and have no designs upon your person, attractive as that may be." And, protesting the while that she was addressing herself only to my spirit, or to some undefined but interior zone of my being, she continually stroked my forehead; later she slipped her hands under my leather jerkin and fondled my pectorals, as if to convince herself that I was really there.

"I know what brings you here, and I want to warn you of a mistake. Your intentions are murderous. You are here to fight my son. I don't know what you may have heard about him, and I don't want to know. Ah, listen to the pleas of my heart! He whom they call the Minotaur may or may not be the monster of whom you have no doubt heard, but he is my son."

At this point I thought it only decent to interject that I had nothing against monsters in themselves; but she went on without listening.

"Please try to understand me. By temperament I am a mystic. Heavenly things alone excite my love. The difficulty, you see, is one never can tell exactly where the god begins and where he ends. I have seen a good deal of my cousin Leda. For her the god hid himself in the guise of a swan. Now, Minos always knew that I wanted to give him a Dioscuros for his heir. But how can one distinguish the animal residue that may remain even in the seed of the gods? If I have since then deplored my mistake—and I realize that to talk of it in this way robs the affair of all grandeur—yet I assure you, Theseus, that it was a celestial moment. For you must understand that my bull was no ordinary beast. Poseidon had sent him. He should have been offered to him as a sacrifice, but he was so beautiful that Minos could not bring himself to do it. That is how I have been able ever since to pass off my desires as an instrument of the god's revenge. And you no doubt know that my mother-in-law, Europa, was carried off by a bull. Zeus was hiding inside him. Minos himself was the fruit of their union. That is why bulls have always been held in great honor in his family. And, if ever, after the birth of the Minotaur, I noticed the king knitting his brows, I had only to say: "What about your mother?" He could only admit that it was a natural mistake. He is very wise. He believes that Zeus has nominated him judge, along with Rhadamanthus, his brother. He takes the view that one must have understood before one can pass judgment, and he thinks that he will not be a good judge until he has experienced everything, either in his own person or through his family. This is a great encouragement for us all. His children, and I myself, in our several ways, are working, by our individual errors of conduct, for the advancement of his career. The Minotaur too, though he doesn't know it. That is why I am begging you here and now, Theseus, not to try to do him any sort of injury, but rather to become intimate with him, and so to end a misunderstanding that has made Crete the enemy of Greece and done great harm to our two countries."

So saying, she became even more attentive, and a point was reached at which I was seriously incommoded, while the exhalations of wine heightened and mingled with the powerful effluvium which, in company with her breasts, was escaping from her corsage.

"Let us return to celestial things," she went on, "as return we always must. You yourself, Theseus—surely you must feel that you are inhabited by one of the gods?"

What put the final touch to my embarrassment was that Ariadne, the elder daughter (and an exceptional beauty, though less attractive to me personally than Phaedra), had made it quite plain to me, before I began to feel so sick—had made it quite plain, as I say, as much by signs as by a whisper, that as soon as I felt better I was to join her on the terrace.

VI

What a terrace! And what a palace! Trance-like under the moon, the gardens seemed to be suspended in readiness for one knew not what. It was the month of March, but I could sense already the delicious half-warmth of spring. Once in the open air, I began to

feel quite well. Never an indoor man, I need to fill my lungs with
fresh air. Ariadne came running toward me, and without a word
clamped her warm lips to mine—so violently that we were both
sent staggering.

"Follow me," she said. "Not that I mind if anyone sees us; but
we can talk more freely under the terebinths." She led me down a
few steps toward a more leafy part of the gardens, where huge trees
obscured the moon, though not its reflection upon the sea. She
had changed her clothes, and now wore, in place of her hooped
skirt and tight surcoat, a sort of loose dress, beneath which she
was palpably naked.

"I can guess what my mother's been telling you," she began.
"She's mad, raving mad, and you can disregard everything she
says. First of all, I must tell this: you are in great danger here. You
came here, as I well know, to fight my half-brother, the Minotaur.
I'm telling you all this for your own good, so listen carefully. You
will win—I'm sure of it. To see you is to banish doubt. (Don't
you think that's rather a good line of poetry? But perhaps you
have no ear.) But nobody to this day has ever managed to get out
of the maze in which the monster lives; and you won't succeed
either, unless your sweetheart (that I am, or shall presently be)
comes to your rescue. You can't begin to conceive how complicated it is, that maze. To-morrow I shall introduce you to Daedalus,
who will tell you about it. It was he who built it; but even he has already forgotten how to get out of it. You'll hear from him how his
son Icarus, who once ventured inside, could only get out on wings,
through the upper air. That I don't dare to recommend to you;
it's too risky. You'd better get it into your head at once that your
only hope is to stick close to me. We shall be together, you and I—
we *must* be together, from now on, in life and in death. Only
thanks to me, by me, and in me will you be able to recapture yourself. You must take it or leave it. If you leave me, so much the
worse for you. So begin by taking me." Whereupon she abandoned
all restraint, gave herself freely to my embrace, and kept me in her
arms till morning.

The hours passed slowly for me, I must admit. I have never been
good at staying in one place, be it even in the very bosom of delight. I always aim to break free as soon as the novelty has worn
off. Afterwards Ariadne used to say: "You promised." I never

gave a promise of any kind. Liberty above all things! My duty is to myself.

Although my powers of observation were still to some extent clouded by drink, Ariadne appeared to me to yield her last reserves with such readiness that I could hardly suppose myself to have done the work of a pioneer. This disposed of any scruples that I might later have had about leaving her. Besides, her sentimentality soon became unendurable. Unendurable her protestations of eternal devotion, and the tender diminutives with which she ornamented me. I was alternately her only treasure, her canary, her puppy, her tercelet, her guinea-fowl—I loathe pet-names. And then she had read too much. "Little heart," she would say, "the irises will wither fast and die." (In point of fact, they'd hardly begun to flower.) I know quite well that nothing lasts forever; but the present is all that matters to me. And then she would say: "I couldn't exist without you." This made me think all the time of how to get rid of her.

"What will the king, your father, say to that?" I had asked her. And her reply: "Minos, sweet chuck, puts up with everything. He thinks it's wisest to allow what cannot be prevented. He didn't complain of my mother's adventure with the bull, but according to my mother he simply remarked: 'Here I have some difficulty in following you.' 'What's done is done, and nothing can undo it,' he added. When it comes to us, he'll do the same. At the most, he'll banish you from the court—and a lot of difference that'll make! Wherever you go, I shall follow."

That remains to be seen, I thought.

After we had taken a light breakfast, I asked her to be kind enough to lead me to Daedalus, and added that I wished to speak to him privately and alone. She agreed to this only after I had sworn by Poseidon that immediately our talk was over, I would rejoin her at the palace.

VII

Daedalus rose to welcome me. I had found him in a dim-lit room, bending over the tablets and working-drawings that were spread before him, and surrounded by a great many peculiar instruments. He was very tall, and perfectly erect in spite of his great age. His beard was silvery in color, and even longer than that of Minos, which was still quite black, or the fairer one of Rhadamanthus. His vast forehead was marked by deep wrinkles across the whole of its width. When he looked downwards, his eyes were half-hidden by the overhanging brushwood of his eyebrows. He spoke slowly, and in a deep voice. His silences had the quality of thought.

He began by congratulating me on my prowess. The echo of this, he said, had penetrated even to him, who lived in retirement, remote from the tumult of the world. He added that I looked to him to be something of a booby; that he took little account of feats of arms, and did not consider that physical strength was the godhead of man.

"At one time I saw quite a lot of your predecessor Hercules. He was a stupid man, and I could never get anything out of him except heroics. But what I did appreciate in him, and what I appreciate in you, is a sort of absorption in the task in hand, an unrecoiling audacity, a temerity even, which thrusts you forward and destroys your opponent, after first having destroyed the coward whom each of us carries within himself. Hercules took greater pain than you do; was more anxious, also, to do well; rather melancholy, especially when he had just completed an adventure. But what I like in you is your enjoyment; that is where you differ from Hercules. I shall commend you for never letting your mind interfere. You can leave that to others who are not men of action, but are clever at inventing sound and good motives for those who are.

"Do you realize that we are cousins? I too (but don't repeat this to Minos, who knows nothing about it)—I too am Greek. I was forced regretfully to leave Attica after certain differences had arisen between myself and my nephew Talos, a sculptor like myself, and my rival. He became a popular favorite, and claimed to uphold the dignity of the gods by representing them with their lower limbs set fast in a hieratic posture, and thus incapable of movement; whereas I was for setting free their limbs and bringing the gods nearer to ourselves. Olympus, thanks to me, became once again a neighbor of the earth. By way of complement, I aspired, with the aid of science, to mold mankind in the likeness of the gods.

"At your age I longed above all to acquire knowledge. I soon decided that man's personal strength can effect little or nothing without instruments, and that the old saying 'Better a good tool than a strong forearm' was true. Assuredly you could never have subdued the bandits of Attica and the Peloponnese without the weapons which your father had given you. So I thought I could not employ myself more usefully than by bringing these auxiliaries nearer to perfection, and that I could not do this without first mastering mathematics, mechanics and geometry to the degree, at any rate, in which they were known in Egypt, where such things are put to great use; also that I must then pass from theory to practice by learning all that was known about the properties and qualities of every kind of material, even of those for which no immediate use was apparent, for in these (as happens also in the human sphere) one sometimes discovers extraordinary qualities one had never expected to find. And so I widened and entrenched my knowledge.

"To familiarize myself with other trades, other crafts and skills, other climates and other living things, I set myself to visit distant countries, put myself to school with eminent foreigners, and remained with them until they had nothing more to teach me. But no matter where I went, or how long I stayed, I remained a Greek. In the same way it is because I know and feel that you are a son of Greece that I am interested in you, my cousin.

"Once back in Crete, I told Minos all about my studies and my travels, and went on to tell him of a project I had cherished. This was to build and equip, not far from his palace (if he approved the plan and would provide the means to carry it out), a labyrinth like the one which I had admired in Egypt, on the shore of lake Moeris; but mine would be different in plan. At the very moment Minos was in an awkward position. His queen had whelped a monster; not knowing how best to look after it, but judging it prudent to isolate it and keep it well away from the public gaze, he asked me to devise a building and a set of communicating gardens which, without precisely imprisoning the monster, would at least contain him and make it impossible for him to get loose. I lavished all my scholarship, all my best thoughts, on the task.

"But, believing that no prison can withstand a really obstinate intention to escape, and that there is no barrier, no ditch, that daring and resolution will not overcome, I thought that the best way of containing a prisoner in the labyrinth was to make it of such a kind, not that he couldn't get out (try to grasp my meaning here), but that he wouldn't want to get out. I therefore assembled in this one place the means to satisfy every kind of appetite. The Minotaur's tastes were neither many nor various; but we had to plan for everybody, whosoever it might be, who would enter the labyrinth. Another and indeed the prime necessity was to fine down the visitor's will-power to the point of extinction. To this end I made up some electuaries and had them mixed with the wines that were served. But that was not enough; I found a better way. I had noticed that certain plants, when thrown into the fire, gave off, as they burned, semi-narcotic vapors. These seemed admirably suited to my purpose, and indeed they played exactly the part for which I needed them. Accordingly I had them fed to the stoves, which are kept alight night and day. The heavy gases thus distributed not only act upon the will and put it to sleep; they induce a delicious intoxication, rich in flattering delusions, and provoke the mind, filled as this is with voluptuous mirages, to a certain pointless activity; 'pointless,' I say, because it has merely an imaginary outcome, in visions and speculations without order, logic or substance. The effect of these gases is not the same for all of those who breathe them; each is led on by the complexities implicit in his own mind to lose himself, if I may so put it, in a labyrinth of his own devising. For my son Icarus, the complexities were metaphysical. For me, they take the form of enormous edifices, palatial buildings heaped upon themselves with an elaboration of corridors and staircases . . . in which (as with my son's speculations) everything leads to a blank wall, a mysterious 'keep out.' But the most surprising thing about these perfumes is that when one has inhaled them for a certain time, they are already indispensable; body and mind have formed a taste for this malicious insobriety; outside of it reality seems charmless and one no longer has any wish to return to it. And that—that above all—is what keeps one inside the labyrinth. Knowing that you want to enter it in order to fight the Minotaur, I give you fair warning; and if I have told you at length of this danger, it was to put you on your guard. You will never bring it off alone; Ariadne must go with you. But she must remain on the threshold and not so much as sniff the vapors. It is important that she should keep a clear head while you are being overcome by drunkenness. But even when drunk, you must keep control of yourself: everything depends on that. Your will alone may not suffice (for, as I told you, these emanations will weaken it), and so I have thought of this plan: to link you and Ariadne by a thread, the tangible symbol of duty. This thread will allow, indeed will compel you to rejoin her after you have been some time away. Be always determined not to break it, no matter what may be the charms of the labyrinth, the seduction of the unknown, or the headlong urging of your own courage. Go back to her, or all the rest, and the best with it, will be lost. This thread will be your link with the past. Go back to it. Go back to yourself. For nothing can begin from nothing, and it is from your past, and from what you are at this moment, that what you are going to be must spring.

"I should have spoken more briefly if I had not been so interested in you. But before you go out to meet your destiny, I want you to hear my son. You will realize more vividly, while listening to him, what danger you will presently run. Although he was able, thanks to me, to escape the witchcraft of the maze, his mind is still most pitiably a slave to its maleficence."

He walked over to a small door, lifted the arras that covered it, and said very loudly:

"Icarus, my dear son, come and tell us of your distress. Or, rather, go on thinking aloud, as if you were alone. Pay no attention to me or to my guest. Behave as if neither of us were here."

VIII

I saw coming in a young man of about my own age, who seemed in the half-light to be great beauty. His fair hair was worn very long and fell in ringlets to his shoulders. He stared fixedly, but seemed not to focus his gaze on anything in particular. Naked to the waist, he wore a tight metal belt and a loincloth, as it seemed to me, of leather and dark cloth; this swathed the top of his thighs, and was held in place by a curious and prominent knot. His white leather boots caught my eye, and seemed to suggest that he was making ready to go out; but his mind alone was on the move. Himself seemed not to see us. Proceeding no doubt with some unbroken chain of argument, he was saying:

"Who came first: man or woman? Can the Eternal One be female? From the womb of what great Mother have you come, all you myriad species? And by what engendering cause can that womb have been made great? Duality is inadmissable. In that case, god himself would be the son. My mind refuses to divide God. If once I allow division, strife begins. Where there are gods, there are wars. There are not gods, but a God. The kingdom of God is peace. All is absorbed, all is reconciled in the Unique Being."

He was silent for a moment and then went on:

"If man is to give a form to the gods, he must localize and reduce. God spreads where he will. The gods are divided. His extension is immense; theirs merely local."

He was silent again, before going on in a voice panting with anguish.

"But what is the reason for all this, O God who art lucidity itself? For so much trouble, so many struggles? And toward what? What is our purpose here? Why do we seek reasons for everything? Where are we to turn, if not toward God? How are we to direct our steps? Where are we to stop? When can we say: so be it; nothing more to be done? How can we reach God, after starting from man? And if I start from God, how can I reach across to myself? Yet if man is the creation of God, is not God the creation of man? It is the exact crossing place of those roads, at the very heart of that cross, that my mind would fix itself."

As he spoke, the veins swelled on his forehead, and the sweat ran down his temples. At least, so it seemed to me, for I could not see him clearly in the half-light; but I heard him gasping, like a man putting forth an immense effort.

He was quiet for a moment, then went on:

"I don't know where God begins, and still less where He ends. I shall even express myself more exactly if I say that His beginning never ends. Ah, how sick I am of 'therefore,' and 'since,' and 'because'! Sick of inference, sick of deduction. I never learn anything, from the finest of syllogisms that I haven't first put into it myself. If I put God in at the beginning, He comes out at the end. I don't find Him unless I do put Him in. I have tramped all the roads of logic. On their horizontal plane I have wandered all too often. I crawl, and I would rather take wings; to lose my shadow, to lose the filth of my body, to throw off the weight of the past! The infinite calls me! I have the sensation of being drawn upwards from a great point. O mind of man, I shall climb to your topmost height. My father, with his great knowledge of mechanics, will provide me with the means to go. I shall travel alone. I'm not afraid. I can pay my way. It's my only chance to escape. O noble mind, too long entangled in the confusion of my problems, an uncharted road is waiting for you now. I cannot define what it is that summons me; but I know that my journey can have only one end: in God."

Then he backed away from us as far as the arras, which he raised and afterwards let drop behind him.

"Poor dear boy," said Daedalus. "As he thought he could never escape from the labyrinth and did not understand that the labyrinth was within himself, at his request I made him a set of wings, with which he was able to fly away. He thought that he could only escape by way of the heavens, all terrestrial routes being blocked. I knew him to be of a mystical turn, so that his longing did not surprise me. A longing that has not been fulfilled, as you will have been able to judge for yourself while listening to him. In spite of my warnings, he tried to fly too high, and overtaxed his strength. He fell into the sea. He is dead."

"How can that be?" I burst out. "I saw him alive only a moment ago."

"Yes," he answered, "you did see him, and he seemed to be alive. But he is dead. At this point, Theseus, I am afraid that your intelligence, although Greek, and as such subtle and open to all aspects of the truth, cannot follow me; for I myself, I must confess, was slow to grasp and concede this fact: those of us whose souls, when weighed in the supreme scale, are not judged of too little account, do not just live an ordinary life. In time, as we mortals measure it, we grow up, accomplish our destiny, and die. But there is another, truer, eternal plane on which time does not exist; on this plane the representative gestures of our race are inscribed, each according to its particular significance. Icarus was, before his birth, and remains after his death, the image of man's disquiet, of the impulse to discovery, the soaring flight of poetry—the things of which, during his short life, he was the incarnation. He played out his hand, as he owed it to himself to do; but he didn't end there. What happens, in the case of a hero, is this: his mark endures. Poetry and the arts reanimate it, and it becomes an enduring symbol. That is how it is that Orion, the hunter, is riding still, across Elysian fields of asphodel, in search of the prey that he has already killed during his life; and meanwhile the night sky bears the eternal, constellated image of him and his baldric. That is how Tantalus' throat is parched to all eternity, and how Sisyphus still rolls upward toward an unattainable summit the heavy and ever-rebounding weight of care that tormented him in the days when he was king of Corinth. For you must realize that in hell the only punishment is to begin over and over again the actions which, in life, one failed to complete.

"In the same way, in the animal kingdom, the death of each creature in no way impoverishes its species, for this retains its habitual shape and behavior; there are no individuals among the beasts. Whereas among men it is the individual alone who counts. That is why Minos is already leading at Knossos the life which will fit him for his career as a judge in hell. That is why Pasiphaë and Ariadne are yielding to their destiny in such exemplary fashion. And you yourself, Theseus, may appear carefree, and you may feel it, but you will not escape the destiny that is shaping you, any more than did Hercules, or Jason, or Perseus. But know this (because my eyes have learned the art of discerning the future through the present)—there remain great things for you to do, and in a sphere quite different from that of your previous exploits; things beside which these exploits will seem, in the future, to have been the amusements of a child. It remains for you to found the city of Athens, and there to situate the supremacy of the human mind.

"Do not linger, therefore, in the labyrinth, or in the embrace of Ariadne, after the hideous combat from which you will emerge triumphant. Keep on the move. Regard indolence as treachery. Seek no rest until, with your destiny completed, it is time to die. It is only thus that, on the farther side of what seems to be death, you will live, forever re-created by the gratitude of mankind. Keep on the move, keep well ahead, keep on your own road, O valiant gatherer of cities."

"And now listen carefully, Theseus, and remember what I say. No doubt you will have an easy victory over the Minotaur. Taken in the right way, he is not so redoubtable as people suppose. (They used to say that he lived on carrion; but since when has a bull eaten anything but grass?) Nothing is easier than to get into the labyrinth, nothing less easy than to get out. Nobody finds his way in there without first he lose it. And for your return journey (for footsteps leave no trace in the labyrinth) you must attach yourself to Ariadne by a thread. I have prepared several reels of this, and you will take them away with you. Unwind them as you make your way inside, and when the reel is exhausted, tie the end of the thread to the beginning of the next, so as never to have a break in the chain. Then on your way back you must re-wind the thread until you come to the end, which Ariadne will have in her hand. I don't know why I insist so much, when all that part of the enterprise is as easy as good-morning. The real difficulty is to preserve unbroken, to the last inch of the thread, the will to come back; for the perfumes will make you forgetful, as will also your natural curiosity, which will conspire to make you weaken. I have told you this already and have nothing to add. Here are the reels. Goodbye."

I left Daedalus and made off to rejoin Ariadne.

IX

Those reels of thread were the occasion of the first dispute between Ariadne and myself. She wanted me to hand over to her, for safe keeping in her corsage, those same reels which Daedalus had entrusted to me, claiming that to wind and unwind such things was a woman's job (one, in fact, in which she was particularly expert) and that she wanted to spare me the bother of attending to it. But in reality she hoped in this way to remain the mistress of my fate, a thing to which I would not consent at any price. Moreover, I had another suspicion: Ariadne would be reluctant to unwind, where every turn of the reel allowed me to stray farther from herself; she might hold back the thread, or pull it toward her; in such a case I should be prevented from going in as far as I wanted. I therefore stood my ground, in the face even of that last argument of women, a flood of tears—knowing well that if one once begins to yield one's little finger, they are quick to snap up the whole arm, and the rest with it.

The thread was neither of linen nor of wool. Daedalus had made it from some unknown material, which even my sword, when I experimented with a little piece, was powerless to cut. I left the sword in Ariadne's care, being determined (after what Daedalus had said to me about the superiority that man owes wholly to his instruments, and the decisive role of these in my victories over the monsters)—being determined, as I say, to subdue the Minotaur with the strength of my bare hands. When, after all this we arrived before the entrance to the labyrinth, a portal embellished with that double axe which one saw everywhere in Crete, I entreated Ariadne on no account to stir from the spot. She insisted that she should herself tie the end of the thread to my wrist, with a knot that she was pleased to call a lover's; she then glued her lips to my own and held them there for what seemed to me an interminable time. I was longing to get on.

My thirteen companions, both male and female, had gone on ahead, Pirithoüs among them; I found them in the first big room, already quite fuddled by the vapors. I should have mentioned that, together with the thread, Daedalus had given me a piece of rag drenched with a powerful specific against the gases, and had pressed me most particularly to employ it as a gag. (This also Ariadne had taken in hand, as we stood before the entrance to the labyrinth.) Thanks to it, and though hardly able to breathe, I was able in the midst of these intoxicating vapors to keep my head clear and my will taut. I was rather suffocated, all the same, because, as I've said before, I never feel really well when I'm not in the open air, and the artificial atmosphere of that place was oppressive to me.

Unreeling the thread, I penetrated into a second room, darker than the first; then into another, still darker; then into a fourth, where I could only grope my way. My hand, brushing along the wall, fell upon the handle of a door. I opened it, and stepped into brilliant sunshine. I was in a garden. Facing me, and stretched at length upon a flowery bed of buttercups, pansies, jonquils, tulips and carnations, lay the Minotaur. As luck would have it, he was asleep. I ought to have hurried forward and taken advantage of this, but something held me back, arrested my arm: the monster was beautiful. As happens with centaurs also, there was in his person a harmonious blending of man and beast. On top of this, he was young, and his youthfulness gave an indefinable bloom to his good looks; and I am more vulnerable to such things than to any show of strength. When faced with them, I needed to call upon all my reserves of energy. For one never fights better than with the doubled strength of hatred; and I could not hate the Minotaur. I even stood still for some time and just looked at him. But he opened one eye. I saw then that he was completely witless, and that it was time for me to set about my task. . . .

What I did next, what happened, I cannot exactly recall Tightly as I had been gagged, my mind had doubtless been benumbed by the gases in the first room; they affected my memory, and if in spite of this I vanquished the Minotaur, my recollection of the victory is confused, though on the whole somewhat voluptuous. That must be my last word, since I refuse to invent. I have also many dreamlike memories of the charms of that garden; it so went to my head that I thought I could never bear to leave it; and it was only reluctantly that, after settling with the Minotaur, I rewound my thread and went back to the first room, there to rejoin my companions.

They were seated at table. Before them a massive repast had been spread (how or by whom I cannot say). They were busy gormandizing, drinking heavily, making passes of love at one another, and braying like so many madmen or idiots. When I made as if to take them away, they replied that they were getting on very well and had no thought of leaving. I insisted, saying that I had come to deliver them. "Deliver us from what?" they shouted; and suddenly they all banded together and covered me with insults. I was very much distressed, because of Pirithoüs. He hardly recognized me, forswore virtue, made mock of his own good qualities, and told me roundly that not for all the glory in the world would he consent to give up his present enjoyments. All the same, I couldn't blame him for it, because I knew too well that, but for Daedalus' precautions, I should have foundered in the same way, and joined in the chorus with him and with the others. It was only by beating them up, it was only by punching them and kicking them hard on their behinds, that I got them to follow me; of course there was also the fact that they were so clogged by drink as to be incapable of resistance.

Once out of the labyrinth, how slowly and painfully they came back to their senses and re-assumed their normal selves! This they did with great sadness. It appeared to them (so they told me afterwards) as if they were climbing down from some high peak of happiness into a dark and narrow valley. Each rebuilt for himself the prison in which every man is his own jailor and from which he could never again escape. Pirithoüs, however, soon showed himself aghast at his momentary degradation, and he promised to redeem himself, in his own eyes and in mine, by excess of zeal. An occasion was offered to him, not long afterwards, to give me proof of his devotion.

X

I hid nothing from him; he knew my feelings for Ariadne, and of their decline. I did not even hide from him that, child though she might still be, I was very much taken with Phaedra. She used often at that time to play on a swing strung up between the trunks of two palm-trees; and when I saw her at the top of her flight, with the wind lifting her short skirts, my heart would miss a beat. But when Ariadne appeared, I looked the other way and dissembled my feelings as best I could, for fear of arousing in her the jealousy of an elder sister. Still, thwarted desires are not healthy. But if I was to abduct her, and thus bring off the audacious project which was beginning to simmer in my heart, I should need to employ a ruse of some sort. Then it was that Pirithoüs was able to help me by devising a plan stamped with all his fertile ingenuity. Meanwhile our stay in the island was dragging on, though both Ariadne and myself were obsessed with the idea of getting away. But what Ariadne didn't know was that I was resolved not to leave without Phaedra. Pirithoüs knew it, and this is how he helped me.

He had more freedom than I—Ariadne stuck to me like a ball-and-chain—and he passed his leisure in the study and observation of the customs of Crete. "I think," he said to me one morning, "that I've got just what we want. You know that Minos and Rhadamanthus, those two model legislators, have drawn up a code of morals for the island, paying particular attention to pederasty. As you know, too, the Cretans are especially prone to this, as is evident from their culture. So much so, in fact, that every adolescent who reaches manhood without having been chosen by some older admirer becomes ashamed and regards his neglect as dishonorable; for if he is good-looking people generally conclude that some vice of heart or mind must be the cause. Young Glaucus, the son of Minos, who is Phaedra's absolute double, confided to me his anxiety in this respect. His friendless state causes him much distress. I made the vain suggestion that no doubt his princely rank has discouraged admirers; he replied that this, though possible, did not make his position in any way less painful, and that people ought to realize that it was also a grief to Minos; and that Minos as a rule disregards all distinctions of rank and position. All the same, he would certainly be flattered if an eminent prince like yourself were to be kind enough to take an interest in his son. It occurred to me that Ariadne, who shows herself so importunately jealous of her sister, would have no such feelings about her brother. There is hardly a single instance of a woman taking serious notice of the love of a man for a boy; in any case, she would think it unbecoming to show resentment. You need have no fear on that score."

"What!" I shouted, "can you think that fear would ever stop me? But though I am a Greek, I do not feel myself drawn in any way toward people of my own sex, however young and attractive they may be. In this I differ from Hercules, and would gladly let him keep his Hylas. Your Glaucus may be like my Phaedra, but it is she whom I desire, not he."

"You haven't grasped what I mean," he resumed. "I'm not suggesting you should take Glaucus in her place, but simply that you should pretend to take him, in order to deceive Ariadne and let her believe, and everybody else, that Phaedra, whom you are carrying off, is Glaucus. Now listen and follow me carefully. One of the customs of the island, and one that Minos himself instituted, is that the lover assumes complete charge of the child whom he covets, and takes him to live with him, under his roof, for two months; after which period the child must announce publicly whether or not his lover has given him satisfaction and treated him properly. To take the supposed Glaucus under your roof, you must put him aboard the ship that brought us here from Greece. Once we are all assembled, with the crypto-Phaedra safe in our hand, we must up-anchor; Ariadne will have to be there since she assumes that she will be going with you; then we shall put out with all speed to the open sea. The Cretans have a large fleet, their ships are not so fast as ours, and if they give chase we can easily out-distance them. Tell Minos about this project. You may be sure that he'll smile on it, provided you let him believe that Glaucus, and not Phaedra, is involved; for, as for Glaucus, he could hardly hope to secure a better master and lover than yourself. But tell me: is Phaedra willing?"

"I don't know, as yet. Ariadne takes good care never to leave me alone with her, so that I've had no chance to sound her . . . . But I don't doubt that she will be ready to follow me, when she realizes that I prefer her to her sister."

It was Ariadne who had to be approached first. I took her into my confidence, but deceitfully of course, and according to our agreed procedure.

"What a wonderful plan!" she cried. "And how I shall enjoy traveling with my small brother! You've no idea how charming he can be. I get on very well with him and in spite of the difference in our ages I am still his favorite playmate. Nothing could be better for broadening his mind than to visit a foreign country. At Athens he can perfect his Greek, which he already speaks passably, though with a bad accent: that will soon be put right. You will set him the best of examples, and I only hope he will grow to be like you."

I let her talk. The wretched girl could not foresee what fate was in store for her.

Glaucus had also to be warned, lest any hitch should occur. Pirithoüs took charge of this, and told me later that the boy was at first bitterly disappointed. Only after an appeal to his better sentiments did he decide to join in the game; or rather, I should say, to drop out of it and yield up his place to his sister. Phaedra had also to be informed. She might have started screaming if we had tried to abduct her by force or by surprise. But Pirithoüs exploited with great skill the malicious pleasure that both children would not fail to take in gulling their elders—Glaucus his parents, and Phaedra her sister.

Phaedra duly rigged herself out in Glaucus' everyday clothes. The two were of exactly the same build, and when she had bound up her hair and muffled the lower part of her face, it was impossible for Ariadne not to mistake her identity.

It was certainly disagreeable for me to have to deceive Minos, who had lavished upon me every mark of his confidence, and had told me of the good influence which he expected me, as an older person, to have upon his son. And I was his guest, too. Of course I was abusing my position. But it was not, and indeed it is never, a part of my character to allow myself to be stopped by scruples. The voices of gratitude and decency were shouted down by the voice of desire. The end justifies the means. What must be must be.

Ariadne was first on board, in her anxiety to secure comfortable quarters. As soon as Phaedra arrived we could make off. Her abduction took place not at nightfall, as had at first been agreed, but after the family dinner, at which she had insisted on appearing. She pleaded that as she had formed the habit of going to her room immediately after dinner her absence could not, she thought, be remarked before the morning of the next day. So everything went off without a hitch, and I was able to disembark with Phaedra, a few days later, in Attica, having meanwhile dropped off her sister, the beautiful and tedious Ariadne, at Naxos.

I learned on arriving at our territory that when Aegeus, my father, had seen in the distance the black sails (those sails which I had omitted to change), he had hurled himself into the sea. I have already touched on this in a few words; I dislike returning to it. I shall add, however, that I had dreamed, that last night of our voyage, that I was already king of Attica. Be that as it may, or as it might have been, this was, for the whole population and for myself, a day of rejoicing for our happy return and my promotion to the throne, and a day of mourning for the death of my father. I therefore gave orders that in the rites for the day lamentations should alternate with songs of joy; and in these songs and dances we took a prominent part—my companions, now so implausibly restored to their homes, and myself. Joy and desolation: it was fitting that the people should be made to explore, at once and the same time, these two extremes of feeling.

XI

People sometimes reproached me afterwards for my conduct toward Ariadne. They said I had behaved like a coward and that I should not have abandoned her, or at any rate not on an island. Possibly; but I wanted to put the sea between us. She was after me, hunting me down, marking me for the kill. When she got wind of my ruse and detected her sister beneath her brother's clothes, she set up the devil's own noise, broke into a series of rhythmical screams, upbraided me for my treachery; and when, in my exasperation, I told her that I did not intend to take her farther than the first island at which the wind, now suddenly risen, would allow or compel us to make landfall, she threatened me with a long poem she proposed to write on the subject of this infamous desertion. I told her at once that she could not do better; the poem promised to be very good, as far as I could judge from her frenzied and lyrical tones; moreover, it would serve as a distraction, and she would undoubtedly soon find in it the best solace for her grief. But all this only vexed her the more. Such are women, when one tries to make them see reason. For my part, I always allow myself to be guided by an instinct in which, by reason of its greater simplicity, I have perfect confidence.

The island in question was Naxos. One story has it that, some time after we had abandoned her, Dionysus went there to join her, and indeed married her; all of which may be a way of saying that she found consolation in drink. People say that on their wedding-day the god made her a present of a crown, the work of Hephaestus, which now forms one of the constellations; and that Zeus welcomed her on Olympus and made her immortal. She was even mistaken, they say, for Aphrodite. I let people talk, and myself, in order to cut short hostile rumors, did my best to confirm her divine rank by founding a cult in her honor. I also went out of my way to be the first to dance my reverences there. May I be allowed to remark that, but for my desertion, she would have enjoyed none of these great advantages?

Certain imaginary incidents have enriched the mythology of my person: the abduction of Helen, the descent into Hell with Pirithoüs, the rape of Proserpine. I took care never to deny these rumors, for they all enhanced my prestige. I even improved upon some of them, in order to confirm the people in beliefs that they are all too inclined, in Attica, to discard. Popular emancipation is a good thing; irreverence quite another.

The truth is that after my return to Athens I remained faithful to Phaedra. I took both the woman and the city for my bride. I was a husband, and the son of a dead king: I was a king. My days of adventure are over, I used to repeat to myself; where I had sought to conquer, I now sought to rule.

This was not easy. Athens at that time really did not exist. In

Attica a mass of petty townships disputed for predominance; whence continual brawling, besieging and strife. The essential thing was to secure a strong central unit of government—a thing I obtained only with great difficulty. I brought both strength and cunning to the task.

Aegeus, my father, thought he could assure his own authority by perpetuating these quarrels. Considering, myself, that the well-being of the citizens is compromised by such discords, I traced the source of most of the evils to the general inequality of wealth and the desire to increase one's own fortune. Myself caring little for the acquisition of wealth, and preoccupied with the public good as much as, if not more than, with my own, I set an example of plain living. By an equal division of all properties, I abolished at one blow both the fact of supremacy and the rivalries it had provoked. This was a drastic measure, which no doubt pleased the poor (the great majority, that is to say) but antagonized the rich, whom I had thereby dispossessed. These, though few in number, were clever men. I summoned the most important among them, and said:

"Personal merit is the only thing to which I attach any importance. I recognize no other scale of values. You have made yourselves rich by ingenuity, practical knowledge and perseverance; but also, and more often, by injustice and abuse. Your private rivalries are compromising the security of a state that I intend to be a great power, beyond the reach of your intrigues. Only thus will it be able to resist foreign invasion, and prosper. The accursed love of money that torments you does not bring you happiness, for one can truly call it insatiable. The more people have, the more they want. I shall therefore curtail your fortunes; and by force (I possess it) if you do not submit peaceably to the curtailment. For myself I shall keep only the preservation of the laws and the command of the army. I care very little for the rest. I mean to live, now that I am king, just as simply as I have lived hitherto, and in the same style as the humblest of my subjects. I shall see that the laws are respected, and that I myself am respected, if not feared. I mean to have it said among our neighbors that Attica is ruled, not by a tyrant, but by a government of the people; for each citizen of the state shall have an equal right to sit on the council, irrespective of his birth. If you do not side willingly with all this, I shall find ways, as I said, to compel you.

"I shall raze and destroy utterly your little courts of local justice and your regional council-chambers, and I shall assemble, beneath the Acropolis, the capital city which already bears the name of Athens. And it is this name of Athens that for the races of the future—and this I promise to the gods who show me favor—will be a name of wonders. I dedicate my city to Pallas. Now go, all of you, and take my words as meant."

Then, suiting my example to my words, I stripped myself of all royal authority, stepped back into the ranks, and was not afraid to show myself to the public without escort, like a simple citizen; but I gave my attention unceasingly to public affairs, maintaining peace and watching over the good order of the state.

Pirithoüs, after hearing me address the men of wealth, said to me that he thought my speech sublime, but ridiculous. Because, he argued: "Equality is not natural among men; I would go farther and say that it is not desirable. It is a good thing that the superior men should rise above the vulgar mass to the full height of their eminence. Without emulation, rivalry and jealousy, that mob will be forever a formless, stagnant, wallowing mass. There must be some leaven to make it rise; take care that it doesn't rise against yourself. Whether you like it or not, and though you may succeed in your wish and achieve an initial levelling by which each man starts on the same plane and with an equal chance, yet differences of talent will soon bring about differences of station; in other words, a downtrodden people and an aristocracy."

"Good Gods!" That set me off again. "I certainly expect that, and I hope it won't be long in coming. But in the first place I don't see why the people should be downtrodden if the new aristocracy to which I shall give all the support in my power is, as I would have it, an aristocracy not of wealth, but of intellect."

And then, in order to increase the power and importance of Athens, I made it known that there would be an impartial welcome for everyone, no matter whence he came, who might choose to come and settle there. And criers were sent throughout the neighboring countries to carry this message: "Peoples all, make haste to Athens!"

The news spread far and wide. And was it not through this that Oedipus, the fallen monarch, saddest and noblest of derelicts, made his way from Thebes to Attica, there to seek help and protection, there to die? Because of that I was able later to secure for

Athens the blessing which the gods had conferred on his ashes. Of this, I shall have more to say.

I promised to all newcomers indifferently the same rights as were enjoyed by those who were natives of Athens or who had settled there earlier; any necessary discrimination could await the proofs of experience. For good tools reveal their quality only after use, and I wish to judge nobody except according to his services.

So that if I was later obliged none the less to admit differences among the Athenians (and consequently to admit a hierarchy), I allowed this only in order to ensure that the state would in general function better. Thus it is that, thanks to me, the Athenians came to deserve, among all the other Greeks, the fine name of "people," which was commonly bestowed upon them and upon them only. There lies my fame, far surpassing that of my earlier feats; a fame to which neither Hercules attained, nor Jason, nor Bellerophon, nor Perseus.

Pirithoüs, alas! the companion of my youthful exuberances, later fell away from me. All those heroes whom I have named, and others too, like Meleager and Peleus, never prolonged their career beyond their first feats, or sometimes beyond a single one. For myself, I was not content with that. "There is a time for conquest," I used to say to Pirithoüs, "a time for cleansing the earth of its monsters, and then a time for husbandry and the harvesting of well-cherished land; a time to set men free from fear, and then a time in which to find employment for their liberty, in which to profit by the moment of ease and coax it into bloom." And that could not be achieved without discipline: I would not admit that, as with the Boeotians, man should make himself his own boundary, or aim merely at a mediocre happiness. I thought that man was not and would never be free, and that it would not be a good thing if he were. But I couldn't urge him forward without his consent: nor could I obtain that consent without leaving him (leaving the people, at any rate) the illusion of liberty. I wanted to educate him. I would not allow him to become in any degree content with his lot, or to resign himself to furrow his brow in perpetuity. Humanity (such was always the cast of my thought) can do more and deserves better. I remembered the teaching of Daedalus, who wanted to enrich mankind with all the spoils of the gods. My great strength was that I believed in progress.

So Pirithoüs and I parted company. In my youth he had been my constant companion, and often an invaluable aide. But I realized that constancy in friendship can prevent a man from advancing—can even pull him backwards; after a certain point one can only go forward alone. As Pirithoüs was a man of sense, I still listened to what he said, but that was all. He himself was growing old, and whereas he had once been enterprise itself, he now allowed wisdom to degenerate into temperance. His advice was now always for restriction and restraint.

"Mankind isn't worth all this trouble," he would say. And I would reply: "Well, what else is there to think about, except mankind? Man has not yet said his last word."

"Don't get excited," he used to reply. "Haven't you done enough? Now that the prosperity of Athens is assured, it is time for you to rest on your laurels and savor the happiness of married life."

He urged me to pay more attention to Phaedra and there for once he was right. For I must now tell of how the peace of my fireside was disturbed, and what a hideous price was expected by the gods in return for my successes and my self-conceit.

XII

I had unlimited confidence in Phaedra. I had watched her grow more beautiful month by month. She was the very breath of virtue. I had withdrawn her at so early an age from the pernicious influence of her family that I never conceived she might carry within her a full dose of inherited poison. She obviously took after her mother, and when she later tried to excuse herself by saying that she was not responsible, or that she was foredoomed, I had to own that there was something in it. But that was not all: I also believe that she had too great a disdain for Aphrodite. The gods avenge themselves, and it was in vain that Phaedra later strove to appease the goddess with an added abundance of offerings and supplications. For Phaedra was pious, in spite of everything. In my wife's family everyone was pious. But it was no doubt regrettable that not everyone addressed his devotions to the same god. With Pasiphaë, it was Zeus; with Ariadne, Dionysus. For my own part, I reverenced above all Pallas Athene, and next Poseidon, to whom I was bound by a secret tie, and who, unfortunately for me, had similarly bound himself always to answer my prayers so that I should never beseech him in vain. My son whose mother had been the Amazon, and whom I set above all the others, devoted himself to Artemis the huntress. He was as chaste as she—as chaste as I, at his age, had been dissolute. He used to run naked through moonlit woods and thickets; detested the court, formal parties, and, above all, the society of women, and was only happy when, with his bearhounds, he could go hunting for wild beasts and follow them to the topmost mountain or the last recesses of a valley. Often, too, he broke in wild horses, tamed them on the seashore, or rode them at a full gallop into the sea. How I loved him then! Proud, handsome, unruly, not to me, whom he held in veneration, nor to the laws: but he despised the conventions that prevent a man from asserting himself and wear out his merits in futility. He it was whom I wanted for my heir. I could have slept quietly, once the reins of state were in his unsullied hands; for I knew that he would be as inaccessible to threats as to flatteries.

That Phaedra might fall in love with him I realized only too late. I should have foreseen it, for he was very like me. (I mean, like what I had been at his age.) But I was already growing old, and Phaedra was still astonishingly young. She may still have loved me, but it was as a young girl loves her father. It is not good, as I have learned to my cost, that there should be such a difference of age between husband and wife. Yet what I could not forgive her was not her passion (natural enough, after all, though half-incestuous), but that, when she realized she could not satisfy her desire, she should have accused my Hippolytus and imputed to him the impure longings that were consuming her. I was a blind father, and a too trustful husband; I believed her. For once in my life I took a woman at her word! I called down the vengeance of the gods upon my innocent son. And my prayer was heard. Men do not realize, when they address themselves to the gods, that if their prayers are answered, it is most often for their misfortune. By a sudden, passionate, mindless impulse I had killed my son. And I am still inconsolable. That Phaedra, awakened to her guilt, should at once afterwards have wrought justice upon herself, well and good. But now that I cannot count even upon the friendship of Pirithoüs, I feel lonely; and I am old.

Oedipus, when I welcomed him at Colonus, had been driven from Thebes, his fatherland: without eyes, dishonored and wretched as he was, he at least had his two daughters with him, and in their constant tenderness he found relief from his sufferings. He had failed in every part of what he had undertaken. I have succeeded. Even the enduring blessing that his ashes are to confer upon the country where they are laid—even this will rest, not upon his ungrateful Thebes, but upon Athens.

I am surprised that so little should have been said about this meeting of our destinies at Colonus, this moment at the cross-roads when our two careers confronted each other. I take it to have been the summit and the crown of my glory. Till then I had forced all life to do obeisance to me, and had seen all my fellow men bow in their turn (excepting only Daedalus, but he was my senior by many years, besides, even Daedalus gave me best in the end). In Oedipus alone did I recognize a nobility equal to my own. His misfortunes could only enhance his grandeur in my eyes. No doubt I had triumphed everywhere and always; but on a level which, in comparison with Oedipus, seemed to me merely human—inferior, I might say. He had held his own with the Sphinx; had stood man upright before the riddle of life, and dared to oppose him to the gods. How then, and why, had he accepted defeat? By putting out his eyes, had he not even contributed to it? There was something, in this dreadful act of violence against himself, that I could not contrive to understand. I told him of my bewilderment. But his explication, I must admit, hardly satisfied me —or else I did not fully understand it.

"True," he said, "I yielded to an impulse of rage—one that could only be directed against myself; against whom else could I have turned? In face of the immeasurable horror of the accusations I had just discovered, I felt an overwhelming desire to make a protest. And besides, what I wanted to destroy was not so much my eyes themselves as the canvas they held before me; the scenery before which I was struggling, the falsehood in which I no longer believed; and this so as to break through to reality.

"And yet, no! I was not really thinking of anything very clearly; I acted rather by instinct. I put out my eyes to punish them for having failed to see the evidence that had, as people say, been staring me in the face. But to speak the truth—ah, how can I put it to you? . . . Nobody understood me when I suddenly cried out 'O darkness, my light!' And you also, you don't understand it—I feel that distinctly. People heard it as a cry of grief; it was a statement of fact. It meant that in my darkness I had found a source of supernatural light, illuminating the world of the spirit. I meant: 'Darkness, thou art henceforth my light.' And at the moment when the blue of the sky went black before me, my inward firmament became bright with stars."

He was silent and for some moments remained deep in meditation. Then he went on:

"As a young man, I passed for one who could see the future. I believed in myself, too. Was I not the first, the only man, to solve the riddle of the Sphinx? Only since my eyes of flesh were torn with my own hand from the world of appearances have I begun, as it seems to me, to see truly. Yes; at the moment when the outer world was hidden forever from the eyes of my body, a kind of new eyesight opened out within myself upon the infinite perspectives of an inner world, which the world of appearances (the only one which had existed for me until that time) had led me to disdain. And this imperceptible world (inaccessible, I mean, to our senses) is, I now know, the only true one. All the rest is an illusion, a deception moreover, that disturbs our contemplation of what is divine. Tiresias, the blind sage, once said to me: 'Who wishes to see God must first cease to see the world;' and I didn't understand him then: just as you, yourself, O Theseus, do not understand me now."

"I shall not attempt to deny," I replied, "the importance of this world beyond temporal things of which your blindness has made you aware; but what I still cannot understand is why you oppose it to the outer world in which we live and act."

"Because," said Oedipus, "for the first time, when with my inward eye I perceived what was formerly hidden from me, I suddenly became aware of this fact: that I had based my earthly sovereignty upon a crime, and that everything which followed from this was in consequence tainted; not merely all my personal decisions, but even those of the two sons to whom I had abandoned my crown—for I at once stepped down from the slippery eminence to which my crime had raised me. You must know already to what new villainies my sons have allowed themselves to stoop, and what an ignominious doom hangs over all that our sinful humanity may engender; of this my unhappy sons are no more than a signal example. For, as the fruits of an incestuous union, they are no doubt doubly branded; but I believe that an original stain of some sort afflicts the whole human race, in such a way that even the best bear its stripe, and are vowed to evil and perdition; from all this man can never break free without divine aid of some sort, for that alone can wash away his original sin and grant him amnesty."

He was silent again for a few moments, as if preparing to plunge still deeper, and then went on:

"You are astonished that I should have put out my eyes. I am astonished myself. But in this gesture, inconsidered and cruel as it was, there may yet be something else: an indefinable secret longing to follow my fortunes to their farthest limit, to give the final turn of the screw to my anguish, and to bring to a close the destiny of a hero. Perhaps I dimly foresaw the grandeur of suffering and its power to redeem; that is why the true hero is ashamed to turn away from it. I think that it is in fact the crowning proof of his greatness, and that he is never worthier than when he falls a victim; then does he exact the gratitude of heaven, and disarm the vengeance of the gods. Be that as it may, and however deplorable my mistakes may have been, the state of unearthly beatitude that I have been able to reach is an ample reward for all the ills that I have had to suffer—but for them, indeed, I should doubtless never have achieved it."

"Dear Oedipus," I said, when it was plain that he had finished speaking, "I can only congratulate you on the kind of superhuman wisdom which you profess. But my thoughts can never march with yours along that road. I remain a child of this world, and I believe that man, be he what he may, and with whatever blemishes you judge him to be stained, is in duty bound to play out his hand to the end. No doubt you have learned to make good use even of your misfortunes, and through them have drawn nearer to what you call the divine world. I can well believe, too, that a sort of benediction now attaches to your person, and that it will presently be laid, as the oracles have said, upon the land in which you will take your everlasting rest."

I did not add that what mattered to me was that this blessing should be laid upon Attica, and I congratulated myself that the god had made Thebes abut upon my country.

If I compare my lot with that of Oedipus, I am content: I have fulfilled my destiny. Behind me I leave the city of Athens. It has been dearer to me even than my wife and son. My city stands. After I am gone, my thoughts will live on there forever. Lonely and consenting, I draw near to death. I have enjoyed the good things of the earth, and I am happy to think that after me, and thanks to me, men will recognize themselves as being happier, better and more free. I have worked always for the good of those who are to come. I have lived.

Selected Readings

Brée, Germaine. *Gide*. New Brunswick, N.J.: Rutgers University Press, 1963.

———. "Time Sequences and Consequences in the Gidian World." *Yale French Studies*, No. 7 (1951), 51–59.

——— and Margaret Guiton. *The French Novel: From Gide to Camus*. A Harbinger Book; New York: Harcourt, Brace & World, Inc., 1962.

Brennan, Joseph G. *Three Philosophical Novelists: James Joyce, André Gide, and Thomas Mann*. New York: The Macmillan Company, 1964.

Fowlie, Wallace. *André Gide: His Life and Art*. New York: The Macmillan Company, 1965.

Freedman, Ralph. *The Lyrical Novel: Studies in Hermann Hesse, André Gide, and Virginia Woolf*. Princeton, N.J.: Princeton University Press, 1963.

Guerard, Albert. *André Gide*. Cambridge, Mass.: Harvard University Press, 1951.

Hytier, Jean. *André Gide*. Trans. Richard Howard. Garden City, N.Y.: Doubleday and Company, Inc., 1962.

IRELAND, G. W. *André Gide.* New York: Grove Press, 1963.

MANN, KLAUS. *André Gide and the Crisis of Modern Thought.* New York: Creative Age Press, 1943.

O'BRIEN, JUSTIN. *Portrait of André Gide, a Critical Biography.* New York: Alfred A. Knopf, Inc., 1953.

WATSON-WILLIAMS, HELEN. *André Gide and the Greek Myth: A Critical Study.* Oxford: Clarendon Press, 1967.

THOMAS MANN

(1875-1955)

Thomas Mann was born in Lubeck, Germany, in 1875. His father, a grain merchant, intended Thomas to enter the business world, but Thomas Mann the merchant warred with Thomas Mann the artist. By 1901 Mann's course was set with the publication of the novel *Buddenbrooks*. His early novels and short stories deal with the bourgeois, provincial background he knew well. The struggle for aesthetic independence in conflict with such a background constitutes one of his chief literary themes.

Disease and death provide two other consistent Mann themes. His novella, *Death in Venice* (1913), explores them both. In his own life Mann experienced his father's early death, his mother's long illness, the suicides of two sisters and his wife's lung infection. German politics provide a fourth major theme. Mann's intense early nationalism resulted in the anti-English and anti-European treatise, *Reflections of a Non-Political Man* (1917). His monumental work *The Magic Mountain* was published in 1924.

By 1929, the year he received a Nobel prize, Mann had evidently undergone a reversal of political sympathy, for in that year his allegorical triumph, *Mario and the Magician,* came out. By 1933 he had denounced the Nazi cause and was living in exile in Europe. He came to America in 1938, became a citizen, and returned to Germany in 1952. He died in Zurich, Switzerland, in 1955.

Thomas Mann was a great and skilled craftsman. As an allegorist he is unequaled in the twentieth century; his allegories are epic in scope. They frequently progress beyond the narrative line to simultaneously sustained levels of psychological, social, political, aesthetic, and spiritual comment.

A Gleam

Hush! Let us look into a human soul. On the wing, as it were, and only in passing; only for a page or so, for we are very busy. We come from Florence, Florence of the old days, where we have been dealing with high and tragic and ultimate concerns. And after that —whither? To court, perhaps, a royal castle? Who knows? Strange, faint-shimmering forms are taking their place on the stage.—Anna, poor little Baroness Anna, we have little time to spare for you.

Waltz-time, tinkling glasses; smoke, steam, hubbub, voices, dance-steps. We all know these little weaknesses of ours. Do we secretly love to linger at life's silliest feasts simply because there suffering wears bigger, more childlike eyes than in other places?

"*Avantageur!*" cried Baron Harry, the cavalry captain. He stopped dancing and called the whole length of the hall, one hand on his hip, the other still holding his partner embraced. "That's not a waltz, man, it's a funeral march! You have no rhythm in your body; you just float and sway about without any sense of time. Let Lieutenant von Gelbsattel play, so that we can feel the rhythm. Come on down, *Avantageur!* Dance, if you can do that better!"

And the *Avantageur* stood up, clapped his spurs together, and without a word yielded the platform to Lieutenant von Gelbsattel, who straightway began to make the piano ring and rattle under the blows from his sprawling white fingers.

Baron Harry, we observe, had music in him: waltz music, march music. He had rhythm, joviality, hauteur, good fortune, and a

From *Stories of Three Decades,* by Thomas Mann and translated by H. T. Lowe-Porter. Copyright 1936 by Alfred A. Knopf, Inc. Reprinted by permission.

conquering-hero air. His gold-braided hussar jacket suited to a T his glowing young face, unmarked by a single care, a single thought. He was burnt red, like a blond, though hair and moustache were dark—a piquant combination that appealed to the ladies—and the red scar across his right cheek gave a bold and dashing look to his open countenance. The scar might be from a wound, or a fall from a horse—in any case it was glorious. He danced divinely.

But the *Avantageur* floated and swayed—to extend the meaning of Baron Harry's phrase. His eyelids were much too large, so that he could never properly open his eyes; also his uniform fitted him rather carelessly and improbably round the waist—and God alone knew how he came to be a soldier. He had not cared much for this affair with the "Swallows" at the Casino, but even so he had come to it; he had to be careful not to give offence, for two reasons: first, because his origins were bourgeois, and second, because there was a book by him, that he had written or put together, or whatever the word is, a collection of stories, that anybody could buy in a book-shop. It must make people feel a little shy of him, of course.

The hall in the officers' Casino was long and wide—much too large for the thirty people who were disporting themselves in it. The walls and the musicians' platform were decorated with imitation draperies in red plaster, and from the ugly ceiling hung two crooked chandeliers, in which the candles stood askew and dripped hot wax. But the board floor had been scrubbed the whole forenoon by seven hussars told off for the job; and, after all, officers in a little hole like Hohendamm could not expect grandeur. Whatever was otherwise lacking to the feast was amply made up by its characteristic atmosphere; it had the sweetness of forbidden fruit, the reckless charm imparted by the presence of the "Swallows." Even the orderlies smirked knowingly as they renewed the supplies of champagne in the ice-tubs beside the white-covered tables which stood ranged along three walls of the room. They looked at each other and then down with a grin, as servants do when they assist irresponsibly at the excesses of their masters. And all this with reference to the "Swallows."

The Swallows, the Swallows? Well, in short, they were the "Swallows from Vienna." Like migratory birds, thirty in the flock, they flew through the country, appearing in fifth-rate variety-theatres and music-halls, where they stood on the stage in easy, unconventional poses and chirped their famous swallows' chorus:

> When the swallows come again
> See them fly—*aren't* they fly?

It was a good song, its humour was not obscure; it was always received with warm applause from the more knowing section of the public.

Well, the Swallows came to Hohendamm and sang in Gugelfing's beer-hall. A whole regiment of hussars were in barracks at Hohendamm, and the Swallows were justified in anticipating a good reception from representative circles. But they got more, they got an enthusiastic one. Evening after evening the unmarried officers sat at the girls' feet, listened to their swallow song, and drank their health in Gugelfing's yellow beer. It was not long before the married officers were there too; one evening Colonel von Rummler appeared in person, followed the programme with the closest interest, and afterwards expressed himself with unlimited approval in various places.

So then the lieutenants and cavalry captains conceived a plan to bring about closer contact with the Swallows: to invite a select group of them—say, ten of the prettiest—to a jolly champagne supper in the Casino. The upper orders could not take any public cognizance of the affair, of course; they had to refrain, however sore at heart. Not only the unmarried lieutenants, however, but also the married first lieutenants and cavalry captains took part, and also—this was the nub of the whole matter, the thing that gave it, so to speak, its "punch"—their wives.

Obstacles and misgivings? First Lieutenant von Levzahn brushed them all away with a phrase: what else, said he, were obstacles for, if not that soldiers might triumph over them! The good citizens of Hohendamm might rage when they heard that the officers were introducing their wives to the Swallows. Of course, they could not have done such a thing themselves. But there were heights, there were aloof and untrammelled regions of existence, where things might freely come to pass that in a lower sphere could only sully and dishonour. It was not as though the worthy natives of Hohendamm were not used to expecting all sorts of unexpectednesses from their hussars. The officers would ride along the middle of the pavement, in broad daylight, if it occurred to them so to do. They had done it. One evening pistols had been fired off in the Markt-platz—nobody but the officers could have done that. And had anyone dared to murmur? The following anecdote was amply vouched for:

One morning, between five and six o'clock, Captain of Cavalry Baron Harry, feeling pretty jolly, was on his way home from a party, with his friends Captain of Cavalry von Huhnemann and Lieutenants Le Maistre, Baron Truchsess, von Trautenau, and von Lichterloh. Riding across the Old Bridge, they met a baker's boy, with a great basket of rolls on his shoulder, taking his way through the fresh morning air and whistling blithely as he went. "Give me that basket!" commanded Baron Harry. He seized it by the handle, swung it three times round his head, so skilfully that not a roll fell out, and sent it flying out into the stream on a great curve that showed the strength of his arm. At first the baker's boy was scared stiff. Then as he saw his rolls swimming about, he flung up his arms with a yell and behaved as though he had gone out of his mind. The gentlemen amused themselves for a while with his childish despair; then Baron Harry tossed him a gold piece which would have paid three times over for his loss and the officers rode laughing away home. Then the boy realized that these were the nobility and ceased his outcry.

This story lost no time in going the rounds—but who would have ventured to look askance? You might gnash your teeth over the pranks of Baron Harry and his friends; outwardly you took them with a smile. They were the lords and masters of Hohendamm. And now the lords and masters were having a party for the Swal-lows.

The *Avantageur* seemed not to know how to dance a waltz any better than to play one. For he did not take a partner, but going up to one of the white tables made a bow and sat down near little Baroness Anna, Baron Harry's wife, to whom he addressed a few shy words. The capacity to amuse himself with a Swallow was simply beyond the poor young man. Actually he was afraid of that kind of girl; he fancied that whatever he said to one she looked at him as though she were surprised—and this hurt the *Avantageur*. But music, even the poorest, always put him into a speechless, re-laxed, and dreamy mood—it is often the way with these flabby and futile characters; and as the Baroness Anna, to whom he was entirely indifferent, made only absent answers to his remarks, they soon fell silent and confined themselves to gazing into the whirling scene, with the same somewhat wry smile, strange to say, on both their faces.

The candles flickered and sputtered so much that they became quite mis-shapen with great blobs of soft wax. Beneath them the couples twisted and turned in obedience to Lieutenant von Gebsattel's inspiring strains. They put out their feet and pointed their toes, swung round with a flourish, then glided away. The gentlemen's long legs bent and balanced and sprang again. Petticoats flew. Gay hussar jackets whirled in abandon; voluptuously the ladies inclined their heads, yielding their waists to their partners' embraces.

Baron Harry held an amazingly pretty young Swallow pressed fairly close to his braided chest, putting his face down to hers and looking unswervingly into her eyes. Baroness Anna's gaze and her smile followed the pair. The long, lanky Lichterloh was trundling along with a plump and dumpy little Swallow in an extraordinary décolletage. But Frau Cavalry Captain von Huhnemann, who loved champagne above all else in life, there she was, dancing round and round under one of the chandeliers, completely absorbed, with another Swallow, a friendly creature whose freckled face beamed all over at the unprecedented honour done her. "My dear Baroness," Frau von Huhnemann said later to Frau First Lieutenant von Truchsess, "these girls are far from ignorant. They know all the cavalry garrisons in Germany off by heart." The pair were dancing together because there were two extra ladies; they were quite unaware that the other couples had gradually left the field to them until they were performing all by themselves. At last, however, they saw what had happened and stood there together in the centre of the hall overwhelmed from all sides by laughter and applause.

Next came the champagne, and the white-gloved orderlies ran from table to table pouring out. After that the Swallows were urged to sing again—they simply had to sing, no matter how out of breath they were.

They stood on the platform that ran along the narrow side of the hall and made eyes at the company. Their shoulders and arms were bare, and they were dressed like the birds they represented, in long dark swallow-tails over pale grey waistcoats. They wore grey clocked stockings, and slippers with very low vamps and very high heels. There were blonde and brunette, there were the fat good-natured and the interestingly lean; there were some whose cheeks were staringly rouged, other with faces chalk-white like clowns. But the prettiest was the little dark one who had almond-shaped eyes and arms like a child's—she it was with whom Baron Harry had just danced. Baroness Anna, too, found that she was the prettiest one, and continued to smile.

The Swallows sang, and Lieutenant von Gelbsattel accompanied them, flinging back his torso and twisting round his head to look, while his long arms reached out after the keys. They sang as with one voice, that they were gay birds, that they had flown the world over and always left broken hearts behind them when they flew away. They sang another very tuneful piece beginning:

> Yes, yes, the arm-y,
> How we love the arm-y,

and ending with the same. And in response to vociferous requests they repeated their Swallow song, and the officers, who knew it by now as well as they did, joined lustily in the chorus:

> When the swallows come again
> See them fly—*aren't* they fly?

The whole hall rang with laughter and song and the stamping and clinking of spurred feet beating out the time.

Baroness Anna laughed too, at all the nonsense and extravagant spirits. She had laughed so much already, all the evening, that her head and her heart ached, and she would have been glad to close her eyes in darkness and quiet had not Harry been so zealous in his pleasures. "I feel so jolly today," she had told her neighbour, at a moment when she believed what she said; but the neighbour had answered only by a mocking look, and she had realized that people do not say such things. If you really feel jolly, you act like it; to proclaim the fact makes it sound queer. On the other hand, it would have been quite impossible to say: "I feel so sad!"

Baroness Anna had grown up in the solitude and stillness of her father's estate by the sea; she was at all times too much inclined to leave out of consideration such home truths as the above, despite her constitutional fear of putting people out and her constitutional yearning to be like them and have them love her. She had white hands and heavy, ash-blond hair—much too heavy for her narrow face with its delicate bones. Between her light eyebrows ran a perpendicular furrow, which gave a pained expression to her smile.

The truth was, she loved her husband. You must not laugh. She loved him even for the prank with the rolls. With a cowering and miserable love, though he betrayed her and daily abused her love like a schoolboy. She suffered for love of him as a woman does who despises her own weak tenderness and knows that power and the happiness of the powerful are justified on this earth. Yes, she yielded herself to love and its torments as once she had yielded herself to him when in a brief attack of tenderness he wooed her; with the hungry yearning of a lonely and dreamy soul, that craves for life and passion and an outlet for its emotions.

Waltz-time, tinkling glasses—hurly-burly and smoke, voices and dancing steps. That was Harry's world and his kingdom. It was the kingdom of her dreams as well: the world of love and life, the happy commonplace.

Social life, harmless, jolly conviviality—what a frightful thing it is, how enervating, how degrading; what a vain, alluring poison, what an insidious enemy to our peace! There she sat, evening after evening, night after night, a martyr to the glaring contrast between the utter emptiness round about her and the feverish excitement born of wine and coffee, of sensual music and the dance. She sat and looked on while Harry exercised his arts of fascination upon gay and pretty ladies—not because of their personal charms but because it fed his vanity to have people see him with them and know what a lucky man he was, how much in the centre of things without one single ungratified longing. His vanity hurt her—and yet she loved it! How sweet to feel how handsome he was, how young, splendid, and bewitching! The infatuation of those other women would bring her own to fever pitch. And when afterwards, at the end of an evening spent by her in suffering for his sake, he would exhaust himself in stupid and self-centered expressions of enjoyment, there would come moments when her hatred and scorn outweighed her love; in her heart she would call him a puppy and a trifler and try to punish him by not talking, by an absurd and desperate dumbness.

Are we guessing right, little Baroness Anna? Are we giving words to all that lay behind that poor little smile of yours as the Swallows sang their song? Behind that pitiable and shameful state, when you lay in bed afterwards in the grey dawn, thinking of the jests, the witticisms, the repartee, the social charms you should have displayed—and did not! Dreams come, in that grey dawn: you, quite worn with anguish, weep on his shoulder, he tries to console you with some of his empty, pleasant, commonplace phrases, and you are suddenly overcome with the mockery of your situation: you, lying on his shoulder, are shedding tears over the whole world!

Suppose he were to fall ill? Are we right in saying that some small trifling indisposition of his could call up a whole world of dreams for you, wherein you see him as your ailing child; in which he lies helpless and broken before you and at last, at last, belongs to you alone? Do not blush, do not shrink away! Trouble does sometimes make us think bad thoughts. But after all you might trouble yourself a little about the young *Avantageur* with the drooping eyelids, sitting there beside you—how gladly he would share his loneliness with you! Why do you scorn him? Why despise? Because he belongs to your own world, not to that other where pride and high spirits reign, and conscious triumph and dancing rhythm. Truly it is hard not to be at home in one world or in the other. We know. But there is no half-way house.

Applause broke in upon Lieutenant von Gelbsattel's final chords. The Swallows had finished their song. They scorned the steps of the platform and jumped down from the front, flopping or fluttering—the gentlemen rushed up to be of help. Baron Harry helped the little brunette Swallow with the childlike arms; he helped her very efficiently and with understanding of such things. He took her by the thigh and the waist, gave himself plenty of time to set her down, then almost carried her to the table, where he brimmed her glass with champagne till it overflowed, and touched his own to it, slowly, meaningfully, gazing into her eyes with a foolish, insistent smile. He had drunk a good deal, and the scar stood out on his forehead, that looked very white next his glowing face. But his mood was a free and hilarious one, unclouded by any passion.

His table stood opposite to Baroness Anna's across the hall. As she sat talking idly with her neighbour she was listening greedily to the laughter over there and sending stolen and reproachful glances to watch every moment—in that painful state of tension which enables a person to carry on a conversation that complies with all the social forms, while actually being elsewhere all the time, and in the presence of the person one is watching.

Once or twice it seemed to her that the little Swallow's eye caught her own. Did she know her? Did she know who she was? How lovely she looked! How provocative, how full of fascination and thoughtless life! If Harry had been in love with her, if he had burned and suffered for her sake, his wife could have forgiven that, she could have understood and sympathized. And suddenly she became conscious that her own feeling for the little Swallow was warmer and deeper than Harry's own.

And the little Swallow herself? Dear me, her name was Emmy, and she was fundamentally commonplace. But she was wonderful too, with black strands of hair framing a wide, sensuous face, shadowed, almond-shaped eyes, a generous mouth full of shining teeth, and those arms like a child's. Loveliest of all were the shoulders—they had a way of moving with such ineffable suppleness in their sockets. Baron Harry took great interest in these shoulders; he would not have them covered, and set up a noisy struggle for the scarf which she would have put about them. And in all this, nobody in the whole hall saw, neither Baron Harry nor his wife nor anyone else, that this poor little waif, made sentimental by the wine she had drunk, had all the evening been casting longing glances at the young *Avantageur* whose lack of feeling for rhythm had caused his demission from the piano-stool. She had been drawn by the way he played, by his drooping lids, she found him noble, poetic, a being from a different world—whereas she was familiar unto boredom with Baron Harry's sort and all its works and ways. She was saddened, she was wretched, because the *Avantageur* cast not a thought in her direction.

The candles burned low and dim in the cigarette smoke and blue wreaths drifted above the company's heads. There was a smell of coffee on the heavy air, and odours and vapours of the feast, made still more heady by the somewhat daring perfume affected by the Swallows, hung about the scene; the white tables and champagne coolers, the men and women, flirting, giggling and guffawing, weary-eyed and unrestrained.

Baroness Anna talked no more. Despair—and that frightful mixture of yearning, envy, love, and self-contempt which we call jealousy and which makes the world no good place at all to live in —had so subdued her heart that she had not power to counterfeit any more. Let him see how she felt, perhaps he would be ashamed —or at least he would have some feeling about her, of whatever kind, in his heart.

She looked across. The game over there was going rather far, everybody was watching and laughing. Harry had thought of a new kind of amorous struggle with the fair Swallow: it consisted in an exchange of rings. Bracing his knee against hers he held her fast to her chair, and snatched and tugged after her hand in a violent effort to open her little clenched fist. In the end he won. Amid noisy applause he wrenched off the narrow circlet she wore —it cost him some trouble—and triumphantly forced his own wedding ring upon her finger.

Then Baroness Anna stood up. Anger and pain, a longing to hide herself away in the dark with her sense of his so dear unworthiness; a desperate desire to punish him by making a scandal by forcing him at all costs to acknowledge her presence—such were the emotions that overpowered her. She pushed back her chair, and pale as death she walked across the hall towards the door.

There was a great sensation. People were sobered, they looked at one another grave-faced. One or two gentlemen called out Harry's name. All at once it became still in the hall.

Then something very odd happened: the little Swallow—Emmy —suddenly and decisively espoused the Baroness's cause. Perhaps she was moved by a natural feminine instinct of pity for suffering love; perhaps her own pangs for the *Avantageur* with the drooping lids made her see in the little Baroness a fellow-sufferer. In any case, she acted—to the amazement of the company.

"You are coarse!" she said loudly, in the hush, and gave the dumbfounded Harry a great push. Just these three words: "You are coarse." And all at once she was at Baroness Anna's side, where the latter stood lifting the latch of the door.

"Forgive!" she breathed—softly, as though no one else in the room were worthy to hear. "Here is the ring," and she slipped Harry's wedding ring into the Baroness's hand. And suddenly

Baroness Anna felt the girl's broad, glowing face bend over this hand of hers; she felt burning on it a soft and passionate kiss. "Forgive!" whispered the little Swallow once more, and ran off.

But Baroness Anna stood outside in the darkness, still quite dazed, and waited for this unexpected event to take on shape and meaning within her. And it did: it was a joy, so warm, so sweet, so comfortable that for a moment she closed her eyes.

We stop here. No more, it is enough. Just this one priceless little detail, as it stands: there she was, quite enraptured and enchanted, simply because a little chit of a strolling chorus-girl had come and kissed her hand!

We leave you, Baroness Anna. We kiss your brow and take our leave; farewell, we must hurry away. Sleep, now. You will dream all night of the Swallow who came to you, and you will have a gleam of happiness.

For it brings happiness, it brings to the heart a little thrill and ecstasy of joy, when two worlds, between which longing plies, for one fleeting, illusory moment touch each other.

The Dilettante

It can all be summed up, beginning, middle, and end—yes, and fitting valediction too, perhaps—in the one word: "disgust." The disgust which I now feel for everything and for life as a whole; the disgust that chokes me, that shatters me, that hounds me out and pulls me down, and that one day may give me strength to break the whole fantastic and ridiculous situation across my knee and finish with it once and for all. I may go on for another month or so, perhaps for six months or a year; eat and drink and fill my days somehow or other. Outwardly my life may proceed as peacefully, regularly, and mechanically as it has been doing all this winter, in frightful contrast to the process of dry rot and dissolution going on within. It would seem that the more placid, detached, and solitary a man's outer life, the more strenuous and violent his inner experiences are bound to be. It comes to the same thing: if you take care not to be a man of action, if you seek peace in solitude, you will find that life's vicissitudes fall upon you from within and it is upon that stage you must prove yourself a hero or a fool.

I have bought this new note-book in order to set down my story in it—but to what end, after all? Perhaps just to fill in the time? Out of interest in the psychological, and to soothe myself with the conviction that it all had to be? There is such consolation in the inevitable! Or perhaps in order to give myself a temporary illusion of superiority and therewith a certain indifference to fate? For even indifference, as I know full well, might be a sort of happiness.

From *Stories of Three Decades*, by Thomas Mann and translated by H. T. Lowe-Porter. Copyright 1936 by Alfred A. Knopf, Inc. Reprinted by permission.

It lies so far behind me, the little old city with its narrow, irregular, gabled streets, its Gothic churches and fountains, its busy, solid, simple citizens, and the big patrician house, hoary with age, where I grew up!

It stood in the centre of the town and had lasted out four generations of well-to-do, respected business men and their families. The motto over the front door was "*Ora et labora*." You entered through a large flagged court, with a wooden gallery, painted white, running round it up above; and mounted the stairs to a good-sized lobby and a dark little columned hall, whence you had access, through one of the tall white-enamelled doors, to the drawing-room, where my mother sat playing the piano.

The room was dull, for thick dark-red curtains half-shrouded the windows. The white figures of gods and goddesses on the wall hangings stood out plastically from their blue background and seemed as though listening to the deep, heavy first notes of a Chopin nocturne which was her favourite piece. She always played it very slowly, as though to enjoy to the full each melancholy cadence. The piano was old and its resonance had suffered; but by using the soft pedal you could give the notes a veiled, dull silvery sound and so produce quite extraordinary effects.

I would sit on the massive, straight-backed mahogany sofa listening, and watching my mother as she played. She was small and fragile and wore as a rule a soft, pale-grey gown. Her narrow face was not beautiful, it was more like that of a quiet, gentle, dreamy child, beneath the parted, slightly waved, indefinitely blond hair. Sitting at the piano, her head a little on one side, she looked like one of those touching little angels who sit in old pictures at the Madonna's feet and play on their guitars.

When I was little she often used to tell me, in her low, deprecatory voice, such fairy-tales as nobody else knew; or she would simply put her hands on my head as it lay in her lap and sit there motionless, not saying a word. Those, I think, were the happiest, peacefullest days of my life.—Her hair did not grey, she became no older; only her figure grew more fragile with the years and her face thinner, stiller, and more dreaming.

But my father was a tall, broad-shouldered gentleman, in fine black broadcloth trousers and coat, with a white waistcoat on which his gold eye-glasses dangled. He wore grey mutton-chop whiskers, with a firm round chin coming out between them, smooth-shaven like his upper lip. Between his brows stood permanently two horizontal folds. He was a powerful man, of great influence in public affairs. I have seen men leave his presence, some with quickened breath and sparkling eyes, others quite broken and in despair. For it sometimes happened that I, and I suppose my mother and my two elder sisters as well, were witnesses at such scenes—either because our father wanted to rouse my ambitions and stimulate me to get on in the world, or else, as I have since suspected, because he needed an audience. He had a way of leaning back in his chair, with one hand thrust into the opening of his waistcoat, and looking after the favoured or the disappointed man, which even as a child led me vaguely to such a conclusion.

I sat in my corner looking at my father and mother, and it was as though I would choose between them: whether I would spend my life in deeds of power or in dreamy musing. And always in the end my eyes would rest upon my mother's quiet face.

Not that I could have been at all like her outwardly, for my occupations were for the most part quite lively and bustling. One of them I still remember, which I vastly preferred to any sort of game with my schoolmates. Even now, at thirty, I still recall it with a heightened sense of pleasure.

I owned a large and well-equipped puppet theatre, and I would shut myself in alone with it to perform the most wonderful musical dramas. My room was in the second storey and had two dark and grisly-bearded ancestral portraits hanging on the wall. I would draw the curtains and set a lamp near the theatre, for it heightened the atmosphere to have artificial light. I, as conductor, took my place directly in front of the stage, my left hand resting upon a large round pasteboard box which was the sole visible orchestral instrument.

The performers would now enter; I had drawn them myself with pen and ink, cut them out, and fitted them into little wooden blocks so that they could stand up. There were the most beautiful ladies, and gentlemen in overcoats and top hats.

"Good evening, ladies and gentlemen," I would say. "Everybody all right? I got here betimes, for there was still some work to do. But it is quite time for you to go to your dressing-rooms."

They went behind the stage and soon came back transfigured, in the gayest and most beautiful costumes, to look through the peep-hole which I had cut in the curtain and see if there was a good house. The house was in fact not so bad; and I rang the bell to let myself know that the performance was about to begin, lifted my baton, and paused to enjoy the sudden stillness which my gesture evoked. Another motion called up the dull warning rumble of the drums with which the overture began—this I performed with my left hand on the top of the box. Then came in the horns, clarinets, and flutes; these I reproduced with my own voice in most inimitable fashion, and so it went on until upon a powerful crescendo the curtain rose and the play began, in a setting of gloomy forest or glittering palace hall.

I would mentally sketch out the drama beforehand and then improvise the details as I went along. The shrilling of the clarinets, the beating of the drums accompanied singing of great passion and sweetness; I chanted splendid bombastic verse with more rhyme than reason; in fact it seldom had any connected meaning, but rolled magnificently on, as I drummed with my left hand, performed both song and accompaniment with my own voice, and directed with my right hand both music and acting down to the minutest detail. The applause at the end of each act was so enthusiastic that there were repeated curtain calls, and even the conductor had sometimes to rise from his seat and bow low in pride and gratitude.

Truly, when after such a strenuous performance I put my toy theatre away, all the blood in my body seemed to have risen to my head and I was blissfully exhausted as is a great artist at the triumphant close of a production to which he has given all that is in him. Up to my thirteenth or fourteenth year this was my favourite occupation.

I recall so very little of my childhood and boyhood in the great house, where my father conducted his business on the ground floor, my mother sat dreaming in her easy-chair, and my sisters, who were two and three years older than I, bustled about in kitchen and laundry.

I am clear that I was an unusually brisk and lively lad. I was well born, I was an adept in the art of imitating my schoolmasters, I knew a thousand little play-acting tricks and had a quite superior use of language—so that it was not hard for me to be popular and respected among my mates. But lessons were a different matter; I was too busy taking in the attitudes and gestures of my teachers to have attention left over for what they were saying, while at home my head was too full of my verses, my theatre, and all sorts of airy trifles to be in a state to do any serious work.

"You ought to be ashamed," my father would say, the furrows in his brow getting deeper as he spoke, when I brought him my report into the drawing-room after dinner and he perused it with one hand stuck in his waistcoat. "It does not make very good reading for me and that's a fact. Will you kindly tell me what you expect will become of you? You will never get anywhere in life like this."

Which was depressing; but it did not prevent me from reading aloud to my parents and sisters after the evening meal a poem which I had written during the afternoon. My father laughed so that his pince-nez bounced about all over his waistcoat. "What sort of fool's tricks are those?" he cried again and again. But my mother drew me to her and stroked my hair. "It is not bad at all, my dear," she said. "I find there are some quite pretty lines in it."

Later on, when I was at an older stage, I taught myself a way of playing the piano. Being attracted by the black keys, I began with the F-sharp major chords, explored modulations over into other scales, and by assiduous practice arrived at a certain skill in various harmonies without time or tune, but imparting all possible expressiveness to my mystical billows of sound.

My mother said that my attack displayed a taste for piano, and she got a teacher for me. The lessons went on for six months, but I had not sufficient manual dexterity or sense of rhythm to succeed.

Well, the years passed, and despite my troubles at school I found life very jolly. In the circle of my relatives and friends I was high-spirited and popular, being amiable out of sheer pleasure in playing the amiable part; though at the same time I began instinctively to look down on all these people, finding them arid and unimaginative.

One afternoon, when I was some eighteen years old and about to enter the highest class at school, I overheard a little conversation between my parents. They were sitting together at the round table in the sitting-room and did not see me dawdling by the window in the adjacent dining-room, staring at the pale sky above the gabled roofs. I heard my own name and slipped across to the half-open white-enamelled folding doors.

My father was leaning back in his chair with his legs crossed and the financial newspaper in one hand while with the other he slowly stroked his chin between the mutton-chops. My mother sat on the sofa with her placid face bent over her embroidery. The lamp was on the table between.

My father said: "It is my view that we ought to take him out of school and apprentice him to some good well-known firm."

"Oh!" answered my mother looking up in dismay. "Such a gifted child!"

My father was silent for a moment, meticulously brushing a speck from his coat. Then he lifted his shoulders and put out his hands, palms up. Said he:

"If you think, my love, that it takes no brains to be a business man you are much mistaken. And besides, I realize to my regret that the lad is accomplishing absolutely nothing at school. His gifts to which you refer are of the dilettante variety—though let me hasten to add that I by no means underestimate the value of that sort of thing. He can be very charming when he likes; he knows how to flatter and amuse his company, and he needs to please and be successful. Many a man has before now made a fortune with this equipment. Possessing it, and in view of his indifference to other fields of endeavour, he is not unadapted to a business career in the larger sense."

My father leaned back in some self-satisfaction, took a cigarette out of his case, and slowly lighted it.

"You are quite right," said my mother, looking about the room with a saddened face. "Only I have often thought and to some extent hoped that we might make an artist of him. I suppose it is true that no importance can be attached to his musical talent, which has remained undeveloped; but have you noticed that since he went to that art exhibition he has been doing a little drawing? It does not seem at all bad to me."

My father blew out smoke from his cigarette, sat erect, and said curtly:

"That is all stuff and nonsense. Anyhow, we can easily ask him."

I asked myself. What indeed did I really want? The prospect of any sort of change was most welcome to me. So in the end I put on a solemn face and said that I was quite ready to leave school and become a business man. I was apprenticed to the wholesale lumber business of Herr Schlievogt, down on the river-bank.

The change was only superficial, of course. I had but the most moderate interest in the lumber business; I sat in my revolving chair under the gas burner in the dark, narrow counting-room, as remote and indifferent as on the bench at school. This time I had fewer cares—that was the great difference.

Herr Schlievogt was a stout man with a red face and stiff grey nautical beard; he troubled himself very little about me, being mostly in the mills, at some distance from the counting-house and yards. The clerks treated me with respect. I had social relations with but one of them, a talented and self-satisfied young man of good family whom I had known when I was at school. His name was Schilling. He made as much fun of everything in the world as I did, but he displayed a lively interest in the lumber business and every day gave utterance to his firm resolve that he would some day and somehow become a rich man.

As for me, I mechanically performed my necessary tasks and for the rest spent my time sauntering among the workmen in the yards, between the stacks of lumber, looking at the river beyond the high wooden lattice, where now and then a freight train rolled past, and thinking about some theatre or concert I had lately attended or some book which I had read.

For I read a great deal, read everything I could lay my hands on, and my capacity for impressions was great. I had an emotional grasp of each character created by an author; in each one I thought to see myself, and identified myself wholly with the atmosphere of a book—until it was the turn of a new one to have its effect upon me. I would sit in my room—with a book on my knee instead of the toy theatre to occupy me—and look up at my two ancestral portraits while I savoured the style of the book in which I was then absorbed, my brain filled with an unproductive chaos of half-thoughts and fanciful imaginings.

My sisters had married in quick succession. When I was not at the office I would often go down to the drawing-room, where my mother sat, now almost always alone. She was a little ailing, her face had grown even more childlike and placid, and when she played Chopin to me or I showed her a new sequence of harmonies which I had discovered, she would ask me whether I was content and happy in my calling.—And there was no doubt that I was happy.

I was not much more than twenty, my choice of a career was still provisional, and the idea was not foreign to me that I need not always spend my life with Herr Schlievogt or with some bigger lumber-dealer. I knew that one day I could free myself, leave my gabled birthplace, and live somewhere more in accordance with my tastes: read good and well-written novels, attend the theatre, make a little music. Was I not happy? Did I not eat excellently well, go dressed in the best? And as in my schooldays I realized that there were poor and badly dressed boys who behaved with subservience to me and my like, so now I was stimulated by the consciousness that I belonged to the upper classes, the rich and enviable ones, born to look down with benevolent contempt upon the unlucky and dissatisfied. Why should I not be happy? Let things take their course. And there was a certain charm in the society of these relations and friends. It gave me a blithe feeling of superiority to smile at their limitations and yet to gratify my desire to please by behaving towards them with the extreme of affability. I basked in the sunshine of their somewhat puzzled approbation— puzzled because while they approved, they vaguely discerned elements of contradiction and extravagance.

A change began to take place in my father. Each day when he came to table at four o'clock the furrows on his brow seemed to have got deeper. He no longer thrust his hand imposingly between his waistcoat buttons, his bearing was depressed and self-conscious. One day he said to me:

"You are old enough now to share with me the cares which are undermining my health. And it is even my duty to acquaint you with them, to prevent you from cherishing false expectations. You know that I made considerable sacrifices to give your sisters their marriage portions. And of late the firm has lost a deal of money as well. I am an old man, and a discouraged one; I do not feel that things will change much for the better. I must ask you to realize that you will be flung upon your own resources."

These things he said some two months before his death. One day he was found sitting in his arm-chair in the office, waxen-faced, paralysed, and unable to articulate. A week later the whole town attended his funeral.

My mother sat by the table in the drawing-room, fragile and silent, with her eyes mostly closed. My sisters and I hovered about her; she would nod and smile, but still be motionless and silent, her hands in her lap and her strange, wide, melancholy gaze directed at one of the white deities on the wall. Gentlemen in frock-coats would come in to tell her about the progress of the liquidation; she would nod and smile and shut her eyes again.

She played Chopin no more. When she passed her pale, delicate hand over her smoothly parted hair it would tremble with fatigue and weakness. Scarcely six months after my father's death she laid herself down and died, without a murmur, without one struggle for life.

So it was all over now—and what was there to hold me to the place? For good or ill, the business of the firm had been liquidated; I turned out to have fallen heir to some hundred thousand marks, enough to make me independent. I had no duties and on some ground or other had been declared unfit for service.

There was no longer any bond between me and those among whom I had grown up. Their point of view was too one-sided for me to share it, and on their side they regarded me with more and more puzzled eyes. Granted that they knew me for what I was, a perfectly useless human being—as such, indeed, did I know myself. But I was cynical and fatalistic enough to look on the bright side of what my father had called my dilettante talents, self-satisfied enough to want to enjoy life in my own way.

I drew my little competence out of the bank and almost without any formal farewell left my native town to pursue my travels.

I remember as though they were a beautiful, far-away dream those next three years, in which I surrendered myself greedily to a thousand new, rich, and varied sensations. How long ago was it that I spent a New Year's Day amid snow and ice among the monks at the top of the Simplon Pass? How long since I was sauntering across Piazza Erbe in Verona? Since I entered the Piazza di San Pietro from the Borgo San Spirito, trod for the first time beneath the colonnades, and let my gaze stray abashed into the distances of that mammoth square? Since I looked down from Corso Vittorio Emmanuele on the city of Naples, white in the brilliant light, and saw far off across the bay the charming silhouette of Capri, veiled in deep-blue haze? All that was some six years ago, hardly more.

I lived very carefully within my means, in simple lodgings or in modest pensions. But what with travelling and the difficulty of giving up all at once the good bourgeois comforts I was used to, my expenses were after all not small. I had set apart for my travels the sum of fifteen thousand marks out of my capital—but I overstepped this limit.

For the rest I fared very well among the people with whom I came into contact: disinterested and often very attractive characters, to whom of course I could not be the object of respect that I had been in my former surroundings, but from whom, on the other hand, I need not fear disapproving or questioning looks.

My social gifts sometimes made me genuinely popular—I recall for instance a scene in Pensione Minelli at Palermo, where there was a circle of French people of all ages. One evening I improvised for them "a music drama by Richard Wagner" with a lavishness of tragic gesture, recitative, and rolling harmonies, finishing amid enormous applause. An old gentleman hurried up to me; he had scarcely a hair on his head, his sparse white mutton-chops straggled down across his grey tweed jacket. He seized my hands, tears in his eyes, and cried:

"But it is amazing! Amazing, my dear sir! I swear to you that not for thirty years have I been so pricelessly entertained. Permit me to thank you from the bottom of my heart. But you must, you certainly must become an actor or a musician!"

Truly, on such an occasion I felt something of the arrogance of a great painter who draws a caricature on the table-cloth to amuse his friends.—But after dinner I sat down alone in the salon and spent a sad and solitary hour trying sustained chords on the piano in an effort to express the mood evoked in me by the sight of Palermo.

Leaving Sicily, I had just touched the African coast, then gone on into Spain. In the country near Madrid, on a gloomy, rainy winter afternoon, I felt the first time the desire—and the necessity —for a return to Germany. For aside from the fact that I began to

crave a settled and regular life, I saw without any prolonged calcu-
lation that however carefully I lived I should have spent twenty
thousand marks before my return.

I did not hesitate many days before setting out on the long journey through France, which was protracted to nearly six months
by lengthy sojourns in this place and that. I recall with painful
distinctness the summer evening of my arrival at the capital city
in the centre of Germany which even before setting out on my
travels I had selected as my home. Hither I had now come: a little
wiser, equipped with a little experience and knowledge, and full of
childish joy at the prospect of here setting up my rest and estab-
lishing—carefree, independent, and in enjoyment of my modest
means—a life of quiet and contemplation.

The spot was not badly chosen. It is a city of some size, yet not
so bustling as a metropolis, nor marred by a too obtrusive business
life. It has some fine old squares and its atmosphere is not lacking
in either elegance or vivacity. Its suburbs are charming; best of all
I liked the well-laid-out promenade leading up to the Lerchenberg,
a long ridge against which most of the town is built. From this
point there is an extended view over houses, churches, and the
river winding gently away into the distance. From some positions,
and especially when the band is playing on a summer afternoon
and carriages and pedestrians are moving to and fro, it recalls the
Pincio.—But I will return to this promenade later on.

It would be hard to overestimate the peculiar pleasure I drew
from the arrangement of the bedroom and sitting-room I had
taken in a busy quarter in the centre of the city. Most of our family
effects had passed into the possession of my sisters, but enough
was left for my needs: adequate and even handsome furniture, my
books, and my two ancestral portraits, even the old grand piano,
which my mother had willed to me.

When everything had been placed and the photographs which
I had acquired on my travels were hung on the walls or arranged
on the heavy mahogany writing-desk and the bow-front chest of
drawers, and when ensconced in my new fastness I sat down in an
arm-chair by the window to survey by turns my abode within and
the busy street life outside, my comfort and pleasure were no small
thing. And yet—I shall never forget the moment—besides my

satisfaction and confidence something else stirred in me, a faint sense of anxiety and unrest, a faint consciousness of being on the defensive, of rousing myself against some power that threatened my peace: the slightly depressing thought that I had now for the first time left behind the temporary and provisional and exchanged it for the definite and fixed.

I will not deny that these and like sensations repeated themselves from time to time. But must they not come, now and then, those afternoon hours in which one sits and looks out into the growing twilight, perhaps into a slowly falling rain, and becomes prey to gloomy foreboding? True, my future was secure. I had entrusted the round sum of eighty thousand marks to the bank, the interest came to about six hundred marks the quarter—my God, but the times are bad!—so that I could live decently, buy books, and now and then visit the theatre or enjoy some lighter kind of diversion.

My days in fact conformed very well to the ideal which I had always had in view. I got up at about ten, breakfasted, and spent the rest of the morning at the piano or reading some book or magazine. Then I strolled up the street to my little restaurant, ate my dinner, and took a long walk, through the city streets, to a gallery, the suburbs, or the Lerchenberg. I came back and resumed the same occupations: read, played the piano, amused myself with drawing of a sort, or wrote a letter, slowly and carefully. Perhaps I attended the theatre or a concert after my evening meal; if not, I sat in a café and read the papers until bedtime. That was a good day, with a solid and gratifying content, when I had discovered a motif on the piano which seemed to me new and pleasing, or when I had carried away from a painting in the gallery or from the book I had read some fine and abiding impression.

I must say too that my programme was seriously conceived with the view of giving my days as much ideal content as possible. I ate modestly, had as a rule only one suit at a time; in short, I limited my material demands in order to be able to get a good seat at the opera or concert, to buy the latest books or visit this or that art exhibition.

But the days went by, they turned into weeks and months—of boredom? Yes, I confess it. One has not always a book at hand which will absorb one for hours on end. I might sit all the morning at the piano and have no success with my improvisations. I

would be seated at the window smoking cigarettes and feel stealing over me a distaste of all the world, myself included. I would
be possessed by fear, spring up and go out of doors, there to shrug
my shoulders and watch with a superior smile the business men
and labourers on the street, who lacked the spiritual and material
gifts which would fit them for the enjoyment of leisure.

But is a man of seven-and-twenty able seriously to believe—
no matter how likely it is—that his days are now fixed and un-
changeable up to the end? A span of blue sky, the twitter of a
bird, some half-vanished dream of the night before—everything
has power to suffuse his heart with undefined hopes and fill it
with the solemn expectation of some great and nameless joy. —I
dawdled from one day to the next—aimless, dreamy, occupied
with this or that little thing to look forward to, even if it were
only the date of a forthcoming publication, with the lively conviction that I was certainly very happy even though now and again
weary of my solitude.

They were not precisely infrequent, those hours in which I was
painfully conscious of my lack of contact with my kind. That I
had none needs no explanation. I was not in touch with society—
neither the first circles nor the second. To introduce myself as a
fêtard among the gilded youth, I lacked means for that, God knew
—and on the other hand, bohemia? But I was well brought up, I
wear clean linen and a whole suit, and it does not amuse me to
carry on anarchistic conversations with shabby young people at
tables sticky with absinthe. In short, there was no one sphere to
which I could naturally gravitate, and the chance connections I
made from time to time were few, slight, and superficial—though
this was largely my own fault, for I held back, I know, being inse-
cure myself and unpleasantly aware that I could not make clear
even to a drunken painter exactly who and what I was.

Besides, of course, I had given up society; I had broken with it
when I took the liberty of going my own way regardless of its
claims upon me. So if in order to be happy I needed "people,"
then I had to ask myself whether I should not have been by now
busy and useful making money as a business man in a large way
and becoming the object of respect and envy.

But meanwhile? The fact remained that my philosophic isolation disturbed me far too much. It refused to fit in with my conception of happiness, with the consciousness or conviction that I was happy—and from this conviction I was utterly unable to part. That I was not happy, that I was in fact unhappy—certainly that was unthinkable. And there the matter rested, until the next time came, when I found myself sitting alone, withdrawn and remote, alarmingly morose—and, in short, in an intolerable state.

But are happy people morose? I thought of my home life in the limited circle where I had moved in the pleasing consciousness of my own talents and parts, sociable, charming, my eyes bright with fun and mockery and good feeling of a rather condescending sort; viewed as a little odd and yet quite generally liked. Then I had been happy, despite Herr Schlievogt and the lumber business, whereas now—?

But some vastly interesting book would appear, a new French novel, which I would spend the money to buy and, sitting in my comfortable arm-chair, would enjoy at my leisure. Three hundred unexplored pages of charming blague and literary art! Certainly life was going as I would have it. Was I asking myself whether I was happy? Such a question is sheer rubbish, nothing else.

So ends another day, undeniably a full one, thank God! Evening is here, the curtains are drawn, the lamp burns on the writing-table, it is nearly midnight, I might go to bed, but I remain sprawled in my arm-chair with idle hands, gazing up at the ceiling in order to concentrate on the vague gnawing and boring of an indefinite ache which I know not how to dispel.

I have spent the past hours immersed in a great work of art: one of those tremendous and ruthless works of genius which rack and deafen, enrapture and shatter the reader with their decadent and dilettante splendours. My nerves still quiver, my imagination is rampant, my mind seethes with strange fancies, with moods mingled of yearning, religious fervour, triumph, and a mystical peace. And with all that the compulsion, which forever urges them upwards and outwards, to display them, to share them, to "make something of them."

Suppose I were an artist in very truth, capable of giving utterance to my feelings in music, in verse, in sculpture—or best of all, to be honest, in all of them at once? It is true that I can do a little of everything. For instance, I can sit at my piano in my quiet little room and express the fullness of my feelings, to my heart's content—ought that not to be enough? Of course, if I needed "people" in order to be happy, then I could understand. But supposing that I set store by success, by recognition, praise, fame, envy, love? My God, when I recall that scene at Palermo I have to admit to myself that something like that at this moment would be a great encouragement to me now!

If I am honest with myself I cannot help admitting the sophistical and ridiculous distinction between the two kinds of happiness, inward and outward. Outward happiness—of what does it consist? There are men, the favourites of the gods, it would seem, whose happiness is genius and their genius happiness; children of light, who move easily through life with the reflection and image of the sun in their eyes; easy, charming, amiable, while all the world surrounds them with praise, admiration, envy, and love —for even envy is powerless to hate them. And they mingle in the world like children, capricious, arrogant, spoiled, friendly as the sunshine, as certain of their genius and their joy as though it were impossible things should be otherwise.

As for me, weak though I may be, I confess that I should like to be like them. Rightly or wrongly I am possessed with the feeling that I once belonged among them—but what matter? For when I am honest with myself I know that the real point is what one thinks of oneself, to what one gives oneself, to what one feels strong enough to give oneself!

Perhaps the truth is that I resigned my claim to this "outward happiness" when I withdrew myself from the demands of society and arranged my life to do without people. But of my inward satisfaction there is no doubt at all—it cannot, it must not be doubted; for I repeat, with the emphasis of desperation, that happy I must and will be. For I conceive too profoundly of happiness as a virtue, as genius, refinement, charm; and of unhappiness as something ugly, mole-like, contemptible—in a word, absurd—to be able to be unhappy and still preserve my self-respect.

I could not permit myself to be unhappy, could not stand the sight of myself in such a role. I should have to hide in the dark like a bat or an owl and gaze with envy at the children of light. I should have to hate them with a hatred which would be nothing but a festered love—and I should have to despise myself!

Hide in the dark! Ah, there comes to my mind all that I have been thinking and feeling these many months about my philosophic isolation—and my fit takes me again, my familiar, my too-much-feared fear! I am conscious of anger against some force which threatens me.

Certainly I found consolations, ameliorations, oblivion for the time and for another time and yet another. But my fear always returned, returned a thousand times in the course of the months and the years.

There are autumn days that are like a miracle. Summer is past, the trees are yellow and brown, all day the wind whistles round the corners, and turbid water fills all the gutters. You have come to terms with the time of year; you have come home, so to speak, to sit by the stove and let the winter go over your head. Then one morning you wake to see with unbelieving eyes a narrow strip of luminous blue shine through your bedroom curtains. You spring astonished out of bed and open your window, a tremulous wave of sunshine streams towards you, while through all the street noises you hear the blithe twitter of a bird. It is as though the fresh light atmosphere of an early October day were to breathe the ineffably sweet and spicy air which belongs to the promiseful winds of May. It is spring—obviously, despite the calendar, a day in spring. You fling on your clothes to hurry through the streets and into the country, out under the open sky.

Now, such an unhoped-for blessing of a day there was, some four months ago—we are now in the month of February. And on that day I saw a lovely sight. I had got up before nine, in a bright and joyful mood, possessed by vague hopes of change, of unexpected and happy events. I took the road to the Lerchenberg, mounting the right side of the hill and following along the ridge on the main road, close to the low stone parapet, in order to keep in sight all the way—it takes perhaps half an hour—the view over the slightly terraced city on the slope below, the river winding and glittering in the sun, and the green hilly landscape dim in the distance.

Hardly anyone was up here. The benches were empty, here and there among the trees a white statue looked out; a faded leaf straggled down. Watching the bright panorama as I walked, I went on undisturbed until I had reached the end of the ridge, where my road slanted down among old chestnut trees. Then I

heard the ringing of horses' hoofs and the rolling of a wagon coming on at a lively trot. It would pass me at about the middle of the
descent, so I moved to one side and stood still.

It was a small, light, two-wheeled cart drawn by two large,
briskly snorting, glossy light bays. A young lady of nineteen or
twenty years held the reins, seated beside a dignified elderly
gentleman with bushy white eyebrows and moustaches brushed
up *á la russe*. A servant in plain black and silver livery adorned the
seat behind.

The pace of the horses had been slowed down at the top of the
descent, which seemed to have made one of them nervous; it
swung out sidewise from the shaft, tucked down its head, and
braced its forelegs, trembling. The old gentleman leaned over to
help his companion, drawing in one rein with his elegantly gloved
hand. The driving seemed to have been turned over to her only
temporarily and half as a game; at least she seemed to do it with
a childish air of mingled importance and inexperience. She made
a vexed little motion of the head as she tried to quiet the shying
and stumbling animal.

She was slender and brunette. Her hair was gathered to a firm
knot in the back of her neck, but lay loose and soft on brow and
temples so that I could see the single bright brown strands; atop
it perched a round dark straw hat trimmed with a ribbon bow.
For the rest she wore a short dark-blue jacket and a simple skirt
of light-grey cloth. The brunette skin of her finely formed oval
face looked freshened and rosy in the morning air; the most attractive features in it were the long, narrow eyes, whose scarcely
visible iris was a shining black, above which arched brows so even
that they looked as though they were drawn with a pen. The nose
was perhaps a little long and the mouth might have been smaller,
though the lips were clear-cut and fine. It was charming to see the
gleaming white well-spaced teeth of her upper jaw, which, in her
efforts to control the struggling horse, she pressed hard upon
her lower lip, lifting her chin, which was almost as round as a
child's.

It would not be true to say that this face possesses any striking
or exceptional beauty. What it had was youth, the charm of gaiety
and freshness, polished, as it were, refined and heightened by ease,
well-being, and luxurious living-conditions. Certainly those bright

narrow eyes, now looking in displeasure at the refractory horse, would assume next minute their accustomed expression of happy security. The sleeves of her jacket, which were wide at the shoulders, came close round the slender wrists and she had an enchantingly dainty and elegant way of holding the reins in her slim ungloved white hands.

I stood by the edge of the path unnoted as the cart drove past, and walked slowly on when the horses quickened their pace again and took it out of sight. I felt pleasure and admiration, but at the same time a strange and poignant pain—was it envy, love, self-contempt? I did not dare to think.

The image in my mind as I write is that of a beggar, a poor wretch standing at a jeweller's window and staring at a costly jewel within. The man will not even feel any conscious desire to possess the stone, the bare idea would make him laugh at his own absurdity.

It came about quite by chance that I saw this same young lady again, only a week later, at the opera, during a performance of Gounod's *Faust*. Hardly had I entered the brightly lighted auditorium to betake myself to my seat in the stalls when I became aware of her seated at the old gentleman's side in a proscenium box on the other side of the stage. To my surprise I felt a little startled and confused, and in consequence perhaps averted my eyes, letting them rove over the other tiers and boxes. It was only when the overture had begun that I summoned resolution to look at the pair more closely.

The old gentleman wore a buttoned-up frock-coat and a black tie. He leaned back in his seat with dignified calm, one of his brown-gloved hands resting on the ledge in front of him while the other slowly stroked his beard or the close-cropped grey hair. The young girl—undoubtedly his daughter—leaned forward with lively interest, clasping her fan with both hands and resting them on the velvet upholstery of the ledge. Now and then with a quick gesture she tossed back the bright, soft brown hair from her brow and temples.

She wore a light-coloured silk blouse with a bunch of violets in her girdle. In the bright light her narrow eyes seemed to sparkle even more than before; and the position of the lips and mouth which I had noticed proved to be habitual with her; for she constantly set her even, shining, well-spaced white teeth on her under lip and drew the chin upwards a little. This innocent little face, quite devoid of coquetry, the detached and merrily roving glance, the delicate white throat, confined only by a ribbon the colour of her blouse, the gesture with which she called the old gentleman's attention to something in the stalls, on the stage, or in a box —all this gave the impression of an unspeakably refined and charming child, though it had nothing touching about it and did not arouse any of those emotions of pity which we sometimes feel for children. It was childlike in an elevated, tempered, and superior way that rested upon a security born of physical well-being and good breeding. Her evident high spirits did not have their source in pride, but in an inward and unconscious poise.

Gounod's music, spirited and sentimental by turns, seemed not a bad accompaniment to this young lady's appearance. I listened without looking at the stage, lost in a mild and pensive mood which without the music might have been more painful than it was. But after the first act there disappeared from his place in the stalls a gentleman of between twenty-five and thirty years who presently with a very easy bow appeared in the box on which my eye was fastened. The old man put out his hand at once, the young lady gave him hers with a gay nod, and he carried it respectfully to his lips as they invited him to sit down.

I was quite ready to admit that this gentleman's shirt-front was the most incomparable I had ever had the pleasure of beholding. It was fully exposed, for the waistcoat was the narrowest of black strips; his dress coat was not fastened save by a single button which came below his middle, and it was cut out from the shoulders in a sweeping curve. A stand-up collar with turned-over points met the shirt-front beneath a wide black tie, and his studs were two large square black buttons, standing out on the admirably starched, dazzlingly white expanse of shirt, which however did not lack flexibility, for it had a pleasing little concavity in the neighbourhood of the waist and swelled out again just as pleasingly and glossily below.

Of course, this shirt-front was what took the eye; but there was a head atop, entirely round and covered with close-cropped very blond hair and boasting such adornments as a pair of eye-glasses without rims or cord, a rather weedy, waving blond moustache, and a host of little duelling scars running up to the temple on one cheek. For the rest the gentleman was faultlessly built and moved with assurance.

In the course of the evening—for he remained in the box—I noted two attitudes characteristic of him. If the conversation languished he sat leaning jauntily back with one leg cocked over the other and his opera-glasses on his knee, bent his head and stuck out his whole mouth as far as it would go, to plunge into absorbed contemplation of his moustache, quite hypnotized, it would seem, and turning the while his head slowly to and fro. On the other hand, taken up in a conversation with the young lady, he would, to be sure, respectfully alter the position of his legs; then leaning even further back and seizing his chair with both hands, he would elevate his chin as high as possible and smile down upon his young neighbour with his mouth wide open, assuming an amiable and slightly superior air. What wonderfully happy self-confidence such a young man must rejoice in!

In all seriousness, I do not undervalue the possession. Upon none of his motions, however airily audacious, did the faintest self-consciousness ensue—he was buoyed up by his own self-respect. And why not? It was plain that he had made his way—not necessarily by pushing—and was on the straight road to a plain and profitable goal. He dwelt in the shade of good understanding with all the world and in the sunshine of general approbation. And so he sat there chatting with a young girl for whose pure and priceless charms he probably had an eye—and if he had he need feel no hesitation in asking for her hand. Certainly I have no desire to utter one contemptuous word in the direction of this young gentleman.

But as for me? I sat far off in the darkness below, sulkily observing that priceless and unobtainable young creature as she laughed and prattled happily with this unworthy male. Shut out, unregarded, disqualified, unknown, *hors ligne—déclassé*, pariah, a pitiable object even to myself!

I stopped on till the end and came on the three in the cloakroom, where they lingered a little getting their furs, chatting with this or that acquaintance, here a lady, there an officer. When they left, the young gentleman accompanied the young lady and her father, and I followed at a little remove through the vestibule.

It was not raining, there were a few stars in the sky, they did not take a cab. Talking easily, the three passed on ahead and I followed, timid, oppressed, tortured by my poignant, mocking, miserable feelings.—They had not far to go; not more than one turning and they stopped in front of a stately house with a plain façade, and father and daughter disappeared after a cordial leave-taking from their companion, who walked off with a brisk tread.

On the heavy, carved house-door was a plate with the name: Justizrat Rainer.

I am determined to see these notes to a finish, though my inward resistance is so great that I am tempted every minute to spring up and escape. I have dug and burrowed into this mess until I am perfectly exhausted. I am sick to death of it all.

Not quite three months since, I read in the paper that a charity bazaar was to be held in the Rathaus under the auspices of the best society in the city. I read the announcement attentively and made up my mind to go. "She will be there," I thought; "perhaps she will have a stall, and nothing can prevent my speaking to her. After all I am a man of good birth and breeding, and if I like this Fräulein Rainer I am just as well qualified as the man with the shirt-front to address her and exchange a few light words."

It was a windy, rainy afternoon when I betook myself to the Rathaus, before whose doors was a press of carriages and people. I made my way into the building, paid the entrance fee, left my hat and coat, and with some difficulty gained the broad and crowded staircase up to the first floor and so into the hall. I was greeted by a waft of heavy scent—wine, food, perfume, and pine needles—and a confused hurly-burly of laughter, talk, cries, and ringing gongs.

The immensely high and large space was gaily adorned with flags and garlands; along the walls and down the middle were the stalls, both open and closed, fantastically arrayed gentlemen acting as barkers in front of the latter and shouting at the top of their lungs. Ladies, likewise in costume, were everywhere selling flowers, embroideries, tobacco, and various refreshments. On the stage at the upper end, decorated with potted plants, a noisy band was in action, while a compact procession of people moved slowly forwards in the narrow lanes between the rows of stalls.

A little confused by the noise of the music, the barkers, and the grab-bags, I joined the procession, and in no time at all, scarcely four paces from the entrance, I found her whom I sought. She was selling wine and lemonade and wore the bright-coloured skirt, the square white head-dress and short stays of the Albanian peasant costume, her tender arms bare to the elbow. She was looking rather flushed, leaning back against her serving-table, playing with her gaudy fan and talking with a group of gentlemen round the stall. Among them I saw at the first glance a well-known face—my gentleman of the shirt-front stood beside her at the table with four fingers of each hand thrust in the side pockets of his jacket.

I pushed my way over, meaning to approach her when she was less surrounded. This was a test: we should see whether I still had in me some remnant of the blithe self-assurance and conscious ability of yore, or whether my present moroseness and pessimism were only too well justified. What was it ailed me? Why did the sight of this girl—I confess it—make my cheeks burn with the same old mingled feelings of envy, yearning, chagrin, and bitter exasperation? A little straightforwardness, in the devil's name, a little gaiety and self-confidence, as befits a talented and happy man! With nervous eagerness I summoned the apt word, the light Italian phrase with which I meant to address her.

It took some time for me to make the circuit of the hall in that slowly moving stream of people; and when once more I stood in front of her booth all the gentlemen save one had gone. He of the shirt-front still leaned against her table, discoursing blithely with the fair vendeuse. I would take the liberty of interrupting their conversation. And turning quickly, I edged myself out of the stream and stood before her stall.

What happened? Ah, nothing at all, or hardly anything. The conversation broke off, the young man stepped aside and, holding his rimless, ribbonless pince-nez with all five fingers, stared at me through them and it, while the young lady swept me with a calm and questioning gaze—from my suit down to my boots. My suit was by no means new and my boots were muddy, as I was well aware. I was hot too, and very likely my hair was ruffled. I was not cool, I was not unconcerned, I was not equal to the occasion. Here was I, a stranger, not one of the elect, intruding and making myself absurd; hatred and helpless hapless misery prevented me from looking at her at all, and in desperation I carried through my stout resolve by saying gruffly, with a scowl and in a hoarse voice:

"I'd like a glass of wine."

What matter whether she really did, as I thought, cast a quick mocking glance at her companion? We stood all three in silence as she gave me the wine; without raising my eyes, red and distraught with pain and fury, a wretched and ridiculous figure, I stood between the two, drank a few sips, laid the money on the table, and rushed out of the hall.

Since that moment it is all up with me; it added but little to my bitter cup when a few days later I read in the paper that Herr Justizrat Rainer had the honour to announce his daughter Anna's engagement to Herr Dr. Alfred Witznagel.

Since that moment it is all up with me. My last remaining shreds of happiness and self-confidence have been blown to the winds, I can do no more. Yes, I am unhappy; I freely admit it, I seem a lamentable and absurd figure even to myself. And that I cannot bear. I shall make an end of it. Today, or tomorrow, or some time, I will shoot myself.

My first impulse, my first instinct, was a shrewd one: I would make copy of the situation, I would contribute my pathetic sickness to swell the literature of unhappy love. But that was all folly. One does not die of an unhappy love-affair. One revels in it. It is not such a bad pose. But what is destroying me is that hope has been destroyed with the destruction of all pleasure in myself.

Was I—if I might ask the question—was I in love with this girl? Possibly . . . . But how—and why? Such love, if it existed, was a monstrosity born of a vanity which had long since become irritable and morbid, rasped into torment at sight of an unattainable prize. Love was the mere pretext, escape, and hope of salvation for my feelings of envy, hatred, and self-contempt.

Yes, it was all superficial. And had not my father once called me a dilettante?

No, I had not been justified, I less than most people, in keeping aloof and ignoring society—I, who am too vain to support her indifference or contempt, who cannot do without her and her applause. But here was not a matter of justification, rather one of necessity; and was it just my impractical dilettantism that made me useless for society? Ah, well, it was precisely my dilettantism that was killing me!

Indifference, I know, would be a sort of happiness. But I cannot be indifferent to myself, I am not in a position to look at myself with other eyes than those of "people"—and all innocent as I am, I am being destroyed by my bad conscience. But is a bad conscience ever anything but a festering vanity?

There is only one kind of unhappiness: to suffer the loss of pleasure in oneself. No longer to be pleasant to oneself—that is the worst that can happen; and I have known it for such a long time! All else is the play of life, it enriches life; any other kind of suffering can leave one perfectly satisfied with oneself, one can get on quite well with it. It is the conflict in oneself, the suffering with a bad conscience, the struggle with one's vanity—it is these make you a pitiable and disgusting spectacle.

An old acquaintance of mine turned up, a man named Schilling, in whose company I had once served society by working in Herr Schlievogt's lumber-yard. He was in the city on business and came to see me: a cynical individual with his hands in his trouser pockets, black-rimmed pince-nez, and a convincingly tolerant shoulder-shrug. He arrived one evening and said: "I am stopping for a few days." We went to a wine-house.

He met me as though I were still the happy and self-satisfied individual he had known; and in the belief that he was merely confirming my own conviction he said:

"My God, young fellow, but you have done yourself well here! Independent, eh? And you are right too, deuce take me if you aren't. Man lives but once, as they say, and that's all there is to it. You are the cleverer of us two, I must say. But you were always a bit of a genius." And went on just as of yore, wholeheartedly recognizing my claims to superiority and being agreeable without suspecting for a moment that I on my side was afraid of his opinion.

I struggled desperately to retain his high opinion of me, to appear happy and self-satisfied. All in vain. I had not the backbone, the courage, or the countenance; I was languid and ill at ease, I betrayed my insecurity — and with astonishing quickness he grasped the situation. He had been perfectly ready to grant my superiority—but it was frightful to see how he saw through me, was first astonished, then impatient, then cooled off and betrayed his contempt and disgust with every word he spoke. He left me early and next day I received a curt note saying that after all he found he was obliged to go away.

It is a fact that everybody is much too preoccupied with himself to form a serious opinion about another person. The world displays a readiness, born of indolence, to pay a man whatever degree of respect he himself demands. Be as you will, live as you like—but be bold about it, display a good conscience and nobody will be moral enough to condemn you. But once suffer yourself to become split, forfeit your own self-esteem, betray that you despise yourself, and your view will be blindly accepted by all and sundry. As for me, I am a lost soul.

I cease to write, fling the pen from me—full of disgust, full of disgust! I will make an end of it—alas, that is an attitude too heroic for a dilettante. In the end I shall go on living, eating, sleeping; I shall gradually get used to the idea that I am dull, that I cut a wretched and ridiculous figure.

Good God, who would have thought, who could have thought, that such is the doom which overtakes the man born a dilettante!

The Wardrobe

It was cloudy, cool, and half-dark when the Berlin-Rome express
drew in at a middle-sized station on its way. Albrecht van der
Qualen, solitary traveller in a first-class compartment with lace
covers over the plush upholstery, roused himself and sat up. He
felt a flat taste in his mouth, and in his body the none-too-agree-
able sensations produced when the train comes to a stop after a
long journey and we are aware of the cessation of rhythmic
motion and conscious of calls and signals from without. It is like
coming to oneself out of drunkenness or lethargy. Our nerves,
suddenly deprived of the supporting rhythm, feel bewildered and
forlorn. And this the more if we have just roused out of the heavy
sleep one falls into in a train.

Albrecht van der Qualen stretched a little, moved to the window, and let down the pane. He looked along the train. Men were
busy at the mail van, unloading and loading parcels. The engine
gave out a series of sounds, it snorted and rumbled a bit, standing
still, but only as a horse stands still, lifting its hoof, twitching its
ears, and awaiting impatiently the signal to go on. A tall, stout
woman in a long raincoat, with a face expressive of nothing but
worry, was dragging a hundred-pound suitcase along the train,
propelling it before her with pushes from one knee. She was saying nothing, but looking heated and distressed. Her upper lip
stuck out, with little beads of sweat upon it—altogether she was
a pathetic figure. "You poor dear thing," van der Qualen thought.
"If I could help you, soothe you, take you in—only for the sake

From *Stories of Three Decades*, by Thomas Mann and translated by H. T. Lowe-
Porter. Copyright 1936 by Alfred A. Knopf, Inc. Reprinted by permission.

of that upper lip. But each for himself, so things are arranged in life; and I stand here at this moment perfectly carefree, looking at you as I might at a beetle that has fallen on its back."

It was half-dark in the station shed. Dawn or twilight—he did not know. He had slept, who could say whether for two, five, or twelve hours? He had sometimes slept for twenty-four, or even more, unbrokenly, an extraordinarily profound sleep. He wore a half-length dark-brown winter overcoat with a velvet collar. From his features it was hard to judge his age: one might actually hesitate between twenty-five and the end of the thirties. He had a yellowish skin, but his eyes were black like live coals and had deep shadows round them. These eyes boded nothing good. Several doctors, speaking frankly as man to man, had not given him many more months.—His dark hair was smoothly parted on one side.

In Berlin—although Berlin had not been the beginning of his journey—he had climbed into the train just as it was moving off —incidentally with his red leather hand-bag. He had gone to sleep and now at waking felt himself so completely absolved from time that a sense of refreshment streamed through him. He rejoiced in the knowledge that at the end of the thin gold chain he wore round his neck there was only a little medallion in his waistcoat pocket. He did not like to be aware of the hour or of the day of the week, and moreover he had no truck with the calendars. Some time ago he had lost the habit of knowing the day of the month or even the month of the year. Everything must be in the air—so he put it in his mind, and the phrase was comprehensive though rather vague. He was seldom or never disturbed in this programme, as he took pains to keep all upsetting knowledge at a distance from him. After all, was it not enough for him to know more or less what season it was? "It is more or less autumn," he thought, gazing out into the damp and gloomy train shed. "More I do not know. Do I even know where I am?"

His satisfaction at this thought amounted to a thrill of pleasure. No, he did not know where he was! Was he still in Germany? Beyond a doubt. In North Germany? That remained to be seen. While his eyes were still heavy with sleep the window of his compartment had glided past an illuminated sign; it probably had the name of the station on it, but not the picture of a single letter had been transmitted to his brain. In still dazed condition he had heard the conductor call the name two or three times, but not a syllable had he grasped. But out there in a twilight of which he knew not so much as whether it was morning or evening lay a strange place, an unknown town.—Albrecht van der Qualen took his felt hat out of the rack, seized his red leather hand-bag, the strap of which secured a red and white silk and wool plaid into which was rolled an umbrella with a silver crook—and although his ticket was labelled Florence, he left the compartment and the train, walked along the shed, deposited his luggage at the cloak room, lighted a cigar, thrust his hands—he carried neither stick nor umbrella—into his overcoat pockets, and left the station.

Outside in the damp, gloomy, and nearly empty square five or six hackney coachmen were snapping their whips, and a man with braided cap and long cloak in which he huddled shivering inquired politely: "*Hotel zum braven Mann?*" Van der Qualen thanked him politely and held on his way. The people whom he met had their coat-collars turned up; he put his up too, nestled his chin into the velvet, smoked, and went his way, not slowly and not too fast.

He passed along a low wall and an old gate with two massive towers; he crossed a bridge with statues on the railings and saw the water rolling slow and turbid below. A long wooden boat, ancient and crumbling, came by, sculled by a man with a long pole in the stern. Van der Qualen stood for a while leaning over the rail of the bridge. "Here," he said to himself, "is a river; here is *the* river. It is nice to think that I call it that because I do not know its name."—Then he went on.

He walked straight on for a little, on the pavement of a street which was neither very narrow nor very broad; then he turned off to the left. It was evening. The electric arc-lights came on, flickered, glowed, sputtered, and then illuminated the gloom. The shops were closing. "So we may say that it is in every respect autumn," thought van der Qualen, proceeding along the wet black pavement. He wore no galoshes, but his boots were very thick-soled, durable, and firm, and withal not lacking in elegance.

He held to the left. Men moved past him, they hurried on their business or coming from it. "And I move with them," he thought "and am as alone and as strange as probably no man has ever been before. I have no business and no goal. I have not even a stick to lean upon. More remote, freer, more detached, no one can be, I owe nothing to anybody, nobody owes anything to me. God has never held out His hand over me, He knows me not at all. Honest unhappiness without charity is a good thing; a man can say to himself: I owe God nothing."

He soon came to the edge of the town. Probably he had slanted across it at about the middle. He found himself on a broad sub-urban street with trees and villas, turned to his right, passed three or four cross-streets almost like village lanes, lighted only by lanterns, and came to a stop in a somewhat wider one before a wooden door next to a commonplace house painted a dingy yel-low, which had nevertheless the striking feature of very convex and quite opaque plate-glass windows. But on the door was a sign: "In this house on the third floor there are rooms to let." "Ah!" he remarked; tossed away the end of his cigar, passed through the door along a boarding which formed the dividing line between two properties, and then turned left through the door of the house itself. A shabby grey runner ran across the entry. He cov-ered it in two steps and began to mount the simple wooden stair.

The doors to the several apartments were very modest too; they had white glass panes with woven wire over them and on some of them were name-plates. The landings were lighted by oil lamps. On the third storey, the top one, for the attic came next, were entrances right and left, simple brown doors without name-plates. Van der Qualen pulled the brass bell in the middle. It rang, but there was no sign from within. He knocked left. No answer. He knocked right. He heard light steps within, very long, like strides, and the door opened.

A woman stood there, a lady, tall, lean, and old. She wore a cap with a large pale-lilac bow and an old-fashioned, faded black gown. She had a sunken birdlike face and on her brow there was an eruption, a sort of fungus growth. It was rather repulsive.

"Good evening," said van der Qualen. "The rooms?"

The old lady nodded; she nodded and smiled slowly, without a word, understandingly, and with her beautiful long white hand made a slow, languid, and elegant gesture towards the next, the left-hand door. Then she retired and appeared again with a key. "Look," he thought, standing behind her as she unlocked the door;

"you are like some kind of banshee, a figure out of Hoffman, madam." She took the oil lamp from its hook and ushered him in.

It was a small, low-ceiled room with a brown floor. Its walls were covered with straw-coloured matting. There was a window at the back in the right-hand wall, shrouded in long, thin white muslin folds. A white door also on the right led into the next room. This room was pathetically bare, with staring white walls, against which three straw chairs, painted pink, stood out like strawberries from whipped cream. A wardrobe, a washing-stand with a mirror . . . . The bed, a mammoth mahogany piece, stood free in the middle of the room.

"Have you any objections?" asked the old woman, and passed her lovely long, white hand lightly over the fungus growth on her forehead.—It was as though she had said that by accident because she could not think for the moment of a more ordinary phrase. For she added at once: " —so to speak?"

"No, I have no objections," said van der Qualen. "The rooms are rather cleverly furnished. I will take them. I'd like to have somebody fetch my luggage from the station, here is the ticket. You will be kind enough to make up the bed and give me some water. I'll take the house key now, and the key to the apartment. . . . I'd like a couple of towels. I'll wash up and go into the city for supper and come back later."

He drew a nickel case out of his pocket, took out some soap, and began to wash his face and hands, looking as he did so through the convex window-panes far down over the muddy, gas-lit suburban streets, over the arc-lights and the villas. —As he dried his hands he went over to the wardrobe. It was a square one, varnished brown, rather shaky, with a simple curved top. It stood in the centre of the right-hand wall exactly in the niche of a second white door, which of course led into the rooms to which the main and middle door on the landing gave access. "Here is something in the world that is well arranged," thought van der Qualen. "This wardrobe fits into the door niche as though it were made for it." He opened the wardrobe door. It was entirely empty, with several rows of hooks in the ceiling; but it proved to have no back, being closed behind by a piece of rough, common grey burlap, fastened by nails or tacks at the four corners.

Van der Qualen closed the wardrobe door, took his hat, turned up the collar of his coat once more, put out the candle, and set forth. As he went through the front room he thought to hear mingled with the sound of his own steps a sort of ringing in the other room: a soft, clear, metallic sound—but perhaps he was mistaken. As though a gold ring were to fall into a silver basin, he thought, as he locked the outer door. He went down the steps and out of the gate and took the way to the town.

In a busy street he entered a lighted restaurant and sat down at one of the front tables, turning his back to all the world. He ate a *soupe aux fines herbes* with croutons, a steak with a poached egg, a compote and wine, a small piece of green gorgonzola and half a pear. While he paid and put on his coat he took a few puffs from a Russian cigarette, then lighted a cigar and went out. He strolled for a while, found his homeward route into the suburb, and went leisurely back.

The house with the plate-glass windows lay quite dark and silent when van der Qualen opened the house door and mounted the dim stair. He lighted himself with matches as he went, and opened the left-hand brown door in the third storey. He laid hat and overcoat on the divan, lighted the lamp on the big writing-table, and found there his hand-bag as well as the plaid and umbrella. He unrolled the plaid and got a bottle of cognac, then a little glass and took a sip now and then as he sat in the arm-chair finishing his cigar. "How fortunate, after all," thought he, "that there is cognac in the world." Then he went into the bedroom, where he lighted the candle on the night-table, put out the light in the other room, and began to undress. Piece by piece he put down his good, unobstrusive grey suit on the red chair beside the bed; but then as he loosened his braces he remembered his hat and overcoat, which still lay on the couch. He fetched them into the bedroom and opened the wardrobe . . . . He took a step backwards and reached behind him to clutch one of the large dark-red mahogany balls which ornamented the bedposts. The room, with its four white walls, from which the three pink chairs stood out like strawberries from whipped cream, lay in the unstable light of the candle. But the wardrobe over there was open and it was not empty. Somebody was standing in it, a creature so lovely that Albrecht van der Qualen's heart stood still a moment and then in long, deep, quiet throbs resumed its beating. She was quite nude and one of her slender arms reached up to crook a forefinger round one of the hooks in the ceiling of the wardrobe. Long waves of brown hair rested on the childlike shoulders—they breathed that charm to which the only answer is a sob. The candlelight was mirrored in her narrow black eyes. Her mouth was a little large, but it had an expression as sweet as the lips of sleep when after long days of pain they kiss our brow. Her ankles nestled and her slender limbs clung to one another.

Albrecht van der Qualen rubbed one hand over his eyes and stared . . . and he saw that down in the right corner the sacking was loosened from the back of the wardrobe. "What—" said he . . . "won't you come in—or how should I put it—out? Have a little glass of cognac? Half a glass?" But he expected no answer to this and he got none. Her narrow, shining eyes, so very black that they seemed bottomless and inexpressive—they were directed upon him, but aimlessly and somewhat blurred, as though they did not see him.

"Shall I tell you a story?" she said suddenly in a low, husky voice.

"Tell me a story," he answered. He had sunk down in a sitting posture on the edge of the bed, his overcoat lay across his knees with his folded hands resting upon it. His mouth stood a little open, his eyes half-closed. But the blood pulsated warm and mildly through his body and there was a gentle singing in his ears. She had let herself down in the cupboard and embraced a drawn-up knee with her slender arms, while the other leg stretched out before her. Her little breasts were pressed together by her upper arm, and the light gleamed on the skin of her flexed knee. She talked . . . talked in a soft voice, while the candle-flame performed its noiseless dance.

Two walked on the heath and her head lay on his shoulder. There was a perfume from all growing things, but the evening mist already rose from the ground. So it began. And often it was in verse, rhyming in that incomparably sweet and flowing way that comes to us now and again in the half-slumber of fever. But it ended badly; a sad ending: the two holding each other indissolubly embraced, and while their lips rest on each other, one stabbing the other above the waist with a broad knife—and not without good cause. So it ended. And then she stood up with an infinitely sweet and modest gesture, lifted the grey sacking at the right-hand corner—and was no more there.

From now on he found her every evening in his wardrobe and listened to her stories—how many evenings? How many days, weeks, or months did he remain in this house and in this city? It would profit nobody to know. Who would care for a miserable statistic? And we are aware that Albrecht van der Qualen had been told by several physicians that he had but a few months to live. She told him stories. They were sad stories, without relief; but they rested like a sweet burden upon the heart and made it beat longer and more blissfully. Often he forgot himself.—His blood swelled up in him, he stretched out his hands to her, and she did not resist him. But then for several evenings he did not find her in the wardrobe, and when she came back she did not tell him anything for several evenings and then by degrees resumed, until he again forgot himself.

How long it lasted—who knows? Who even knows whether Albrecht van der Qualen actually awoke on that grey afternoon and went into the unknown city; whether he did not remain asleep in his first-class carriage and let the Berlin–Rome express bear him swiftly over the mountains? Would any of us care to take the responsibility of giving a definite answer? It is all uncertain. "Everything must be in the air . . . . "

Selected Readings

AMES, VAN METER. "The Humanism of Thomas Mann." *Journal of Aesthetics and Art Criticism*, X (1952), 247–57.

BRENNAN, JOSEPH G. *Thomas Mann's World*. New York: Columbia University Press, 1942.

Germanic Review, XXV (1950). [A Thomas Mann issue]

HATFIELD, HENRY (ed.). *Thomas Mann: A Collection of Critical Essays*. Englewood Cliffs, N.J.: Prentice-Hall, Inc., 1964.

————. *Thomas Mann*. rev. ed. Norfolk, Conn.: New Directions, 1962.

HELLER, ERICH. *The Ironic German: A Study of Thomas Mann.* Boston: Little, Brown and Company, 1958.

KAUFMAN, FRITZ. *Thomas Mann: The World as Will and Representation.* Boston: Beacon Press, 1957.

LINDSEY, JOHN M. *Thomas Mann.* Oxford: Blackwell, 1954.

LUKÁCS, GYORGY S. *Essays on Thomas Mann.* Trans. Stanley Mitchell. New York: Grosset and Dunlap, Inc., 1964.

NEIDER, CHARLES (ed.). *The Stature of Thomas Mann: A Critical Anthology by Many Hands.* Norfolk, Conn.: New Directions, 1947.

THOMAS, RICHARD H. *Thomas Mann: The Mediation of Art.* Oxford: Clarendon Press, 1956.

WEST, RAY B., JR. "Thomas Mann: Moral Precept as Psychological Truth." *Sewanee Review*, LX (1952), 310–17.

FRANZ KAFKA

(1883-1924)

"The Judgment," written in one sitting on September 22, 1912, was one of the few of Kafka's stories published during his lifetime. He had asked Max Brod, his friend and biographer, to burn all his manuscripts after his death, but fortunately Mr. Brod did not comply. Some of his works that appeared after his death were the novels, *The Trial*, 1925 (translated into English in 1937); *The Castle*, 1926 (translated in 1930); *Amerika*, 1927 (translated in 1938); and the short story collection, *The Great Wall of China*, collected in 1931 (translated in 1933).

Franz Kafka was born in 1883 in Prague, where his father owned a warehouse. After taking a law degree from the University of Prague in 1906, Kafka went to work at the workman's compensation office. He had already begun to write. In 1912 he met a young German girl, but in 1917 broke off his engagement to her for the second and final time. He felt mentally and physically inadequate for marriage. Severe headaches and insomnia persisted and by 1917 he also realized he had tuberculosis. It was the beginning of many years in sanitariums. He died of tuberculosis in June, 1924, at the age of forty-one.

Kafka's stories are filled with the neurotic symbolism of a dream world. The characters themselves, obsessed with guilt, seem to be symbols of psychological states of being. The stories are all permeated by the brooding remoteness of a towering father image. But accept the premise of a dream world where the unpredictable is unsurprising and undisturbing, and the narrative level of a Kafka story makes sense. His apparently nonrational psychic symbolism appeals to man's subconscious level of perception. The real danger in Kafka lies in the possibility of his irrational world becoming commonplace, understandable, predictable, and hence rational; the real miracle of Kafka is his conscious control of the unconscious, his manner of objectively controlling the subjective world through his style: consistent point of view, matter of fact tone, simple diction and sentence structures.

Give it Up!

It was very early in the morning, the streets clean and deserted, I was on my way to the station. As I compared the tower clock with my watch I realized it was much later than I had thought and that I had to hurry; the shock of this discovery made me feel uncertain of the way, I wasn't very well acquainted with the town as yet; fortunately, there was a policeman at hand, I ran to him and breathlessly asked him the way. He smiled and said: "You asking me the way?" "Yes," I said, "since I can't find it myself." "Give it up! Give it up!" said he, and turned with a sudden jerk, like someone who wants to be alone with his laughter.

Reprinted by permission of Schocken Books Inc. from *Description of a Struggle* by Franz Kafka, Copyright 1958 © by Schocken Books Inc.

The Refusal

Our little town does not lie on the frontier, nowhere near; it is so far from the frontier, in fact, that perhaps no one from our town has ever been there; desolate highlands have to be crossed as well as wide fertile plains. To imagine even part of the road makes one tired, and more than part one just cannot imagine. There are also big towns on the road, each far larger than ours. Ten little towns like ours laid side by side, and ten more forced down from above, still would not produce one of these enormous, overcrowded towns. If one does not get lost on the way one is bound to lose oneself in these towns, and to avoid them is impossible on account of their size.

But what is even further from our town than the frontier, if such distances can be compared at all—it's like saying that a man of three hundred years is older than one of two hundred—what is even further than the frontier is the capital. Whereas we do get news of the frontier wars now and again, of the capital we learn next to nothing—we civilians that is, for of course the government officials have very good connections with the capital; they can get news from there in as little as three months, so they claim at least.

Now it is remarkable and I am continually being surprised by the way we in our town humbly submit to all orders issued in the capital. For centuries no political change has been brought about by the citizens themselves. In the capital great rulers have superseded each other—indeed, even dynasties have been deposed

Reprinted by permission of Schocken Books Inc. from *Description of a Struggle* by Franz Kafka, Copyright © 1958 by Schocken Books Inc.

or annihilated, and new ones have started; in the past century even the capital itself was destroyed, a new one was founded far away from it, later on this too was destroyed and the old one rebuilt, yet none of this had any influence on our little town. Our officials have always remained at their posts; the highest officials came from the capital, the less high from other towns, and the lowest from among ourselves—that is how it has always been and it has suited us. The highest official is the chief tax-collector, he has the rank of colonel, and is known as such. The present one is an old man; I've known him for years, because he was already a colonel when I was a child. At first he rose very fast in his career, but then he seems to have advanced no further; actually, for our little town his rank is good enough, a higher rank would be out of place. When I try to recall him I see him sitting on the veranda of his house in the Market Square, leaning back, pipe in mouth. Above him from the roof flutters the imperial flag; on the sides of the veranda, which is so big that minor military maneuvers are sometimes held there, washing hangs out to dry. His grandchildren, in beautiful silk clothes, play around him; they are not allowed down in the Market Square, the children there are considered unworthy of them, but the grandchildren are attracted by the Square, so they thrust their heads between the posts of the banister and when the children below begin to quarrel they join the quarrel from above.

This colonel, then, commands the town. I don't think he has ever produced a document entitling him to this position; very likely he does not possess such a thing. Maybe he really is chief tax-collector. But is that all? Does that entitle him to rule over all the other departments in the administration as well? True, his office is very important for the government, but for the citizens it is hardly the most important. One is almost under the impression that the people here say: "Now that you've taken all we possess, please take us as well." In reality, of course, it was not he who seized the power, nor is he a tyrant. It has just come about over the years that the chief tax-collector is automatically the top official, and the colonel accepts the tradition just as we do.

Yet while he lives among us without laying too much stress on his official position, he is something quite different from the ordinary citizen. When a delegation comes to him with a request, he stands there like the wall of the world. Behind him is nothingness, one imagines hearing voices whispering in the background, but this is probably a delusion; after all, he represents the end of all things, at least for us. At these receptions he really was worth seeing. Once as a child I was present when a delegation of citizens arrived to ask him for a government subsidy because the poorest quarter of the town had been burned to the ground. My father the blacksmith, a man well respected in the community, was a member of the delegation and had taken me along. There's nothing exceptional about this, everyone rushes to spectacles of this kind, one can hardly distinguish the actual delegation from the crowd. Since these receptions usually take place on the veranda, there are even people who climb up by ladder from the Market Square and take part in the goings-on from over the banister. On this occasion about a quarter of the veranda had been reserved for the colonel, the crowd filling the rest of it. A few soldiers kept watch, some of them standing round him in a semicircle. Actually a single soldier would have been quite enough, such is our fear of them. I don't know exactly where these soldiers come from, in any case from a long way off, they all look very much alike, they wouldn't even need a uniform. They are small, not strong but agile people, the most striking thing about them is the prominence of their teeth which almost overcrowd their mouths, and a certain restless twitching of their small narrow eyes. This makes them the terror of the children, but also their delight, for again and again the children long to be frightened by these teeth, these eyes, so as to be able to run away in horror. Even grownups probably never quite lose this childish terror, at least it continues to have an effect. There are, of course, other factors contributing to it. The soldiers speak a dialect utterly incomprehensible to us, and they can hardly get used to ours—all of which produces a certain shut-off, unapproachable quality corresponding, as it happens, to their character, for they are silent, serious, and rigid. They don't actually do anything evil, and yet they are almost unbearable in an evil sense. A soldier, for example, enters a shop, buys some trifling object, and stays there leaning against the counter; he listens to the conversations, probably does not understand them, and yet gives the impression of understanding; he himself does not say a word, just stares blankly at the speaker, then back at the listeners, all the while keeping his hand on the hilt of the long knife in his belt. This is revolting, one loses the desire to talk, the customers start leaving the shop, and only when it is quite empty does the soldier also leave. Thus wherever the soldiers appear, our lively people grow silent. That's what happened this time, too. As on all solemn occasions the colonel stood upright, holding in front of him two poles of bamboo in his outstretched hands. This is an ancient custom implying more or less that he supports the law, and the law supports him. Now everyone knows, of course, what to expect up on the veranda, and yet each time people take fright all over again. On this occasion, too, the man chosen to speak could not begin; he was already standing opposite the colonel when his courage failed him and, muttering a few excuses, he pushed his way back into the crowd. No other suitable person willing to speak could be found, albeit several unsuitable ones offered themselves; a great commotion ensued and messengers were sent in search of various citizens who were well-known speakers. During all this time the colonel stood there motionless, only his chest moving visibly up and down to his breathing. Not that he breathed with difficulty, it was just that he breathed so conspicuously, much as frogs breathe—except that with them it is normal, while here it was exceptional. I squeezed myself through the grownups and watched him through a gap between two soldiers, until one of them kicked me away with his knee. Meanwhile the man originally chosen to speak had regained his composure and, firmly held up by two fellow citizens, was delivering his address. It was touching to see him smile throughout this solemn speech describing a grievous misfortune—a most humble smile which strove in vain to elicit some slight reaction on the colonel's face. Finally he formulated the request—I think he was only asking for a year's tax exemption, but possibly also for timber from the imperial forests at a reduced price. Then he bowed low, remaining in this position for some time, as did everyone else except the colonel, the soldiers, and a number of officials in the background. To the child it seemed ridiculous that the people on the ladders should climb down a few rungs so as not to be seen during the significant pause and now and again peer inquisitively over the floor of the veranda. After this had lasted quite a while an official, a little man, stepped up to the colonel and tried to reach the latter's height by standing on his toes. The colonel, still motionless save for his deep breathing, whispered something in his ear, whereupon the little man clapped his hands and everyone rose. "The petition has been refused," he announced. "You may go." An undeniable sense of relief passed through the crowd, everyone surged out, hardly a soul paying any special attention to the colonel, who, as it were, had turned once more into a human being like the rest of us. I still caught one last glimpse of him as he wearily let go of the poles, which fell to the ground, then sank into an armchair produced by some officials, and promptly put his pipe in his mouth.

This whole occurrence is not isolated, it's in the general run of things. Indeed, it does happen now and again that minor petitions are granted, but then it invariably looks as though the colonel had done it as a powerful private person on his own responsibility, and it had to be kept all but a secret from the government—not explicitly of course, but that is what it feels like. No doubt in our little town the colonel's eyes, so far as we know, are also the eyes of the government, and yet there is a difference which it is impossible to comprehend completely.

In all important matters, however, the citizens can always count on a refusal. And now the strange fact is that without this refusal one simply cannot get along, yet at the same time these official occasions designed to receive the refusal are by no means a formality. Time after time one goes there full of expectation and in all seriousness and then one returns, if not exactly strengthened or happy, nevertheless not disappointed or tired. About these things I do not have to ask the opinion of anyone else, I feel them in myself, as everyone does; nor do I have any great desire to find out how these things are connected.

As a matter of fact there is, so far as my observations go, a certain age group that is not content—these are the young people roughly between seventeen and twenty. Quite young fellows, in fact, who are utterly incapable of foreseeing the consequences of even the least significant, far less a revolutionary, idea. And it is among just them that discontent creeps in.

An Old Manuscript

It looks as if much had been neglected in our country's system of defense. We have not concerned ourselves with it until now and have gone about our daily work; but things that have been happening recently begin to trouble us.

I have a cobbler's workshop in the square that lies before the Emperor's palace. Scarcely have I taken my shutters down, at the first glimmer of dawn, when I see armed soldiers already posted in the mouth of every street opening on the square. But these soldiers are not ours, they are obviously nomads from the North. In some way that is incomprehensible to me they have pushed right into the capital, although it is a long way from the frontier. At any rate, here they are; it seems that every morning there are more of them.

As is their nature, they camp under the open sky, for they abominate dwelling houses. They busy themselves sharpening swords, whittling arrows and practicing horsemanship. This peaceful square, which was always kept so scrupulously clean, they have made literally into a stable. We do try every now and then to run out of our shops and clear away at least the worst of the filth, but this happens less and less often, for the labor is in vain and brings us besides into danger of falling under the hoofs of the wild horses or of being crippled with lashes from the whips. Speech with the nomads is impossible. They do not know our language, indeed they hardly have a language of their own. They communicate with each other much as jackdaws do. A screeching

Reprinted by permission of Schocken Books Inc. from *The Penal Colony* by Franz Kafka, Copyright © 1948 by Schocken Books Inc.

as of jackdaws is always in our ears. Our way of living and our institutions they neither understand nor care to understand. And so they are unwilling to make sense even out of our sign language. You can gesture at them till you dislocate your jaws and your wrists and still they will not have understood you and will never understand. They often make grimaces; then the whites of their eyes turn up and foam gathers on their lips, but they do not mean anything by that, not even a threat; they do it because it is their nature to do it. Whatever they need, they take. You cannot call it taking by force. They grab at something and you simply stand aside and leave them to it.

From my stock, too, they have taken many good articles. But I cannot complain when I see how the butcher, for instance, suffers across the street. As soon as he brings in any meat the nomads snatch it all from him and gobble it up. Even their horses devour flesh; often enough a horseman and his horse are lying side by side, both of them gnawing at the same joint, one at either end. The butcher is nervous and does not dare to stop his deliveries of meat. We understand that, however, and subscribe money to keep him going. If the nomads got no meat, who knows what they might think of doing; who knows anyhow what they may think of, even though they get meat every day.

Not long ago the butcher thought he might at least spare himself the trouble of slaughtering, and so one morning he brought along a live ox. But he will never dare to do that again. I lay for a whole hour flat on the floor at the back of my workshop with my head muffled in all the clothes and rugs and pillows I had, simply to keep from hearing the bellowing of that ox, which the nomads were leaping on from all sides, tearing morsels out of its living flesh with their teeth. It had been quiet for a long time before I risked coming out; they were lying overcome round the remains of the carcass like drunkards round a wine cask.

This was the occasion when I fancied I actually saw the Emperor himself at a window of the palace; usually he never enters these outer rooms but spends all his time in the innermost garden; yet on this occasion he was standing, or so at least it seemed to me, at one of the windows, watching with bent head the goings on before his residence.

"What is going to happen?" we all ask ourselves. "How long

can we endure this burden and torment? The Emperor's palace has drawn the nomads here but does not know how to drive them away again. The gate stays shut; the guards, who used to be always marching out and in with ceremony, keep close behind barred windows. It is left to us artisans and tradesmen to save our country; but we are not equal to such a task; nor have we ever claimed to be capable of it. This is a misunderstanding of some kind; and it will be the ruin of us."

The Judgment

It was a Sunday morning in the very height of spring. Georg
Bendemann, a young merchant, was sitting in his own room on
the first floor of one of a long row of small, ramshackle houses
stretching beside the river which were scarcely distinguishable
from each other except in height and coloring. He had just finished
a letter to an old friend of his who was now living abroad, had
put it into its envelope in a slow and dreamy fashion, and with
his elbows propped on the writing table was gazing out of the
window at the river, the bridge and the hills on the farther bank
with their tender green.

He was thinking about his friend, who had actually run away
to Russia some years before, being dissatisfied with his prospects
at home. Now he was carrying on a business in St. Petersburg,
which had flourished to begin with but had long been going downhill, as he always complained on his increasingly rare visits. So
he was wearing himself out to no purpose in a foreign country;
the unfamiliar full beard he wore did not quite conceal the face
Georg had known so well since childhood, and his skin was
growing so yellow as to indicate some latent disease. By his own
account he had no regular connection with the colony of his
fellow countrymen out there and almost no social intercourse
with Russian families, so that he was resigning himself to becoming a permanent bachelor.

What could one write to such a man, who had obviously run

Reprinted by permission of Schocken Books Inc. from *The Penal Colony* by
Franz Kafka, Copyright © 1948 by Schocken Books Inc., trans. by Willa
and Edwin Muir.

off the rails, a man one could be sorry for but could not help? Should one advise him to come home, to transplant himself and take up his old friendships again—there was nothing to hinder him—and in general to rely on the help of his friends? But that was as good as telling him, and the more kindly the more offensively, that all his efforts hitherto had miscarried, that he should finally give up, come back home, and be gaped at by everyone as a returned prodigal, that only his friends knew what was what and that he himself was just a big child who should do what his successful and home-keeping friends prescribed. And was it certain, besides, that all the pain one would have to inflict on him would achieve its object? Perhaps it would not even be possible to get him to come home at all—he said himself that he was now out of touch with commerce in his native country—and then he would still be left an alien in a foreign land embittered by his friends' advice and more than ever estranged from them. But if he did follow their advice and then didn't fit in at home—not out of malice, of course, but through force of circumstances—couldn't get on with his friends or without them, felt humiliated, couldn't be said to have either friends or a country of his own any longer, wouldn't it have been better for him to stay abroad just as he was? Taking all this into account, how could one be sure that he would make a success of life at home?

For such reasons, supposing one wanted to keep up correspondence with him, one could not send him any real news such as could frankly be told to the most distant acquaintance. It was more than three years since his last visit, and for this he offered the lame excuse that the political situation in Russia was too uncertain, which apparently would not permit even the briefest absence of a small business man while it allowed hundreds of thousands of Russians to travel peacefully abroad. But during these three years Georg's own position in life had changed a lot. Two years ago his mother had died, since then he and his father had shared the household together, and his friend had of course been informed of that and had expressed his sympathy in a letter phrased so dryly that the grief caused by such an event, one had to conclude, could not be realized in a distant country. Since that time, however, Georg had applied himself with greater determination to the business as well as to everything else.

Perhaps during his mother's lifetime his father's insistence on having everything his own way in the business had hindered him from developing any real activity of his own, perhaps since her death his father had become less aggressive, although he was still active in the business, perhaps it was mostly due to an accidental run of good fortune—which was very probable indeed —but at any rate during those two years the business had developed in a most unexpected way, the staff had had to be doubled, the turnover was five times as great, no doubt about it, further progress lay just ahead.

But Georg's friend had no inkling of this improvement. In earlier years, perhaps for the last time in that letter of condolence, he had tried to persuade Georg to emigrate to Russia and had enlarged upon the prospects of success for precisely Georg's branch of trade. The figures quoted were microscopic by comparison with the range of Georg's present operations. Yet he shrank from letting his friend know about his business success, and if he were to do it now retrospectively that certainly would look peculiar.

So Georg confined himself to giving his friend unimportant items of gossip such as rise at random in the memory when one is idly thinking things over on a quiet Sunday. All he desired was to leave undisturbed the idea of the home town which his friend must have built up to his own content during the long interval. And so it happened to Georg that three times in three fairly widely separated letters he had told his friend about the engagement of an unimportant man to an equally unimportant girl, until indeed, quite contrary to his intentions, his friend began to show some interest in this notable event.

Yet Georg preferred to write about things like these rather than to confess that he himself had got engaged a month ago to a Fräulein Frieda Brandenfeld, a girl from a well-to-do family. He often discussed this friend of his with his fiancée and the peculiar relationship that had developed between them in their correspondence. "So he won't be coming to our wedding," said she, "and yet I have a right to get to know all your friends." "I don't want to trouble him," answered Georg. "Don't misunderstand me, he would probably come, at least I think so, but he would feel that his hand had been forced and he would be hurt, perhaps he would envy me and certainly he'd be discontented and without being able to do anything about his discontent he'd have to go away again alone. Alone—do you know what that means?" "Yes, but may he not hear about our wedding in some other fashion?" "I can't prevent that, of course, but it's unlikely, considering the way he lives." "Since your friends are like that, Georg, you shouldn't ever have got engaged at all." "Well, we're both to blame for that; but I wouldn't have it any other way now." And when, breathing quickly under his kisses, she still brought out: "All the same, I do feel upset," he thought it could not really involve him in trouble were he to send the news to his friend. "That's the kind of man I am and he'll just have to take me as I am," he said to himself, "I can't cut myself to another pattern that might make a more suitable friend for him."

And in fact he did inform his friend, in the long letter he had been writing that Sunday morning, about his engagement, with these words: "I have saved my best news to the end. I have got engaged to a Fräulein Frieda Brandenfeld, a girl from a well-to-do family, who only came to live here a long time after you went away, so that you're hardly likely to know her. There will be time to tell you more about her later, for today let me just say that I am very happy and as between you and me the only difference in our relationship is that instead of a quite ordinary kind of friend you will now have in me a happy friend. Besides that, you will ac-quire in my fiancée, who sends her warm greetings and will soon write you herself, a genuine friend of the opposite sex, which is not without importance to a bachelor. I know that there are many reasons why you can't come to see us, but would not my wedding be precisely the right occasion for giving all obstacles the go-by? Still, however that may be, do just as seems good to you without regarding any interests but your own."

With this letter in his hand Georg had been sitting a long time at the writing table, his face turned towards the window. He had barely acknowledged, with an absent smile, a greeting waved to him from the street by a passing acquaintance.

At last he put the letter in his pocket and went out of his room across a small lobby into his father's room, which he had not entered for months. There was in fact no need for him to enter it, since he saw his father daily at business and they took their midday meal together at an eating house; in the evening, it was true, each did as he pleased, yet even then, unless Georg—as mostly happened—went out with friends or, more recently, visited his fiancée, they always sat for a while, each with his newspaper, in their common sitting room.

It surprised Georg how dark his father's room was even on this sunny morning. So it was overshadowed as much as that by the high wall on the other side of the narrow courtyard. His father was sitting by the window in a corner hung with various mementoes of Georg's dead mother, reading a newspaper which he held to one side before his eyes in an attempt to overcome a defect of vision. On the table stood the remains of his breakfast, not much of which seemed to have been eaten.

"Ah, Georg," said his father, rising at once to meet him. His heavy dressing gown swung open as he walked and the skirts of it fluttered round him.— "My father is still a giant of a man," said Georg to himself.

"It's unbearably dark here," he said aloud.

"Yes, it's dark enough," answered his father.

"And you've shut the window, too?"

"I prefer it like that."

"Well, it's quite warm outside," said Georg, as if continuing his previous remark, and sat down.

His father cleared away the breakfast dishes and set them on a chest.

"I really only wanted to tell you," went on Georg, who had been vacantly following the old man's movements, "that I am now sending the news of my engagement to St. Petersburg." He drew the letter a little way from his pocket and let it drop back again.

"To St. Petersburg?" asked his father.

"To my friend there," said Georg, trying to meet his father's eye.— In business hours he's quite different, he was thinking. How solidly he sits here with his arms crossed.

"Oh, yes. To your friend," said his father, with peculiar emphasis.

"Well, you know, Father, that I wanted not to tell him about my engagement at first. Out of consideration for him, that was the only reason. You know yourself he's a difficult man. I said to myself that someone else might tell him about my engagement, although he's such a solitary creature that that was hardly likely—I couldn't prevent that—but I wasn't ever going to tell him myself."

"And now you've changed your mind?" asked his father, laying his enormous newspaper on the window sill and on top of it his spectacles, which he covered with one hand.

"Yes, I've been thinking it over. If he's a good friend of mine, I said to myself, my being happily engaged should make him happy too. And so I wouldn't put off telling him any longer. But before I posted the letter I wanted to let you know."

"Georg," said his father, lengthening his toothless mouth, "listen to me! You've come to me about this business, to talk it over with me. No doubt that does you honor. But it's nothing, it's worse than nothing, if you don't tell me the whole truth. I don't want to stir up matters that shouldn't be mentioned here. Since the death of our dear mother certain things have been done that aren't right. Maybe the time will come for mentioning them, and maybe sooner than we think. There's many a thing in the business I'm not aware of, maybe it's not done behind my back—I'm not going to say that it's done behind my back—I'm not equal to things any longer, my memory's failing, I haven't an eye for so many things any longer. That's the course of nature in the first place, and in the second place the death of our dear mother hit me harder than it did you. —But since we're talking about it, about this letter, I beg you, Georg, don't deceive me. It's a trivial affair, it's hardly worth mentioning, so don't deceive me. Do you really have this friend in St. Petersburg?"

Georg rose in embarrassment. "Never mind my friends. A thousand friends wouldn't make up to me for my father. Do you know what I think? You're not taking enough care of yourself. But old age must be taken care of. I can't do without you in the business, you know that very well, but if the business is going to undermine your health, I'm ready to close it down tomorrow forever. And that won't do. We'll have to make a change in your way of living. But a radical change. You sit here in the dark, and in the sitting room you would have plenty of light. You just take a bite of breakfast instead of properly keeping up your strength. You sit by a closed window, and the air would be so good for you. No, Father! I'll get the doctor to come, and we'll follow his orders.

We'll change your room, you can move into the front room and I'll move in here. You won't notice the change, all your things will be moved with you. But there's time for all that later. I'll put you to bed now for a little; I'm sure you need to rest. Come, I'll help you to take off your things, you'll see I can do it. Or if you would rather go into the front room at once, you can lie down in my bed for the present. That would be the most sensible thing."

Georg stood close beside his father, who had let his head with its unkempt white hair sink on his chest.

"Georg," said his father in a low voice, without moving.

Georg knelt down at once beside his father. In the old man's weary face he saw the pupils, over-large, fixedly looking at him from the corners of the eyes.

"You have no friends in St. Petersburg. You've always been a leg-puller and you haven't even shrunk from pulling my leg. How could you have a friend out there! I can't believe it."

"Just think back a bit, Father," said Georg, lifting his father from the chair and slipping off his dressing gown as he stood feebly enough, "it'll soon be three years since my friend came to see us last. I remember that you used not to like him very much. At least twice I kept you from seeing him, although he was actually sitting with me in my room. I could quite well understand your dislike of him, my friend has his peculiarities. But then, later, you got on with him very well. I was proud because you listened to him and nodded and asked him questions. If you think back you're bound to remember. He used to tell us the most incredible stories of the Russian Revolution. For instance, when he was on a business trip to Kiev and ran into a riot, and saw a priest on a balcony who cut a broad cross in blood on the palm of his hand and held the hand up and appealed to the mob. You've told that story yourself once or twice since."

Meanwhile Georg had succeeded in lowering his father down again and carefully taking off the woollen drawers he wore over his linen underpants and his socks. The not particularly clean appearance of this underwear made him reproach himself for having been neglectful. It should have certainly been his duty to see that his father had clean changes of underwear. He had not yet explicitly discussed with his bride-to-be what arrangements should be made for his father in the future, for they had both of them silently taken it for granted that the old man would go on living alone in the old house. But now he made a quick, firm decision to take him into his own future establishment. It almost looked, on closer inspection, as if the care he meant to lavish there on his father might come too late.

He carried his father to bed in his arms. It gave him a dreadful feeling to notice that while he took the few steps towards the bed the old man on his breast was playing with his watch chain. He could not lay him down on the bed for a moment, so firmly did he hang on to the watch chain.

But as soon as he was laid in bed, all seemed well. He covered himself up and even drew the blankets farther than usual over his shoulders. He looked up at Georg with a not unfriendly eye.

"You begin to remember my friend, don't you?" asked Georg, giving him an encouraging nod.

"Am I well covered up now?" asked his father, as if he were not able to see whether his feet were properly tucked in or not.

"So you find it snug in bed already," said Georg, and tucked the blankets more closely round him.

"Am I well covered up?" asked the father once more, seeming to be strangely intent upon the answer.

"Don't worry, you're well covered up."

"No!" cried his father, cutting short the answer, threw the blankets off with a strength that sent them all flying in a moment and sprang erect in bed. Only one hand lightly touched the ceiling to steady him.

"You wanted to cover me up, I know, my young sprig, but I'm far from being covered up yet. And even if this is the last strength I have, it's enough for you, too much for you. Of course I know your friend. He would have been a son after my own heart. That's why you've been playing him false all these years. Why else? Do you think I haven't been sorry for him? And that's why you had to lock yourself up in your office—the Chief is busy, mustn't be disturbed—just so that you could write your lying little letters to Russia. But thank goodness a father doesn't need to be taught how to see through his son. And now that you thought you'd got him down, so far down that you could set your bottom on him and sit on him and he wouldn't move, then my fine son makes up his mind to get married!"

Georg stared at the bogey conjured up by his father. His friend in St. Petersburg, whom his father suddenly knew too well, touched his imagination as never before. Lost in the vastness of Russia he saw him. At the door of an empty, plundered warehouse he saw him. Among the wreckage of his showcases, the slashed remnants of his wares, the falling gas brackets, he was just standing up. Why did he have to go so far away!

"But attend to me!" cried his father, and Georg, almost distracted, ran towards the bed to take everything in, yet came to a stop halfway.

"Because she lifted up her skirts," his father began to flute, "because she lifted her skirts like this, the nasty creature," and mimicking her he lifted his shirt so high that one could see the scar on his thigh from his war wound, "because she lifted her skirts like this and this you made up to her, and in order to make free with her undisturbed you have disgraced your mother's memory, betrayed your friend and stuck your father into bed so that he can't move. But he can move, or can't he?"

And he stood up quite unsupported and kicked his legs out. His insight made him radiant.

Georg shrank into a corner, as far away from his father as possible. A long time ago he had firmly made up his mind to watch closely every least movement so that he should not be surprised by any indirect attack, a pounce from behind or above. At this moment he recalled this long-forgotten resolve and forgot it again, like a man drawing a short thread through the eye of a needle.

"But your friend hasn't been betrayed after all!" cried his father, emphasizing the point with stabs of his forefinger. "I've been representing him here on the spot."

"You comedian!" Georg could not resist the retort, realized at once the harm done and, his eyes starting in his head, bit his tongue back, only too late, till the pain made his knees give.

"Yes, of course I've been playing a comedy! A comedy! That's a good expression! What other comfort was left to a poor old widower? Tell me—and while you're answering me be you still my living son—what else was left to me, in my back room, plagued by a disloyal staff, old to the marrow of my bones? And my son strutting through the world, finishing off deals that I had pre-

pared for him, bursting with triumphant glee and stalking away
from his father with the closed face of a respectable business man!
Do you think I didn't love you, I, from whom you are sprung?"

Now he'll lean forward, thought Georg. What if he topples and
smashes himself! These words went hissing through his mind.

His father leaned forward but did not topple. Since Georg
did not come any nearer, as he had expected, he straightened
himself again.

"Stay where you are, I don't need you! You think you have
strength enough to come over here and that you're only hanging
back of your own accord. Don't be too sure! I am still much the
stronger of us two. All by myself I might have had to give way, but
your mother has given me so much of her strength that I've
established a fine connection with your friend and I have your
customers here in my pocket!"

"He has pockets even in his shirt!" said Georg to himself, and
believed that with this remark he could make him an impossible
figure for all the world. Only for a moment did he think so, since
he kept on forgetting everything.

"Just take your bride on your arm and try getting in my way!
I'll sweep her from your very side, you don't know how!"

Georg made a grimace of disbelief. His father only nodded,
confirming the truth of his words, towards Georg's corner.

"How you amused me today, coming to ask me if you should
tell your friend about your engagement. He knows it already, you
stupid boy, he knows it all! I've been writing to him, for you forgot
to take my writing things away from me. That's why he hasn't been
here for years, he knows everything a hundred times better than
you do yourself, in his left hand he crumples your letters unopened
while in his right hand he holds up my letters to read through!"

In his enthusiasm he waved his arm over his head. "He knows
everything a thousand times better!" he cried.

"Ten thousand times!" said Georg, to make fun of his father,
but in his very mouth the words turned into deadly earnest.

"For years I've been waiting for you to come with some such
question! Do you think I concern myself with anything else?
Do you think I read my newspapers? Look!" and he threw Georg
a newspaper sheet which he had somehow taken to bed with him.
An old newspaper, with a name entirely unknown to Georg.

"How long a time you've taken to grow up! Your mother had to die, she couldn't see the happy day, your friend is going to pieces in Russia, even three years ago he was yellow enough to be thrown away, and as for me, you see what condition I'm in. You have eyes in your head for that!"

"So you've been lying in wait for me!" cried Georg.

His father said pityingly, in an offhand manner: "I suppose you wanted to say that sooner. But now it doesn't matter." And in a louder voice: "So now you know what else there was in the world besides yourself, till now you've known only about yourself! An innocent child, yes, that you were, truly, but still more truly have you been a devilish human being!—And therefore take note: I sentence you now to death by drowning!"

Georg felt himself urged from the room. The crash with which his father fell on the bed behind him was still in his ears as he fled. On the staircase, which he rushed down as if its steps were an inclined plane, he ran into his charwoman on her way up to do the morning cleaning of the room. "Jesus!" she cried, and covered her face with her apron, but he was already gone. Out of the front door he rushed, across the roadway, driven towards the water. Already he was grasping at the railings as a starving man clutches food. He swung himself over, like the distinguished gymnast he had once been in his youth, to his parents' pride. With weakening grip he was still holding on when he spied between the railings a motor-bus coming which would easily cover the noise of his fall, called in a low voice: "Dear parents, I have always loved you, all the same," and let himself drop.

At this moment an unending stream of traffic was just going over the bridge.

Selected Readings

BROD, MAX. *Franz Kafka, A Biography.* Trans. G. Humphreys Roberts. 2nd ed. New York: Schocken Books, 1960.

FLORES, ANGEL (ed.). *The Kafka Problem.* New York: Octagon Books, Inc., 1963.

———— and HOMER SWANDER (eds.). *Franz Kafka Today.* Madison, Wisc.: University of Wisconsin Press, 1958.

FOULKES, A. P. "Dream Pictures in Kafka's Writings." *Germanic Review,* XL (1965), 17–30.

FRAIBERG, SELMA. "Kafka and the Dream." *Partisan Review,* XXIII (1956), 47–69.

GRAY, RONALD D. (ed.). *Kafka, A Collection of Critical Essays.* Englewood Cliffs, N.J.: Prentice-Hall, Inc., 1962.

MAGNY, CLAUDE-EDMONDE. "The Objective Depiction of Absurdity." *Quarterly Review of Literature,* II (1945), 211–27.

NEIDER, CHARLES. *The Frozen Sea, a Study of Franz Kafka.* New York: Russell and Russell, Inc., 1948.

POLITZER, HEINRICH. *Franz Kafka: Parable and Paradox.* rev. ed. Ithaca, N.Y.: Cornell University Press, 1966.

SPAHR, BLAKE LEE. "Franz Kafka: The Bridge and the Abyss." *Modern Fiction Studies,* VIII (1962), 3–15.

STEINBERG, ERWIN R. "The Judgment in Kafka's 'The Judgment.'" *Modern Fiction Studies,* VIII (1962), 23–30.

VIVAS, ELISEO. "Kafka's Distorted Mask." *Creation and Discovery.* rev. ed. Gateway Editions; Chicago: Henry Regnery Co., 1965.

WARREN, AUSTIN. "Kosmos Kafka." *Southern Review,* VII (1941), 350–65.

JEAN-PAUL SARTRE

(1905-   )

Jean-Paul Sartre was born in Paris on June 21, 1905. His education was a continuous process until 1929 when he received his degree in philosophy. Two years of military service followed his graduation. He taught in Germany and France from 1933 to 1939, at which time he was drafted into the French army.

Sartre was a prisoner of war in 1940–41; upon his release, he returned to teaching. By 1944, however, he had given up teaching to devote himself to writing—novels, plays, literary critiques, short stories, philosophical tracts, and political theories. Sartre's earliest works dealt with his philosophical ideas: *Psychology and Imagination,* 1936; *The Transcendence of the Ego,* 1936–37. His important *Being and Nothingness* appeared in France in 1943. These same philosophical principles began to appear in dramatic form in his novel *Nausea,* written in 1938, and in his short story collection, *The Wall and Other Stories,* compiled in France in 1939. (This collection, published in the United States in 1948, bears the title *Intimacy.*)

By the early '40's, following the appearance of these works, Sartre's philosophical approach was coming to be labeled "existential" (a term first appearing in Kierkegaard), and Sartre himself was called an existentialist. Sartre had clearly philosophized and dramatized his view of the human condition: that man's existence precedes his essence. Since man can be sure only of his own consciousness, man can (and must) define himself; he is responsible for defining himself through free choice, commitment, involvement, engagement. Freed from essences and intelligent Being, man becomes the *Dasein* of being; and being is the existence of man. This sense of engagement reveals itself repeatedly in Sartre's works, especially in his plays relating to the

German occupation of France—for example, *The Flies* (1943) and *No Exit* (1944)—and in the novels of his trilogy *Roads to Freedom: The Age of Reason* (1947), *The Reprieve* (1947), and *Troubled Sleep* (1951).

The Room

Mme. Darbedat held a *rahat-loukoum* between her fingers. She brought it carefully to her lips and held her breath, afraid that the fine dust of sugar that powdered it would blow away. "Just right," she told herself. She bit quickly into its glassy flesh and a scent of stagnation filled her mouth. "Odd how illness sharpens the sensations." She began to think of mosques, of obsequious Orientals (she had been to Algeria for her honeymoon) and her pale lips started in a smile: the *rahat-loukoum* was obsequious too.

Several times she had to pass the palm of her hand over the pages of her book, for in spite of the precaution she had taken they were covered with a thin coat of white powder. Her hand made the little grains of sugar slide and roll, grating on the smooth paper: "That makes me think of Arcachon, when I used to read on the beach." She had spent the summer of 1907 at the seashore. Then she wore a big straw hat with a green ribbon; she sat close to the jetty, with a novel by Gyp or Colette Yver. The wind made swirls of sand rain down upon her knees, and from time to time she had to shake the book, holding it by the corners. It was the same sensation: only the grains of sand were dry while the small bits of sugar stuck a little to the ends of her fingers. Again she saw a band of pearl grey sky above a black sea. "Eve wasn't born yet." She felt herself all weighted down with memories and precious as a coffer of sandalwood. The name of the book she used to read suddenly came back to mind: it was called *Petite Madame*, not at

Jean-Paul Sartre, *Intimacy*. Translated by Lloyd Alexander. Copyright 1948 by New Directions. Reprinted by permission of New Directions Publishing Corporation.

all boring. But ever since an unknown illness had confined her to her room she preferred memories and historical works.

She hoped that suffering, heavy readings, a vigilant attention to her memories and the most exquisite sensations would ripen her as a lovely hothouse fruit.

She thought, with some annoyance, that her husband would soon be knocking at her door. On other days of the week he came only in the evening, kissed her brow in silence and read *Le Temps,* sitting in the armchair across from her. But Thursday was M. Darbedat's *day:* he spent an hour with his daughter, generally from three to four. Before going he stopped in to see his wife and both discussed their son-in-law with bitterness. These Thursday conversations, predictable to their slightest detail, exhausted Mme. Darbedat. M. Darbedat filled the quiet room with his presence. He never sat, but walked in circles about the room. Each of his outbursts wounded Mme. Darbedat like a glass splintering. This particular Thursday was worse than usual: at the thought that it would soon be necessary to repeat Eve's confessions to her husband, and to see his great terrifying body convulse with fury, Mme. Darbedat broke out in a sweat. She picked up a *loukoum* from the saucer, studied it for a while with hesitation, then sadly set it down: she did not like her husband to see her eating *loukoums.*

She heard a knock and started up. "Come in," she said weakly.

M. Darbedat entered on tiptoe. "I'm going to see Eve," he said, as he did every Thursday. Mme. Darbedat smiled at him. "Give her a kiss for me."

M. Darbedat did not answer and his forehead wrinkled worriedly: every Thursday at the same time, a muffled irritation mingled with the load of his digestion. "I'll stop in and see Franchot after leaving her, I wish he'd talk to her seriously and try to convince her."

He made frequent visits to Dr. Franchot. But in vain. Mme. Darbedat raised her eyebrows. Before, when she was well, she shrugged her shoulders. But since sickness had weighted down her body, she replaced the gestures which would have tired her by plays of emotion in the face: she said *yes* with her eyes, *no* with the corners of her mouth: she raised her eyebrows instead of her shoulders.

"There should be some way to take him away from her by force."

"I told you already it was impossible. And besides, the law is very poorly drawn up. Only the other day Franchot was telling me that they have a tremendous amount of trouble with the families: people who can't make up their mind, who want to keep the patient at home; the doctors' hands are tied. They can give their advice, period. That's all. He would," he went on, "have to make a public scandal or else she would have to ask to have him put away herself."

"And that," said Mme. Darbedat, "isn't going to happen tomorrow."

"No." He turned to the mirror and began to comb his fingers through his beard. Mme. Darbedat looked at the powerful red neck of her husband without affection.

"If she keeps on," said M. Darbedat, "she'll be crazier than he is. It's terribly unhealthy. She doesn't leave his side, she only goes out to see you. She has no visitors. The air in their room is simply unbreathable. She never opens the window because Pierre doesn't want it open. As if you should ask a sick man. I believe they burn incense, some rubbish in a little pan, you'd think it was a church. Really, sometimes I wonder . . . she's got a funny look in her eyes, you know."

"I haven't noticed," Mme. Darbedat said. "I find her quite normal. She looks sad, obviously."

"She has a face like an unburied corpse. Does she sleep? Does she eat? But we aren't supposed to ask her about those things. But I should think that with a fellow like Pierre next to her, she wouldn't sleep a wink all night." He shrugged his shoulders. "What I find amazing is that we, her parents, don't have the right to protect her against herself. Understand that Pierre would be much better cared for by Franchot. There's a big park. And besides, I think," he added, smiling a little, "he'd get along much better with people of his own type. People like that are children, you have to leave them alone with each other; they form a sort of freemasonry. That's where he should have been put the first day and for his own good, I'd say. Of course it's in his own best interest."

After a moment, he added, "I tell you I don't like to know she's alone with Pierre, especially at night. Suppose something happened. Pierre has a very sly way about him."

"I don't know," Mme. Darbedat said, "if there's any reason to worry. He always looked like that. He always seemed to be making fun of the world. Poor boy," she sighed, "to have had his pride and then come to that. He thought he was cleverer than all of us. He had a way of saying 'You're right' simply to end the argument . . . It's a blessing for him that he can't see the state he's in."

She recalled with displeasure the long, ironic face, always turned a little to the side. During the first days of Eve's marriage, Mme. Darbedat asked nothing more than a little intimacy with her son-in-law. But he had discouraged her: he almost never spoke, he always agreed quickly and absent-mindedly.

M. Darbedat pursued his idea. "Franchot let me visit his place," he said. "It was magnificent. The patients have private rooms with leather arm-chairs, if you please, and day-beds. You know, they have a tennis court and they're going to build a swimming pool."

He was planted before the window, looking out, rocking a little on his bent legs. Suddenly he turned lithely on his heel, shoulders lowered, hands in his pockets. Mme. Darbedat felt she was going to start perspiring: it was the same thing every time: now he was pacing back and forth like a bear in a cage and his shoes squeaked at every step.

"Please, please won't you sit down. You're tiring me." Hesitating, she added, "I have something important to tell you."

M. Darbedat sat in the armchair and put his hands on his knees; a slight chill ran up Mme. Darbedat's spine: the time had come, she had to speak.

"You know," she said with an embarrassed cough, "I saw Eve on Tuesday."

"Yes."

"We talked about a lot of things, she was very nice, she hasn't been so confiding for a long time. Then I questioned her a little, I got her to talk about Pierre. Well, I found out," she added, again embarrassed, "that she is *very* attached to him."

"I know that too damned well," said M. Darbedat.

He irritated Mme. Darbedat a little: she always had to explain things in such detail. Mme. Darbedat dreamed of living in the company of fine and sensitive people who would understand her slightest word.

"But I mean," she went on, "that she is attached to him *differently* than we imagined."

M. Darbedat rolled furious, anxious eyes, as he always did when he never completely grasped the sense of an allusion or something new.

"What does that all mean?"

"Charles," said Mme. Darbedat, "don't tire me. You should understand a mother has difficulty in telling certain things."

"I don't understand a damned word of anything you say," M. Darbedat said with irritation. "You can't mean . . ."

"Yes," she said.

"They're still . . . now, still . . . ?"

"Yes! Yes! Yes!" she said, in three annoyed and dry little jolts.

M. Darbedat spread his arms, lowered his head and was silent.

"Charles," his wife said, worriedly, "I shouldn't have told you. But I couldn't keep it to myself."

"Our child," he said slowly. "With this madman! He doesn't even recognize her any more. He calls her Agatha. She must have lost all sense of her own dignity."

He raised his head and looked at his wife severely. "You're sure you aren't mistaken?"

"No possible doubt. Like you," she added quickly, "I couldn't believe her and I still can't. The mere idea of being touched by that wretch . . . So . . . " she sighed, "I suppose that's how he holds on to her."

"Do you remember what I told you," M. Darbedat said, "when he came to ask for her hand? I told you I thought he pleased Eve *too much*. You wouldn't believe me." He struck the table suddenly, blushing violently. "It's perversity! He takes her in his arms, kisses her and calls her Agatha, selling her on a lot of nonsense about flying statues and God knows what else! Without a word from her! But what in heaven's name's between those two? Let her be sorry for him, let her put him in a sanitorium and see him every day,—fine. But I never thought . . . I considered her a widow. Listen, Jeannette," he said gravely, "I'm going to speak frankly to you; if she had any sense, I'd rather see her take a lover!"

"Be quiet, Charles!" Mme. Darbedat cried.

M. Darbedat wearily took his hat and the cane he had left on the stool. "After what you've just told me," he concluded, "I don't have much hope left. In any case, I'll have a talk with her because it's my duty."

Mme. Darbedat wished he would go quickly.

"You know," she said to encourage him, "I think Eve is more headstrong than . . . than anything. She knows he's incurable but she's obstinate, she doesn't want to be in the wrong."

M. Darbedat stroked his beard absently.

"Headstrong? Maybe so. If you're right, she'll finally get tired of it. He's not always pleasant and he doesn't have much to say. When I say hello to him he gives me a flabby handshake and doesn't say a word. As soon as they're alone, I think they go back to his obsessions: she tells me sometimes he screams as though his throat were being cut because of his hallucinations. He sees statues. They frighten him because they buzz. He says they fly around and make fishy eyes at him."

He put on his gloves and continued, "She'll get tired of it, I'm not saying she won't. But suppose she goes crazy before that? I wish she'd go out a little, see the world: she'd meet some nice young man—well, someone like Schroeder, an engineer with Simplon, somebody with a future, she could see him a little here and there and she'd get used to the idea of making a new life for herself."

Mme. Darbedat did not answer, afraid of starting the conversation up again. Her husband bent over her.

"So," he said, "I've got to be on my way."

"Goodbye, Papa," Mme. Darbedat said, lifting her forehead up to him. "Kiss her for me and tell her for me she's a poor dear."

Once her husband had gone, Mme. Darbedat let herself drift to the bottom of her armchair and closed her eyes, exhausted. "What vitality," she thought reproachfully. As soon as she got a little strength back, she quietly stretched out her pale hand and took a *loukoum* from the saucer, groping for it without opening her eyes.

Eve lived with her husband on the sixth floor of an old building on the Rue du Bac. M. Darbedat slowly climbed the 112 steps of the stairway. He was not even out of breath when he pushed the bell. He remembered with satisfaction the words of Mlle. Dormoy: "Charles, for your age, you're simply marvelous." Never did he feel himself stronger and healthier than on Thursday, especially after these invigorating climbs.

Eve opened the door: that's right, she doesn't have a maid. No girls *can* stay with her. I can put myself in their place. He kissed her. "Hello, poor darling."

Eve greeted him with a certain coldness.

"You look a little pale," M. Darbedat said, touching her cheek. "You don't get enough exercise."

There was a moment of silence.

"Is Mamma well?" Eve asked.

"Not good, not too bad. You saw her Tuesday? Well, she's just the same. Your Aunt Louise came to see her yesterday, that pleased her. She likes to have visitors, but they can't stay too long. Aunt Louise came to Paris for that mortgage business. I think I told you about it, a very odd sort of affair. She stopped in at the office to ask my advice. I told her there was only one thing to do: sell. She found a taker, by the way: Bretonnel. You remember Bretonnel. He's retired from business now."

He stopped suddenly: Eve was hardly listening. He thought sadly that nothing interested her any more. It's like the books. Before you had to tear them away from her. Now she doesn't even read any more.

"How is Pierre?"

"Well," Eve said. "Do you want to see him?"

"Of course," M. Darbedat said gaily, "I'd like to pay him a little call."

He was full of compassion for this poor young man, but he could not see him without repugnance. *I detest unhealthy people.* Obviously, it was not Pierre's fault: his heredity was terribly loaded down. M. Darbedat sighed: *All the precautions are taken in vain, you find out those things too late.* No, Pierre was not responsible. But still he had always carried that fault in him; it formed the base of his character; it wasn't like cancer or tuberculosis, something you could always put aside when you wanted to judge a man as he is. His nervous grace, the subtlety which pleased Eve so much when he was courting her were the flowers of madness. He was already mad when he married her only you couldn't tell.

It makes you wonder, thought M. Darbedat, *where responsibility begins, or rather, where it ends.* In any case, he was always analysing himself too much, always turned in on himself. But was it the cause or effect of his sickness? He followed his daughter through a long, dim corridor.

"This apartment is too big for you," he said. "You ought to move out."

"You say that every time, Papa," Eve answered, "but I've already told you Pierre doesn't want to leave his room."

Eve was amazing. Enough to make you wonder if she realized her husband's state. He was insane enough to be in a strait-jacket and she respected his decisions and advice as if he still had good sense.

"What I'm saying is for your own good." M. Darbedat went on, somewhat annoyed, "It seems to me that if I were a woman I'd be afraid of these badly lighted old rooms. I'd like to see you in a bright apartment, the kind they're putting up near Auteuil, three airy little rooms. They lowered the rents because they couldn't find any tenants; this would be just the time."

Eve quietly turned the doorknob and they entered the room. M. Darbedat's throat tightened at the heavy odor of incense. The curtains were drawn. In the shadows he made out a thin neck above the back of an armchair: Pierre's back was turned. He was eating.

"Hello, Pierre," M. Darbedat said, raising his voice. "How are we today?" He drew near him: the sick man was seated in front of a small table; he looked sly.

"I see we had soft boiled eggs," M. Darbedat said, raising his voice higher. "That's good!"

"I'm not deaf," Pierre said quietly.

Irritated, M. Darbedat turned his eyes toward Eve as his witness. But Eve gave him a hard glance and was silent. M. Darbedat realized he had hurt her. Too bad for her. It was impossible to find just the right tone for this boy. He had less sense than a child of four and Eve wanted him treated like a man. M. Darbedat could not keep himself from waiting with impatience for the moment when all this ridiculous business would be finished. Sick people always annoyed him a little—especially madmen because they were wrong. Poor Pierre, for example, was wrong all along the line, he couldn't speak a reasonable word and yet it would be useless to expect the least humility from him, or even temporary recognition of his errors.

Eve cleared away the eggshells and the cup. She put a knife and fork in front of Pierre.

"What's he going to eat now," M. Darbedat said jovially.

"A steak."

Pierre had taken the fork and held it in the ends of his long, pale fingers. He inspected it minutely and then gave a slight laugh.

"I can't use it this time," he murmured, setting it down, "I was warned."

Eve came in and looked at the fork with passionate interest.

"Agatha," Pierre said, "give me another one."

Eve obeyed and Pierre began to eat. She had taken the suspect fork and held it tightly in her hands, her eyes never leaving it; she seemed to make a violent effort. How suspicious all their gestures and relationships are! thought M. Darbedat.

He was uneasy.

"Be careful, Pierre, take it by the middle because of the prongs."

Eve sighed and laid the fork on the serving table. M. Darbedat felt his gall rising. He did not think it well to give in to all this poor man's whims—even from Pierre's viewpoint it was pernicious. Franchot had said: "One must never enter the delirium of a madman." Instead of giving him another fork, it would have been better to have reasoned quietly and made him understand that the first was like all the others.

He went to the serving table, took the fork ostentatiously and tested the prongs with a light finger. Then he turned to Pierre. But the latter was cutting his meat peacefully: he gave his father-in-law a gentle, inexpressive glance.

"I'd like to have a little talk with you," M. Darbedat said to Eve.

She followed him docilely into the salon. Sitting on the couch, M. Darbedat realized he had kept the fork in his hand. He threw it on the table.

"It's much better here," he said.

"I never come here."

"All right to smoke?"

"Of course, Papa," Eve said hurriedly. "Do you want a cigar?"

M. Darbedat preferred to roll a cigarette. He thought eagerly of the discussion he was about to begin. Speaking to Pierre he felt as embarrassed about his reason as a giant about his strength when playing with a child. All his qualities of clarity, sharpness, precision, turned against him; *I must confess it's somewhat the same with my poor Jeannette.* Certainly Mme. Darbedat was not insane, but this illness had . . . stultified her. Eve, on the other hand, took after her father . . . a straight, logical nature; discussion with her was a pleasure; *that's why I don't want them to ruin her.* M. Darbedat raised his eyes. Once again he wanted to see the fine intelligent features of his daughter. He was disappointed with this face; once so reasonable and transparent, there was now something clouded and opaque in it. Eve had always been beautiful. M. Darbedat noticed she was made up with great care, almost with pomp. She had blued her eyelids and put mascara on her long lashes. This violent and perfect make-up made a painful impression on her father.

"You're green beneath your rouge," he told her. "I'm afraid you're getting sick. And the way you make yourself up now! You used to be so discreet."

Eve did not answer and for an embarrassed moment M. Darbedat considered this brilliant, worn-out face beneath the heavy mass of black hair. He thought she looked like a tragedian. *I even know who she looks like. That woman . . . that Roumanian who played* Phèdre *in French at the Mur d'Orange.* He regretted having made so disagreeable a remark: *It escapes me! Better not worry her with little things.*

"Excuse me," he said smiling, "you know I'm an old purist. I don't like all these creams and paints women stick on their face today. But I'm in the wrong. You must live in your time."

Eve smiled amiably at him. M. Darbedat lit a cigarette and drew several puffs.

"My child," he began, "I wanted to talk with you: the two of us are going to talk the way we used to. Come, sit down and listen to me nicely; you must have confidence in your old Papa."

"I'd rather stand," Eve said. "What did you want to tell me?"

"I am going to ask you a single question," M. Darbedat said a little more dryly. "Where will all this lead you?"

"All this?" Eve asked astonished.

"Yes . . . all this whole life you've made for yourself. Listen," he went on, "don't think I don't understand you (he had a sudden illumination) but what you want to do is beyond human strength. You want to live solely by imagination, isn't that it? You don't want to admit he's sick. You don't want to see the Pierre of today, do you? You have eyes only for the Pierre of before. My dear, my darling little girl, it's an impossible bet to win," M. Darbedat continued. "Now I'm going to tell you a story which perhaps you don't know. When we were at Sables-d'Olonne—you were three years old—your mother made the acquaintance of a charming young woman with a superb little boy. You played on the beach with this little boy, you were thick as thieves, you were engaged to marry him. A while later, in Paris, your mother wanted to see this young woman again; she was told she had had a terrible accident. That fine little boy's head was cut off by a car. They told your mother, 'Go and see her, but above all don't talk to her about the death of her child, she *will not* believe he is dead.' Your mother went, she found a half-mad creature: she lived as though her boy was still alive; she spoke to him, she set his place at the table. She lived in such a state of nervous tension that after six months they had to take her away by force to a sanitorium where she was obliged to stay three years. No, my child," M. Darbedat said, shaking his head, "these things are impossible. It would have been better if she had recognized the truth courageously. She would have suffered once, then time would have erased with its sponge. There is nothing like looking things in the face, believe me."

"You're wrong," Eve said with effort. "I know very well that Pierre is . . . "

The word did not escape. She held herself very straight and put her hands on the back of the armchair: there was something dry and ugly in the lower part of her face.

"So . . . ?" asked M. Darbedat, astonished.

"So . . . ?"

"You . . . ?"

"I love him as he is," said Eve rapidly and with an irritated look.

"Not true," M. Darbedat said forcefully. "It isn't true: you don't love him, you can't love him. You can only feel that way about a healthy, normal person. You pity Pierre, I don't doubt it, and surely you have the memory of three years of happiness he gave you. But don't tell me you love him. I won't believe you."

Eve remained wordless, staring at the carpet absently.

"You could at least answer me," M. Darbedat said coldly. "Don't think this conversation has been any less painful for me than it has for you."

"More than you think."

"Well then, if you love him," he cried, exasperated, "it is a great misfortune for you, for me and for your poor mother because I'm going to tell you something I would rather have hidden from you: before three years Pierre will be sunk in complete dementia, he'll be like a beast."

He watched his daughter with hard eyes: he was angry at her for having compelled him, by stubbornness, to make this painful revelation.

Eve was motionless; she did not so much as raise her eyes.

"I knew."

"Who told you?" he asked stupefied.

"Franchot. I knew six months ago."

"And I told him to be careful with you," said M. Darbedat with bitterness. "Maybe it's better. But under those circumstances you must understand that it would be unpardonable to keep Pierre with you. The struggle you have undertaken is doomed to failure, his illness won't spare him. If there were something to be done, if we could save him by care, I'd say yes. But look: you're pretty, intelligent, gay, you're destroying yourself willingly and without profit. I know you've been admirable, but now it's over . . . done, you've done your duty and more; now it would be immoral to continue. We also have duties to ourselves, child. And then you aren't thinking about us. You must," he repeated, hammering the words, "send Pierre to Franchot's clinic. Leave this apartment where you've had nothing but sorrow and come home to us. If you want to be useful and ease the sufferings of someone else, you have your mother. The poor woman is cared for by nurses, she needs someone closer to her, and *she*," he added, "can appreciate what you do for her and be grateful."

There was a long silence. M. Darbedat heard Pierre singing in the next room. It was hardly a song, rather a sort of sharp, hasty recitative. M. Darbedat raised his eyes to his daughter.

"It's no then?"

"Pierre will stay with me," she said quietly. "I get along well with him."

"By living like an animal all day long?"

Eve smiled and shot a glance at her father, strange, mocking and almost gay. *It's true,* M. Darbedat thought furiously, *that's not all they do; they sleep together.*

"You are completely mad," he said, rising.

Eve smiled sadly and murmured, as if to herself, "Not enough so."

"Not enough? I can only tell you one thing, my child. You frighten me."

He kissed her hastily and left. Going down the stairs he thought: *we should send out two strong-arm men who'd take the poor imbecile away and stick him under a shower without asking his advice on the matter.*

It was a fine autumn day, calm and without mystery; the sunlight gilded the faces of the passers-by. M. Darbedat was struck with the simplicity of the faces; some weather-beaten, others smooth, but they reflected all the happiness and care with which he was so familiar.

I know exactly what I resent in Eve, he told himself, entering the Boulevard St. Germain. *I resent her living outside the limits of human nature. Pierre is no longer a human being: in all the care and all the love she gives him she deprives human beings of a little. We don't have the right to refuse ourselves to the world; no matter what, we live in society.*

He watched the faces of the passers-by with sympathy; he loved their clear, serious looks. In these sunlit streets, in the midst of mankind, one felt secure, as in the midst of a large family.

A woman stopped in front of an open-air display counter. She was holding a little girl by the hand.

"What's that?" the little girl asked, pointing to a radio set.

"Mustn't touch," her mother said. "It's a radio; it plays music."

They stood for a moment without speaking, in ecstasy. Touched, M. Darbedat bent down to the little girl and smiled.

II

"He's gone." The door closed with a dry snap. Eve was alone in the salon. *I wish he'd die.*

She twisted her hands around the back of the armchair: she had just remembered her father's eyes. M. Darbedat was bent over Pierre with a competent air; he had said "That's good!" the way someone says when they speak to invalids. He had looked and Pierre's face had been painted in the depths of his sharp, bulging eyes. *I hate him when he looks at him because I think he sees him*.

Eve's hands slid along the armchair and she turned to the window. She was dazzled. The room was filled with sunlight, it was everywhere, in pale splotches on the rug, in the air like a blinding dust. Eve was not accustomed to this diligent, indiscreet light which darted from everywhere, scouring all the corners, rubbing the furniture like a busy housewife and making it glisten. However, she went to the window and raised the muslin curtain which hung against the pane. Just at that moment M. Darbedat left the building; Eve suddenly caught sight of his broad shoulders. He raised his head and looked at the sky, blinking, then with the stride of a young man he walked away. *He's straining himself,* thought Eve, *soon he'll have a stitch in the side.* She hardly hated him any longer: there was so little in that head; only the tiny worry of appearing young. Yet rage took her again when she saw him turn the corner of the Boulevard St. Germain and disappear. *He's thinking about Pierre.* A little of their life had escaped from the closed room and was being dragged through the streets, in the sun, among the people. *Can they never forget about us?*

The Rue du Bac was almost deserted. An old lady crossed the street with mincing steps; three girls passed, laughing. Then men, strong, serious men carrying briefcases and talking among themselves. *Normal people,* thought Eve, astonished at finding such a powerful hatred in herself. A handsome, fleshy woman ran heavily toward an elegant gentleman. He took her in his arms and kissed her on the mouth. Eve gave a hard laugh and let the curtain fall.

Pierre sang no more but the woman on the fourth floor was playing the piano; she played a Chopin Etude. Eve felt calmer; she took a step toward Pierre's room but stopped almost immediately and leaned against the wall in anguish; each time she left the room, she was panic-stricken at the thought of going back. Yet she knew she could live nowhere else: she loved the room. She looked around it with cold curiosity as if to gain a little time: this shadowless, odorless room where she waited for her courage to return. *You'd think it was a dentist's waiting room.* Armchairs of pink silk, the divan, the tabourets were somber and discreet, a little fatherly; man's best friends. Eve imagined those grave gentlemen dressed in light suits, all like the ones she saw at the window, entering the room, continuing a conversation already begun. They did not even take time to reconnoiter, but advanced with firm step to the middle of the room; one of them, letting his hand drag behind him like a wake in passing knocked over cushions, objects on the table, and was never disturbed by their contact. And when a piece of furniture was in their way, these poised men, far from making a detour to avoid it, quietly changed its place. Finally they sat down, still plunged in their conversation, without even glancing behind them. *A living-room for normal people,* thought Eve. She stared at the knob of the closed door and anguish clutched her throat: *I must go back. I never leave him alone so long.* She would have to open the door, then stand for a moment on the threshold, trying to accustom her eyes to the shadow and the room would push her back with all its strength. Eve would have to triumph over this resistance and enter all the way into the heart of the room. Suddenly she wanted violently to see Pierre; she would have liked to make fun of M. Darbedat with him. But Pierre had no need of her; Eve could not foresee the welcome he had in store for her. Suddenly she thought with a sort of pride that she had no place anywhere. *Normal people think I belong with them. But I couldn't stay an hour among them. I need to live out there, on the other side of the wall. But they don't want me out there.*

A profound change was taking place around her. The light had grown old and greying: it was heavy, like the water in a vase of flowers that hasn't been changed since the day before. In this aged light Eve found a melancholy she had long forgotten: the melancholy of an autumn afternoon that was ending. She looked around her, hesitant, almost timid: all that was so far away: there was neither day nor night nor season nor melancholy in the room. She vaguely recalled autumns long past, autumns of her childhood, then suddenly she stiffened: she was afraid of memories.

She heard Pierre's voice. "Agatha! Where are you?"

"Coming!" she cried.

She opened the door and entered the room.

The heavy odor of incense filled her mouth and nostrils as she opened her eyes and stretched out her hands—for a long time the perfume and the gloom had meant nothing more to her than a single element, acrid and heavy, as simple, as familiar as water, air or fire—and she prudently advanced toward a pale stain which seemed to float in the fog. It was Pierre's face: Pierre's clothing (he dressed in black ever since he had been sick) melted in obscurity. Pierre had thrown back his head and closed his eyes. He was handsome. Eve looked at his long, curved lashes, then sat close to him on the low chair. *He seems to be suffering*, she thought. Little by little her eyes grew used to the darkness. The bureau emerged first, then the bed, then Pierre's personal things: scissors, the pot of glue, books, the herbarium which shed its leaves onto the rug near the armchair.

"Agatha?"

Pierre had opened his eyes. He was watching her, smiling. "You know, that fork?" he said. "I did it to frighten that fellow. There was *almost* nothing the matter with it."

Eve's apprehensions faded and she gave a light laugh. "You succeeded," she said, "You drove him completely out of his mind."

Pierre smiled. "Did you see? He played with it a long time, he held it right in his hands. The trouble is," he said, "they don't know how to take hold of things; they grab them."

"That's right," Eve said.

Pierre tapped the palm of his left hand lightly with the index of his right.

"They take with that. They reach out their fingers and when they catch hold of something they crack down on it to knock it out."

He spoke rapidly and hardly moving his lips; he looked puzzled.

"I wonder what they want," he said at last, "that fellow has already been here. Why did they send him to me? If they want to know what I'm doing all they have to do is read it on the screen, they don't even need to leave the house. They make mistakes. They have the power but they make mistakes. I never make any, that's my trump card. *Hoffka!*" he said. He shook his long hands before his forehead. "The bitch Hoffka! Paffka! Suffka! Do you want any more?"

"Is it the bell?" asked Eve.

"Yes. It's gone." He went on severely. "This fellow, he's just a subordinate. You know him, you went into the living-room with him."

Eve did not answer.

"What did he want?" asked Pierre. "He must have told you."

She hesitated an instant, then answered brutally. "He wanted you locked up."

When the truth was told quietly to Pierre he distrusted it. He had to be dealt with violently in order to daze and paralyze his suspicions. Eve preferred to brutalize him rather than lie: when she lied and he acted as if he believed it she could not avoid a very slight feeling of superiority which made her horrified at herself.

"Lock me up!" Pierre repeated ironically. "They're crazy. What can walls do to me. Maybe they think that's going to stop me. I sometimes wonder if there aren't two groups. The real one, the negro—and then a bunch of fools trying to stick their noses in and making mistake after mistake."

He made his hand jump up from the arm of the chair and looked at it happily.

"I can get through walls. What did you tell them?" he asked, turning to Eve with curiosity.

"Not to lock you up."

He shrugged. "You shouldn't have said that. You made a mistake too . . . unless you did it on purpose. You've got to call their bluff."

He was silent. Eve lowered her head sadly: "*They grab things!*" *How scornfully he said that—and he was right. Do I grab things too? It doesn't do any good to watch myself, I think most of my movements annoy him. But he doesn't say anything.* Suddenly she felt as miserable as when she was fourteen and Mme. Darbedat told her "You don't know what to do with your hands." She didn't dare make a move and just at that time she had an irresistible desire to change her position. Quietly she put her feet under the chair, barely touching the rug. She watched the lamp on the table—the lamp whose base Pierre had painted black—and the chess set. Pierre had left only the black pawns on the board. Sometimes he would get up, go to the table and take the pawns in his hands one by one. He spoke to them, called them Robots and they seemed to stir with a mute life under his fingers. When he set them down, Eve went and touched them in her turn (she always felt somewhat ridiculous about it). They had become little bits of dead wood again but something vague and incomprehensible stayed in them, something like understanding. *These are his things*, she thought. *There is nothing of mine in the room.* She had had a few pieces of furniture before; the mirror and the little inlaid dresser handed down from her grandmother and which Pierre jokingly called "*your* dresser." Pierre had carried them away with him; things showed their true face to Pierre alone. Eve could watch them for hours: they were unflaggingly stubborn and determined to deceive her, offering her nothing but their appearance —as they did to Dr. Franchot and M. Darbedat. *Yet*, she told herself with anguish, *I don't see them quite like my father. It isn't possible for me to see them exactly like him.*

She moved her knees a little: her legs felt as though they were crawling with ants. Her body was stiff and taut and hurt her; she felt it too alive, too demanding. *I would like to be invisible and stay here seeing him without his seeing me. He doesn't need me; I am useless in this room.* She turned her head slightly and looked at the wall above Pierre. Threats were written on the wall. Eve knew it but she could not read them. She often watched the big red roses on the wallpaper until they began to dance before her eyes. The roses flamed in shadow. Most of the time the threat was written near the ceiling, a little to the left of the bed; but sometimes it moved. *I must get up. I can't . . . I can't sit down any longer.* There were also white discs on the wall that looked like slices of onion. The discs spun and Eve's hands began to tremble: *Sometimes I think I'm going mad. But no,* she thought, *I can't go mad. I get nervous, that's all.*

Suddenly she felt Pierre's hand on her's.

"Agatha," Pierre said tenderly.

He smiled at her but he held her hand by the ends of his fingers with a sort of revulsion, as though he had picked up a crab by the back and wanted to avoid its claws.

"Agatha," he said, "I would so much like to have confidence in you."

She closed her eyes and her breast heaved. *I musn't answer anything, if I do he'll get angry, he won't say anything more.*

Pierre had dropped her hand. "I like you, Agatha," he said, "but I can't understand you. Why do you stay in the room all the time?"

Eve did not answer.

"Tell me why."

"You know I love you," she said dryly.

"I don't believe you," Pierre said. "Why should you love me? I must frighten you: I'm haunted." He smiled but suddenly became serious. "There is a wall between you and me. I see you, I speak to you, but you're on the other side. What keeps us from loving? I think it was easier before. In Hamburg."

"Yes," Eve said sadly. Always Hamburg. He never spoke of their real past. Neither Eve nor he had ever been to Hamburg.

"We used to walk along the canal. There was a barge, remember? The barge was black; there was a dog on the deck."

He made it up as he went along; it sounded false.

"I held your hand. You had another skin. I believed all you told me. Be quiet!" he shouted.

He listened for a moment. "They're coming," he said mournfully.

Eve jumped up. "They're coming? I thought they wouldn't ever come again."

Pierre had been calmer for the past three days; the statues did not come. Pierre was terribly afraid of the statues even though he would never admit it. Eve was not afraid: but when they began to fly, buzzing, around the room, she was afraid of Pierre.

"Give me the ziuthre," Pierre said.

Eve got up and took the ziuthre: it was a collection of pieces of cardboard Pierre had glued together; he used it to conjure the statues. The ziuthre looked like a spider. On one of the cardboards Pierre had written "Power over ambush" and on the other, "Black." On a third he had drawn a laughing face with wrinkled eyes: it was Voltaire.

Pierre seized the ziuthre by one end and looked at it darkly.

"I can't use it any more," he said.

"Why?"

"They turned it upside down."

"Will you make another?"

He looked at her for a long while. "You'd like me to, wouldn't you," he said between his teeth.

Eve was angry at Pierre. *He's warned every time they come: how does he do it? He's never wrong.*

The ziuthre dangled pitifully from the ends of Pierre's fingers. *He always finds a good reason not to use it. Sunday when they came he pretended he'd lost it but I saw it behind the paste pot and he couldn't fail to see it. I wonder if he isn't the one who brings them.* One could never tell if he were completely sincere. Sometimes Eve had the impression that despite himself Pierre was surrounded by a swarm of unhealthy thoughts and visions. But at other times Pierre seemed to invent them. *He suffers. But how much does he believe in the statues and the negro. Anyhow, I know he doesn't see the statues, he only hears them: when they pass he turns his head away; but he still says he sees them; he describes them.* She remembered the red face of Dr. Franchot: "But my dear madame, all mentally unbalanced persons are liars; you're wasting your time if you're trying to distinguish between what they really feel and what they pretend to feel." She gave a start. *What is Franchot doing here? I don't want to start thinking like him.*

Pierre had gotten up. He went to throw the ziuthre into the wastebasket: *I want to think like you,* she murmured. He walked with tiny steps, on tiptoe, pressing his elbows against his hips so as to take up the least possible space. He came back and sat down and looked at Eve with a closed expression.

"We'll have to put up black wallpaper," he said. "There isn't enough black in this room."

He was crouched in the armchair. Sadly Eve watched his meagre body, always ready to withdraw, to shrink: the arms, legs and head looked like retractable organs. The clock struck six. The piano downstairs was silent. Eve sighed: the statues would not come right away; they had to wait for them.

"Do you want me to turn on the light?"

She would rather not wait for them in darkness.

"Do as you please," Pierre said.

Eve lit the small lamp on the bureau and a red mist filled the room. Pierre was waiting too.

He did not speak but his lips were moving, making two dark stains in the red mist. Eve loved Pierre's lips. Before, they had been moving and sensual; but they had lost their sensuality. They were wide apart, trembling a little, coming together incessantly, crushing against each other only to separate again. They were the only living things in this blank face; they looked like two frightened animals. Pierre could mutter like that for hours without a sound leaving his mouth and Eve often let herself be fascinated by this tiny, obstinate movement. *I love his mouth.* He never kissed her any more; he was horrified at contacts: at night they touched him—the hands of men, hard and dry, pinched him all over; the longnailed hands of women caressed him. Often he went to bed with his clothes on but the hands slipped under the clothes and tugged at his shirt. Once he heard laughter and puffy lips were placed on his mouth. He never kissed Eve after that night.

"Agatha," Pierre said, "don't look at my mouth."

Eve lowered her eyes.

"I am not unaware that people can learn to read lips," he went on insolently.

His hand trembled on the arm of the chair. The index finger stretched out, tapped three times on the thumb and the other fingers curled: this was a spell. *It's going to start,* she thought. She wanted to take Pierre in her arms.

Pierre began to speak at the top of his voice in a very sophisticated tone.

"Do you remember Sao Paulo?"

No answer. Perhaps it was a trap.

"I met you there," he said, satisfied. "I took you away from a Danish sailor. We almost fought but I paid for a round of drinks and he let me take you away. All that was only a joke."

He's lying, he doesn't believe a word of what he says. He knows my name isn't Agatha. I hate him when he lies. But she saw his staring eyes and her rage melted. *He isn't lying,* she thought, *he can't stand it any more. He feels them coming; he's talking to keep from hearing them.* Pierre dug both hands into the arm of the chair. His face was pale; he was smiling.

"These meetings are often strange," he said, "but I don't believe it's by chance. I'm not asking who sent you. I know you wouldn't answer. Anyhow, you've been smart enough to bluff me."

He spoke with great difficulty, in a sharp, hurried voice. There were words he could not pronounce and which left his mouth like some soft and shapeless substance.

"You dragged me away right in the middle of the party, between the rows of black automobiles, but behind the cars there was an army with red eyes which glowed as soon as I turned my back. I think you made signs to them, all the time hanging on my arm, but I didn't see a thing. I was too absorbed by the great ceremonies of the Coronation."

He looked straight ahead, his eyes wide open. He passed his hand over his forehead very rapidly, in one spare gesture, without stopping his talking. He did not want to stop talking.

"It was the Coronation of the Republic," he said stridently, "an impressive spectacle of its kind because of all the species of animals that the colonies sent for the ceremony. You were afraid to get lost among the monkeys. I said among the monkeys," he repeated arrogantly, looking around him, "I could say *among the negroes!* The abortions sliding under the tables, trying to pass unseen, are discovered and nailed to the spot by my Look. The password is silence. To be silent. Everything in place and attention for the entrance of the statues, that's the countersign. Tralala . . . " he shrieked and cupped his hands to his mouth. "Tralalala, tralalalala!"

He was silent and Eve knew that the statues had come into the room. He was stiff, pale and distrustful. Eve stiffened too and both waited in silence. Someone was walking in the corridor: it was Marie the housecleaner, she had undoubtedly just arrived. Eve thought, *I have to give her money for the gas.* And then the statues began to fly; they passed between Eve and Pierre.

Pierre went "Ah!" and sank down in the armchair, folding his legs beneath him. He turned his face away; sometimes he grinned, but drops of sweat pearled his forehead. Eve could stand the sight no longer, this pale cheek, this mouth deformed by a trembling grimace; she closed her eyes. Gold threads began to dance on the red background of her eyelids; she felt old and heavy. Not far from her Pierre was breathing violently. *They're flying, they're buzzing, they're bending over him.* She felt a slight tickling, a pain in the shoulder and right side. Instinctively her body bent to the left as if to avoid some disagreeable contact, as if to let a heavy, awkward object pass. Suddenly the floor creaked and she had an insane desire to open her eyes, to look to her right, sweeping the air with her hand.

She did nothing; she kept her eyes closed and a bitter joy made her tremble: *I am afraid too,* she thought. Her entire life had taken refuge in her right side. She leaned towards Pierre without opening her eyes. The slightest effort would be enough and she would enter this tragic world for the first time. *I'm afraid of the statues,* she thought. It was a violent, blind affirmation, an incantation. She wanted to believe in their presence with all her strength. She tried to make a new sense, a sense of touch out of the anguish which paralysed her right side. She *felt* their passage in her arm, in her side and shoulder.

The statues flew low and gently; they buzzed. Eve knew that they had an evil look and that eyelashes stuck out from the stone around their eyes; but she pictured them badly. She knew, too, that they were not quite alive but that slabs of flesh, warm scales appeared on their great bodies; the stone peeled from the ends of their fingers and their palms were eaten away. Eve could not *see* all that: she simply thought of enormous women sliding against her, solemn and grotesque, with a human look and compact heads of stone. *They are bending over Pierre*—Eve made such a violent effort that her hands began trembling—*they are bending over me.* A horrible cry suddenly chilled her. They had touched him. She opened her eyes: Pierre's head was in his hands, he was breathing heavily. Eve felt exhausted: *a game,* she thought with remorse; *it was only a game. I didn't sincerely believe it for an instant. And all that time he suffered as if it were real.*

Pierre relaxed and breathed freely. But his pupils were strangely dilated and he was perspiring.

"Did you see them" he asked.

"I can't see them."

"Better for you. They'd frighten you," he said. "I am used to them."

Eve's hands were still shaking and the blood had rushed to her head. Pierre took a cigarette from his pocket and brought it up to his mouth. But he did not light it:

"I don't care whether I see them or not," he said, "but I don't want them to touch me: I'm afraid they'll give me pimples."

He thought for an instant, then asked, "Did you hear them?"

"Yes," Eve said, "it's like an airplane engine." (Pierre had told her this the previous Sunday.)

Pierre smiled with condescension. "You exaggerate," he said. But he was still pale. He looked at Eve's hands. "Your hands are trembling. That made quite an impression on you, my poor Agatha. But don't worry. They won't come back again before tomorrow." Eve could not speak. Her teeth were chattering and she was afraid Pierre would notice it. Pierre watched her for a long time.

"You're tremendously beautiful," he said, nodding his head. "It's too bad, too bad."

He put out his hand quickly and toyed with her ear. "My lovely devil-woman. You disturb me a little, you are too beautiful: that distracts me. If it weren't a question of recapitulation . . . "

He stopped and looked at Eve with surprise.

"That's not the word . . . it came . . . it came," he said, smiling vaguely. "I had another on the tip of my tongue . . . but this one . . . came in its place. I forget what I was telling you."

He thought for a moment, then shook his head.

"Come," he said, "I want to sleep." He added in a childish voice, "You know, Agatha, I'm tired. I can't collect my thoughts any more."

He threw away his cigarette and looked at the rug anxiously. Eve slipped a pillow under his head.

"You can sleep too," he told her, "they won't be back."

. . . *Recapitulation* . . .

Pierre was asleep, a candid, half-smile on his face; his head was turned to one side: one might have thought he wanted to caress his cheek with his shoulder. Eve was not sleepy, she was thoughtful: *Recapitulation*. Pierre had suddenly looked stupid and the word had slipped out of his mouth, long and whitish. Pierre had stared ahead of him in astonishment, as if he had seen the word and didn't recognize it; his mouth was open, soft: something seemed broken in it. He stammered. *That's the first time it ever happened to him: he noticed it, too. He said he couldn't collect his thoughts any more.* Pierre gave a voluptuous little whimper and his hand made a vague movement. Eve watched him harshly: *how is he going to wake up.* It gnawed at her. As soon as Pierre was asleep she had to think about it. She was afraid he would wake up wild-eyed and stammering. *I'm stupid,* she thought, *it can't start before a year; Franchot said so.* But the anguish did not leave her; a year: a winter, a springtime, a summer, the beginning of another autumn. One day his features would grow confused, his jaw would hang loose, he would half open his weeping eyes. Eve bent over Pierre's hand and pressed her lips against it: *I'll kill you before that.*

Selected Readings

ALBERÈS, RENE MARILL. *Jean-Paul Sartre: Philosopher Without Faith.* Trans. Wade Baskin. New York: Philosophical Library, 1961.

BUCK, STRATTON. "The Uses of Madness." *Tennessee Studies in Literature,* III (1958), 63–71. [Sartre's "The Room" and Balzac's "Louis Lambert"]

CRANSTON, MAURICE W. *Jean-Paul Sartre.* New York: Grove Press, 1962.

DESAN, WILFRID. *The Tragic Finale: an Essay on the Philosophy of Jean-Paul Sartre.* Cambridge, Mass.: Harvard University Press, 1954.

FELL, JOSEPH P. *Emotion in the Thought of Sartre.* New York: Columbia University Press, 1965.

JAMESON, FREDRIC. *Sartre: The Origins of a Style.* New Haven, Conn.: Yale University Press, 1961.

GREENE, NORMAN N. *Jean-Paul Sartre: The Existentialist Ethic.* Ann Arbor, Mich.: University of Michigan Press, 1960.

HARDRE, JACQUES. "Sartre's Existentialism and Humanism." *Studies in Philology,* XLIX (1952), 534–37.

KERN, EDITH (ed.). *Sartre: A Collection of Critical Essays.* Englewood Cliffs, N.J.: Prentice-Hall, Inc., 1962.

KLEPPNER, AMY M. "Philosophy and the Literary Medium: The Existentialist Predicament." *Journal of Aesthetics and Art Criticism,* XXIII (1964), 207–17.

MURDOCH, IRIS. *Sartre: Romantic Rationalist.* New Haven, Conn.: Yale University Press, 1953.

THODY, PHILIP. *Jean-Paul Sartre: A Literary and Political Study.* London: H. Hamilton, 1960.

ALBERTO MORAVIA

(1907-   )

Alberto Moravia is the pseudonym for Alberto Pincherle, born in Rome in 1907, son of an architect. Moravia spent much of his youth, from 1916 to 1925, in tuberculosis sanitariums. As an adolescent he lived with sickness, ennui, boredom, frustration, and loneliness. He may be considered the first great continental writer of adolescence and the loss of innocence. His early works reflect this theme: the novel, *The Indifferent Ones;* the short story, "A Sick Boy's Winter;" and the novella, *Agostino.* In Moravia's works sensuality seems to provide a potent connecting link between reality and the knowledge of one's own existence.

Moravia has been a lifelong anti-fascist. Many of his works record the gradual fascistic takeover of Italy in the 1930's, the result of the moral and political indifference of the middle class. When man relinquishes individual responsibility, corruption, anguish, and decay flourish. *The Fancy Dress Party,* written in 1940 and published in translation in America in 1950, satirized dictatorship; when Mussolini had it recalled, that action marked the beginning of a ban on Moravia's works. He continued writing under pseudonyms but after his marriage in 1941 and the German occupation of Italy, Moravia and his wife escaped to the mountainous country where they lived in a chicken coop and where Moravia continued writing until his supplies ran out. With the coming of the allied forces in 1944, Moravia returned to Rome. Since the American publication of *The Woman of Rome* in 1949 and *Agostino* in 1951, Moravia's reputation has continued to grow in this country.

The Fall

Tancredi's illness had lasted a couple of months, and as soon as he was able to get up his parents decided to send him to the seaside. No sooner had they found a villa near a beach than they started making the usual preparations for departure. But the boy felt uneasy when he saw the unseasonable suitcases, the clothes that had not had time to get impregnated with the pungent smell of camphor. The idea of this premature holiday disturbed some hidden sense of order within him, and the interruption of his studies weighed on him, even though he felt unfit to go on with them; it was all a leap in the dark. In other words, he was unable to appreciate that his childhood was over and that he was on the threshold of his turbid and troubled adolescence. When he had taken to his bed his hair had been curly and he himself wilful and capricious; when he got up his hair was cropped and smooth, his neck scrawny, and he was listless and delicate, a victim of obsessions. At one time he hadn't known the meaning of revulsion, fear or remorse; now there were a hundred reasons for revulsion, fear had caught up with him and didn't give him a moment's respite, and he was beset by remorse, though, try as he might, he couldn't conceive what he was guilty of. Despite these changes, in his mother's eye he was still the same Tancredi, and throughout the journey she treated him as a child—and this made him grind his teeth with shame. When they reached the sea, his mother, who liked playing cards and had found some other people who shared her tastes, put him in charge of Veronica, the maid, whose task it was to keep an eye on him and accompany him to the beach. At first Veronica did this regularly, but after a while she became slack and in the end ceased entirely to bother about him. Tancredi was left alone and completely free.

The villa, the last on that strip of coast, was a massive, three-storeyed building of the beginning of the century, with sloping roof of slate, round attic skylights, oblong windows, and balconies, bulges and balustrades. A green-and-red decoration representing a tangle of water-lilies writhing like serpents covered the whole façade, the stalks beginning at ground-level, twisting round the windows and bursting into bloom under the roof. The villa belonged to an antique dealer, a friend of Tancredi's family, who had loaned it to them in return for good turns they had done him in the past; and it contained all his ugliest, most spurious and unsellable possessions, serving him as a kind of storehouse.

There were rooms on the ground floor containing four wardrobes, one for each wall; there were others with whole battle-lines of tables, great and small; yet others were crammed with cabinets, brackets and minor knick-knacks. In the overcrowded living-rooms on the second floor there were mirrors of all sizes with over-ornate frames and green reflections. In the bedrooms there were two, three or even four beds ranged side by side, as in a hospital. The lobbies and passages were cluttered up with marble torsos, chests and pieces of armour; on the walls were huge blackening seventeenth-century pictures; by the staircase hung a series of pale tapestries with a whole population of soft and flowery figures. Everything was dark, dank, creaking and shadowy. The feeling of the sea never penetrated, nor the radiant light of the coast; for the antique dealer had put some of his pieces of stained glass into the windows, for want of a better place. A musty, tomblike smell of old wood, mould and mice hovered in those air tight rooms, and the furniture with its strange arbitrary arrangement seemed to rebuff human intrusion with surly self-sufficiency. For Tancredi's mother the house was uncomfortable—impossible to keep it clean, impossible to move about without knocking into something—and, as she was always saying, not without complacency, it was a great responsibility living in such a museum, for it would be a disaster if anything got broken. But for Tancredi, given his inclinations, it was worse than uncomfortable; it was

terrifying: though not without that background of delicious anguish that fear inspires when it ceases to be an abnormal state
and becomes the rule. How this terror had taken root he wouldn't
have been able to explain; perhaps it was the terror of death
which had come with his illness and survived his recovery; perhaps it was caused by his break from childhood and by the feeling
that his strength was not equal to the demands made on it by
his new condition. He had a kind of chronic apprehension or
feeling of foreboding; as if everything concealed a trap; and he
was oppressed by a mystery that he was powerless to solve. This
state of mind might possibly have diminished had they taken up
residence elsewhere, but the dark house full of furniture seemed
made to aggravate his morbid and melancholy states of mind. As
always happens in such cases, Tancredi was attracted by everything that helped to keep him immersed in the terror-charged
atmosphere. Moreover, he was deeply aware that the atmosphere
pervaded not only the whole villa, but the neighbouring enclosure
—and beyond that it faded away and evaporated. Soon he came
to prefer the house and the enclosure to the silly bathing hut with
its crooked sunshade facing the sea, and the sand that you could
trickle through your fingers hour after hour.

Little by little he took possession of his domain. He was especially attracted by the attic rooms on the top floor. They were
like cells, and their whitewashed ceilings and rough, paved floors
suggested tragic, forgotten loves whose secrets had remained
locked up with the dust and decay. The antique dealer's huge
black pictures, most of them unframed, covered the walls from
floor to ceiling, and the figures depicted in violent attitudes among
clouds and darkness seemed out-of-place in those low-ceilinged
cells. Tancredi unrolled the mattresses and lay flat on his back
with his legs in the air for hours on end, letting his imagination
run riot—gazing dreamily at the tonsured St. Antonys kneeling
at the feet of dusky Madonnas, at the rapacious Judiths sitting
on the decapitated torsos of Holofernes, at the big-bellied Danaës
whose beds, curtains, cushions, and even the divine rain of coins,
had been blacked out by the patina of time, so that it was impossible to see what they were waiting for as they lay there in
voluptuous attitudes. Tancredi was even more fascinated by what
was lacking in the pictures than by what they were intended to
signify; the cold faces, the disproportionate limbs, and the false

postures. It did not matter to him whether the subjects were sacred or profane so long as he could abandon himself to his imaginings and invent haunting terrors in which he gradually came to believe.

Now, one day, while he was lying on his back, his attention was held by a huge picture hanging on the wall facing him, for it seemed to be almost a reflection of himself. It was probably a copy of a Caravaggio and represented St. Paul's fall on the way to Damascus. A bright, smoky shaft of light like the trail of a thunderbolt lit up the saint's naked and emaciated body and hurled him backwards, blinded, legs in air, arms outstretched. All the rest of the picture was in darkness, though it was still just possible to discern the saddle, the mane, the horse's head and a calm, beardless attendant in a turban—things that seemed to belong to a different world, a reign of peace. Tancredi found this picture astonishing, as though he were seeing it for the first time, and he liked it particularly perhaps because he was lying in the same position as the figure in the picture and thus felt better able to probe its inner meaning. Head down, feet in air, he began thinking, with the dizzy sensation of falling over backwards into an abyss—the lightning in his eyes. But after the event came perfect faith, so that the world which had been simple was now double, for the lightning had laid bare the soul hidden beneath appearances. This was what Tancredi was thinking or, rather, working out in some dim way deep down inside him, when, suddenly, he felt something hard in his pocket and remembered that the day before he had made a much-longed-for catapult with a fork of pinewood and a piece of bicycle tyre, and with the speed of a child his thoughts and wishes suddenly changed their direction—he experienced an irresistible desire to go to the enclosure near the villa and try out his new toy. No sooner thought than done: he leapt from the bed, giddy, flung down the stairs and went out at the back door of the villa. But as soon as he was out of doors the heavy, sultry air undermined his confidence, and it was with slow, uneasy footsteps that he made his way towards the gap in the wall through which he passed every day into the neighbouring enclosure. On reaching the gap, he had to make his way through brambles that he had already trodden down and pushed aside on previous occasions, but this time a bramble caught his arm and pinned him back—and this, in view of his habit of endowing objects with intelligence, seemed to him a bad omen. "Don't you want me to get through?" he murmured as he unhooked the thorns one by one from his sleeve. "Tell me, why don't you want me to get through?" The wall was much higher on the other side than on the garden side. Tancredi sat on the top, swung himself round, stuck out his legs and, resting his chest on the wall, slid down.

The wall bounded the enclosure on three sides; the side opposite Tancredi's villa was bounded by the smooth white end of a mansion, a slice of house without any windows, so that the enclosure was quite hidden from view unless someone happened to look out of the upper windows of the villa—which wasn't often. The whole extent of the sunk enclosure was rough with mounds and pitted with holes and littered with tins and every kind of crumbling refuse: in one corner a tree of medium size stretched its branches over the wall into the road; tangled shrubs such as are to be found near the sea grew in patches in the sandy soil. That day the sky, overcast and dark and presaging a storm, withheld all light from the sand and stubble, and the acrid smell from still-fresh heaps of refuse lay heavy in the motionless air.

As he entered the enclosure Tancredi underwent his usual transformation. His movements became circumspect, he walked on tiptoe, looking from side to side in terror. It was partly a game; but his nervous wariness—and the bramble that had held him back by the arm—warned him that the game was a façade and what was real were the traps, though he had no idea where they lay concealed. He looked up at the sky and saw that, passing over him obliquely, was a dark cloud with a smoky fringe—beginning over the pinewood and slanting gradually upward till it reached its greatest height over the sea, like a badly-raised theatre curtain, so that the whole sky looked lopsided. In the silence his foot struck noisily on a tin can; with a kick, he booted it away. Then, with deliberation though without enthusiasm, he took up a heap of sharp stones that he had collected the day before and went to sit on a mound not far from the wall: here, with the missiles between his legs, he began to practise with the catapult. The target was a food tin balanced on the top of the wall. Every time he hit the tin and it fell on the further side of the wall, Tancredi methodically put another in its place. It was not easy to hit the tins with their rounded, run-away surfaces, but as the stones hit the target

Tancredi little by little warmed up to the game he had started so half-heartedly. Then, unexpectedly, at the moment of raising his eyes to take aim after bending down for a stone, he saw a big cat pass cautiously along the ridge of the wall just behind the tin, its blue-greyness standing out against the thicker darker grey of the sky. "I'll aim at that," he thought. This was pure showing-off, because he was sure he would not hit it, nor did he want to; he did not even pull the catapult back to its full extent, and he let fly almost gently. As if there was a tenuous nerve attached to the missile and communicating its every vibration to him, he distinctly felt that the stone had hit, not the target, but something soft and living that could only be the cat. In terror he got up from the mound and approached cautiously. The blow seemed to have stunned the cat; it stood there motionless with its astonished face turned in his direction. But on looking more carefully he saw that only one of its eyes sent forth its green rays in wide-open surprise; the other was extinguished and in its place a little bleeding cross deep set in the fur seemed to heighten the glassiness of the eye that remained open; a round convex piece of glass, living and sensitive, had been smashed to pieces.

When he saw this he was speechless with terror. He was less frightened by the clot of blood in the grey fur than by the animal's stillness, as it stood as if turned to stone, and by the gaze of the one eye. His fear was not so much that the beast might spring at him as that it might attach itself to him with a vindictive loyalty —the horror of this was already on him. The cat's expression was one of surprise rather than of hatred, and in the surprise a singular affection seemed already present, as if with the catapult shot that had blinded it in one eye the cat recognised an unbreakable bond between Tancredi and itself. There followed a hollow clap of thunder from the oblique cloud crossing the sky; and with a shout of "Get off! Get off!" Tancredi waved his arms at the cat. He saw it draw back with an almost pained expression as if to say, "What harm have I done you that you should chase me away?" and, in a frenzy of terror, he bent down to pick up a stone. But when he stood up again there was only the tin on the wall that had served him as target; the cat had disappeared.

Trembling all over, he threw down the catapult in disgust and made for the gap in the wall. The fading light was grey and gloomy; he noticed, when he had vaulted the wall, that under the leafy trees it was almost dark. Midges were buzzing in the already rain-laden shadows. A smell of washed plates and dead fires came up from the thick, black grating of the kitchen. Tancredi knew that at this time of day the cat usually sat in the corner of the fireplace under the chimney, and as he was about to go into the kitchen he was seized by the craven fear of meeting it. He was convinced for some reason that the beast would never leave his heels from now onwards, that to get rid of it he would have to kill it, and that even after he had killed it the persecution would persist, for there would remain the remorse for an act which he already foresaw would be drawn-out and horrible. However, he screwed up his courage, pulled himself together, and, after trying to pierce the darkness, charged blindly across the kitchen and fumbled at the door leading from that room to the dining-room. The cat was waiting for him in the passage; he felt its fur against his naked legs. The confined space made it more unbearable, and with a shudder and scream he fled into the dining-room.

Here it was no less dark and deserted. By now he had lost his nerve completely, and though there was no sign of the cat he couldn't stop shaking. He picked his way cautiously out of the dining-room and hurried across the entrance hall, trembling in every limb as if his body were trying to run away from him, like a horse from a rider who has lost control; he felt frantically for the light switch, flicked it on and looked around. The cat was the first thing he saw; it was between the legs of an armchair, facing him.

It fixed him with its one green eye, staring and terrified now and quite unlike the shy affection of its first advances. His heart beating wildly, Tancredi retreated, backing upstairs on the stair carpet. Immediately the cat came out from its refuge and followed him, deliberately lifting its face up to him. Still backing up the stairs, Tancredi reached the landing, where there stood a table strewn with ancient weapons: one of these—a pistol or a dagger—he intended to seize and hurl at the cat. The cat continued to climb towards him, fixing him with something that looked like hope. Tancredi's hand fumbled on the table behind him. He clutched a pistol and hurled it blindly. There was a sharp crash followed by the tinkle of broken glass: the pistol had hit the dining-room door. Panic-stricken, Tancredi turned on his heels and fled.

He ran up the two flights of stairs to the third floor landing. A dusky light filtered in from the two windows at the end of the passage and fell on the red brickwork floor. In this halo of grey light Tancredi saw the cat turning round watchfully with its back up, its fur raised. He gave a leap and reached a doorway. With his fingers on the handle, he watched the animal's movements. It did not seem to be aware of his presence, but in the dim light was turning round and round with arched back and tail erect. It might have been looking at its reflection in the floor, for all of a sudden it leapt aside as if in play with its own image. It was then that it first caught sight of Tancredi and made for him with a calm and trusting trot. Tancredi, who had kept his eyes on it all this time, hurriedly entered the room and very slowly, without making a sound, closed the door.

The room in which he found himself was the same as all the others on the third floor. It was almost entirely filled with a great walnut bed whose grey striped mattress looked comforting in the twilight under the low ceiling. On the bedside table stood a candlestick of bright blue glass, but the walls, strangely enough, were bare. Tancredi sat down on the edge of the bed and listened to the furtive nibbling and scurrying of the rats in the space between ceiling and roof. After a moment he felt reassured, and was just going to lie down in his usual way when the deep silence was broken by a strange sound. It was the noise of low chatting voices, engaged in urgent discussion; and it seemed to come from the next room, whose door appeared to be ajar. For a while Tancredi listened, motionless, to the whispering which had an inhuman, improbable quality in the silence of the attic, as if the pieces of antique furniture were talking rather than two people. Suddenly one of the voices was raised, revealing itself as not only human, but that of a man. His curiosity aroused, Tancredi got up and went to take a look through the crack in the door.

At first he saw only a little room in all respects similar to the one he was in; then on the far wall he recognised the picture of the fall of St. Paul looking gloomier and eerier than ever. The bed on which his fancy had run riot a few hours earlier as he lay staring at the picture was empty, and he could not conceive where the low voices had come from. The voices had now stopped, and yet the room looked alive and inhabited as if the dark enclosed atmosphere had retained an imprint of the presences so recently within it. What prevented Tancredi from entering the room was a very precise sensation that he would be violating an intimacy that was private and in some way clandestine, and as he watched he had a feeling he had never experienced before—of committing a shameless indiscretion. While he was still looking there began a long, dry, melancholy creaking such as is made when unoiled hinges are being slowly turned by the cautious shutting of a door. There was no doubt about it—at that very moment someone was leaving the room with the least possible noise, but the door with its long high creak was betraying him. Then there was silence again. Suddenly, as if precautions were no longer necessary, the person remaining in the room dropped on to the bed, with a groaning of springs and a creaking of wood. And Tancredi saw two legs stretching along the mattress towards the bottom of the bed, naked and shining white and as if weighed down with langour and the desire for repose. Veronica's legs, Tancredi thought involuntarily, remembering the white face, blue eyes and fair hair of his mother's maid. The legs, long slender and slightly convex at the knees, couldn't keep still, though their movements were heavy, weary and voluptuous. The attic window beyond the bed began now to be spattered with dark drops of rain. The legs stopped moving. Tancredi was overcome with a growing and intolerable sense of shameful prying; his cheeks burned and he drew away from the door and sat on his own bed.

He didn't know what to make of what he had seen, but experienced an acute sense of ambiguity and doubt. There was nothing odd about it at first sight. But why should Veronica go to sleep in a room that wasn't hers? And what was all the chattering and the man's voice? But when he embarked on these questionings he again experienced the acute sense of shame that had beset him while he was peeping, and in disgust he tried to think of something else.

He got up from the bed and went to sit on the floor in the embrasure of the window; there, feeling utterly safe and happy, he began watching the rain streaking down the window. The little room was almost dark by now, but he thought that the cat might well be waiting for him outside in the passage, whereas in here under the low ceiling and against that big bed he felt secure. Crouched, with his lips against his knees, he watched the rain falling for a long time. When he began dozing he got up automatically and lay on the bed. The mattress, though hard and flat, felt soft after the tiles. He lay on his back and stared at the ceiling listening to the swishing of the rain and the rats scurrying in the rafters. At last his eyelids grew heavy and he fell asleep.

For a while he slumbered dreamlessly and when he reawakened he found himself in darkness. It was already nightfall, but by his reckoning still too early for supper; so he did not stir from the bed. From some point in the ceiling, above his head almost, there came a persistent noise, the stubborn gnawing of a rodent ferociously at work on dry, hard wood. The noise had a rhythm, first loud, then soft, then almost silent— "It's gone," thought Tancredi—then loud again and fiercer than ever. After he had lain in wait a little while he felt something falling on top of him— something like a piece of plaster. Convulsed with fear, he groped for the lamp on the bedside table, lit it and looked.

It was as he thought: some plaster had fallen and there was a black hole in the middle of the ceiling. It was small and jagged, but its flaky edges suggested that some vast den lay beyond, so that if the plaster fell Heaven knew what tunnels might not be disclosed. He gazed; and then suddenly something appeared in the hole, something dark, soft and swollen, and with a swift motion there glared the red and raging eye of a rat. A split second —then the hole became black and empty again; but it was enough for Tancredi. He leapt trembling from the bed and ran headlong to call Veronica from the next room. She was no longer on the bed, but sitting on a stool busy sewing.

"Veronica," he said, his voice throbbing with unspeakable joy. "Veronica, there's a rat up there . . . . "

She looked at him without a word and then put down her work and followed him, or, to be more precise, preceded him into the room.

"Up there," said Tancredi, staying by the door and pointing to the ceiling.

The maid looked at the hole and still without a word went back to her room and returned armed with a broom. Tancredi watched her get on to the bed and, holding the broom by the brush end, begin to explore the hole with the handle. Heartened by her calmness, Tancredi advanced several steps into the room. The broom-handle went in and out, rubbing with a dull sound against the sides of the hole.

"There. I can feel it," she said almost with delight. "Yes; it really is a rat." But the broom fell from her hands and down fell something large and dark; she fell headlong back on to the bed, her legs open, grasping her loins with her hands, pulling her clothes round her thighs and shouting:

"It jumped on top of me! I've got it on top of me."

She struggled and her naked legs emerged from her clothes. Tancredi saw that they really were the legs that he had seen lying languidly twitching on the mattress. But amid this display of whiteness there was no rat to be seen, and this gave rise to the suspicion that it must have hidden under a chair, unless it had got under the woman's clothes—and how could it? Tancredi was so terrified that the infuriated rat would bite his legs that he leapt on to a chair.

The woman was still struggling: Tancredi, distraught, jumped from the first chair to another without touching the ground. Breathless, his heart beating frantically, he tried to reach the door and call for help; but it was dark, and this time he really did wake up, trembling and sweating all over—not on the chair as in his dream, nor on the bed where he was when he went to sleep, but in an unknown part of the room. Though he realised that the business of the rat had all been a dream, a frenzied terror was still upon him and he tried wildly to get out of the room or to find a light. But the room seemed to have changed its shape; his outstretched arms met with unforeseen walls and unfamiliar corners; he seemed to be not in the villa at all, but many feet underground, shut up in a tomb. At last the door burst open, the wavering light of a candle broke through the darkness, and while he was turning distractedly two shadows were cast upon the ceiling.

"But he's here," said his mother's voice with relief. "I've been looking for you for an hour . . . . What on earth made you hide up here in the dark?"

Trembling and weeping, Tancredi ran blindly to the refuge of the two women.

"He must have been frightened by the storm," said Veronica, stroking his hair. "He's trembling all over . . . . Come. There's nothing to cry about."

"The rat," Tancredi couldn't help stammering. "The rat . . . . "

"What rat?" asked his mother without interest. "If only you wouldn't go and hide as you're always doing."

"The rat," Tancredi said again, and meanwhile, still entangled in the atmosphere of his dream, he couldn't help pressing his shoulder against the maid's belly as if to make really sure that the rat hadn't taken refuge there. He noticed her legs, too, despite his terror, and they seemed strange. There was no doubt but that they were the legs he had seen in the adjoining room; but how different they looked. They had then seemed languid and nervously sensitive; now they seemed tall, strong, muscular, like two chiselled pillars of virtue. In the grip of these disturbed sensations, he let himself be consoled a little by the two women; and, drying his eyes mechanically, he followed them out of the room.

It emerged, as they were going downstairs, that a fuse had blown in the storm, and the house had been plunged in darkness.

"Stop crying," said his mother, walking downstairs with the composure of a woman of the world, preceded by the maid with the candle, "and go and get your tools . . . . We need your help."

Here it must be mentioned that Tancredi was very clever with electricity and all mechanical things, and it had long been the custom to seek him out when simple breakdowns occurred that did not require a mechanic.

"Yes, Mother," he said obediently.

"We were looking for you all over the house," the maid admonished him in an unusually affectionate tone of voice. "What a thoughtless boy you are."

But Tancredi imagined that she was intending a reference to the scene he had espied through the door, with an obvious desire that he shouldn't tell his mother; and, filled with a feeling of deep complicity, he said nothing.

When they reached the ground floor Tancredi went to fetch his tools from the nook where he kept them, and said he was ready. The fuse-box was under the stairs above a cupboard, on top of which all sorts of junk was stored, as if it was an attic. Veronica went to look for a step-ladder, set it against the wall and held it steady with one hand while she manipulated a candle with the other. Tancredi's mother steadied the ladder on the other side and she too held a candlestick above her head. Between these two guardian angels, Tancredi mounted to the top rung holding a third candle that he was going to fix on the top of the cupboard. When he reached the top of the ladder he tilted the candle for some of the grease to drop and then as best he could fixed the candle on a dusty corner of the cupboard. The flickering light revealed a whole heap of odds and ends—a bronze lamp, innumerable curtain rings, dust-clotted bottles of every size, a legless armchair with the stuffing bulging out from the torn cover. As soon as he had fixed the candle, Tancredi bent down and asked his mother to pass him the screwdriver and two other small tools he had placed on a chair. His mother handed them up to him; but in the moment of straightening up to unfasten some of the screws, Tancredi heard a rustle. He turned and saw—Heaven knows how it had got there—the grey cat advancing on him between the pieces of junk; it had one cautious paw upraised, one wide staring eye, and its violet-coloured lip was drawn back above its teeth. When he saw it panic gripped him, and a fearful anger. "This time I'll kill it," he thought, and aimed the screwdriver at the beast. But at that moment there was a dry snap, a flash shot from the fuse-box and, blinded, with a cry of dismay he fell headlong back between the two women. The candles went out; in the darkness he felt himself being carried by his feet and shoulders like a dead man to the dining-room. He just heard his mother's voice saying to Veronica: "In here." But the blood was already ebbing from his temples, fleeing from his body, and while around him the light returned, an icy blackness robbed him of his last fraction of strength, and he closed his eyes.

Two days later, in the summer-house overlooking the sea, his mother was telling her friends:

"For a moment I was afraid he was hurt . . . but he didn't have a scratch—he had merely fainted. The over-excitement . . . . I must admit that for a moment I was quite alarmed. The queerest thing was that afterwards we found out that the flash had been caused by the house cat. The poor creature had somehow got itself tangled up with the wire . . . . We found it electrocuted. It seems to have got the shock instead of Tancredi. Anyway, I've strictly forbidden him ever to go near the electricity again. Boys are so reckless."

"I couldn't agree more," said one of her friends.

"Your shuffle," said his mother.

And the game began.

The Triple Looking-Glass

The maid had gone out to do the shopping; his wife could not hear the bell because she was out on the roof-terrace with the baby; so Giovanni went to open the door himself, and was faced by two men in shirtsleeves carrying a wrapped-up object which looked like a screen. "It's the mirror," said one of the two men; "where shall we put it?" Feeling very cheerful because he had slept well and also because it was Saturday and he did not have to go to his office, Giovanni led the two men in, whistling as he went, and showed them a corner in the bedroom, beside his wife's dressing-table. The men put down the mirror in the corner and went away. Giovanni tore the paper from the mirror, which was a triple one just like those in dressmakers' shops, and then looked at himself in it. And then his good humour vanished, for he became conscious of a fact of which he had never been ignorant but which, for some time, he had almost forgotten: not merely was his face unpleasing to him but it also appeared to him to be, in a disagreeable way, an entirely new face, with the result that he had difficulty in believing that so unpleasing a face could be his own.

Evidently, he thought, turning first in profile, then three-quarter-face, evidently he had a different idea of himself, a better, a flattering idea. But what idea? Thinking it over, he realized that in reality he did not have any idea of himself; it was simply that he did not want, on any account, to recognize himself in that unpleasing face. Gradually, slowly changing position, he again started looking at himself, as if hoping, by closer examination, to discover some likeable quality; but he became conscious that, the more he looked at himself, the more his aversion grew. His fore-head was hard, compact and unsymmetrical, his nose undecided and ungainly in shape, his eye lacked intelligence, the expression of his mouth inspired disgust, his complexion was inclined to be red and shiny, and even less expressive features such as his ears and chin aroused in him a feeling of repulsion. Struck all of a sudden by an acute sense of unhappiness, Giovanni looked at him-self again three or four times, then left the glass and went out on to the terrace.

They lived in a pent-house flat surrounded by roof-terraces from which one enjoyed a view of the Tiber, jade-coloured as it wound between low green banks, of the Ponte Milvio with its ancient golden stonework and of the white and yellow modern buildings lined up on the far shore. Half-closing his eyes in the luminous, pale sunshine of the fine spring day, Giovanni crossed the terrace, which looked like a garden owing to the numerous vases and boxes of flowers along the parapets, and went towards the corner where his wife was sitting reading beside the baby's cradle. Sitting down beside her, he said: "The mirror has arrived. I took off the paper it was wrapped in."

"The cheval-glass," said his wife absent-mindedly, continuing to read.

"Strictly speaking," said Giovanni, "a cheval-glass is one of those antique mirrors, movable, and mounted on a stand. This is a triple looking-glass."

"Well," said his wife, "*I* call triple looking-glasses cheval-glasses."

The scorching sunshine was conducive to silence. Giovanni, however, persisted. "It's not very beautiful," he said. "It looks like a dressmaker's mirror."

"That's just what it is," his wife confirmed.

"I looked at myself," Giovanni went on, hoping that his wife would reassure him, "and, to tell the truth, I didn't like myself at all."

But his wife appeared not to have heard him and said nothing. Giovanni, too, was silent; then he remembered that an elderly female relation had come to see them the day before, who had declared emphatically, as soon as she saw the boy, that he was the very image of his father. At the moment, this declaration had given him great pleasure; but now, thinking it over, he was aware of a feeling almost of terror at the idea that this, his first child, so dearly loved by him, might really resemble him. It was a strange kind of terror that seemed to go beyond the physical resemblance and hint at the child's destiny. At that moment there was a thin, clear wailing sound: the baby had woken up. His wife rose at once and hurried to the cradle. Giovanni also rose.

Once again he admired the extreme delicacy with which his wife inserted her two hands underneath the little wrapped-up body of the baby, lifted him from the cradle and then carried him in her arms to the chair near the parapet. She rested her foot on one of the flower-boxes and laid the baby in her lap, raising him to a sloping position with her left arm. Giovanni sat down beside her and gazed intently at the child who now, as soon as his mother had taken him from the cradle, had immediately quieted down. He was really a very beautiful baby; his fine, soft hair reminded one of the down on a coconut just torn from its husk; his brow was white and free from thought; his eyes looked out from pupils of a dark, limpid blue; his pink mouth wore a grave expression, between cheeks of remarkable firmness and rotundity. The baby clasped his foot with his hand and stared with ecstatic fixity at some unspecifiable point in the air in front of him. Almost without thinking, Giovanni said: "I wonder which of us two he'll look like when he grows up."

"He'll look like you," his wife answered with assurance.

"I hope not," said Giovanni sharply.

"Why not?"

"Because I don't like myself."

His wife waved away a bee which had come buzzing close to the baby, then said in a good-natured way: "I assure you there's nothing unpleasant about you. In fact, on the whole, everyone finds you very likeable."

"Everyone, I daresay, but not myself."

She leant over the baby and repeated in an affectionate and instructive tone of voice: "Ma-ma . . . Ma-ma . . ." The baby, letting go of his foot, stretched out his hand eagerly towards his mother's face and almost succeeded in catching hold of her nose. Giovanni realized that his wife, wholly taken up with her baby, was not interested in his troubles. He went on, nevertheless: "I dislike myself as I might dislike a stranger or someone one doesn't know. By which I mean that to the dislike is added the idea of strangeness. The first thing that came into my mind a short time ago, when I looked at myself in the mirror, was: how on earth is it possible that that man there is myself?"

"And yet," said his wife with careless cruelty, "it's not only possible, but it's certain."

"That's why I hope my son won't resemble me."

His wife lowered her face again towards the baby's hand, seeking its hesitant caress; then she raised her head, looked at her husband and started laughing: "You know you're very funny. You're the only father in the world that doesn't want his son to look like him."

Giovanni thought for a moment and was forced to admit, inwardly, that his wife was right. However, the fact remained, he felt an aversion for himself and a genuine fear that his son would resemble him. He said emphatically: "The mere thought that in the future I might look on my son with the same dislike that I look upon myself makes me feel sick."

"But why? Come on: be rational."

"Dislikes aren't rational; otherwise they wouldn't exist. They're dislikes, and that's that."

His wife put out her hand and gently tickled the chin of the baby, who at once smiled, but without altering the expression of gravity on his face. For a long time she sat contemplating this smile which she had provoked and won, with the look, almost, of a painter who pauses to gaze at the picture he is painting; then, in an access of tenderness, she bent over her son, kissing him and repeating with passionate determination: "But *he's* lovable, oh yes, yes, he's very very lovable, yes, he's very lovable indeed." Finally, having given vent to her mother love, she seemed to remember her husband and said hurriedly: "Why, why? You have a mania for self-destruction. Why do you dislike yourself? Now come on, let's make a joint examination of your personality. You're a good lawyer with a practice that's doing very well; as a man you're clever, gentlemanly, reliable, well-balanced, intelligent, cultivated; you're young, you're good-looking, you also come of a rich family, which is a further asset; you're esteemed and highly thought-of by your colleagues, you have lots of friends, you go in for several kinds of sport, you have a taste for beautiful things: what more do you want? Why in the world should you dislike yourself? I tell you, I should be really pleased for our son to resemble you in every point."

His wife had spoken with so much energy that Giovanni suddenly felt doubtful. Supposing that he had made a mistake and that his wife was right? Then all at once he remembered having read in the paper that morning a matrimonial advertisement in which a man described himself with almost the same words as his wife had used about him; and he also remembered having thought, as he read this eulogy at so much a line: "Goodness knows, I daresay he's really an odious type." He said sourly: "You've painted a very external, conventional portrait of me. If you'd gone a little deeper you would have seen that things aren't like that."

With a touch of irritation, his wife answered: "I see you like that because I love you. How ever deeply I dig I don't find anything else. Dig deeper yourself, seeing that you want to so much."

Giovanni thought again, but found nothing. Shaking his head, he said: "I don't know, I don't find anything. I feel that this dislike has a reason but I don't know what it is."

His wife replied in an absent-minded and at the same time triumphant tone of voice: "There, you see, you contradict yourself. You dislike yourself and at the same time you can't discover any defect in yourself, which is as much as to say that you consider yourself perfect. What are we to suppose?"

"I dislike myself," answered Giovanni, "as one dislikes certain people that one meets in the train, people about whom one knows nothing and whom one has nothing to reproach with, and yet one dislikes them. The fact that I have nothing to reproach myself with and that I find myself, as you say, perfect, merely proves that it is not a small or a large part of myself that I dislike, but the complete whole. In other words, if I looked at this alleged perfection from a correct point of view, it would be transformed into its opposite, into a complete imperfection."

"And why don't you look at it from this correct point of view?"

Giovanni replied bitterly: "Because there isn't one, or at any rate I don't know it."

The baby had now gone to sleep again. His mother rose slowly to her feet, so as not to awaken him, and then went and deposited him, with cautious movements, in the cradle. She came back to her husband and, before sitting down, gave him a quick caress, saying: "It's simply that you're not content with yourself, that's all. You'll get over it."

Giovanni shook his head. "No, it's not like that."

"What is it, then?"

Giovanni thought intensely, trying for a moment to identify his own feeling precisely and to grasp its whole significance. Finally he said: "It's as though there were some deception between me and myself; or as though I had been cheating myself in a fraudulent manner, continually, always. The dislike I feel for myself is like the antipathy one feels for someone who has pretended to us to be something that he was not, for interested, or anyhow obscure, motives. But I don't know what the deception is. I feel it, that's all; it's in the air, like a smell, but that's all I can say about it."

Serenely, his wife answered: "I understand. In you there must be two people, one who deceives and one who is deceived. I'm for the second one; he's the one I love."

The Go-Between

As we were going up the great staircase of the palace, Antonio, the butler, warned me: "Don't imagine you'll get much out of the Princess, she's so mean you wouldn't believe it . . . . Ever since her husband died, she's had a passion for interfering in the management of everything, and she won't leave anyone in peace."

"But why . . . is she old?" I asked casually.

"She—old? No, she's young and beautiful . . . . She can't be more than twenty-five or so . . . . To look at her, you'd think she was an angel . . . . But appearances are deceptive."

"Well," I replied, "she can look like a devil, for all I care. All I want is the money that's due to me . . . . I'm a house agent, the Princess has an apartment to sell, I sell it for her, I take my commission and that's that."

"Ah, it's not as simple as that . . . she'll make you sweat blood . . . . Now wait while I go and tell her you're here."

He left me in the anteroom and went to find the Princess, whom he called "Excellency", as though she were a man. I waited for some time in the icy anteroom, typical of an ancient palace, with its tapestry-hung walls and frescoed ceiling. At last Antonio came and told me that Her Excellency was ready for me. We went through a suite of reception-rooms and then, in a room larger that the others, I saw, in a window embrasure, a desk and the Princess herself sitting writing. Antonio went over to her, respectfully, and said: "Here is Signor Proietti, Excellency." Without raising her eyes, she answered: "Come in, Proietti." As I came

"The Go-Between" from *Roman Tales* by Alberto Moravia. Copyright © 1956, 1957 by Valentino Bompiani & Co.

close to her, I was able to examine her at my leisure and was at once forced to admit that Antonio had not exaggerated when he compared her to an angel. She had a pure, pale, delicate, sweet face, with black hair and long black eyelashes that shadowed her cheeks. Her nose, slightly turned up, was slender and transparent, as though accustomed to smelling nothing but perfumes. Her mouth was small, the upper lip bigger than the lower, like a rose. I lowered my glance to her figure: she was dressed in black, with a close-fitting jacket; broad in the hips and bosom, she had a wasp waist, so small that you could have put your two hands round it. She was writing: and I noticed that her hand was white, thin and elegant, with a diamond ring on the forefinger. Then she looked up at me and I saw that her eyes were extremely beautiful—enormous, dark, at the same time both velvety and liquid. "Well then, Proietti," she said, "shall we go and look at the apartment?"

She had a soft, caressing voice. "Yes, Princess," I stammered.

"Come then, Proietti, this way," she said, taking up a big iron key.

We went back through the same series of reception-rooms, and in the anteroom she said to Antonio, as he moved forward to open the door for her: "Antonio, tell the people who look after the heating not to put on any more coal . . . . The heat in here is stifling"; and I was astonished, because the anteroom was icy and so were all the other rooms. We started off up the main staircase, she in front and I behind, and as she walked ahead I could see that her figure, too, was very beautiful—tall and slim, with straight legs; and the black dress emphasized the whiteness of her neck and hands. We went up two flights of the main staircase and then two more flights of a back staircase, and finally, at the far end of a garret, reached the iron corkscrew stairs that led up to the apartment. She clambered up this little staircase and I followed behind, lowering my eyes because I knew I could have looked at her legs and I did not wish to do so, and already I respected her as one respects a woman one loves. We came into the apartment, which consisted, as I at once saw, of two big rooms with brick-paved floors and windows with fixed shutters open only at the top, right under the ceiling, so that you could see nothing but the sky. A third, smaller room, circular in shape, had been devised inside a belvedere tower, and gave, through a french window, on to a balcony with a railing which hung over a wide expanse of brown-tiled roof. She opened the french window and went out on the the balcony, saying: "Come, Proietti, come and see what a view there is." And indeed there was a fine panorama: from that balcony you could see the whole of Rome, with its endless roofs and domes and towers. It was a clear day, and, far away against the blue sky, between one roof and another, you could see the great dome of St. Peter's. I looked idly at the view, but in truth I hardly saw it and thought only of her, as though she were something that preoccupied me and that I could not forget. She, in the meantime, had gone in again; and I swung round and asked her, automatically: "How about the conveniences?"

"You'd like to see the bathroom? Here it is." And she went to a small door that I had not noticed and showed me a little low, square, windowless room which she had converted into a bathroom. I was able to see at a glance that the fittings were of a cheap kind, the sort of thing you see in a working-class house. She closed the bathroom door again and, stopping in the middle of the big room, her hands in her jacket pockets, asked me: "Well, Proietti, how much d'you think we can ask?"

I was so much preoccupied with her beauty and with the disturbing fact of finding myself alone with her in this garret, that for a moment, as I stood looking at her, I made no answer. She perhaps became aware of what was passing through my head, for, tapping the floor with a small, nervous foot, she added: "May I ask what you are thinking about?"

I said hastily: "I was calculating . . . . There are three rooms . . . but no lift, and whoever buys it will have to do it up . . . . I suggest three and a half million lire."

"But, Proietti," she immediately exclaimed, raising her voice, "Proietti, I intended to ask seven million!"

To tell the truth, for a moment I was stupefied. This combination of beauty and spurious business acumen was disconcerting. Finally I stammered: "Princess, at seven million no one will take it."

"But this isn't the Parioli district," she replied. "This is a historic palace . . . . This is the centre of Rome."

Well, we discussed the matter for some time, she standing in the middle of the room and I at a safe distance from her, so as not to be led into temptation. I talked and talked, but in reality I was only thinking about *her,* and—since it was all I could do— I devoured her with my eyes. In the end she allowed herself, very unwillingly, to be convinced that four million was all she could ask, though this was already a high price. As a matter of fact, allowing a million lire for the necessary work to be done, and adding on taxes and other things, the apartment would ultimately cost the buyer almost six million. I already had a possible client, so I told her the matter could be considered settled, and left the house.

Next day I presented myself at the palace with a young architect who was looking for just such an unusual and picturesque place. The Princess took her key and showed us over the apartment. The architect argued a little about the price but in the end agreed to the sum already fixed—four million lire.

Early the following morning, however—it wasn't even eight o'clock—my wife came and woke me up, telling me that the Princess was on the telephone. I was so sleepy I could hardly see; but her voice, her sweet, delicate voice, seemed to me like music as she spoke. I listened to this music in my pyjamas, standing barefooted on the floor, while my wife knelt down to put my slippers on my feet, and then threw an overcoat over my shoulders. I understood little or nothing of what the Princess was saying, but, amongst her flood of words, two, all of a sudden, struck me: " . . . Five million."

I said at once: "Princess, we've pledged ourselves for four million . . . we can't go back on that . . . . "

"In business there's no such thing as a pledge . . . . It's five million or nothing."

"But, Princess, he'll back out of it . . . . "

"Don't be a damned fool, Proietti . . . . Five million or nothing."

To tell the truth, the words "damned fool", when pronounced by that voice, did not seem to me either vulgar or insulting but almost a compliment. I said I would do as she wished, and immediately afterwards telephoned my client and told him the new figure. I heard him exclaim at once, at the other end of the wire: "Are you people having a joke? The price goes up by a million in one day!"

"I can't help it . . . those are my orders."

"Well, I'll see . . . . I'll think about it."

"Then you'll let me know . . . ?"

"Yes, I'll think about it, I'll see."

That, naturally, was the last of *him*. And then began what was, so to speak, the most intimate period of my relations with the Princess. She telephoned me, on an average, three times a day, and, each time my wife called out ironically: "It's the usual princess," I was as excited as if it had been a telephone-call between lovers. Far from it. She loved money to an extent that was hardly believable; she was mercenary, mean, pig-headed, cunning— worse than a usurer. It must be confessed that she had a money-box in place of a heart: she saw nothing and she thought of nothing but money. Every day now, on the telephone, she invented some new pretext for raising the price, even it is was only by a trifle of five or ten thousand lire. One day it would be the bathroom, in order to recompense herself for plumbing expenses, next day it would be the view, another day the fact that the bus stopped right in front of the main door of the palace, and so on. But I held fast to the figure of five million, which was already enormous; so much so that possible buyers, as soon as they heard it, vanished and were never seen again. At last, by a lucky chance, I found her someone who really fell in love with the place—a business man from Milan who wanted to put a girl friend of his into it. He was a curt, practical man who knew the market and the value of money: a middle-aged man, tall, with a long, brown face and a mouth full of gold teeth. He came to see the apartment, examined everything carefully and then said to the Princess, without much ceremony: "It's nothing but a mouse's nest, and in Milan we'd put in water and use it as a laundry . . . . If it's worth five million, I'm a Dutchman . . . . By the time I've done the necessary alterations, such as renewing the floors and the fixtures, putting in windows, getting rid of this cheap stuff" —and he pointed to the porcelain fittings in the bathroom—"it will cost me seven or eight millions . . . . Never mind . . . . The law of the market is ruled by supply and demand . . . . You've met the person who really wants this apartment, so you're quite right."

But he did wrong to talk in this frank, brutal, businesslike way.

For, as soon as he had gone, she said to me sorrowfully: "Proietti, we've made an enormous mistake."

"What?"

"In asking only five million . . . that man would have paid seven."

"Princess," I answered, "I'm afraid you didn't quite understand his type: he's a man who's full of money, it's true, and he's very fond of his mistress, I don't doubt; but he'll never give more than that much."

"You don't know what a man cannot do for a woman he loves," said she, looking at me with those wonderfully beautiful eyes in which there was nothing at all except greed and money. I became confused, and replied: "It may be so . . . but I'm convinced I'm right."

Well, next day the Milanese business man presented himself at the palace with a lawyer, and the Princess, as soon as we were seated, said at once: "Signor Casiraghi, I'm sorry, but, on thinking it over, I cannot accept the figure I mentioned yesterday."

"How d'you mean?"

"I mean that I want six million."

You should have seen Casiraghi. With great simplicity he rose to his feet and said: "Princess, my most sincere and respectful greetings!" Then he bowed and went out. As soon as he had disappeared, I said: "Well, you see? Who was right?"

But she was not in the least disconcerted. "Don't worry," she said; "we shall find a buyer all right, even at six million."

I wanted to tell her to go to the devil, but alas, I was properly in love. Perhaps it was just because I was in love that I did not notice the strangeness of the buyer whom I found for her, at five and a half millions, a few days later. The figure, high as it was, failed to make him gasp. He was a country gentleman, a big, tall young man who looked like a bear, by name Pandolfi. I took a dislike to him at once, as though I felt a presentiment about him. When I took him to see the Princess, I realized at once why it was that he had made no protest at the price. To begin with, they had, it seemed, a whole lot of friends in common. And further, he looked at her in a kind of way that left no possible doubts. We made our usual examination of the three rooms and the bath-room, and then she opened the french window and went out with him on to the balcony to show him the view. I stayed inside the room and so was able to observe them. They were both resting their hands on the railing; and then I saw his hand approach hers as though by chance and place itself on top of it, covering it completely. I started counting, slowly, and reached twenty. Twenty seconds of stroking—it doesn't sound much but you just try counting them! At twenty, with perfect naturalness, she disengaged her hand and came back into the room. He—to put it briefly—said that the apartment suited him, and went away. We were left alone and she, quite shamelessly, said: "You see, Proietti? Five and a half million . . . but we'll raise it yet."

Next morning I went back and found her awaiting me, as usual, at her desk in the drawing-room. She said to me briskly: "D'you know what I discovered yesterday, Proietti, while I was looking at the view with that client of yours?"

"That he's in love with you," I should have liked to reply; but I restrained myself. "I discovered," she went on, "that in one corner you can see quite a good piece of the Borghese Gardens. Proietti, we must strike while the iron is hot . . . . Today we'll ask Signor Pandolfi six and a half millions."

You see? She knew Pandolfi was in love with her, and was ready to speculate on it. She was now making him pay a round million for those twenty seconds that he had held her hand— fifty thousand lire a second. What an appetite! But this time I realized that she would get her price, and suddenly I was filled with rage and jealousy and disgust all at the same time. Hitherto I had been the go-between in a matter of business; but now she was forcing me to become the go-between in a love intrigue. Before I was fully aware of what I was saying, I burst out violently: "Princess, I'm a house-agent, not a pimp," and, red in the face, ran out of the room. I heard her say, in a tone that was not in the least offended: "But, Proietti, what's the matter with you?" And that was the last time I ever heard that sweet voice.

Some months afterwards I ran into Antonio, the butler, and asked him: "And how's the Princess?"

"She's getting married."

"Who to? I bet she's marrying that man Pandolfi who bought the apartment in the attic."

"Pandolfi indeed! . . . She's marrying a prince from South Italy, an old stick who might be her grandfather . . . but he's rich; she says he owns half Calabria . . . . Like attracts like, in fact,"

"Is she still beautiful?"

"An angel."

Selected Readings

BALDANZA, FRANK. "The Classicism of Alberto Moravia." *Modern Fiction Studies*, III (1957), 309–20.

BERGIN, THOMAS G. "The Moravian Muse." *Virginia Quarterly Review*, XXIX (1953), 215–25.

DeDOMINICIS, ANNA MARIA, and BEN JOHNSON. "The Art of Fiction—VI: Alberto Moravia." *Paris Review*, No. 6 (1955), 17–37.

GOLINO, CARLO L. "Alberto Moravia." *Modern Language Journal*, XXXVI (1952), 334–40.

KEENE, FRANCES. "Moravia, Moralist." *The Nation*, CLVI (May 23, 1953), 438–40.

LEWIS, R. W. B. "Alberto Moravia: Eros and Existence." *Picaresque Saint: Representative Figures in Contemporary Fiction*. Philadelphia: J. B. Lippincott Company, 1959.

PACIFICI, SERGIO J. "The Fiction of Alberto Moravia: Portrait of a Wasteland." *Modern Language Quarterly*, XVI (1955), 68–77.

————. "Alberto Moravia." *A Guide to Contemporary Italian Literature: From Futurism to Neorealism*. New York: The World Publishing Company, 1962.

ROLO, CHARLES. "Alberto Moravia." *The Atlantic*, CXCV (February, 1955), 69–74.

ALBERT CAMUS

(1913-1960)

Another great existentialist writer, Albert Camus found the meaning of man's existence in his spirit of revolt where Sartre found it in man's consciousness and Moravia in man's sensuality. Like these writers he too was a resistance writer. During the war years in France he edited the underground paper *Combat*.

Camus' life began in 1913 in Mondoni, Algeria, in great poverty. By the time he was twenty he was already writing—journalism and fiction—and working in theatre. He continued his journalistic and theatrical activities in France during the war and in 1942, in occupied France, he published *The Myth of Sisyphus*. The myth functions as an objective correlative for Camus' work—Sisyphus' absurd effort in the face of a meaningless cosmos to roll the stone eternally up the hill only to have it crash down again symbolizes man's absurd passion for revolt and freedom in action.

These three terms—passion, revolt, freedom—typify Camus' attitude toward life. Man, caught in the delicate balance of the extremities of life—light–dark, innocence–guilt, sentiment–nihilism, life–death—without hope of appeal, must create and live by his own responsible moral-ethical code. He must help his fellow man. Absurdly enough, Death becomes the final bond, linking man to man. Death becomes the purpose of life.

Camus' *The Stranger*, published in 1942, dramatizes the plight of the absurd man: a chance happening jars the protagonist into an awareness of his hopeless situation. Though he is a dull fellow, made so by an indifferent world, he must nevertheless be punished for behaving spiritlessly. He has no appeal but the reality of death. A play, *The Misunderstanding* (1944), deals with the same theme. In 1957, with the appearance of his collection *Exile and the Kingdom*, Camus received the Nobel Prize. He was killed in an automobile accident in 1960.

The Guest

The schoolmaster was watching the two men climb toward him. One was on horseback, the other on foot. They had not yet tackled the abrupt rise leading to the schoolhouse built on the hillside. They were toiling onward, making slow progress in the snow, among the stones, on the vast expanse of the high, deserted plateau. From time to time the horse stumbled. He could not be heard yet but the breath issuing from his nostrils could be seen. The schoolmaster calculated that it would take them a half hour to get onto the hill. It was cold; he went back into the school to get a sweater.

He crossed the empty, frigid classroom. On the blackboard the four rivers of France, drawn with four different colored chalks, had been flowing toward their estuaries for the past three days. Snow had suddenly fallen in mid-October after eight months of drought without the transition of rain, and the twenty pupils, more or less, who lived in the villages scattered over the plateau had stopped coming. With fair weather they would return. Daru now heated only the single room that was his lodging, adjoining the classroom. One of the windows faced, like the classroom windows, the south. On that side the school was a few kilometers from the point where the plateau began to slope toward the south. In clear weather the purple mass of the mountain range where the gap opened onto the desert could be seen.

Somewhat warmed, Daru returned to the window from which

he had first noticed the two men. They were no longer visible. Hence they must have tackled the rise. The sky was not so dark, for the snow had stopped falling during the night. The morning had dawned with a dirty light which had scarcely become brighter as the ceiling of clouds lifted. At two in the afternoon it seemed as if the day were merely beginning. But still this was better than those three days when the thick snow was falling amidst unbroken darkness with little gusts of wind that rattled the double door of the classroom. Then Dary had spent long hours in his room, leaving it only to go to the shed and feed the chickens or get some coal. Fortunately the delivery truck from Tadjid, the nearest village to the north, had brought his supplies two days before the blizzard. It would return in forty-eight hours.

Besides, he had enough to resist a siege, for the little room was cluttered with bags of wheat that the administration had left as a supply to distribute to those of his pupils whose families had suffered from the drought. Actually they had all been victims because they were all poor. Every day Daru would distribute a ration to the children. They had missed it, he knew, during these bad days. Possibly one of the fathers or big brothers would come this afternoon and he could supply them with grain. It was just a matter of carrying them over to the next harvest. Now shiploads of wheat were arriving from France and the worst was over. But it would be hard to forget that poverty, that army of ragged ghosts wandering in the sunlight, the plateaus burned to a cinder month after month, the earth shriveled up little by little, literally scorched, every stone bursting into dust under one's foot. The sheep had died then by thousands, and even a few men, here and there, sometimes without anyone's knowing.

In contrast with such poverty, he who lived almost like a monk, in his remote schoolhouse, had felt like a lord with his whitewashed walls, his narrow couch, his unpainted shelves, his well, and his weekly provisioning with water and food. And suddenly this snow, without warning, without the foretaste of rain. This is the way the region was, cruel to live in, even without men, who didn't help matters either. But Daru had been born here. Everywhere else, he felt exiled.

He went out and stepped forward on the terrace in front of

the schoolhouse. The two men were now halfway up the slope. He recognized the horseman to be Balducci, the old gendarme he had known for a long time. Balducci was holding at the end of a rope an Arab walking behind him with hands bound and head lowered. The gendarme waved a greeting to which Daru did not reply, lost as he was in contemplation of the Arab dressed in a faded blue *jellaba*, his feet in sandals but covered with socks of heavy raw wool, his head crowned with a narrow, short *cheche*. Balducci was holding back his horse in order not to hurt the Arab, and the group was advancing slowly.

Within earshot, Balducci shouted, "One hour to do the three kilometers from El Ameur!" Daru did not answer. Short and square in his thick sweater, he watched them climb. Not once had the Arab raised his head. "Hello," said Daru when they got up onto the terrace. "Come in and warm up." Balducci painfully got down from his horse without letting go of the rope. He smiled at the schoolmaster from under his bristling mustache. His little dark eyes, deep-set under a tanned forehead, and his mouth surrounded with wrinkles made him look attentive and studious. Daru took the bridle, led the horse to the shed, and came back to the two men who were now waiting for him in the school. He led them into his room. "I am going to heat up the classroom," he said. "We'll be more comfortable there."

When he entered the room again, Balducci was on the couch. He had undone the rope tying him to the Arab, who had squatted near the stove. His hands still bound, the *cheche* pushed back on his head, the Arab was looking toward the window. At first Daru noticed only his huge lips, fat, smooth, almost Negroid; yet his nose was straight, his eyes dark and full of fever. The *cheche* uncovered an obstinate forehead and, under the weathered skin now rather discolored by the cold, the whole face had a restless and rebellious look. "Go into the other room," said the schoolmaster, "and I'll make you some mint tea." "Thanks," Balducci said. "What a chore! How I long for retirement." And addressing his prisoner in Arabic, he said, "Come on, you." The Arab got up and, slowly, holding his bound wrists in front of him, went into the classroom.

With the tea, Daru brought a chair. But Balducci was already sitting in state at the nearest pupil's desk, and the Arab had squatted against the teacher's platform facing the stove, which stood between the desk and the window. When he held out the glass of tea to the prisoner, Daru hesitated at the sight of his bound hands. "He might perhaps be untied." "Sure," said Balducci. "That was for the trip." He started to get to his feet. But Daru, setting the glass on the floor, had knelt beside the Arab. Without saying anything, the Arab watched him with his feverish eyes. Once his hands were free, he rubbed his swollen wrists against each other, took the glass of tea and sucked up the burning liquid in swift little sips.

"Good," said Daru. "And where are you headed?"

Balducci withdrew his mustache from the tea. "Here, son."

"Odd pupils! And you're spending the night?"

"No. I'm going back to El Ameur. And you will deliver this fellow to Tinguit. He is expected at police headquarters."

Balducci was looking at Daru with a friendly little smile.

"What's this story?" asked the schoolmaster. "Are you pulling my leg?"

"No, son. Those are the orders."

"The orders? I'm not . . ," Daru hesitated, not wanting to hurt the old Corsican. "I mean, that's not my job."

"What! What's the meaning of that? In wartime people do all kinds of jobs."

"Then I'll wait for the declaration of war!"

Balducci nodded. "O.K. But the orders exist and they concern you too. Things are bubbling, it appears. There is talk of a forthcoming revolt. We are mobilized, in a way."

Daru still had his obstinate look.

"Listen, son," Balducci said. "I like you and you've got to understand. There's only a dozen of us at El Ameur to patrol the whole territory of a small department and I must be back in a hurry. He couldn't be kept there. His village was beginning to stir; they wanted to take him back. You must take him to Tinguit tomorrow before the day is over. Twenty kilometers shouldn't faze a husky fellow like you. After that, all will be over. You'll come back to your pupils and your comfortable life."

Behind the wall the horse could be heard snorting and pawing the earth. Daru was looking out the window. Decidedly the weather was clearing and the light was increasing over the snowy plateau. When all the snow was melted, the sun would take over again and once more would burn the fields of stone. For days still, the unchanging sky would shed its dry light on the solitary expanse where nothing had any connection with man.

"After all," he said, turning around toward Balducci, "what did he do?" And, before the gendarme had opened his mouth, he asked, "Does he speak French?"

"No, not a word. We had been looking for him for a month, but they were hiding him. He killed his cousin."

"Is he against us?"

"I don't think so. But you can never be sure."

"Why did he kill?"

"A family squabble, I think. One owed grain to the other, it seems. It's not at all clear. In short, he killed his cousin with a billhook. You know, like a sheep, *kreezk!*"

Balducci made the gesture of drawing a blade across his throat, and the Arab, his attention attracted, watched him with a sort of anxiety. Daru felt a sudden wrath against the man, against all men with their rotten spite, their tireless hates, their blood lust.

But the kettle was singing on the stove. He served Balducci more tea, hesitated, then served the Arab again, who drank avidly a second time. His raised arms made the *jellaba* fall open, and the schoolmaster saw his thin, muscular chest.

"Thanks, son," Balducci said. "And now I'm off."

He got up and went toward the Arab, taking a small rope from his pocket.

"What are you doing?" Daru asked dryly.

Balducci, disconcerted, showed him the rope.

"Don't bother."

The old gendarme hesitated. "It's up to you. Of course, you are armed?"

"I have my shotgun."

"Where?"

"In the trunk."

"You ought to have it near your bed."

"Why? I have nothing to fear."

"You're crazy, son. If there's an uprising, no one is safe; we're all in the same boat."

"I'll defend myself. I'll have time to see them coming."

Balducci began to laugh, then suddenly the mustache covered the white teeth. "You'll have time? O.K. That's just what I was saying. You always have been a little cracked. That's why I like you; my son was like that."

At the same time he took out his revolver and put it on the desk. "Keep it; I don't need two weapons from here to El Ameur." The revolver shone against the black paint of the table. When the gendarme turned toward him, the schoolmaster caught his smell of leather and horseflesh.

"Listen, Balducci," Daru said suddenly, "all this disgusts me, beginning with your fellow here. But I won't hand him over. Fight, yes, if I have to. But not that."

The old gendarme stood in front of him and looked at him severely.

"You're being a fool," he said slowly. "I don't like it either. You don't get used to putting a rope on a man even after years of it, and you're even ashamed—yes, ashamed. But you can't let them have their way."

"I won't hand him over," Daru said again.

"It's an order, son, and I repeat it."

"That's right. Repeat to them what I've said to you: I won't hand him over."

Balducci made a visible effort to reflect. He looked at the Arab and at Daru. At last he decided.

"No, I won't tell them anything. If you want to drop us, go ahead; I'll not denounce you. I have an order to deliver the prisoner and I'm doing so. And now you'll just sign this paper for me."

"There's no need. I'll not deny that you left him with me."

"Don't be mean with me. I know you'll tell the truth. You're from around these parts and you are a man. But you must sign; that's the rule."

Daru opened his drawer, took out a little square bottle of purple ink, the red wooden penholder with the "sergeant-major" pen he used for models of handwriting, and signed. The gendarme carefully folded the paper and put it into his wallet. Then he moved toward the door.

"I'll see you off," Daru said.

"No," said Balducci. "There's no use being polite. You insulted me."

He looked at the Arab, motionless in the same spot, sniffed peevishly, and turned away toward the door. "Good-by, son," he said. The door slammed behind him. His footsteps were muffled by the snow. The horse stirred on the other side of the wall and several chickens fluttered in fright. A moment later Balducci reappeared outside the window leading the horse by the bridle. He walked toward the little rise without turning around and disappeared from sight with the horse following him.

Daru walked back toward the prisoner, who, without stirring, never took his eyes off him. "Wait," the schoolmaster said in Arabic and went toward the bedroom. As he was going through the door, he had a second thought, went to the desk, took the revolver, and stuck it in his pocket. Then, without looking back, he went into his room.

For some time he lay on his couch watching the sky gradually close over, listening to the silence. It was this silence that had seemed painful to him during the first days here, after the war. He had requested a post in the little town at the base of the foothills separating the upper plateaus from the desert. There rocky walls, green and black to the north, pink and lavender to the south, marked the frontier of eternal summer. He had been named to a post farther north, on the plateau itself. In the beginning, the solitude and the silence had been hard for him on these wastelands peopled only by stones. Occasionally, furrows suggested cultivation, but they had been dug to uncover a certain kind of stone good for building. The only plowing here was to harvest rocks. Elsewhere a thin layer of soil accumulated in the hollows would be scraped out to enrich paltry village gardens. This is the way it was: bare rock covered three quarters of the region. Towns sprang up, flourished, then disappeared; men came by, loved one another or fought bitterly, then died. No one in this desert, neither he nor his guest, mattered. And yet, outside this desert neither of them, Daru knew, could have really lived.

When he got up, no noise came from the classroom. He was amazed at the unmixed joy he derived from the mere thought that the Arab might have fled and that he would be alone with no decision to make. But the prisoner was there. He had merely stretched out between the stove and the desk and he was staring at the ceiling. In that position, his thick lips were particularly noticeable, giving him a pouting look. "Come," said Daru. The Arab got up and followed him. In the bedroom the schoolmaster pointed to a chair near the table under the window. The Arab sat down without ceasing to watch Daru.

"Are you hungry?"

"Yes," the prisoner said.

Daru set the table for two. He took flour and oil, shaped a cake in a frying pan, and lighted the little stove that functioned on bottled gas. While the cake was cooking, he went out to the shed to get cheese, eggs, dates, and condensed milk. When the cake was done he set it on the window sill to cool, heated some condensed milk diluted with water, and beat up the eggs into an omelette. In one of his motions he bumped into the revolver stuck in his right pocket. He set the bowl down, went into the classroom, and put the revolver in his desk drawer. When he came back to the room, night was falling. He put on the light and served the Arab. "Eat," he said. The Arab took a piece of the cake, lifted it eagerly to his mouth, and stopped short.

"And you?" he asked.

"After you. I'll eat too."

The thick lips opened slightly. The Arab hesitated, then bit into the cake determinedly.

The meal over, the Arab looked at the schoolmaster. "Are you the judge?"

"No, I'm simply keeping you until tomorrow."

"Why do you eat with me?"

"I'm hungry."

The Arab fell silent. Daru got up and went out. He brought back a camp cot from the shed and set it up between the table and the stove at right angles to his own bed. From a large suitcase which, upright in a corner, served as a shelf for papers, he took two blankets and arranged them on the cot. Then he stopped, felt useless, and sat down on his bed. There was nothing more to do or to get ready. He had to look at this man. He looked at him therefore, trying to imagine his face bursting with rage. He couldn't do so. He could see nothing but the dark yet shining eyes and the animal mouth.

"Why did you kill him?" he asked in a voice whose hostile tone surprised him.

The Arab looked away. "He ran away. I ran after him."

He raised his eyes to Daru again and they were full of a sort of woeful interrogation. "Now what will they do to me?"

"Are you afraid?"

The Arab stiffened, turning his eyes away.

"Are you sorry?"

The Arab stared at him openmouthed. Obviously he did not understand. Daru's annoyance was growing. At the same time he felt awkward and self-conscious with his big body wedged between the two beds.

"Lie down there," he said impatiently. "That's your bed."

The Arab didn't move. He cried out, "Tell me!"

The schoolmaster looked at him.

"Is the gendarme coming back tomorrow?"

"I don't know."

"Are you coming with us?"

"I don't know. Why?"

The prisoner got up and stretched out on top of the blankets, his feet toward the window. The light from the electric bulb shone straight into his eyes and he closed them at once.

"Why?" Daru repeated, standing beside the bed.

The Arab opened his eyes under the blinding light and looked at him, trying not to blink. "Come with us," he said.

In the middle of the night, Daru was still not asleep. He had gone to bed after undressing completely; he generally slept naked. But when he suddenly realized that he had nothing on he wondered. He felt vulnerable and the temptation came to him to put his clothes back on. Then he shrugged his shoulders after all, he wasn't a child and, if it came to that he, could break his adversary in two. From his bed, he could observe him lying on his back, still motionless, his eyes closed under the harsh light. When Daru turned out the light, the darkness seemed to congeal all of a sudden. Little by little the night came back to life in the window where the starless sky was stirring gently. The schoolmaster soon made out the body lying at his feet. The Arab was still motionless but his eyes seemed open. A faint wind was prowling about the schoolhouse. Perhaps it would drive away the clouds and the sun would reappear.

During the night the wind increased. The hens fluttered a little and then were silent. The Arab turned over on his side with
his back to Daru, who thought he heard him moan. Then he listened for his guest's breathing which had become heavier and
more regular. He listened to that breathing so close to him and
mused without being able to go to sleep. In the room where he had
been sleeping alone for a year, this presence bothered him. But
it bothered him also because it imposed on him a sort of brotherhood he refused to accept in the present circumstances; yet he was
familiar with it. Men who share the same rooms, soldiers or
prisoners develop a strange alliance as if having cast off their
armor with their clothing, they fraternized every evening, over
and above their differences, in the ancient community of dream
and fatigue. But Daru shook himself; he didn't like such musings,
and it was essential for him to sleep.

A little later, however, when the Arab stirred slightly, the
schoolmaster was still not asleep. When the prisoner made a second move, he stiffened, on the alert. The Arab was lifting himself
slowly on his arms with almost the motion of a sleepwalker. Seated
upright in bed, he waited motionless without turning his head toward Daru as if he were listening attentively. Daru did not stir;
it had just occurred to him that the revolver was still in the drawer
of his desk. It was better to act at once. Yet he continued to observe the prisoner, who, with the same slithery motion, put his feet
on the ground, waited again, then stood up slowly. Daru was about
to call out to him when the Arab began to walk, in a quite natural but extraordinary silent way. He was heading toward the
door at the end of the room that opened into the shed. He lifted
the latch with precaution and went out, pushing the door behind
him but without shutting it.

Daru had not stirred. "He is running away," he merely thought.
"Good riddance!" Yet he listened attentively. The hens were not
fluttering; the guest must be on the plateau. A faint sound of
water reached him, and he didn't know what it was until the
Arab again stood framed in the doorway, closed the door carefully,
and came back to bed without a sound. Then Daru turned his
back on him and fell asleep. Still later he seemed, from the depths
of his sleep, to hear furtive steps around the schoolhouse. "I'm
dreaming! I'm dreaming!" he repeated to himself. And he went
on sleeping.

When he awoke, the sky was clear; the loose window let in a cold, pure air. The Arab was asleep, hunched up under the blankets now, his mouth open, utterly relaxed. But when Daru shook him he started dreadfully, staring at Daru with wild eyes as if he had never seen him and with such a frightened expression that the schoolmaster stepped back. "Don't be afraid. It is I. You must eat." The Arab nodded his head and said yes. Calm had returned to his face, but his expression was vacant and listless.

The coffee was ready. They drank it seated together on the cot as they munched their pieces of the cake. Then Daru led the Arab under the shed and showed him the faucet where he washed. He went back into the room, folded the blankets on the cot, made his own bed, and put the room in order. Then he went through the classroom and out onto the terrace. The sun was already rising in the blue sky; a soft, bright light enveloped the deserted plateau. On the ridge the snow was melting in spots. The stones were about to reappear. Crouched on the edge of the plateau, the schoolmaster looked at the deserted expanse. He thought of Balducci. He had hurt him, for he had sent him off as though he didn't want to be associated with him. He could still hear the gendarme's farewell and, without knowing why, he felt strangely empty and vulnerable.

At that moment, from the other side of the schoolhouse, the prisoner coughed. Daru listened to him almost despite himself and then, furious, threw a pebble that whistled through the air before sinking into the snow. That man's stupid crime revolted him, but to hand him over was contrary to honor; just thinking of it made him boil with humiliation. He simultaneously cursed his own people who had sent him this Arab and the Arab who had dared to kill and not managed to get away. Daru got up, walked in a circle on the terrace, waited motionless, and then went back into the schoolhouse.

The Arab, leaning over the cement floor of the shed, was washing his teeth with two fingers. Daru looked at him and said, "Come." He went back into the room ahead of the prisoner. He slipped a hunting jacket on over his sweater and put on walking shoes. Standing, he waited until the Arab had put on his *cheche* and sandals. They went into the classroom, and the schoolmaster pointed to the exit saying, "Go ahead." The fellow didn't budge.

"I'm coming," said Daru. The Arab went out. Daru went back
into the room and made a package with pieces of rusk, dates, and
sugar in it. In the classroom, before going out, he hesitated a second
in front of his desk, then crossed the threshold and locked the
door. "That's the way," he said. He started toward the east,
followed by the prisoner. But a short distance from the schoolhouse he thought he heard a slight sound behind him. He retraced his steps and examined the surroundings of the house;
there was no one there. The Arab watched him without seeming
to understand. "Come on," said Daru.

They walked for an hour and rested beside a sharp needle of
limestone. The snow was melting faster and faster and the sun was
drinking up the puddles just as quickly, rapidly cleaning the plateau, which gradually dried and vibrated like the air itself. When
they resumed walking, the ground rang under their feet. From time
to time a bird rent the space in front of them with a joyful cry.
Daru felt a sort of rapture before the vast familiar expanse, now
almost entirely yellow under its dome of blue sky. They walked
an hour more, descending toward the south. They reached a sort
of flattened elevation made up of crumbly rocks. From there on,
the plateau sloped down—eastward toward a low plain on which
could be made out a few spindly trees, and to the south toward
outcroppings of rock that gave the landscape a chaotic look.

Daru surveyed the two directions. Not a man could be seen.
He turned toward the Arab, who was looking at him blankly.
Daru offered the package to him. "Take it," he said. "There are
dates, bread, and sugar. You can hold out for two days. Here are
a thousand francs too."

The Arab took the package and the money but kept his full
hands at chest level as if he didn't know what to do with what
was being given him.

"Now look," the schoolmaster said as he pointed in the direction of the east, "there's the way to Tinguit. You have a two-
hour walk. At Tinguit are the administration and the police. They
are expecting you."

The Arab looked toward the east, still holding the package
and the money against his chest. Daru took his elbow and turned
him rather roughly toward the south. At the foot of the elevation
on which they stood could be seen a faint path. "That's the trail

across the plateau. In a day's walk from here you'll find pasture-
lands and the first nomads. They'll take you in and shelter you
according to their law."

The Arab had now turned toward Daru, and a sort of panic
was visible in his expression. "Listen," he said.

Daru shook his head. "No, be quiet. Now I'm leaving you."
He turned his back on him, took two long steps in the direction
of the school, looked hesitantly at the motionless Arab, and started
off again. For a few minutes he heard nothing but his own step
resounding on the cold ground, and he did not turn his head. A
moment later, however, he turned around. The Arab was still
there on the edge of the hill, his arms hanging now, and he was
looking at the schoolmaster. Daru felt something rise in his throat.
But he swore with impatience, waved vaguely, and started off
again. He had already gone a distance when he again stopped and
looked. There was no longer anyone on the hill.

Daru hesitated. The sun was now rather high in the sky and
beginning to beat down on his head. The schoolmaster retraced
his steps, at first somewhat uncertainly, then with decision. When
he reached the little hill, he was bathed in sweat. He climbed it as
fast as he could and stopped, out of breath, on the top. The rock
fields to the south stood out sharply against the blue sky, but on
the plain to the east a steamy heat was rising. And in that slight
haze, Daru, with heavy heart, made out the Arab walking slowly
on the road to prison.

A little later, standing before the window of the classroom
the schoolmaster was watching the clear light bathing the whole
surface of the plateau. Behind him on the blackboard, among the
winding French rivers, sprawled the clumsily chalked up words he
has just read: "You handed over our brother. You will pay for
this." Daru looked at the sky, the plateau, and, beyond, the invisible lands stretching all the way to the sea. In this vast landscape he had loved so much he was alone.

Selected Readings

BARNES, HAZEL E. *Humanistic Existentialism: The Literature of Possibility.* Bison Book; Lincoln, Neb.: University of Nebraska Press, 1962.

BRÉE, GERMAINE. *Camus.* New Brunswick, N.J.: Rutgers University Press, 1959.

———(ed.). *Camus: a Collection of Critical Essays.* Englewood Cliffs, N.J.: Prentice-Hall, Inc., 1962.

CRUICKSHANK, JOHN. *Albert Camus and the Literature of Revolt.* London: Oxford University Press, 1959.

HANNA, THOMAS. *The Lyrical Existentialists.* New York: Atheneum Publishers, 1962.

———. *The Thought and Art of Albert Camus.* A Gateway Edition; Chicago: Henry Regnery Company, 1966.

KING, ADELE, *Albert Camus.* New York: Grove Press, 1964.

LOY, J. R. "Prometheus, Theseus, the Uncommon Man and an Eagle." *Yale French Studies,* No. 7 (1951), 32–43.

PERRINE, LAURENCE. "Camus' 'The Guest': A Subtle and Difficult Story." *Studies in Short Fiction,* I (1963), 52–58.

ST. AUBYN, F. C. "Albert Camus and the Death of the Other: An Existentialist Interpretation." *French Studies,* XVI (1962), 124–41.

SCOTT, NATHAN A. *Albert Camus.* New York: Hillary House Publishers, 1962.

THODAY, PHILIP. *Albert Camus, 1913–1960.* London: H. Hamilton, 1961.

WEST, PAUL. "Albert Camus and the Aesthetic Tradition." *New World Writings.* 13th Mentor Selection; New York: New American Library, 1958.

NB

PART I

THE SQUEEZE

CHAPTER ONE

SIGNAL FIRES

PATIENTLY, the donkey trotted down the Champs Elysées. It had the run of the broad avenue. There were no speeding motorcars to frighten it. In the last five months motorcars had all but vanished from the streets of Paris. They were replaced by bicycles, or simply by shanks' mare. Occasionally a horse-and-buggy rattled by. A donkey, however, was a new means of transportation. Passers-by gave it startled glances. They were surprised that the donkey neither carried a load, nor pulled a cart. Two shiny, high boots were tied to its sides. They hit the animal at every stride. Sometimes the donkey brayed painfully. Yet it trotted on without showing the slightest sign of resistance. Only an ass could be as patient as that.

Right and left of the donkey marched a group of boys, Sorbonne students, to judge from their hatlessness, their uncombed hair, their young, furrowed faces, and their worn-out

3

clothes. They marched in silence and dignity, as if in a funeral procession.

The day was November 11, Armistice Day, of 1940. Memorial celebrations for the victims of the first war were *verboten*. They might have led to trouble. General Joachim von Stülpnagel, Commander of the army of occupation in France, did not give the people entrusted to his protection any opportunity to get out of hand. Besides, the French people themselves did not feel like celebrating. After all, who were the victims of the senseless victory of 1918? Were they heroes— or just dead fools? Most of the passers-by on the Champs Elysées, on this November 11, 1940, at eleven A.M., were heartily glad that, as far as they were concerned, the second war was over. *Gagner la vie*, to make a living, was all they now wanted. They were resigned and patient—like the ass.

There must have been some, however, who found the donkey too patient for their taste. Why did the poor animal not throw off the empty, shining, high boots? By the time the silent procession passed the Avenue Dutuit a small crowd was following it. At the corner of the Avenue de Marigny the procession was no longer silent, and the crowd no longer small. Thousands had joined the ranks. They did not dare to sing a patriotic song. The sight of German officers strolling along the Champs Elysées terrified them. Field-gray was a magic color, and the monocle seemed invincible. Moreover, Parisians had little reason to sing. After five months of occupation the bread ration had shrunk to two hundred grams a week, and the listless children cried for milk.

Suddenly a voice burst out: "Vive l'âne!"

The call resounded a thousandfold. "Vive l'âne!" shouted the Paris street.

The ambling German officers were still smiling. "Long live the ass!" one of them translated to his comrades. Chuckling, they shook their square heads. So this was gay Paree!

Major Johann Schmidt, Infantry Regiment 344, insisted

afterward that he had been for drawing sabers immediately. He did not understand, he admitted, what all the shouting was about, but on general principles he was for drawing sabers or using service revolvers whenever a mob began to shout. His friends, however, had prevailed upon him. The chief, General von Stülpnagel, had instructed his officers to behave considerately and politely. Under no conditions must the prestige of the German army, famous for its discipline and reticence, be lowered. If there was any dirty work to be done, the Gestapo would do it. In fact, the General had issued an order that German uniforms were to disappear the moment street riots flared up.

But was this, indeed, a street riot? The people simply cheered an ass. The French were making asses of themselves. That was all.

The Rond Point was heavily policed. It is not recorded how the French police agents felt when they dutifully attacked their compatriots. Probably they did not feel at all. The rubber truncheon is not sentimental. It follows its own logic. Besides, it was well known that M. Chiappe, then Police Prefect of Paris, did not tolerate any trouble in the streets. Under the various republican governments which he had faithfully served, he had always had to curb his disciplinary measures. Now, having sold out to the Nazis, his savage instincts, perhaps a heritage from his Corsican bandit ancestors, had free rein. The chief expected every Paris agent to do his duty with the rubber truncheon.

It took the police ten minutes, all told, to disperse the crowd. The whole incident would have been quickly forgotten, and probably laughed off with the famous Paris shrug, had it not been for the donkey. In the midst of the pandemonium the frightened animal, it appears, ran amuk. It galloped—"like a race horse," Major Johann Schmidt related later—through the general brawl. "It came dangerously close to me as I stood on the pavement, entirely unconcerned in this affair between the French police and the Paris mob. The ass almost struck me with its head. A German officer can, of course, not tolerate such an insult. I drew my service revolver—"

"You cannot do that!" Robert Louis Yomais, aged twenty-six, student of philosophy, shouted, throwing himself between the major and the donkey.

Major Johann Schmidt, Infantry Regiment 344, fired. He hit the young man in the right shoulder. He did not believe, he said, that the wound he inflicted on Yomais or whatever he was called, could have been very serious. He did not shoot to kill, he emphasized, but only to get the impertinent fellow out of the way. Then, he admitted proudly, he emptied his service revolver with deadly precision into the donkey.

Robert Louis Yomais was carried off by his comrades. No police agent interfered. Dr. Maxime Rubinstein, who was subsequently sentenced to twelve years' hard labor for having aided and abetted a political criminal, bandaged Yomais's shoulder. After a few hours' rest the patient was able to walk to the Café de la Coupole, on Montparnasse, where a young intellectual belongs. The other intellectuals in the "Coupole," young and old, asked no questions about the bandage around his right shoulder. They had been sitting out the war, the debacle, the invasion, in their own café, and they were completely uncurious. Robert Louis Yomais, the first victim of the German terror in France, disappeared unnoticed among the crowd in the "Coupole."

Paris honored the donkey as the first victim. The story of the assassinated ass spread like wildfire through the city. The crime had been committed toward eleven-thirty A.M. At two P.M. two German soldiers, walking through a side street of Saint Denis, the "red" suburb, were greeted by a band of workers with shouts that sounded unmistakably like "hee-haw." It was the asses' cry. The soldiers, both elderly men and both unarmed, accelerated rapidly in the direction of